ENGINEERING DESIGN FOR PROCESS FACILITIES

AUSTIN et al. · *Shreve's Chemical Process Industries*
CHOPEY · *Environmental Engineering in the Process Plant*
CHOPEY · *Handbook of Chemical Engineering Calculations*
COOK, DuMONT · *Process Drying Practice*
DEAN · *Lange's Handbook of Chemistry*
DILLON · *Materials Selection for the Chemical Process Industries*
FREEMAN · *Hazardous Waste Minimization*
FREEMAN · *Standard Handbook of Hazardous Waste Treatment and Disposal*
GRANT, GRANT · *Grant & Hackh's Chemical Dictionary*
KISTER · *Distillation Design*
KISTER · *Distillation Operation*
McGEE · *Molecular Engineering*
MILLER · *Flow Measurement Handbook*
PERRY, GREEN · *Perry's Chemical Engineers' Handbook*
REID et al. · *Properties of Gases and Liquids*
REIST · *Introduction to Aerosol Science*
RYANS, ROPER · *Process Vacuum Systems and Design Operation*
SANDLER, LUCKIEWICZ · *Practical Process Engineering*
SATTERFIELD · *Heterogeneous Catalysis in Practice*
SHINSKEY · *Process Control Systems*
SHUGAR, BALLINGER · *The Chemical Technicians' Ready Reference Handbook*
SHUGAR, DEAN · *The Chemist's Ready Reference Handbook*
SMITH, VAN LAAN · *Piping and Pipe Support Systems*
STOCK · *AI in Process Control*
TATTERSON · *Fluid Mixing and Gas Dispersion in Agitated Tanks*
YOKELL · *A Working Guide to Shell-and-Tube Heat Exchangers*

ENGINEERING DESIGN FOR PROCESS FACILITIES

Scott Mansfield

McGraw-Hill, Inc.

New York   San Francisco   Washington, D.C.   Auckland   Bogotá
Caracas   Lisbon   London   Madrid   Mexico City   Milan
Montreal   New Delhi   San Juan   Singapore
Sydney   Tokyo   Toronto

Library of Congress Cataloging-in-Publication Data

Mansfield, Scott, date.
    Engineering design for process facilities / Scott Mansfield.
       p.   cm.
    Includes bibliographical references and index.
    ISBN 0-07-040010-5 (alk. paper)
    1. Production management. 2. Engineering design. 3. Industrial
engineering. I. Title.
TS155.M33325   1993
620′.0042—dc20   93-18663
                                                   CIP

1 2 3 4 5 6 7 8 9 0 KGP/KGP 9 9 8 7 6 5 4 3

ISBN 0-07-040010-5

The sponsoring editor for this book was Gail F. Nalven, the editing supervisor was Stephen M. Smith, the designer was Susan Maksuta, and the production supervisor was Suzanne W. Babeuf. It was set in Bookman by Carol Woolverton, Lexington, Massachusetts, in cooperation with Warren Publishing Services, Eastport, Maine.

Printed and bound by Arcata Graphics/Kingsport.

This book is printed on acid-free paper.

To my wife Claudia Larralde, and our children Michelle and Paul

Also, to those men and women who labor in engineering/design and who know that professional satisfaction and pride in a job well done is of utmost importance

Contents

Chapter 14. Paper

Preface

How to ensure a good job—this is a prime consideration that needs to be reviewed constantly.

To be a good job, it must, of course, be well done. Also, it must leave the participants with a sense of satisfaction and pride—a desire to do more *good* jobs.

A good job requires technical ability and a spirit of cooperation. A few of the technical requirements are

- A reliable mass balance
- Complete, easy-to-read P&IDs
- Complete vendor drawings
- Clear understanding of equipment operation

Cooperation is exemplified by

- Teamwork between the owner/operator and the engineers/designers
- Process engineers helping instrument engineers and vice versa; piping designers helping structural engineers and vice versa
- A clear understanding, among all participants, that the *primary* objective is a safe, reliable, economic facility

Technical ability and a spirit of cooperation can be nurtured or thwarted by project and corporate management. *Good technical work and a spirit of cooperation are not possible in the absence of good management.* Gulfs separating technical and nontechnical people must be bridged at all levels, including the highest levels. Just as the CEO wants the engineers/designers to understand problems facing the business, the engineers/designers want the CEO to appreciate business at the drafting tables.

This means that good management requires an understanding of technical matters and team building. For this reason, the best management is by people who have worked into supervisory positions from technical assignments. Indeed, the manager whose sole "qualification" is *management* will be viewed as an imposter by the majority of the technical people under him or her.

As used here, *good management* means not only good administrative skills, but also good leadership capabilities. Such management will inspire. Such management will nurture creativity. Such management will *not* make unreasonable demands, but *will* expedite, facilitate, and enable the project participants in the execution of their work.

Major corporate expenditures as well as the whole basis for product quality are planned during the engineering/design effort. Thus, a wholehearted, professional effort is easily justified by even the smallest organizations. After all, engineering/design is what will determine the future.

It is my firm conviction that good projects are *inevitable* when the technical input is adequate and management has enough understanding of both the business aspects and the technical aspects to knit individual efforts together into a whole, strong fabric.

At one point early in my career, one of my bosses suggested that I make an attempt to "understand the big picture." By this, he meant that I should make an attempt to understand how my efforts were a part of the larger company strategy of developing new products, improving products, reducing costs, and so on.

His advice was well received (in no small part, I am sure, due to my innate desire to analyze and explore all things). For whatever reason, I have continually tried not only to do my job, but also to look beyond the immediate, never accepting the world at face value, always coming to grips with it on my own terms. Thus I am interested in learning estimating techniques, pouring concrete, finding out how diodes work, contemplating those things that lead to pride in one's work, noting things that were palpable on good jobs that were not evident on bad jobs, etc.

Through the years, the result not only has been personally satisfying, but also has augmented my confidence and effectiveness.

Thus my recommendation to all people working on process facilities jobs, or any work for that matter is: *Seek the big picture.* Look at the job the way your boss, or your boss's boss, might view it. Look at it from the point of view of the equipment vendor. Look at it from the point of view of the "other side," that is, the owner/operator versus engineer/designer. Think how the finished project might affect the neighborhood, the city, the state, people who aren't born yet, etc.

This advice is particularly important to young professionals starting their careers. Even the so-called lone technical specialist must understand how his or her work fits with the work of others.

At this point, it should be obvious that a broad view is more conducive to desirable results than a shortened view. This book gives the broad view. A good many chapters do not involve technical considerations. These chapters are important nevertheless, because good technical work is not accomplished in a world that is entirely technical.

This is the book that I wish I had had 25 years ago as I set forth into the exciting field of engineering/design for process facilities. This book can lead the way to *good projects.*

Scott Mansfield

═Chapter 1═
Design

A design is a vision. It is an image that can be marked in sand or soft clay, or described in words, or sketched on a piece of paper. When things are built, the design is a plan for *action.*

In the creative process of building anything, be it a blue bootee or a bubblecap column, first comes knowledge, next design, and finally action.

Design is very much embedded in human experience—so much so that it is often taken for granted. In philosophy and religion, meaning is sought in "the *design* of the universe" and "God's *design.*"

Cost advantages that result from specialization of labor are the ultimate justification for making *design* a separate field of application. Two hundred years ago cabinetmakers not only did their own design work but also made tools and nails. Since then, the economies of specialization have been recognized and cultivated with astounding results.

It is widely accepted that the best way to build a process plant, no matter how simple, is to employ a specialist at each phase. Design is the planning part. Construction is the execution part.

In Chap. 2, *Quality,* we will see that in the United States, design, as a subpractice of engineering, has fallen behind other areas of practice. Among other things, importance and prestige have been lacking. Design does not have the strong influence it merits. There is no single cause of this state of affairs, but the following three causes stand out:

- Lack of emphasis in colleges and the workplace. (This is traceable to priorities that stress the abstract, computerization, and management technique. Even a reasonable text describing design cannot be found.)

- Adversarial relationships between engineering firms and operating companies.

- Elitism (favoring the abstract versus hands-on).

These topics are touched upon throughout this book, but a few more words about elitism are needed here.

The notion of elitism has been with us for a long time. The basic tenet is that *ideas* are clean and pure, but that the *physical world* in which we live is contaminated. Those of us who deal in ideas for a living are superior to those of us who deal with the real world. The highly readable *A History of* π *(Pi)* by Petr Beckman [1] tells how Archimedes' great insights were based on experiments, but that historians chose to make it appear that Archimedes would never have stooped to deal with physical realities.

This author recalls all too clearly the review meeting in which procedures for removing heavy metals from wastewater were being considered. On one hand were three design engineers. On the other hand were two consulting scientists from Oak Ridge, Tennessee, and two administrators from Washington, D.C. It was obvious that the scientists and administrators had no design experience. Questions of raising pH and filtering or centrifuging or settling were being discussed. The scientists wanted to filter the sticky gel that would result from precipitation. The design engineers favored sedimentation. Finally, an administrator stepped in and said, "Well, it's plain to see what we need here is a *systems* approach." The scientists nodded dutifully. The meeting was over. Here, a purely abstract analysis was adopted when the situation screamed for experimental work.

To some it may come as a surprise that the elitism of "pure" thinking should be an obstacle to doing a good job of designing process facilities, but it is. Among other things, good intellects that could have been of great service have shunned design. This view seems to be stronger in the United States than in Europe or the Orient.

This is a relatively modern trend, and it is all the more surprising given our so-called Yankee ingenuity. The surprise increases when one considers that Albert Einstein admitted that ultimately science must connect to reality. Yes, he also said that the great truths about the universe would be revealed through abstract thinking, *but* he insisted on a tie to reality [2].

If science must find a bedrock in reality, then where should engineering find its bedrock?

ATTENTION TO DETAIL

Attention to detail (ATD) is an important part of design. Throughout this book, the initials *ATD* have been added to show where attention to detail has been of benefit.

Some of the worst advice ever given to young engineers is that they need not worry over the details, "Let someone else do that. It will take care of itself." The fact is that details never take care of themselves. The attitude created by this idea is that someone else will do your job for you. The other problem is the fuzziness of what constitutes a detail. Is a drain valve on a 100,000-gal gasoline storage tank a detail? Is the gasket selection for 11,000 ft of flanged piping a detail?

Much harm is done by assuming that design details will take care of themselves. When such attitudes are adopted, the door is opened to fakes and charlatans to pretend they are doing or administering engineering and design. It is a good way for ignorant and incapable people to hold down jobs that are beyond their capabilities.

Somehow this notion doesn't seem to apply to banking or baseball. Top banking executives don't have any inhibitions about getting into the tiniest of details. Top baseball managers don't hesitate to put in their two cents' worth for such things as signals from catcher to pitcher (two fingers for a fastball, etc.).

That details are demeaning is an echo from ancient Rome where manual labor and, ultimately, details of construction were done by slaves. The notion that details are demeaning is encountered far too frequently in engineering.

Misunderstandings of the concept of delegation of responsibility do not help. The way young engineers are nurtured is by handing them increasing amounts of responsibility. The way senior engineers grow in stature is by running bigger and bigger jobs—something they can do only by delegating responsibility. Engineers at the highest levels are able to delegate the majority of work, and so it seems their environment is free of details. This is an illusion, however.

First, the top engineers must know to whom various parts of a big job must be delegated. Thus they must mate parts of the job to team members having different strengths and weaknesses. This can only be done from experience—by having done parts of the job and knowing what each entails. Second, the top engineers must sense when one of their engineers may need help. Also they must choose between options when two or more engineers differ on jurisdictional matters or matters of mutual concern. Third, the best of the top engineers have good memories and can offer advice from their own experience to younger engineers and designers in all phases of the job.

Engineering company executives on a tour of a jobsite for a major chemical company stopped to watch while a piping mechanic and his helper struggled to fit a 4-in line between a reactor and its supporting structure. It was a tight fit. One of the vice presidents said, "Let's check into our standards for framing around vessels and reactors to see if we can leave more space." A quick review showed that 2 to 4 in more could easily be allowed. The standards were changed.

H. Ross Perot of GM/EDS fame is an example of the hands-on, problem-solving, details-oriented leader. Speaking figuratively, he liked to say, "When you see a snake, kill it." It makes sense. Don't assume that someone else will do the job or even notice the snake. Plenty of snakes will remain even after those that are seen are killed. Why leave *any* that are known? If you see a snake and feel incapable of killing it, at least call someone else's attention to it. Never imagine that someone else will take care of it. Never ignore it [ATD].

DESIGN ACTIVITIES

In design work, there is no substitute for a good imagination. Furthermore, this must be coupled with an ability to communicate via drawings and in writing.

The essence of design is *planning and communication.* Planning takes place in the conceptual thinking and the exploratory calculations. During this early stage, many sketches are made, and many discussions are held over those sketches. Later the calculations become definitive, and the sketches are incorporated into formal drawings. Head scratching continues: "What if we lose air pressure?" Along the way, descriptions of ideas are written down as notes on drawings or as requirements on specifications. Discussions continue. Memos, letters, and reports steadily flow.

If there is one thing that characterizes design work and sets it apart from other engineering practice, it is the constant need for sketches and drawings. The first impression one has in entering an area where design is being done is that drafting equipment and drawings (that is, *product**) in various stages of development are everywhere.

Another characteristic of design is the constant use of sketches during conversations. Both parties often have notepads and are showing sketches to each other as they speak. Latins are said to lend emphasis to their speech with hand gestures. Design people do it with sketches. The conversation often ends with a visit to a copy machine.

---

*This theme is repeated several times, namely, a drawing is a *product* of a design effort.

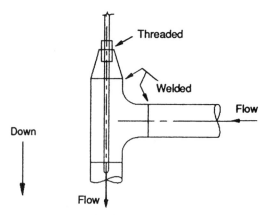

Figure 1-1 Example of a thermocouple in a tee.

"See, on lines 3 in and smaller, if you go to a ½-in screwed connection for your thermocouple and put it into the fluid through a tee, like this, it will drain easily. It will also have good contact with the process, and it will be thrifty—a flanged connection would be exorbitant!" These words backed by the sketch in Fig. 1-1 have great meaning. Without the sketch they are almost useless.

The need to sketch is so great that meetings of six or more people around a small 8½ by 11 in piece of paper become uncomfortable and are often reconvened to a room having a chalkboard. The chalkboard format is good to get creative juices flowing.

Two other characteristic tasks of design work are calculations and writing.

The typical design engineer will spend at least a few minutes a day doing calculations. In the early part of a project, this can extend to a week or two of calculations defining operating limits on a piece of equipment such as a fluid bed. Some mass balances take months. A process "package" for a refinery project often fits into this category. Discipline engineers, such as structural engineers, may spend more time calculating than doing any other activity.

The typical design engineer also writes a good deal. First is the perennial specification (see App. H for an example). Next come process descriptions, scopes of work, and the (sometimes) strong demands of project reporting. There are periods of time, as long as a month or so, when the design engineer can spend more than 70 percent of his or her time writing.

No engineer who is "writing-impaired" can go far in design. A designer who cannot write well cannot aspire to a good position.

By way of contrast, a brief look at engineers in two other subpractices is worthwhile. Engineers working in manufacturing are almost never required to do a calculation. Whatever writing they must do tends to be brief: short memos, daily reports, entries in the logbook, etc. Engineers in manufacturing spend a good deal of time troubleshooting, thinking on their feet, and helping operators run the plant. Engineers working in research and development can encounter some extended periods of mathematical calculation and even an excursion into advanced mathematics, but generally are faced with the more routine sort of mathematics: tests of significance, correlations, etc. The writing of reports of investigation can make great demands, but they occur at most two or three times a year.

ENGINEERS/DESIGNERS

Up to now the term *design* has been used to describe a creative process involving different talents of an undefined nature. From this point on, the term *engineering/design* is used. This is in recognition of the fact that the heart of a design team for process facilities consists of *engineers* and *designers*.

In an ideal situation, each can do goodly portions of the other's work. They work as equals, helping each other. They have different strengths, however. The division of strengths seems to occur somewhere in the vicinity where mechanics and art overlap. And the overlap is large. Some people function remarkably well in both areas. The most exalted example is Leonardo da Vinci whose work with mechanical contrivances is known to have been quite extensive, and, of course, his artworks are among the most highly prized.

Other distinctions are to be found in educational level and mathematical capability. The engineer usually has a college degree; the designer occasionally has a college degree. The engineer usually has had more than 20 college-level units of mathematics. The designer will have had perhaps as many as 10 units at the same level.

The engineer spends a fair amount of time thinking about capacity relationships, and the designer spends a good deal of time thinking about spatial relationships. Here are examples:

Capacity or intensity	Spatial relations
Gallons per minute	Above, below, alongside, etc.
Pounds per hour	Access: walkways, manways, handholes
Tons	Location of equipment
Kips	Location of piping
Amperes	Location of light fixtures
Lumens	Nozzle locations on a vessel

But it must be remembered that these efforts overlap greatly.

Also, and this is important enough to repeat: It is the mutual effort of engineers and designers that produces effective results. Both exist to make life easy for one another. Key "engineering" problems are routinely solved by a correct assessment of *spatial* relationships.

Both designers and engineers will have worked under the supervision of senior colleagues before having achieved competence to work on their own.

The roles of designers and drafters must not be confused. Designers can act on their own; drafters must be guided. With training and study, a drafter can become a designer.

ENGINEERING/DESIGN

The term *engineering/design* is used here because either word, by itself, raises mental images that can obscure realities. By itself, the word *engineering* sometimes evokes images of long computer printouts about abstruse matters. The word *design* can evoke an image of an artist designing a label for a soup can.

As used here, engineering/design is the wholly pragmatic occupation of defining how something *will actually be built*. It is not an exercise, a trial run, or a training experience. It is the real thing. The engineering/design will constitute instructions to real craftspeople, earning well-deserved substantial wages, who will put together a

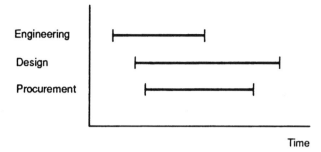

Figure 1-2 Three major activities of engineering design.

manufacturing facility that will be lived in and operated by real people. There will be a well-founded expectation that the facility will perform exactly as planned—*not* a "Well, let's see if it works" attitude.

Truth always triumphs in engineering/design. A lie is impossible to build.*

As used here, engineering/design consists of all the activities that precede the actual construction of the process facility. There are three major categories: engineering, design, and procurement. See Fig. 1-2.

This entire book is about engineering/design. Chapter 12 is devoted to procurement.

The old, established processes and the new, revolutionary ones alike are designed by using the methods described in this book—so this book is also for a completely new facility or a remodeling job.

In Chap. 2, *Quality*, we will see how engineering/design is of great importance to product quality. However, in the next section we will see how engineering/design is equally important to preventing environmental harm.

UNIFICATION OF PROCESS AND ENVIRONMENTAL OBJECTIVES

The following statement is based solely on economic arguments:

> A reasonable job of engineering/design cannot treat process requirements and environmental requirements separately.

Time and again this author has seen plans for a new facility based on a similar facility from forty years earlier, with a huge electrostatic precipitator (or some such unit) hooked onto the tail end. Typically, this is not an economic solution.

The following example shows how rethinking a process can save money (and improve reliability by eliminating superfluous equipment). In this case, a ball mill was to be included in a crystallizer loop to make fines. The client just wanted a duplicate of what he knew worked. He did not know that crystallization is no longer an art. A crystallizer can be designed to give a desired particle size distribution. Forty years earlier such knowledge was not available. Currently, a ball mill is not needed.

Many problems with pollution are like the case just described. By

---

*A plant that cannot be run does not qualify as being finished. A bridge that collapses into a river is not a bridge.

looking at the whole process and the body of knowledge that exists today, a potential problem can be avoided by designing around it.

It makes no difference with either new facilities or facilities being remodeled: environmental needs should drive the process design to arrive at an economic result. The afterthought, retrofit ("Well, this little baby is for pollution control"), is rarely the economic choice.

The following example from the *secondary* metals industry is illustrative. Pure metal can be recovered from scrap metal by using a series of steps that begin with melting in a direct-fired furnace. During this procedure many impurities are removed as oxides, formed as part of an insoluble, glassy layer (slag) that floats on top of the melt.

A particularly troublesome form of scrap is bales of scrap containing plastics such as PVC, Kynar, Teflon, nylon, and so on. When a bale is placed in the furnace, products of decomposition are generated rapidly and mix with the combustion gases headed for the atmosphere.

The knee-jerk reaction is to install a venturi scrubber and a baghouse. A far better approach is to rethink the whole process so that the environmental requirement becomes part of the overall design. Here are some ideas that should be explored:

- Install a small electric melting furnace off to one side of the reverberatory furnace; provide it with its own (tiny) scrubber.

- Install a small decomposition furnace; use it to heat bales to, say, 600°F for several hours, until the plastics are carbonized. This, too, would need only a tiny scrubber.

- Work with companies that buy scrap and compress it into bales; see if a good way can be found to carbonize before baling.

The next example also concerns a metal, but in this case copper is to be made from copper ore.

The following blue-sky thinking is presented. Admittedly, this is on a rather grandiose scale, but it shows the type of thinking needed. Companies that intend to be in business 20 years from now must entertain such ideas.

> Would it not make sense to build hydrometallurgical copper operations and chlor-alkali operations together? This way the chlorine from the chlor-alkali plant would be used to drive the oxidative leach. The two *plant equations** would be

$$\text{8NaCl} + \text{8H}_2\text{O} \xrightarrow{\text{(elect.)}} \text{8NaOH} + \text{4Cl}_2 + \text{4H}_2 \qquad (1\text{-}1)$$

$$\text{4Cl}_2 + \text{CuFeS}_2 + \text{4H}_2\text{O} \longrightarrow \text{Cu}^0 + \text{S}^0 + \text{FeSO}_4 + \text{8HCl} \qquad (1\text{-}2)$$

> By-products of one reaction would be consumed as ingredients by the companion reaction. The net overall reaction would be

$$\text{CuFeS}_2 + \text{4H}_2\text{O} \xrightarrow{\text{(elect.)}} \text{Cu}^0 + \text{S}^0 + \text{FeSO}_4 + \text{4H}_2 \qquad (1\text{-}3)$$

Much simpler symbioses have already developed between cement plants and generators of organic waste with heat value—and between coal-burning power plants and specialty cement producers.

Legislation against high tides does not stem them. Dikes do. King Canute, of course, failed when he ordered a halt in the rise of the tide.

---

*See page 96 for a description of the *plant equation.*

But, as the Dutch have proved, where high tides are concerned, solid, pragmatic engineering/design works.

Legislation against pollution does serve to express a worthwhile sentiment, but it will take engineering/design to guarantee environmental compatibility while maintaining a good standard of living.

It is not hard to envision a scenario where today's air and water would be better than they are now, if only the money spent legislating and anti-legislating had instead been spent on redesigning and remodeling processes.

An important avenue toward environmental soundness and economic good sense is that of *waste minimization.* Some of the simplest waste minimization methods have phenomenal returns on investment. The addition of a countercurrent wash tank and a small electric evaporator in a metal plating operation is an example. One is inclined to wonder why environmental consciousness should precipitate an action that is obviously economical. *Somewhere, a lack of knowledge is at work, or a priority is misplaced, and capital expenditures are stifled while managers are winking at operating costs.*

Waste minimization is best incorporated during the engineering/design effort, and not retrofitted as an afterthought. For example, when a reactor is to be used for making multiple products, the plans for changing from one product to another must be worked out to minimize waste. Another example is the use of solvents for cleaning. A small solvent distillation unit might become part of the project. A simple thing like maintaining a container of solvent-laden rags might save thousands of dollars per month. An invention such as the one shown in Fig. 1-3 is probably worth developing.

The basic operation would be as follows. Initially, say at the start of a day, the unit is cool. The valve on the side is opened, and solvent from the small, internal receptacle is spilled onto the top of the rags. Some solvent-laden rags (maybe one-half or one-third of them) are then removed from the top of the basket. Greasy rags, from the previous day, are placed in the bottom of the basket. A controller is turned on. This starts a heater, and, at the same time, cooling water flow to the upper coil is turned on, too. The heater vaporizes the solvent. The upper cooling coil condenses it. The drops fall onto the rags in the basket and extract the grease. The device is planned so that some drops find their way into the receptacle, eventually filling it, making it ready to start the cycle again. After a few hours, the heater turns off automatically, and cooling water is put through the lower coil until the whole unit has cooled. The unit is back in its initial state, ready to dispense solvent-laden rags while accepting greasy

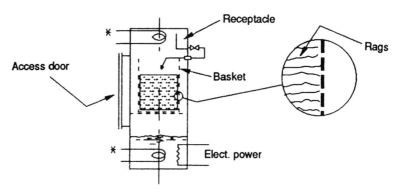

Figure 1-3 Rag cleaner. * = cooling water, connected to a controller.

ones. Every week or so, rags could be removed, without saturating them, and laundered in water to remove solid particles, by now starting to accumulate [ATD].

The unit is patterned after vapor degreasers. In a mass-production operation, a unit for handling 50 rags per day could probably be retailed for less than $1000.

This shows a small example of engineering/design. It contains imagination coupled with communication. It shows individual operations tied together to make a whole *greater* than the sum of the parts.

ORIGINS OF THIS BOOK

This book began 29 years ago when the demands of *real* engineering were perceived to be in stark contrast, if not conflict, with what had been presented as an education in chemical engineering. "Somebody has to tell what this is really all about."

Over the intervening years, a good deal of perspective and unremitting assessment have softened the initial reaction somewhat. Yet, the idea that "Somebody has to tell what this is really all about" has obviously persisted.

Little things seen and heard along the way have provided impetus:

- A grimacing plant operator grumbles, "If I ever catch the person who designed this," as she stands on tiptoes and gropes toward an inaccessible spot to shut a valve.

- A plant engineer is put in charge of running a project out of his back pocket while his other jobs consume him.

- An owner says he won't hire an engineer to work on staff, because "all they do is call vendors to do the work, and *I* can do that."

- An owner declares that engineering/design should not be held back "just because some information is lacking."

- A manager declares that a design is "frozen" before some fundamental details have been resolved.

- Drawings are issued "for construction" before even the first vendor drawing is seen, much less approved.

- There is widespread disdain for all things that are simple.

In the mid-1980s engineering/design for process facilities probably went through the biggest shakeup it has ever experienced. Large, well-established companies such as Fluor and R. M. Parsons Co. underwent severe readjustments. The prestigious industry leader C. F. Braun was reduced to a pitiful shell of what it once was *in only a few years.*

During that same time, some operating companies tried to take advantage of engineering companies. Often the operating people in charge of these efforts were fellow engineers. In a few cases, operating companies were able to get the engineering companies to unwittingly invest capital, by taking on lump-sum, turnkey jobs at a loss. In a few cases, the operating companies wound up having acquired some free engineering. The overall result was a degradation of engineering/design.

The worst part of all this is that the most seasoned, older employees, who were the best-qualified part of the engineering/design workforce, were put in early retirement or laid off, because they were the highest-paid. *These were the people who should have been training the next generation of talent.* Make no mistake, those who remain in the engineering/design industry today are not nearly as well trained as those in the industry twenty years ago.

While all this was taking place, U.S. competitiveness in world markets was on the decline, leveraged buyouts were taking place, junk bonds were being touted as instruments of true genius, and the standard of living was rapidly plunging.

In 1984 this author read *In Search of Excellence,* by Peters and Waterman [3]. Here at last were two people who, while they didn't know the story of engineering/design, certainly were homing in on some ideas that struck a strong chord. This was the start of a process of continual examination, of reflection. What is excellence in engineering/design? How is it acquired? Where are the most serious problems? How can these problems be solved?

With the framework for thinking set into place by Peters and Waterman, articles could be read and practices observed, and suddenly clear patterns of difficulty in engineering/design began to emerge. One pattern, for example, was the inability to put priorities in order so that a job could be performed correctly. Anyone with at least a few years in engineering/design has heard the ironic comment "There's never enough time or money to do it right the first time, but they always seem to be available the second time." Obviously, whoever holds the purse strings sees a strategic need for the work, tries to get it done for very little money; then when *that* fails, the serious effort is begun. Meanwhile, someone gets a black mark, and some bad blood is made.

Another pattern that emerges is lack of knowledge. Once the older, experienced hands left engineering/design, things that had been taken for granted ceased to exist. The problem was compounded because it wasn't obvious immediately. The dead time (to use a process control term) was two years. Then, with excuses being made and all, another year or two went by before the realization occurred: "This would have never happened, if Walt had been on the job."

In the period from 1984 to 1985 the terms *statistical quality control* and *just in time* began gaining currency with some operating companies. The terminology was found in engineering/design, but was not really understood, and even today is mostly misunderstood. These were methods that operating companies wanted to use. A fellow by the name of Deming, who taught smart ways of running production operations to the Japanese, advocated statistical quality control.

In due time Deming's name began to appear with great regularity. The word *quality* caught on as a buzzword for sales presentations made by engineering companies. Finally came the day when the emperor was seen without his clothes.

This was the president of a substantial roofing material company who was looking for engineers to help him make a new product. He was unaccompanied by any staff people. He was relatively new on the job, having been in the position for only a few years. An influential person (a member of the board of directors?) was pushing him to look at the profitability of a new product. A very sketchy process scheme, done by an unknown, lone consulting engineer, was presented. A sample of the material was available for examination. The basic work had apparently been done before the CEO's tenure. During this session the following great revelation slowly emerged: This man knew how to invest in the stock market, but did not know how to invest in his own company!

Originally, the thought was regarded as preposterous, but worth checking. Months went by, while recollections were sorted and fitted into the "preposterous" framework.

The thinking was roughly as follows: This would explain why U.S. industry was not investing at a rate sufficient to replace worn-out capital equipment [4]. It would explain why companies did not see fit to keep project teams on their payrolls. It would explain why in any major bookstore, in the business section, not a book could be found concerning spending on capital projects whereas hundreds could be found on financial manipulations, stock purchases, management, planning, biographical subjects, marketing, humor, etc.

This phenomenon has not gone unnoticed by others. It has been the subject of an intense study by Tom Nourse, a business consultant and investment analyst, who was a member of the Financial Accounting Standard Board's Task Force on Cash Flow Reporting. He has compared performance of companies whose CEOs have purely business and/or finance educations against those with combined business and technical education as well as against those whose CEOs also have only a technical education (see Table 1-1).

Nourse comments [5] that " . . . the MBA group is the poorest performing. CEOs with solely a business background tend to prop up return on investment (ROI) over the short run by cutting back on investment."* Among other things, this impairs the growth rate, but the impairment is not immediately evident. It is seen over the long run, as a decline in competitive capabilities. Nourse believes that excess emphasis on ROI causes myopic planning and that a focus on other performance factors will encourage a longer view.

Nourse has made these studies for more than a decade. In all, he has looked at more than 2000 companies.

The bottom line of all this is that the attitude toward investment of capital in machinery and equipment is not what it should be. Many people today seem to think that an *investment* is a conversion of cash to some sort of a security, not the purchase of equipment and labor to build a manufacturing facility. The connection between capital and manufacturing capacity has been blurred.

The classic college text of the 1920s by David F. Jordan [6], *Investments,* presented this connection with great clarity. At the start of the

---

*To understand how this works, recall that ROI is the ratio of return to investment. The ROI can be increased by cutting investment. As a matter of fact, ROI *suffers* briefly when investment is *increased,* before its benefits can be realized. This effect surely must be daunting to company executives.

TABLE 1-1 Company Performance according to CEO Education* (Courtesy Nourse Associates, Inc.)

	MBA only	Technical + MBA	Technical only
Capital expenditures†	7.4	10.5	9.2
Overhead†	20.5	21.6	17.6
Sales growth rate	10.0	13.5	13.1
Net worth growth rate	9.8	9.9	12.2
Average sales ($ billions)	5.1	6.5	5.4
Market value†	68	61	75
Number of companies‡	80	48	126

*Averages from 1986 to 1990. Similar results are seen in periods from 1985 to 1989 and from 1984 to 1988.

†As percentage of sales.

‡These companies were selected from the top 1000 companies in terms of market value.

book Jordan first leads the reader by stating on page 6: "Investment has previously been defined as the productive employment of capital. While this statement generally holds good, not all commitments for productive employment are investments in the more restrictive sense of the word." On page 9 he completes the definition:

A true investment may now be defined as a commitment of capital:

1. For use in production;
2. Entrusted to management of another;
3. For which the primary purpose of the capitalist . . . is to receive income by reason of the use in production, and
4. In which the estimated risk for use in production is not so great that the premium for risk is greater than the true income.

The repeated use of the word *production* is worthy of note. Jordan's definition would exclude leveraged buyouts as investments. Stock trading would also not qualify as a true investment. The purpose of the stock market is to provide a means by which the public can own diverse kinds of capital. It is also the means by which companies can raise capital to build facilities: factories, toxic waste eliminators, hotels, restaurants, etc. It should not be the refuge of a CEO who does not know how to invest in his or her own company.

Is it possible that the setbacks in the standard of living of the past twenty years coincide with the retirement of executives who were brought up in the Jordan philosophy?

UNDERSTANDING THIS BOOK

The material presented in subsequent chapters is drawn from 29 years of service in industry, of which 25 years or so have been in engineering/design. Virtually all the material presented is drawn from actual experience. The most notable exception is the use of statistical methods in Chap. 2. The form, Figure 2-2, has been used on occasion to keep records of hours, but the data have never been used in a culture emphasizing quality for statistical analysis and control. As a matter of fact, no known engineering/design effort is presently controlled by the methods described. The section entitled *Control* is, therefore, speculative. It has been included to give the reader an idea of the cultural changes that would be required to introduce Deming's methods into engineering/design.

Some of the examples given in this book are negative. This is because good engineering/design consists of *not* repeating mistakes. Mistakes, when they happen, can be used as opportunities for learning. A piping designer might reflect: "In construction, we constantly run into* cross-bracing and girts at building walls and roofs. Let's sit down with the structural group and work up a list of actions both groups can take to minimize changes to the drawings and maximize chances of not running into steel."

It *really* is as easy as that.

Throughout this book, the material presented is the grist of daily life. If something unusual or special is presented, it is labeled as such.

In many cases, there are many ways of performing a project task. In this book, one way among many has been chosen for simplicity's

---

*When pieces being assembled run into each other, the phenomenon is described as *interference* or *collision*. This constitutes a design error.

sake. A good example is the handling of vendor data. The method given here (Chap. 14 and App. B) was the method used by Du Pont in years past. No better method has been found, so it is given here.*

In discussions concerning paperwork, most of the attention has been focused on drawings and specifications. This is to shorten the discussion. There are other documents. Presumably, if the handling of these two is understood, comprehension of the remaining ones will quickly follow.

The question "What is the most common way of doing this?" has been foremost in the planning of this book. Therefore, the reader should not conclude that what is offered here are hard-and-fast rules. On the contrary, the methods are stated as benchmarks for comparison with existing practices.

In a few cases, where great guidance is obviously needed, such as the "disciplined" approach to mass balances (Chap. 8), the author firmly believes lesser measures lead to perdition, so the reader is admonished to do as the method instructs.

The emphasis on coverage in these pages has been driven by the following criterion:

What will improve project work on process facilities?

The word *improve* is laden with meaning. It means to

- Improve the facility being built
- Improve the attitudes and morale of the people doing the work
- Improve the stature of engineering/design
- Improve conditions for suppliers of equipment, construction labor, and operating labor
- Reassure investors and executives of the soundness of proven methods of engineering/design

This book, therefore, is a *whole* treatment of engineering/design. Advice is given to the CEO as well as to the drafter filing vendor drawings.

The coverage is specifically targeted at areas not included in college courses, but nevertheless areas that are of constant use. The two chapters that address equipment considerations, Chaps. 9 and 10, stand out in this regard. In particular, coverage is meant to avoid duplicating material given in *Plant Design and Economics for Chemical Engineers* by Peters and Timmerhaus [7] and *Project Engineering of Process Plants* by Rase and Barrow [8]. Practicing engineers will nonetheless recognize the material presented here as highly pertinent to the business of engineering/design. These engineers may also feel more at home with the treatment accorded here than in the aforementioned texts. An attempt has been made to give the reader a sense that nuts, bolts, and lubricating oil are not too far away.

On those subjects where a great fount of information exists in current literature, such as estimating, scheduling, and economic analysis, coverage has been purposely light. For the most part, in these areas, the discussion centers on aspects not covered in current books or magazine articles. To simplify descriptions, most explanations treat the owners and engineers as separate companies. One can eas-

---

*Modified to conform with what would be accepted by today's typical engineering firm.

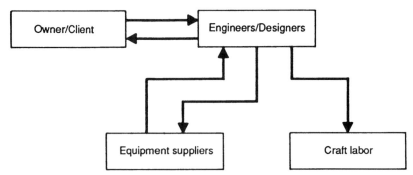

Figure 1-4 Major project participants.

ily imagine, however, owners and engineers being different divisions of a single company.

Figure 1-4 shows the major project participants. The arrows show how design information flows as it is developed. At the beginning of a project the communication is solely between owner/client and engineers/designers. This is where the two parties sort out what is to be done. Later the engineers/designers begin communications with equipment suppliers (also called vendors). The ultimate destination for all the information is with craft labor at the construction site.

—Chapter 2—
Quality
(and Productivity)

INTRODUCTION

Upon first hearing the word *quality,* most people will not hesitate to assert their comprehension of its meaning. For the most part this understanding is associated with cost. Diamonds are a higher-quality gem than opals. Cadillacs are higher-quality cars than Chevrolets.

In process operations the operators often have very strong opinions concerning the quality of some of the ingredients: "Brand X blends in easily and makes good product. Brand Y is a real dog. It's hard to blend and makes a lumpy product." The operators also have some firm ideas about the quality of such things as pumps, valves, pressure gauges, flow controllers, etc. These examples are not associated with cost. The favorite choices reveal a *capability to produce a desired result reliably.*

To draw on an experience from everyday life, the shoe is a good example of two different kinds of quality for a single type of product. In one instance a pair of shoes is needed for the winter ball. Here they must look good, but reliability is not a great concern. In a separate instance, a pair of work boots is needed for work on roofing jobs. Reliability and foot protection are important. The two products both fall into the category of footwear, but the difference ends there. In one case, quality means appearance. In the other case, quality means reliability and protection.

A paint manufacturer, given the choice between two different brands of TiO_2 whitener (identical in every respect except cost) will choose the lower-priced whitener. Over long periods, this lower price can be offered only by the manufacturer whose production methods result in a lower cost, i.e., the manufacturer with the greater productivity. In discussing quality, the experts (Tribus, Deming, etc.) treat productivity and quality as inseparable. That is the treatment here, too.

What is *quality?* Probably the most widely accepted definition in industry (as well as construction) is that quality is *conformance to established requirements.* Deming's definition [9] is that quality is the *economic manufacture of product that meets the demands of the market.* The focus of both statements is the same, but the second is more concrete. Both statements arrive at the idea that the customer deserves a hearing.

Each of these statements is good to establish bases for measurement of quality, but quality has an emotive side, too. Bennis [10] points out that "Feelings of quality are connected intimately with our experience of meaning, beauty, and value in our lives." This aspect can show itself in pride of workmanship.

Finally, we should not lose sight of the fact that quality is often associated with degree of excellence. This latter definition is prominent among the definitions found in common dictionaries. Excellent products will often be chosen over lesser ones, even when a premium must be paid—consider the down pillow compared to the polyester one.

What is quality when engineering/design is being considered?

The quality lies in two things: (1) the quality of the facility that is built and (2) the quality of the products made at the facility. Item 1 depends mostly on the quality of the design and to a lesser extent on the quality of the construction. Item 2 is highly dependent on item 1.

All too often misguided attempts at economy insist that quality 2 be maintained while sharply cutting back on quality 1. More is said concerning this dichotomy later in this chapter and throughout this book.

Why is quality an issue? The answer is simple. Quality goods sell.

Without quality, a manufacturer faces a huge competitive disadvantage. European manufacturers, for example, are promulgating adherence to a new set of quality standards, going under the name of the ISO 9000 standards. If U.S. products are to stay in the European market, they must meet the requirements of ISO 9000 standards.

How is quality achieved?

The achievement of quality during a creative process is tied to three things: *knowledge, materials (including tools),* and *time.* Chinese pottery was unrivaled in quality for centuries. The main reason was the extensive knowledge possessed by the Chinese potters.* Using this knowledge, they were able to exploit superior clay deposits and develop tools and techniques. The role that *time* plays is obvious. Given more time, more care can be exercised. Here a practical limit is required, however. Da Vinci spent thirty years putting the finishing touches on the *Mona Lisa.* In such a case, the search for quality, most people would agree, went beyond reason. Or did it? Witness the popularity of the painting.

The last five years have seen a proliferation of books and magazine articles on how to obtain quality. Many reiterate the thoughts of W. Edwards Deming, regarded by many as the father of the Japanese quality miracle.

Companies that have established quality programs have been forthcoming with information describing their programs. Typical of these is the program used successfully by Xerox. As reported by the Conference Board [11], Xerox uses a technique called *benchmarking* in which it compares its products, services, and practices to competitors and noncompetitors. Xerox lists these factors for gauging and improving performance:

- Improved knowledge
- Improved practices
- Improved processes
- Management commitment
- Organization commitment
- Employee participation

---

*The fact that they could read and write was important to possessing knowledge. By this means, knowledge was passed from generation to generation.

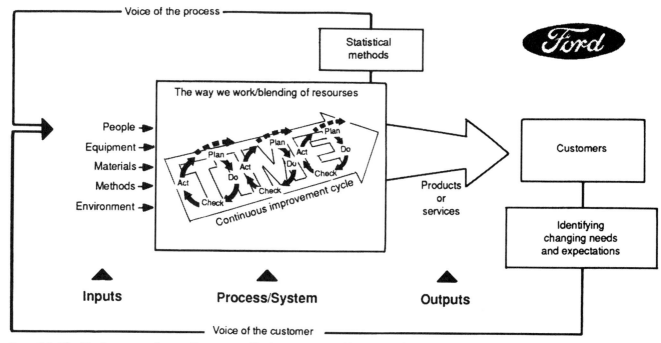

Figure 2-1 The Ford program for continuous quality improvement. (*Courtesy of Ford Motor Company.*)

Figure 2-1 is a diagram showing how Ford Motor Company views its program of continuous quality improvement.

The themes that occur most frequently in quality programs are

- Customer feedback
- Training, education, knowledge
- Leadership
- Design and redesign of products and processes
- Measurement and feedback (by using statistical methods and incorporating a mechanism for correcting problems)
- Management-labor cooperation with a commitment to continuous improvement

It is with the last point above, having to do with commitment, that most quality programs differ at this time. The range in commitment is from total to halfhearted to "What is the ROI that I may expect from my quality program?" Many companies in Japan, at the urging of Deming, have undertaken a total commitment to quality.* Few companies in the United States have done so, but many seem poised to take the plunge.† Ford is a notable example of a company proceeding with total commitment.

The Deming approach is one that requires total commitment to quality (productivity). The next section examines the Deming approach to quality and focuses on a few high spots relating to engineering/design.

---

*Probably a more apt description is the *culture* of total quality.

†Innumerable companies have *declared* total commitment to quality, but the consummation remains to be seen.

THE DEMING WAY

The Deming way is best understood by comparing it to the "old" (existing) way. Such a comparison has been done by Myron Tribus [12], using a hypothetical trucking firm. The example is a good one because it shows the cultural change that is required for *true* total commitment.

The example begins with a quick review of how a trucking firm is run using classic, non-Deming management. Tribus states that in the "old" culture the main concern of management is maximization of profits. Another management function is establishing goals and, in particular, production targets. Among the tools used by classic management are management by objective (MBO) and the hiring of consultants to establish procedures.

Tribus' narrative then switches over to the Deming quality culture, in which the procedures are established and implemented (and continuously improved) by the same employees that do the work. The Deming quality culture is not chaos, as some imagine. It is orderly, methodical, studious, and scientific. It consists of modifications and experimentation with procedures, and constantly watching the ensuing results. It is guided by application of statistical methods.

Tweak a method. Watch for what happens. Is the result an improvement? Why? In Tribus' words,

> *All* employees learn to keep their own statistics. Truck drivers keep track of how long they have to wait and the circumstances of each event. They develop their own control charts and look for trends and correlations with other events, usually events beyond their control. The drivers meet with each other, and sometimes the dispatcher, to compare notes. They keep data on performance of their trucks and discuss their statistical charts with the purchasing agent and with each other. The manager makes changes in the system based on these data, and the workers use their statistical information to help him learn how effective the changes have been. When the manager instructs the purchasing agent to buy on "quality," not just on first cost, the purchasing agent uses the information from the drivers to do just that, and to demonstrate that he has done so.
>
> *Everyone* in the system is involved in studying it and suggesting ways to improve it. *Everyone* spends about 5 percent of his time on this, but only the company statisticians spend 100 percent of their time on it. The employees will see the practice of setting work standards as a dumb idea, since it inhibits their ability to improve the system. They will not need to manage by objective, because they will be engaged in continually refining their own objectives and recording the performance of the system.

The manager in the Deming culture understands that profits are necessary for a business. Furthermore, this manager understands that high profits are preferred over low profits. One more thing is considered, however: long-term commitment to the business. The Deming manager is willing to pursue a long-term strategy—*even at the expense of short-term profits.*

With Tribus' comparison in mind, we now take a look at Deming's 14 points and see how they might apply to engineering and design. It is important to note that in engineering/design the so-called workers are the engineers and designers. The managers are department heads, group leaders, project managers, client project managers, and such. The downstream *product* is a process facility yet to be built. The immediate product is instructions on how to build the facility: drawings, specifications, scopes of work, etc.

DEMING'S 14 POINTS

1. *Create constancy of purpose for improvement of product and service.* The meaning of this point is evident. Even so, a good example is given to drive the point home.

In the late 1960s, the author spent 26 months on various assignments for the Du Pont company in Argentina. The rate of inflation at the time climbed from a 12 percent annual rate to about 110 percent. The projects being evaluated became very difficult to judge. What return on investment should you seek in such circumstances? How can costs be forecast? How can revenues be forecast?

Depending on assumptions, one could envision a bust or a bonanza. Eventually it was decided to do all evaluations based on constant dollars.

Slick financial manipulations could not be part of a rational scheme for a major chemical manufacturer. The view adopted was that industry in Argentina would continue to require the products we presently were making, that we should continue to fill the demand, and that the product line would require continual improvement to meet our customers' needs. ROI? Well, who knows? If we make money, it will be reinvested. If we don't, then we will review our options.*

2. *Adopt the new philosophy.* The "old philosophy" grew up as a result of the de facto monopoly that the United States enjoyed after World War II. In that situation, we often lost sight of the needs and desires of the marketplace. The results of the old style of thinking are exemplified by the declining fortunes of Texas Instruments (TI).

In the early 1980s TI seemingly had a star ascending rapidly on the horizon. It was at the cutting edge of the dawning age of personal computers. It appeared that TI might be capable of taking 25 to 50 percent of the market for personal computers (PCs). Late in 1983 TI withdrew from the battle of personal computers. Today, TI's brief omnipresence is only a dim memory.

TI erred in employing a monopolistic management philosophy: We will give you what we want to give you. Their approach was to make fair amounts of money at huge margins by selling PC components piecemeal and keeping their operating system proprietary. "Oh, you want to run a program in Basic? Here. Our special memory module will get you in business. That will be $299, plus tax."

Overnight, small companies stepped in to offer whole operating systems based on the S-100 bus and the accessible, powerful Z-80 microprocessor. Osborne Computer exploded onto the scene with a complete portable that included a disk operating system, QWERTY keyboard, and a built-in 7-in monitor. TI had already been defeated by these upstarts when IBM introduced the PC.

By concentrating more on market share instead of trying to maximize margins, TI might have been the leader in personal computers today.

3. *Cease dependence on inspection to achieve quality.* Inspection† can only record an error; it cannot prevent one. However, inspection has a valid function when it is used to acquire information to improve the process.‡

---

*Note: Du Pont continues its operations to the present time.

†Called *checking* in engineering/design.

‡*Process* in this context, for engineering/design, is the process of producing drawings and specifications, a major topic of this book.

4. *End the practice of awarding business on the basis of price tag alone. Instead minimize total cost by working with a single supplier.* Leeway must be given so that vendors are not selected based on price alone. Suggested approaches of accomplishing this are given in Chaps. 12 and 13.

5. *Improve constantly, and forever, every process for planning, production, and service.* The majority of materials and methods commonly employed in everyday life today are constantly undergoing improvement. Your competitor won't wait.

Point 5 can be paraphrased, with an emphasis on engineering/design: Improve constantly, and forever, production processes and the servicing of the processes (maintenance).* Improve, likewise, the planning (that is, the *design*) of the processes. This entire book is devoted to this topic.

6. *Institute training on the job.* No engineer or designer will ever achieve a state where training is not needed. Methods, tastes, materials, and knowledge all change. Who heard of CADD twenty years ago? Who ever heard of high-efficiency packings with HTUs† of 6 in and less? In a competitive situation the trained employee will outperform the untrained one without fail.

We all know that in a court of law as well as on a tennis court *competitiveness requires competence.* Without the latter, the former isn't even a consideration. In turn, competence requires many things, but, rest assured: *training* is among the most important. This is particularly important to engineers and designers.

More experienced employees should be encouraged to train newer employees. Design disciplines should provide mutual training to one another, concentrating on those areas where they most often come together—the *interface* areas.

Cost is often cited as a reason for not carrying out training programs. Some of the best training programs can be instituted at no cost. One method is to assign a newcomer to work directly under the supervision of a more experienced engineer or designer. Another method is to hold weekly meetings where three or four members of the design team spend 15 minutes each, describing some of the more interesting and challenging features of their particular niche in the project. Some of these meetings will turn into good, productive brainstorming sessions that will have the effect of saving money while improving the design. After some weeks, all project personnel will have made such a presentation. The three or four who started out will be called upon again. Eventually all project participants will be called again, too. The cycle should continue for the duration of the job.

At the start of a job that will consist of working in or duplicating an existing facility, the owner should invite engineers and designers to visit the facility. The engineers and designers should be shown how the operators and maintenance personnel do their jobs. The engineers/designers should be taken on tours through the existing facility, stopping to review good and bad features. Desired features should be mentioned by the operating personnel.

Site visits during the construction phase and later during start-up and operation benefit both the operating company and the engineering company. Both parties should work together to implement these

---

*As well as providing service to clients who buy products.

†Height of transfer unit.

visits. In the case where an engineering company is hired by an operating company, there must be an accord as to what training methods will be in place during the work. A suggested approach is that both share costs, if any.

7. *Adopt and institute leadership.* Deming uses the word *leader* in the sense of leading—not pushing. He means inspiring people to perform well. This type of leadership requires technical as well as administrative *knowledge.* More is said below.

8. *Drive out fear.* As a stimulus for accomplishing results, fear is the worst tool. Results are never predictable. Fear creates resentment, which in turn destroys cooperation. The very well-being of a project can be compromised if the level of resentment is present. At the very least, costs will rise as turnover on the job increases.

Fear can come from unexpected sources. Change can bring fear. New knowledge can bring fear until the benefits are seen. A good leader will sense fear in others and drive it out.

9. *Break down barriers between staff areas.* Engineering/design should be involved in the development of the process, selection of the equipment, and selection of materials as early as possible. Too often the process is fixed by the time it reaches the engineers and designers. *Yet it is the profession of engineers/designers to put processes together!* Their view of the panorama is not nearly as parochial as that of plant engineers, or R&D engineers, in most cases.

A plant process engineer tends to be a specialist with equipment at the particular worksite. An R&D engineer often doesn't even think in terms of equipment. It is the design engineer who has probably visited hundreds of operations, who has seen techniques in unrelated industries, and who can often suggest solutions to some very thorny problems during the development phase. The design engineer can also make suggestions about the type of data that should be acquired so that the engineering effort can proceed without delays.

10. *Eliminate slogans, exhortations, and targets for the workforce.* Exhortations do not help a person do a better job. Better tools do. Increased levels of knowledge do, as do training, leadership, information, etc. Talk is cheap and produces corresponding results.

11. *Eliminate numerical quotas for the work force and numerical goals for management.* The most common embodiment of this problem in engineering/design is inflexibility regarding cost and schedule. "You promised it would only take 34,000 man-hours and that you would wind it up in June!"

The engineer/designer will sense this inflexibility and will leave small tasks undone and facts unverified. Some of this will be done consciously with one rationale or another. Mostly, however, it will be done unconsciously in choices that will speed up the job and reduce the time required to finish. The engineer/designer will view problems with rose-colored glasses. By doing these things, he can get back on budget, within schedule, but the job as a whole will suffer. The higher costs during construction, lower-quality products over the life of the plant, higher operating costs, and difficulty during start-up are the terribly costly consequences of "management by numbers."

There should be no doubt that a failure to correctly forecast cost and schedule is serious. Obviously something is wrong. Perhaps the original estimate and/or schedule was defective. If so, then the solution is to improve estimating and scheduling skills.

The point here is that, rather than try to force adherence to an unrealistic situation, the conditions that caused a deviation from the forecast should be identified and eliminated. As a matter of fact, strict adherence to the *numbers* will backfire, and cost/schedule problems, of the job as a whole, will suffer.

Many Federal government jobs are controlled strictly by formulas and rating schemes. Award fees are then calculated from the numbers. Schedule and cost are highly important. Technical success, because it is difficult to assess, is diluted to inconsequence. Any thoughtful person who has worked on these jobs knows that quality is an immense problem.

12. *Remove barriers that rob people of pride of workmanship. Eliminate the annual rating or merit system.* In the author's experience, 100 percent of engineers/designers who have more than 5 years' experience take pride in their work. For those with less than 5 years' experience, the vast majority do take pride in their work; the few who don't will move on to other careers before their fifth anniversary.

Good leaders will understand job requirements, on one hand, and capabilities of people under their responsibility, on the other. These leaders will allow their people to be creative. They will express faith in them. They will guide their workers when needed.

Project leaders, by treating people as responsible adults who occasionally need guidance, can create a "can do" atmosphere on projects. On such projects, the barriers that rob people of pride in their work have been removed. Such a project is a marvel to behold.

The key here, though, is *knowledge* on the part of the leaders.

13. *Institute a vigorous program of education and self-improvement for everyone.* This point should come as no surprise. We tell our children that their schooling is all-important. At graduation ceremonies, the graduates invariably hear that their education has just begun.

Walton [13] quotes Deming as stating, "People are afraid to take a course. It might not be the right one. My advice is take it. Find the right one later." Deming himself [14] states:

> In respect to self-improvement, it is wise for anyone to bear in mind that there is no shortage of good people. *Shortage exists at the high levels of knowledge,** and this is true in every field. One should not wait for promise of reimbursement for a course of study. Moreover, study that is directed toward immediate need may not be the wisest course. There is widespread fear of knowledge . . . *but advances in competitive position will have their roots in knowledge.*†

Then he goes on to say: "Management must go through new learning."

In the process industries, the need for self-improvement and continuing education has long been recognized. As a matter of fact, professional societies such as the American Institute of Chemical Engineers organize and present courses under the rubric of continuing education. In general, large firms (both operating and engineering) have programs to sponsor advanced educational courses. Some of these firms will also give time off and pay expenses for employees to attend periodic professional meetings.

14. *Put everybody in the company to work to accomplish the transformation.* Organizations that are managed in accordance with the bad habits developed after World War II must undergo a complete change in their approach to business. It is essential that top management participate in the transformation.

---

*Emphasis added.

†Emphasis added.

The approach to quality, via the thirteen points outlined above, will not work unless a critical mass of people in an organization converts to the new way of looking at the business.

For engineering/design this will require some cultural changes and changes in attitude.

The culture of a transformed engineering effort is such that engineers/designers keep records of how they spend their time and then concentrate on how to spend less time to accomplish the same result. In the new culture, the electrical engineer might think:

> On average it takes me 6.4 h to rewrite the motor specification on each new project. I can probably improve on this. I am going to ask the secretary to read through my last five specifications and note what has been changing and what has been staying the same.
>
> Then, the next time I rewrite the specification, I will just have a cursory look at the material that doesn't change, and I will spend more time on the material that does change. Maybe I can spot a pattern that repeats itself for different conditions.
>
> Who knows? Maybe at some point I can get the time down to 3 or 4 h.
>
> I will keep a record of changes that occur with subsequent specifications. If it looks like I'm onto something, I will expand the technique to motor control centers and electric switchgear. I will present my results to project leaders and other design disciplines.

IMPORTANCE OF ENGINEERING/DESIGN

Time after time in *Out of the Crisis* [14], Deming uses the word *design* in the sense that *engineering/design* is used here. This author was able to count 68 instances in which Deming used the word *design* (or *redesign*) in his book. Of course, not all usage was in the sense of engineering/design (design of experiments, for example), but in most cases the sense was as used here. What follows is a selection of quotes from the 68 instances which are pertinent to engineering/design for process facilities.

> People in research, design, sales and production must work as a team to foresee problems of production and in use that may be encountered with the product or service [p. 24].
>
> A theme that appears over and over in this book is that quality must be built in at the design stage [p. 49].
>
> Engineers get blamed perennially for engineering changes. I myself have criticized their failure to get onto the factory floor to understand the difficulties of producing. . . . The fact is, they tell me, that they are forced to cut corners. . . . They never have time to finish anything. Push for production robs them of the chance to go into the production area to learn the problems created by the designs that they construct. They are rated on numbers [pp. 63–64].
>
> It is thus not sufficient to improve processes. There must also be constant improvement of design of product and service, along with introduction of new product and service and new technology. All this is management's responsibility [p. 135].

At this point Deming is not alone. A blue-ribbon committee established at the Massachusetts Institute of Technology calling itself The MIT Commission on Industrial Productivity, in its final report [15], had these comments:

> U.S. industrial performance has suffered not only from a failure to coordinate the design and manufacturing functions effectively, but also from a lack of attention to the manufacturing process itself. Process design

and production operations have been neglected by management and held in low esteem by the technical community. This is in sharp contrast to industrial practice in Japan and other countries, where production has far higher stature and attracts some of the most qualified and competent technical and managerial professionals [p. 72].

Successful mass producers recognize that price competitiveness must be matched by attention to quality and service, and indeed, they stress quality of design and production engineering as a means of reducing manufacturing costs [p. 119].

None of this comes as a surprise to dedicated, competent professionals who have labored long and hard in engineering/design. In the late 1960s British engine designer Keith Duckworth set the European racing community on its ear with some Formula 1 and Formula 2 engines that were hard to beat. When interviewed, Duckworth [16] commented:

Design has been a backwood of engineering for so long that the normal scheme is to accept that the design will be relatively poor and that a power of development will make it a useful thing in the end. Somebody draws something, usually without adequate thought, and then tries it. When it doesn't work the way he hoped it would he looks at the bits that break and tries to improve on those bits by continuous development. Ninety percent of it is lack of thought at the design stage. I have a principle that development is only required because of the ignorance of designers!

A little farther on he continued, "It is not worth something if you have a grave doubt in your mind on a fundamental point that you are fairly certain is important. It is obviously better, before proving in metal it *doesn't* work, to scrap it in paper form."

Duckworth's comments, although specifically directed at engine design, are equally applicable to process design and plant design.

The importance of design (and its current state of neglect) was stressed by the National Research Council. As reported in *Engineering Times* [17], one of the findings was that "The decline of U.S. international competitiveness has been ascribed to many factors. A crucial factor that is not often recognized is the quality of engineering design in the U.S." The entire article is worth reading and is included in App. I.

REALITIES

At this time a total quality engineering/design effort could only be undertaken in two circumstances: (1) when the engineering/design group is a division of an operating company that has embraced total quality or (2) when an engineering company that has embraced total quality is hired by an operating company that also has embraced total quality. Given these realities, there are probably few total-quality engineering/design efforts in the United States today. Nonetheless the trend seems to be headed in the direction of total-quality engineering/design. Also the number today must be vastly greater than it was only five short years ago.

What facets of engineering/design are weakest from the standpoint of quality? The answer is summarized in the following list (not in any special order):

- Control (via statistics and feedback)
- Leadership

- Knowledge
- Communication

The first three topics are covered below. The last topic, communication, is covered in Chaps. 11 and 14.

CONTROL

In today's engineering/design workplace, *control,* in the Deming sense, is nonexistent. Here and there a few measurements are made, but the culture of measurement for control purposes is not yet in place. Signs of quickening are beginning to show, however.

Control will have many inputs. Some will emerge years after the engineering design has been completed. Others will come from experience on previous projects. Still others will originate on the same project while it is being executed. Examples include

- Operators' comments years hence when an operation is upgraded
- Comments during review of drawings
- The conclusion that a certain design group cannot proceed due to lack of data

Figure 2-2 is presented as a tool for acquiring input data during the course of a job. The data can then be used by the project team to spot problem areas or improve performance on the job. The data should also be used as a reference for estimates or for comparison to other jobs.

The objective of using the form is to understand the engineering/design process and make the process more efficient. Every person in an engineering/design effort should fill out the form religiously, daily. The form can be filled out in less than five minutes. The entries need only be approximate, but the daily total must be correct.

In a manufacturing environment, daily records of a group's performance are often posted, while individuals keep their own records for consultation. In engineering/design, a weekly or biweekly posting is adequate. The form displayed in Fig. 2-2 should be turned in weekly (or biweekly) to a clerk or secretary whose duty it is to enter the data in a computer, run a sorting program, print a report, and publish the results (*without* editing) on the same day. This is a raw data report, and it can contain errors. It should be accompanied with a report from the previous period where errors have been corrected. The typical report consists of individuals' sheets (sent only to the individual, in confidence), and group reports sent to all individuals and posted prominently in the work areas. Group reports, of course, are sent to the client also.*

Whole copies (that is, individuals' sheets plus group reports) are sent to project leaders. These leaders meet with designers and engineers to assess flow of information and document production on the project as a whole. A typical conclusion might be: "Let's not start architectural work yet. There is not enough information. Schedule for two weeks from next Monday." or "Steel fabrication drawings are in. Have a junior piper check for interferences."

One of the statistics in the weekly report should be a difference

---

*On cost-plus work only, see Chap. 13, *Hiring the Engineers,* to understand why.

Project Name: _____ Project No: _____ Week Ending: _____

	Activity	Mon.	Tues.	Wed.	Thus.	Fri.	Sat.	Sun.
1	Read (study, investigate)	– –	– –	– –	– –	– –	– –	– –
2	For Item No.							
3	Discuss: 1. Client							
4	2. Internal							
5	3. Vendor							
6	4.							
7	Calculate							
8	Write: 1. Memo							
9	2. Letter							
10	3. Specification							
11	4. Requisition							
12	5.							
13	Sketch (or doodle, and analyse with sketches)	– –	– –	– –	– –	– –	– –	– –
14	For Item No.							
15	Draw: 1.							
16	2.							
17	3.							
18	4.							
19	Meetings (formal only)							
20	Review	– –	– –	– –	– –	– –	– –	– –
21	For Item No.							
22	Checking others' work	– –	– –	– –	– –	– –	– –	– –
23	For Item No.							
24	On the road							
25	Other projects: 1.							
26	2.							
27	3.							
28	Not assignable *							
29								
30								
31								
32		▬	▬	▬	▬	▬	▬	▬
33	Totals							
34								
35								
36	Availability of information (0 or 1) * *	– –	– –	– –	– –	– –	– –	– –
37	(If 0 only) For Item No.							
38								

	Notes:			
39	1. _____	6. _____		
40	2. _____	7. _____		
41	3. _____	8. _____		
42	4. _____	9. _____		
43	5. _____	10. _____		

44	Documents Issued:	R –	R –	R –	R –	R –
45		R –	R –	R –	R –	R –
46						
47	See attachments (mark if something is attached)					

* i.e., mail, walk, file, copy, etc.

* * 1 – satisfactory ; 0 – unsatisfactory

Employee No.: _____

Figure 2-2 Raw data report.

between planned and actual staffloading for the previous week. This statistic should be reported for each discipline.

The intent of this scheme is to avoid putting people on the job too early, thus causing wasted effort, or putting people on the job too late, causing delays.

> This technique of timing entry to and exit from a project for the different disciplines—and individuals with special skills—is the secret to high productivity and quality for engineering/design of process facilities.

For a truly efficient effort, entry and exit by the same individual should occur several times. Putting an instrument engineer on board at day one of the project and pulling him off when he has run out of scheduled hours does not make sense. Assigning him part-time on day one, so that he can receive correspondence and build an instrument file while his duties on another job lessen, is smart. He will be available to help with piping and instrument diagrams (P&IDs). His involvement will increase and eventually become full-time until the budget estimate is produced. Then the whole job goes on hold while the client reviews and approves the project (see Fig. 14-4a to c). When this happens, the instrument engineer is assigned work on other projects, helping out until "his" project gets the go-ahead. Then, when approval becomes a fact, he can start full-time (and can take on some additional help as needed). Eventually a point will be reached where his full attention will no longer be required, and he can be given a new assignment on the next job getting under way. Thus as duties increase on one job, they will decline on the previous one.

When historical records have been acquired from several projects, the quality of man-hour estimates will be greatly improved. Engineering firms can have much more confidence in their lump-sum work, and owners can engage in cost-plus work, knowing how their money is being spent.

The Deming approach to quality requires statistical analysis of the data acquired with Fig. 2-2. Specifically, all project participants should have learned basic skills in statistics. They should be capable of distinguishing whether the time required to produce a project document is within a normal pattern of variation or whether a special cause is at work.

A professional statistician is needed to train project personnel and to carry out special statistical tests.

The use of Fig. 2-2 and similar measurement/control devices and methods will only be successful as long as they are not perverted to become a tool for management by numbers. The use of devices such as Fig. 2-2 will only succeed in a total-quality culture.*

LEADERSHIP

Leadership and management should not be confused. Leadership inspires. Management obligates. Leadership shows the way. Management points fingers.

In *Leaders* [19], Bennis and Nanus present a message published in

---

*Such a culture exists in very few U.S. firms. Walton [18] states that attempts at *total quality* can only be tried after statistical control has been achieved—something that in Japan takes at least 3 to 5 years of concerted effort.

the *Wall Street Journal* by United Technologies Corporation. It reads as follows:

> *Let's get rid of management.* People don't want to be managed. They want to be led. Who ever heard of a world manager? World leader, yes. Educational leader. Political leader. Religious leader. Scout leader. Community leader. Labor leader. Business leader. They lead. They don't manage. The carrot always wins over the stick. Ask your horse. You can lead your horse to water, but you can't *manage* him to drink. If you want to manage somebody, manage yourself. Do that well and you'll be ready to stop managing. And start leading.

In project work for process facilities it is not unusual to be confronted with managers whose technical skills are low, but whose confidence level and aggressiveness are high. Such managers usually report to superiors with similar skills and personality traits. The mysterious thing, "the project," will be whipped into submission.

On one project, the client project manager targeted a certain type of reflux condenser and made the flat statement that it would not work. This was in a review meeting. Everyone's mouths went dry. The process engineer who had specified the condenser was dumbstruck. He tried arguing, but was no match against the bombast of the attacker. For one thing, he did not have the mantle of authority, the title *manager*. After the meeting, the engineer was able to demonstrate that what he had presented was good practice and would even perform in a superior manner. Later, the manager retreated somewhat by saying the design would work, but "wasn't good."

The manager on the engineering side, to whom the engineer reported, was technically weak and somewhat retiring, so he was useless. From then onward the process engineer was inhibited and adopted an attitude seen all too often: If you stick to doing only what others tell you to do, you can always pass the buck. He completely ran out of ideas and required a good deal of guidance for the rest of the job.

On a completely different job, the client manager (his title was engineer, but his function was to impose his will, that is, to manage) insisted that design work begin before some fundamental engineering problems were solved. "I want to see lead going onto paper." The engineering project manager resisted these entreaties, but at client insistence was removed from the job. His position was filled by a manager acquiescent to client demands.*

Expenditures of no less than $3 million were made. The whole thing came to a halt when one of the phases of a magnetic pump burned out, catastrophically, during a difficult start-up. It was only due to good fortune that no one was standing close enough to be killed.

The destruction and cost of this management approach are huge, yet will never be known, as they cannot be measured. Suffice it to say that the fortunes of this entire country have declined while this type of management has become more prevalent.

Up the Organization by Robert Townsend took this country by storm 20 or so years ago. Townsend spoke from an historical perspective that goes back to ancient philosophers and from the immediate perspective of the boardroom of a major corporation. His

---

*Typical clients rarely comprehend the huge amount of clout they have when they hire an engineering company. If they say, "Black is white," at least half of the staff people at the engineering company will repeat, "Black is white."

observations gain stature with time. Under "Message to Chief Executives," he states irreverently [20]:

> Probably whenever Sitting Bull, Geronimo, and the other chiefs powwowed, the first topic of conversation was the shortage of Indians. Certainly today, no meeting of the high and mighty is complete until someone polishes the conventional wisdom: "Our trouble today is getting enough good people."
>
> This is crystal-clear nonsense. Your people aren't lazy and incompetent. They just look that way. They're beaten by all the overlapping and interlocking policies, rules and systems encrusting your company.
>
> Do you realize that your people can't make long-distance calls without filling out a report? Do you know what they have to go through to hire somebody—or buy something? Stop running down your people. It's your fault they're rusty from underwork. Start tearing down the system where it has defeated and imprisoned them. They'll come to life fast enough. Be the Simon Bolivar of your industry. Ole!

Townsend's whole book is about *leadership.* It must be read and reread.

When the fortunes of engineering companies went on the decline in the early 1980s, operating companies took advantage of the situation by demanding contracts with onerous terms. Engineering companies responded by assigning project managers whose duty was to maximize profits for the engineering company. These managers were hard-nosed, good businesspeople. Highly paid, supremely competent designers were sent into early retirement and replaced by low-paid novices.

The engineering companies survived. Project quality took a nosedive.

The best approach to avoid this sort of trap is to make it plain that quality is important—not with words but with deeds. The owner should choose as project manager an individual with a high degree of technical competence combined with a good deal of professional pride. Then the owner should make it plain that selection of the engineering company will place a premium on technical competence and professional pride, not only at the designer/engineer level, *but also at the project manager level.*

A recurrent and highly destructive idea is the one that implies that managers can manage without knowing what they are managing.* During the selection process, the owner should make it plain that there will be an accord between the owner's project manager and the engineering project manager, based on trust, and that the goal is quality work which will enable quality construction and quality operation. The accord will also contain the specific understanding that neither the engineers nor the owner is trying to maximize profit at the expense of the other.

There is nothing new in the idea that managers should be technically competent. In *Out of the Crisis* [21], Deming brings this out repeatedly. He says, for example, "To manage one must lead. To lead one must understand the work he and his people are responsible for." In an article in *Chemical Engineering* [22], Dalton makes the point that "doing it the right way" requires management with technical competence:

> In this age of high mobility and decreased loyalty to the corporate employer, many professional managers have not learned the process for which they are responsible. *They are isolated from the real product or*

---

*This idea is similar to the one that says a teacher need not know the subjects being taught, but need only know the theory of education.

*service that they are responsible for.** Many organizational structures serve to isolate managers by creating additional reporting layers between the manager and the actual product. This insidious practice has caused many companies to forget how to do their own business.

Today's leader must not be a "professional manager" or a "technical manager." Instead he or she must relate to a specific process by thinking "I design reactors"† or "I make resins." Today's leader must develop a vision of the perfect product or service, one which can be reduced to a quantitative set of product and process specifications. These specifications allow us to do the right thing in the right way.

Doing it the right way can't be subjugated to the demands to "get product out the door." Work should not be done with the wrong materials, substandard materials, nor with in-process work that is imperfect. It cannot be done differently on a given day as a matter of expediency.

Technical competence can even extend to the office of the CEO and have likely beneficial effects. The MIT Commission concluded [23]:

> For too long business schools have taken the position that a good manager could manage anything, regardless of its technological base. If technological judgements were necessary, experts could be consulted, but it was not essential for top executives to understand the technologies they were investing in or managing. Among the consequences was that courses on production or operations management became less and less central to business-school curricula. It is now clear this view is wrong.

Richard Foster in his book *Innovation* [24] reports a comparison study by McKinsey suggesting that companies led by technical or marketing people outperform, by a large margin, companies run by financial people.

The morale of an organization grows from its type of leadership. The George Patton, Ross Perot, Robert Townsend type of organization evolves from a conviction down in the ranks that the boss knows what is going on. This leadership can be compared to the management techniques of Robert McNamara, Secretary of Defense under Lyndon Johnson. Initially McNamara was lauded as a genius. Later, he was reviled and eventually he quit, but his management style did not leave with him. This was (and is) management by the numbers at its apogee.

When managers‡ are not sufficiently knowledgeable about engineering/design, they are in a poor position to sort through the many versions of the truth that will be presented to them. One example occurred when the question arose as to whether interlocks should be numbered on P&IDs. The project manager ran into one of the instrument designers in the hallway and asked his opinion. The instrument designer was thinking only of making life easy for himself, not project requirements, when he stated that numbering interlocks was a waste of time. Had the project manager asked the same question of a field electrical superintendent, he would have gotten an answer that closely reflected project needs. Had he convened a mini meeting with at least one senior instrument engineer present to sort through the pros and cons, he would have also arrived at an answer more consonant with project needs. If he had ever spent time trying to find a

---

*Emphasis by this author.

†Author's note: or "I design process plants."

‡What is said regarding managers in this section applies equally well to project engineers, as they are the heirs apparent—tomorrow's managers.

particular ladder diagram among scores on electrical elementary sheets, he would never have asked the question at all.

When managers are technically weak, they are easier to deceive. Perhaps it is this author's prejudice, but it seems that technically weak managers will put technically strong members off to the side and seek council from their own kind. A project can be managed by a person lacking technical competence, but it cannot be *led* by such a person. The project team will play roles, but they will not truly follow.

When it is said that technical competence should accompany leadership on efforts leading to the construction of process facilities, the degree of competence implied is not high. Yet the level must be such that communication is not a problem and that the "worker" does not sense that she or he is dealing with an inferior. A leader role is difficult to establish if the boss cannot lend an idea or two to a creative effort. H. Wallace Caruthers, the inventor of nylon, was not under the thumb of an MBA.

An engineering project manager should have the following curricula or capabilities:

- A degree in physics, chemistry, engineering, or architecture*
- Successful completion of assignments as process engineer and project engineer
- An understanding of critical path method
- An understanding of Figs. 14-4, 14-5a to c, 5-4, and 5-6
- An understanding of the importance of vendor drawings (how to obtain, how to use, when they will be available)
- An exposure to plant operations (preferably some operating and start-up experience)
- A broad exposure to construction, from excavation and underground work through equipment setting to punch lists (from this the manager should have acquired a rough idea of construction sequence)

In the great majority of cases, project managers should be capable of plotting a pump/system curve having a throttling valve on the pump discharge (see Fig. 10-5). Likewise, managers should also be capable of performing a reliable mass balance on a straightforward process (see Chap. 8).

A fundamental duty of project managers is to promote teamwork. They can only do this if they possess a working knowledge of the many different disciplines to help illuminate blind spots between design disciplines. This does not mean they could substitute for civil engineers, for example, but it does mean that project managers have to know what the civil engineer thinks about: rainfall, flow lines, gradient, fill, compaction, RCP, vitrified clay pipe, and so on.

Project managers must also possess knowledge specific to the type of facility being engineered. Examples:

- *Pharmaceutical:* clean in place, sterile, clean room, class 100 air, pyrogens, WFI, FDA, validation, TIG welding, etc.
- *Refinery:* flare system, gas system, crude units, cat crackers, reformers, cogeneration, cutter stock, sweeteners, pump-arounds, heat balances, etc.

---

*Occasionally, a highly competent project designer can become a project manager.

- *Cyanidation:* vat leach, carbon-in-pulp (CIP), heap leach, counter-current decantation, drum filters, belt filters, deaeration, Merrill-Crowe, etc.

- *Synthetic fibers:* filter pack, spinnerette, metering pump, spinning position, draw ratio, windup, finish rolls, synchronous motors, etc.

- *Copper smelter:* chalcopyrite, iron-copper ratio, heat balances, matte, white metal, converter, blister, poling, flash smelter, acid plant, selenium bleed, etc.

The list, of course, could fill volumes and still be incomplete.

The point is, project managers and their project engineers should have skills suited to the task at hand. Great competence is not needed, but competence that enables leaders and those who work under the leaders is needed.

Bennis [25] says, "*Learning and competence matter. Leaders value learning and mastery, and so do people who work for leaders. Leaders make it clear that there is no failure, only mistakes that give us feedback and tell us what to do next.*"

Next on the list of skills of project leaders is the ability to delegate. The delegation cannot be token in nature. It must be wholly granted, such as when Robert E. Lee entrusted Jeb Stuart with cavalry maneuvers that sometimes took a week and often required days before messages could be exchanged. The authority must accompany the responsibility, or the act of delegation is a farce. Specifically, the project manager must delegate to the project engineers the authority to approve drawings, specifications, requisitions, purchase orders, etc.

Table 2-1 is a summary list of documents for an $18 million project. It is presented here to demonstrate how delegation is a necessity.

If the project manager were the sole authority for approving project documents, he or she would be faced with about 3300 approvals over about an 8-month period. At the time the project activity reaches a peak level, the project manager would have to approve as many as 30 documents in a single day. This load is too heavy. He or she would be signing documents without becoming familiar with what they meant.

A project manager should spend no more than 20 percent of the time reviewing and signing documents. In this example, the project workforce would reach a maximum in the eighth and ninth months after the start of engineering. At that point 31 people would be on board. If three people were to share the load at the peak effort (manager plus two project engineers), about 10 min per document would be available for review and approval. This is not much time, but is manageable in view of the fact that 30 documents per day is a maximum. The average at peak effort will probably be closer to 20.

TABLE 2-1 Summary List of Drawings and Specifications

		Drawings		
	Specifications	**B size**	**D, E size**	**Comments**
Process	32		44	P&IDs + PFDs
Mechanical	11		18	
Instruments	45	188	17	B size are loop diagrams.
Electrical	11		26	
Piping	6	304	35	B size are isometric drawings.
Civil	8		16	
Structural	8		42	
Architectural	9		17	
	130	492	215	

The method for handing out responsibility is to subdivide the job into areas (mostly by function, partly by geography) between the project manager and the project engineers (see Chap. 6, *Project Organization*). Then each is made wholly responsible for *all project work* in his or her area. This responsibility would include the following items, for example: underground piping and conduit, grounding cable, building foundations, building steel, bathrooms, doors, door hardware, equipment, instruments, water fountains, and so on.

The project manager has the additional responsibility of unifying efforts in all three areas.

LEADER OR LACKEY?

A serious problem that often goes unnoticed on projects is the role to be assumed by the engineering group. Are they to be leaders or lackeys?

As pointed out earlier, some engineers, designers, and even managers adopt a submissive attitude whereby they seek to avoid making decisions. An insecurity hampers their ability to make decisions. They prefer to have others do their thinking for them.

"What is the holdup, Joe?"

"I don't know where to run the monorail for the hoist."

"Why don't you run it straight above the center of the aisle between the reactors?"

This sort of behavior can be expected of a few cub engineers or designers. However, it can grow and become endemic from attitudes of the project manager. If the project manager is a shirker, the shirkers will be in control. This behavior also can be easily imposed on a design team by an overly assertive client unless tempered by leadership from within the design team. By far, the majority of clients want the engineering organization to assume a leadership role. There are a few who seek submission, however. More is said about this shortly.

The leadership role is a more natural one, as project work is the lifeblood of an engineering organization. It is the *raison d'être*. "Our job is to tell others how to build things. Shrinking violets are not permitted entry."

Once the possibility of this potential problem is known, steps can be taken to prevent it. Very early in a project, and all the way through it, project leaders should make an effort to help team members make their own decisions.

"Where should I run the discharge line, boss?"

"Well, John, why don't you tell me. Look at the options. Write them down, too. Then make notes of the pros and cons of each choice. Next make a selection. Check with me, once you've done it, and let's talk about it."

Project leaders should also state at weekly meetings and in one-on-one conversations, "We are paid to make decisions for the client. We are looked upon as experts. It is our job to take a leadership role. We are leaders, not lackeys."

There will be the occasional clients who will wish to impose their will on the engineering organization and use it as a drafting service. This should be established when qualifications are being reviewed (see Chap. 13, *Hiring the Engineers*). In such a case, passive managers, engineers, and designers can be assigned to work under close guidance of client managers and engineers.

It is important never to start work until the desired role has been specified. Major misunderstandings have made a surprise appearance when an engineering group assumed a passive, show-me attitude and the clients expected dynamism and creativity. Even worse is when the engineers are playing the passive role and the client engineers lack experience and fail to see that the project is really standing still. It is akin to the situation where there are two chess players, each supposing it is the other's turn to move. Months can go by with nothing being accomplished! In this situation verbal requests and memos asking for guidance are flying, and studies are being generated by the gross, so it looks as though progress is being made. It is all false, however, because no decisions are being made. There exists a crisis of leadership unbeknownst to all.

To avoid this trap, the *scope of work* and *design basis* documents can be extremely useful.* First, the clients can state in the scope of work that they expect the engineering organization to assume a leadership role. Second, the clients can turn these documents over to the engineers and say, "Our part is done. The rest is up to you. We will monitor progress, and we will be available for questions and reviews, but you are responsible from this point on."

The importance of obtaining input, during research and development, from engineering/design was mentioned above. Another advantage of involving engineers/designers during the research and development stage is that they will be committed to a leadership position. Development of fundamental design features without involving the engineers puts them in an inferior position to start with. To come along later and start demanding leadership stretches the limits of credibility.

KNOWLEDGE

Given enough time to do a good job, the key to putting together a good process plant is *knowledge.* There is no superior requisite. This is so fundamental, so obvious, and so often ignored. The reasons for losing sight of this fact are several. First is the idea in the minds of nonengineers and nonscientists that engineering is all formulas and known quantities not requiring investigation, analysis, and judgment. Second is the idea that because project management schemes have been used successfully for saving money and reporting progress, they can be used as a substitute for knowledge. Third is the fact that in many business schools, students are taught that trained people are always available. This implies they are walking the streets and will walk through the door just when needed, looking for a job. This also implies that a good business person will understand job requirements sufficiently to spot an engineer qualified for the proposed task.† Finally, there is that kernel of thought nestled in the minds of the lazy or cynical that there really is no such thing as *knowledge,* just others pretending and playing one-upmanship.

Thus the obvious and fundamental is sullied.

Throughout *Out of the Crisis,* Deming homes in on the value of knowledge as an essential ingredient of quality. Walton [26] quotes Deming:

---

*See examples in App. A.

†This author once gracefully exited a job interview for a responsible position with a major company when he discovered the sole interview was to be with the personnel department. To the author, this was a giant red flag waving off qualified engineers. The company was looking for meat, not brains.

How to improve quality and productivity? "By everyone doing his best." Five words—and it is *wrong.* That is not the right answer. You have to know what you do.

The system is such that almost nobody can do his best. You have to know what to do, *then* do your best. Sure we need everybody's best—everybody working together with a common aim. And knowing something about how to achieve it.

The following example shows how knowledge works. The operation was a small one. It consisted of drying soggy magnetite powder in a rotary dryer, about 4 ft by 25 ft. Heat to drive off the moisture came from a burner stuck through the feed end. A good deal of magnetite went up the stack along with the combustion gases, and, quite rightly, people nearby complained. Under this stimulus, the plant manager called in a dust collector manufacturer and asked for a quote. The quote stunned him, being about 6 times the annual wage of a professional employee. An engineer was assigned to see what might be done. Using his knowledge of project work for process plants, the engineer performed a material balance on the dryer. He then wrote a specification for a dust collector and used his material balance to state capacities for the fan and baghouse. He included some sketches and a P&ID. The same vendor was asked to rebid. His new quote was half of his first quote. His second quote was not padded with fear and uncertainty. With one week's work the engineer had saved his company 3 times his annual salary.

Eventually the unit was installed. And it proved to be a money-maker! It paid for itself in 2 years with revenues from previously lost product.

Many kinds of knowledge must be drawn upon during the engineering of a process plant. On the nontechnical side, foremost in importance is knowing how to read, listen, and speak. On the technical side, a store of knowledge based on past experience, physics, and chemistry is essential. Acquisition of this knowledge can come from formal study, from casual observation, from trips to the library, and so on. The knowledge base of a dedicated individual expands over a lifetime.

Here a pause is needed to briefly view an enticing pitfall: *mathematics.* It should suffice to say, but never has, that mathematics is the tool, not the end product. Particularly in this age of electronics, the physical world can be washed away by seductive mathematical abstractions.

There is the backlash end, too, the people who scoff at the mathematics and say, "Wasn't all that calculus a waste of time?" The answer, of course, is a resounding, "*No!*" This author has used, beneficially, every course he ever took in mathematics and a good number of other studies on the side. Einstein often complained that physics was limited by mathematics. The same can be said about the pedestrian vocation of building process plants.

In summary, then, the mathematics must be used with gusto, studied, and modified as needed, but the engineer must remember at some point that concrete has to be poured, machines installed, and raw materials transformed to products.

Returning from the digression, then, we note that *knowledge* for putting together a process plant fits into three broad categories: past observations, physics, and chemistry. Past observations include physical data from journals, client preferences (for product purity, type of package, etc.), toxicity and corrosivity of materials, how to make a P&ID, critical path method, cost estimating, etc. Physics is the classic newtonian type: $F = mA$, statics, dynamics, mass and energy conservation, etc. Chemistry centers mostly on mole and mass balances, thermodynamics, physical chemistry (properties, equilibria, etc.), kinetics, and so on, again mostly along classical lines.

Knowledge from these sources can be used to

- Characterize raw materials and products
- Understand the operation
- Understand the equipment
- Determine reasonable expectations of cost and schedule
- Determine staffing requirements

among other things. Knowledge in some parts of engineering is highly standardized. For example, in structural engineering, load conditions on structural members have been cataloged for hundreds of cases.

Also *usual* electric power work (such as wiring of residences and commercial establishments) can largely be done by using a few codebooks, some plan and elevation drawings, and some up-to-date manufacturer's catalogs.

The average process job, on the other hand, commonly draws data from nonstandard, uncertified sources (reports by unknown authors, journals from far-away places, and journals more than a century old). Here, as in few other fields, checking the knowledge base is essential. Judgment based on experience must be rigorously exercised.

The point here, rather obviously, is that technical knowledge *does* matter. *Know-how* is important. Millions of dollars are spent purchasing enterprises that appear marginal from their balance sheet but represent a store of knowledge. Knowledge of rebar* and concrete is fine and, make no mistake, very necessary. Knowledge of man-hour estimates† is fine and necessary, too. Knowledge of Newton's third law is even finer and *more* necessary. But none of these reach the level of importance enjoyed by knowledge of the process and the equipment to be used in the process.

This leads to the following maxim:

> On process plant projects, knowledge of the mass balance and of the equipment is the most important kind of knowledge.

Both these are given special attention in subsequent chapters.

Equipment (be it process equipment, material handling equipment, boilers, fans for HVAC systems, etc.) is singled out for special attention as opposed to the lesser pieces, but these pieces matter too. The smaller pieces such as valves, pressure gauges, etc. (given the status of commodity) usually can be applied with less knowledge. The chance that these items might affect the process is minor and is usually well understood. The lesser status of these pieces does not mean they should be ignored, however. A questioning attitude toward all pieces, big or small, must constantly be put to work. *Every* component for a process plant must be thought out ahead of time. Knowledge that the component will work as desired is a requirement. On more than a few occasions, the pros and cons of using carbon-steel bolts on stainless-steel flanges have been a subject of discussion over lunch. The carbon-steel bolts are often selected because they are far thriftier and do not gall [ATD].

---

*Steel reinforcing rod is often referred to as rebar.

†Estimate of time required for engineers, designers, and staff personnel to do their work.

Chapter 10, *Equipment Examples,* is devoted to some fundamental aspects about a few different types of equipment. The purpose is to show the level of detail with which one must be conversant to properly understand and apply equipment. Knowledge is acquired over long periods from many sources. Access to the knowledge can occur only if a good filing system has been set up. Appendix J contains the file index of the author's file as an example. Some comments about acquiring the information are included.

Where project controls* are concerned, note that all the computer software in the world is worth nothing without appropriate knowledge of design and construction. A sad reality today is that the supply of software far outpaces the knowledge to run it intelligently.

Take the case of a schedule. The project was to install wastewater filtration for a petroleum refinery, a $6 million project. The first version of the schedule submitted for review completely omitted vendor drawing submittals and the accompanying fuss over them. The copies of the printout were impressive† but were flawed to the core because they lacked activities for dealing with the vendor information. The clerk who input the data had the title *project scheduler.* His knowledge of engineering/design was slight, and he had never set foot on a construction site. He knew how to run some scheduling software on a computer. Given a choice between a clerk running a $1000 software package on a $2500 system or a knowledgeable scheduler‡ with an adding machine, this author would not hesitate to select the latter as the superior choice by far. The results would be more accurate and available sooner, would cost less, and would not require heavy supervision.

Of course, the best of all worlds would be to have a knowledgeable scheduler running a great program on a good system. Speed, accuracy, readability, and variety of information would be greatly enhanced. The project would prosper. Leave out the knowledgeable individual, and you have nothing. The descriptive acronym from the 1950s is equally true today—GIGO: *garbage in begets garbage out.*

After having spent a day or two studying drawings, a knowledgeable individual can visit a construction jobsite and take note of

- Whether any equipment is installed
- How many of the buildings are ready to receive equipment
- The number of pipe racks that are installed and have pipe in them
- Whether the electrical contractor is on board yet
- Some more key indicators

Then in a few hours, after walking around, asking questions and looking at the drawings while he or she does so, this individual can state the entire job duration (construction portion) to within 1 month in most cases and to within 2 months in all cases. Furthermore, the scheduler can state the percentage of the job that is complete and the probable date for mechanical completion. This is not magic or chicanery. There are very simple sequences that are followed on all jobs. An experienced person can see where the job is at present, and by asking

---

*The two main documents of project control are the schedule and the cost report. The use of these documents is sometimes erroneously referred to as "project management."

†The schedule listed 1400 different activities.

‡A person with an understanding of the required jobs, job sequences, and job durations.

questions can get a good idea of whether the job is being rushed or done at a reasonable pace. He or she can also get a barometer on morale. By having studied the drawings ahead of time, the scheduler has a good idea of what the job requires in normal circumstances. Then the scheduler compensates for the actual conditions seen.

No computer can do what this experienced individual can do. It is amusing to see an inexperienced project scheduler on a jobsite reviewing progress with an experienced construction manager (CM). Unless the scheduler is really foolish (and most aren't), the computer-generated reports will be tailored to agree with what the CM says. This undoubtedly enhances the reputation of the software and the clerks who run it.

On the engineering/design portion of the job, the story is the same. Once a budget estimate is available, and after a day or two of studying project documents, a knowledgeable design professional can look at design statistics, such as

- Whether piping on the P&IDs is labeled with sizes and numbers
- Whether instruments are numbered
- The number of purchase orders issued
- The number of drawings issued and their status (that is, issued for review, approval, construction, etc.)
- How many vendor prints have been approved

Then in a day the professional can state (within 20 percent) the total man-hour requirement, the percentage of the design that is complete, the total time required for engineering/design, and the time remaining for completion. To do this, the individual will make use of Fig. 14-4.

In both these cases, it is assumed that the work is well led and is not being executed out of sequence. Likewise, it is assumed that the design and the construction are performed by competent people. Furthermore, it is assumed that lists of drawings, equipment, instruments, and such are accurate.

Knowledge is peerless for accurate determination of job status. All else is secondary. Knowledge gained while using the Raw Data Report (Fig. 2-2) in the engineering/design phase will greatly assist determination of job status.

CAUSE OF LACK OF KNOWLEDGE

As this chapter comes to a close, it is worth pausing to consider the chief cause of lack of knowledge. The major contributor is poor selection of priorities. This cause, as a matter of fact, may lie at the heart of others that come to mind, such as laziness and inexperience. Thus there is one cause of lack of knowledge: *poor ordering of priorities.* The recent discussion contrasting a computer clerk and a knowledgeable professional contains a good example. Instead of training a novice scheduler to run software, he or she should be taken to the field and shown some stark realities. Scheduling is not the entry of numbers into a screen at a keyboard. It is trying to predict the future, armed with *known* past performance.

The tie between knowledge and priorities is easy to see by considering students with a penchant for watching television. Their knowledge level will stay low until they put a high priority on their studies.

—Chapter 3— For Company Executives

REINVESTMENT OF EARNINGS

One of the most important tasks facing an executive officer of a company is reinvestment of earnings. The most common ways of doing this are:

- Acquisition of another business
- Expansion or improvement of the existing business
- Initiation of a new line of business
- Purchase of securities or financial instruments

For a time in the 1960s and 1970s, investments in nonrelated businesses were quite popular. That time saw the rise of the conglomerate. Although investments of this type still exist, they are not nearly as numerous today. Peters and Waterman [27] used the phrase *stick to the knitting* to describe fealty to the traditional business. Their phrase certainly caught on; moreover, one is tempted to assume it has served as a guide to company executives and stemmed the excesses of the 1960s and 1970s.

Today, most CEOs will try to build upon what they already have and will therefore favor reinvestment in the second category: expansion or improvement of the existing business. Furthermore when acquisitions and new lines of business are considered, often they are in areas which are compatible with the existing business. The last option, securities, is used on a daily basis to keep money working while decisions are made concerning the first three options.

Given the importance of reinvestment in the existing business, it is surprising how infrequently it is discussed in popular business publications. It is not uncommon to read through a whole issue of *Fortune* and catch only an oblique reference. The bulk of articles concern personalities, descriptions (of businesses, companies, or industries), and matters relating to stocks, bonds, and other paper investments.

This book is mainly a guide, providing an organized view of project tasks, for the engineers and designers who will have a heavy role in reinvesting earnings. *And* it is also meant to pave the way to smoother projects by promoting better communications between all project participants, *including upper management.* Company executives must be able to glimpse behind the scenes and comprehend how company money is being used.

This last point is rarely appreciated. Most project participants fail to realize that the executives probably come from a background that did not include project work. In reality, the average executive on his or her first project is in for something of a shock with the massive spending, rapid pace, and pressure cooker atmosphere. In some cases, more than half the money is gone before any equipment shows up on site. Meanwhile the buildings have hardly become more than empty skeletons. In spite of assurances from old project hands, this can be quite unsettling. To this, add unfamiliar jargon and the utilitarian frankness that must accompany this kind of work, and you have all the ingredients of a cardiac case.

One executive vice-president commented, after his first review meeting, that he had never been through anything so depressing. Nothing seemed to be going right. The entire meeting consisted of one revelation after another of something amiss: behind schedule or excessive in cost or likely not to operate properly. He was advised that the things going well are rarely discussed because that is a waste of time. The focus is on problems. When steel must mate with concrete and machines must mate with steel, all discussions must be highly utilitarian. The performance with the cane and softshoe will not suffice.

EARLY EXECUTIVE TASKS

The what and when of executive duties are best understood by reviewing a schedule of a whole venture, see Fig. 3-1. The schedule depicts the phases leading up to and through a capital investment. It usually begins with research and development and ends with a new unit in operation.

It is important that the executive understand preliminary and budget estimates. The preliminary and budget estimates may only be a few months apart from each other, but differ greatly in definition. The preliminary estimate results from a group of perhaps three senior people conjuring an estimate, using examples from the past. The budget estimate results from an abbreviated full effort, using perhaps 25 percent of the engineering/design staff to be expected at full force and for only a brief period. The preliminary estimate is accurate to within about ±25 percent while the budget estimate is in the neighborhood of ±15 percent.

The amount of engineering/design that goes into each kind of estimate differs sharply. For a preliminary estimate, the required amount of engineering* is in the neighborhood of 2 percent of the total for

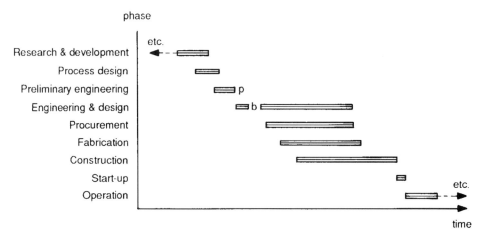

Figure 3-1 Venture schedule. p = preliminary estimate, b = budget estimate.

---

*This does not include process development.

engineering/design. For a budget estimate it is 20 percent. That is, for a $10 million total constructed value (TCV), where engineering runs 12 percent of the TCV, the required work for an estimate will cost:*

- Preliminary: (10,000,000)(0.12)(0.02) = $24,000
- Budget: (10,000,000)(0.12)(0.20) = $240,000

It invariably makes good sense to embark on a major engineering effort with a preliminary estimate. This is an inexpensive way of becoming acquainted with the engineering/design organization while you obtain an estimate. Once this has been done, if the venture appears favorable, additional funds should be spent to obtain a more reliable estimate (the budget estimate). Some funds for vendors may be needed, too; this is covered below.

This method of obtaining estimates keeps spending in check as information is developed.

OVERSTEPPING BOUNDS

Unless measures are taken to prevent this, some profound technical decisions can be made by nontechnical people. In one case, a senior vice-president chose an architectural firm to take the lead on a process job. In another case, an owner scheduled the end of a job to occur where he felt it should end. These requirements were accommodated fully, without so much as a peep from the project people. These same executives never realized how much their requirements had cost them.

Nontechnical executives are advised to sensitize themselves in this matter and to seek technical advice when in doubt. A few examples of technical areas in which nontechnical executives often infringe are

- Schedule
- Assignment of personnel
- Product requirements
- Site selection
- Selection of engineers and constructors

Without a doubt, the executive *must* exert influence, but it must be in an informed fashion. A process plant project, in its execution, is a highly technical effort. Ignorance or disparagement of this fact will ultimately lead to great difficulties.

Executives do best for themselves in selecting an appropriate team to serve their needs.

OWNER'S PROJECT TEAM

The company executive should have access to a project manager or a project engineer at all times—even during the research and development phase. During research and development, the nature of the work will require only an occasional consultation with the project person, who must advise as to the status of the R&D effort, as this must *not* solely be determined by R&D personnel. This project person

---

*The percentages given here are for the sake of the example given. Ranges of these values can be found in Chap. 5.

should have the lead in determining the type of effort, the duration, and the correct funding for process design and preliminary engineering.

Once the project moves into the preliminary engineering phase, the project person should be assigned full-time to the project. On larger projects, this manager/engineer may even require a small staff. A heavy involvement will continue until the construction effort begins to wind down. By the time start-up begins, the owner's project manager might be needed only on a part-time basis.

An owner's project manager need not have as much experience as the engineering project manager, but should have experience both designing and building small plant projects. The project manager should at least have a degree in engineering or a professional engineer's license.

Small companies sometimes hire outside help as owner's engineers. The best course, however, is to avoid total dependence on outside engineering. Astute executives will understand that they need their own project teams—perhaps one individual, but at least *someone on their payroll.* A good rule for determining the size of an owner's engineering staff is to review costs of engineering over a 10-year period, find the year where engineering requirements were the lowest, and staff up to the point where those requirements (or somewhat less) might be met by in-house staff.

It is bad practice to reassign a production person without project experience and convert him or her, overnight, into the owner's project manager. It is unspeakably bad practice to do the same thing without relieving the person of regular duties.

It is good practice to regularly put production people on temporary assignment to work under the direction of an experienced project manager, helping on the larger jobs. Some will take to the work quite naturally—these individuals should be identified as trainable to become owner project managers.

During the course of a project, company executives will find themselves relying heavily on their project managers. Executives should make no mistake: This reliance can be total at times, so they had better have chosen a reliable individual. Furthermore, this selection must take place at the earliest stages. As a matter of fact, executives' influence on a project will largely occur long before the project is started. Once it is under way, the types of things an executive can do are limited.

EARLY FUNDING

The dollars spent during research and development and during preliminary studies will go farther than any other money spent on the project. This is so because only a few people will shape the whole job. Later hordes of people will be lustily spending money along the lines set down earlier.

Research and development funds are usually allocated at the highest level of a company. In a great number of cases, the funds are used mainly for R&D with nothing left for process design and preliminary engineering. Executives should examine this situation. By involving people with *project* credentials, this will not happen. Here is a crucial area where a company executive can make a difference.

Correct funding for preliminary engineering should usually be in the range of 1 to 3 percent of the total constructed value. This can be lower if there are recent projects largely similar to the one in question, or it can be greater if there are unusual aspects to consider.

The correct funding of preliminary work has ample returns. A recent study of start-up times on process plants shows a strong correlation with the degree of preliminary work on process instrumentation. Inadequate early work would result in tripling or quadrupling of the start-up time [28].

POLICY REGARDING VENDORS

The equipment used in a process operation is what makes the process unique. In some businesses the same brand of equipment has been used for generations. In mining/metallurgy it might be Dorr, or in pharmaceuticals it might be Pfaudler; in sugar, Diedert; in evaporation, Swenson; and so on. The jargon of project work has evolved a name for equipment suppliers. They are called *vendors.*

Most vendors enjoy excellent reputations and are exceedingly conscientious in their business dealings. As businesspeople they will try to maximize their profits, without being obscene. They do, after all, know what it takes to win a client. There are always a few rotten apples in the bunch, but these can generally be identified by experienced project people.

All too frequently vendors are abused by unethical practices. Most commonly they are employed to perform free engineering on the false promise of an impending order. Their natural response will be to be as parsimonious as possible with any and all information. Another practice is to have vendors pare back their quotes—after they have already presumably quoted in a competitive situation. This paring back will probably involve a reduction in what is provided.

If your company has a reputation for toying with vendors, your chances of getting full cooperation are diminished and along with them the profitability and quality of your project.

You, as an executive, can cast your company as being fair with vendors, not wishing to take advantage of them. The way to do this is to advise your project team that you seek fair dealings with vendors (and suppliers of raw materials, for that matter). After all, it makes no sense to drive a good vendor out of business. Who gains?

FUNDS FOR VENDORS

Once a project has been approved for engineering/design (see Fig. 3-1), even though it does not have final approval, funds should be set aside for the major pieces of equipment—not for the whole purchase price, but for the portion that covers the vendor's cost of engineering. In project jargon this is called *vendor engineering* (sometimes the coined expression "vendoneering" is used). Typically what is needed for vendor engineering is 10 to 20 percent of the cost of the individual equipment piece. The actual amount is arranged through negotiation.

What this funding accomplishes is a shortening of the schedule by obtaining needed information at an early date. Fair compensation for work performed is the means. Without this compensation, the drawings are not delivered until the equipment order is placed in its entirety. This delays final design work, because the vendor drawings are the key. If the designers continue charging to the project while they wait for drawings—which is difficult to avoid, for the sake of holding

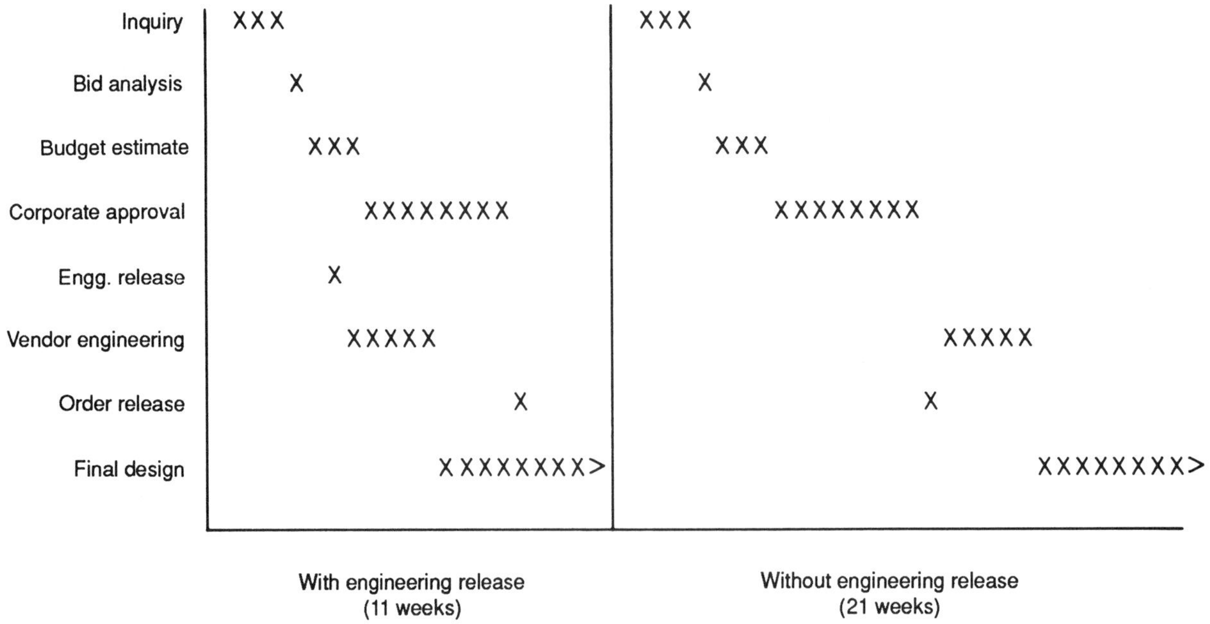

	With engineering release	Without engineering release
Inquiry	X X X	X X X
Bid analysis	X	X
Budget estimate	X X X	X X X
Corporate approval	X X X X X X X X	X X X X X X X X
Engg. release	X	
Vendor engineering	X X X X X	X X X X X
Order release	X	X
Final design	X X X X X X X X >	X X X X X X X X >

With engineering release
(11 weeks)

Without engineering release
(21 weeks)

Figure 3-2 Start of design with and without engineering release. Horizontal axis is time; each x represents 1 week.

the same people on the job—a sizable *waste* of money will result. This is covered further in Chap. 14.

The fragment of schedule shown in Fig. 3-2 shows how this works. In the first case (with engineering release), vendor engineering can commence 6 weeks after inquiry, and final design can get going in the 11th week after starting inquiries. In the second case (without the release), design cannot get under way until the 21st week, because vendor drawings must wait for the estimate and corporate approval.

This is a case where the approved funds will stretch a long way. Take a $10 million project, and say that major equipment might constitute $2 million. The amount to set aside would be $200,000 to $400,000. Sustaining a design effort for 10 weeks will cost approximately the same, but in the end there will be nothing tangible to show for it. More importantly, though, by funding vendor engineering, the whole project completion gets moved ahead by 10 weeks.

The risk is that the project may be canceled. Adequate preliminary work and previously arranged trigger levels can reduce this risk to acceptable levels. Here is how:

- Make sure preliminary work is adequate
- Set trigger levels to kill, rethink, or authorize:

  Kill: more than 50 percent over preliminary estimate
  Rethink: more than 20 percent over estimate
  Authorize: anything less than estimate plus 20 percent

ECONOMIC EVALUATION CRITERIA

Of the hundreds of projects this author has seen, he has yet to find one where criteria were given describing company policy for economic evaluations. This stands out as an embarrassing oversight.

Under the heat of deadlines and without client guidance, after-tax ROIs of 15 percent have been used. When these "bootleg" ROIs were checked with owner engineers, invariably the response was decidedly one of surprise and annoyance: "Oh, yeah, sure . . . sure. . . . Go ahead and use 15 percent." Obviously the economic policy, if it existed at all, was not passed on to the project team.

The requirements during the course of engineering and design are not to be confused with overall project evaluation and strategic planning of a company's resources. The day-to-day need for an economic yardstick will frequently surface during bid evaluation, for example, an expensive agitator that draws less power than a cheap agitator (see Chap. 5, *Cost and Schedule,* for more examples).

Economic studies in the midst of the project must be kept simple. Discounted cash flow analyses should be eschewed unless obviously necessary. This is so mainly because the simple return is adequate, but also because a project is the wrong forum for raising issues such a project life and salvage values. Things must be kept simple.

FLEXIBLE BID ANALYSES

A fact of life in all business dealings is the *bid.* It is a foundation of modern society (and ancient society as well). Prices of hamburgers and airline tickets can be traced (in a few short steps) to bids.

Perhaps because of its fundamental nature, this topic is continually ignored. To appreciate what this means, just imagine a cattle buyer for Burger King who decides to pay only the lowest dollar for beef on the hoof. Or imagine Boeing engineers awarding a contract for gyroscopic compasses based on the lowest bid.

It is quite possible that by not issuing a policy statement on this matter, your company might already be locked into this mode. As a business person, you surely know the importance of marketing your own product on merits other than price.

Company executives are advised to review the parts in Chaps. 12 and 13 having to do with selection of goods and services based on competitive bidding.

While it is obvious that the bidding method will achieve the lowest first cost, this is not necessarily the most economic choice over the long term. Operating cost and ability to impart quality to the product are more important in most cases—those where bids are comparable.

A company that acquires a reputation for selecting only on low first cost will not receive bids from higher-priced suppliers, *even though the higher price is justified.* In this way, the low-bid-only company will find itself dealing with the derelicts more often than not.

When price is the sole measure, low bids result from *leaving out* as much as possible while still meeting the specification. With regard to obtaining engineering/design services, company executives should ask themselves whether they prefer a job staffed mostly by $15-per-hour drafters with 3 years' experience or feel more comfortable with *designers* having 15 years' experience earning $29 per hour.

Executives can do a great deal for their companies by devoting a small part of their time to reviewing how goods and services are obtained. This activity should be persistent, not once only. Executives should make it their duty to find where crucial team efforts with suppliers of goods and services make sense. Then executives should facilitate these team efforts.

Executives should make it known that selections based on price alone are not condoned and that, furthermore, in general, without further guidance, if quoted prices are within 7 percent of each other, a selection based solely on discretion is valid.

MORE DUTIES

Here are a few more duties to occupy the company executive:

- Firm guidance must be provided for determining plant capacity; principal company executives must have a hand in its determination; marketing and manufacturing groups must agree; the procedure for capacity determination should be a formal one.

- Firm guidance must be provided for determining the product specification (see App. G for an example); principal company executives must have a hand in its determination; marketing and manufacturing groups must agree; the procedure for its determination should be a formal one.

- Executives should issue a statement every 3 years or so reminding their employees that it is beneath their dignity to ask for free goods and services.

- Similarly, a statement should be issued stating whether company policy favors the use of an engineering/design organization as a drafting service or whether it should be brought on board as partners and leaders (see section "Leader or Lackey" in Chap. 2).

- The engineering/design group, whether external to your own company or not, should be encouraged to sit down with sales and production people on a regular basis—maybe twice a year, but regularly—the "what's happening" interchange is necessary. An ideal location for the meeting would be at an operating plant and would include a tour to look at some design questions; these meetings should occur even when there are no projects on the horizon.

Chapter 4
Priorities

Each human being has priorities. These individual priorities will override project priorities unless the project priorities are clearly stated, and benefits made evident for all to see, during the course of a job. A haphazard or poor choice of priorities drives up costs and squanders precious resources.

Consider this occurrence. An engineer, very concerned about the environment and with little practical experience, was asked to do calculations concerning a filter for oily waste. Rather than approach this in an objective fashion, the engineer biased the study such that an inordinate amount of equipment was needed. Yes, a superbly clean stream would have resulted, but as it was, the project was killed and the producer of the oily sludge was able to continue (*without filtering*), because the producer was able to show that undertaking the filtration scheme would have been an unreasonable hardship.

A good project engineer or project manager will constantly state project priorities and will constantly review priorities of others to make sure their priorities are not in conflict with project priorities. An excellent way of keeping priorities in the proper order is to constantly compare things in pairs *and* decide whether the more important of two things is *crucial.* Here is an example:

Unordered	Ordered
Heat recovery	Safe to use (crucial)
Easy to fix	Fix, build, operate (all equal)
Cheap to build	Heat recovery
Safe to use	
Cheap to operate	
Easy to operate	

Taking the first two items in the unordered list, we see that it is easy to imagine that ease of repair is more important than heat recovery. Comparing *easy to fix* with *cheap to build,* we see the choice is not so evident, so we rank them on an equal level. Comparing *easy to fix* with *safe to use,* we see that safety deserves the higher rank, and with a little reflection, we conclude that safety is crucial. This process is continued until all elements have been put in order of importance.

Here is another example of comparisons and rankings:

Unordered	Ordered
Schedule	Salable product (crucial)
Salable product	Project cost
Monthly reports	Schedule
Project cost	Monthly reports

Salable product not only tops the list but also is crucial. Compared to the next item, we can see that a project will fail completely unless the product is marketable. This is crucial whereas project cost is not. If project cost is overrun, even significantly, the project can still be quite viable, though not as attractive as originally imagined. That schedule is even less important (under normal circumstances) can be appreciated by understanding that an occasional delay can have a beneficial effect, for example, halting one craft so that another one may finish and get out of the way. Sticking mercilessly to a schedule, however, can be harmful. Least in importance are the monthly reports, but on more than one occasion, mostly on government jobs, one comes away with the idea that the whole reason for doing the project is to generate exhaustive project reports.

This ordering does not mean that cost, schedule, and reports are not important. On the contrary, they are important, but they rank way behind salable product.

A distinction between items of primary importance and items of secondary importance is very useful for setting priorities. Here are some examples:

Primary	Secondary
New plant	Capital cost
New production line	Operating cost
Product description*	Schedule
A good mass balance	Cost accounting
Principal	Interest

This ranking draws spirited remarks such as, "You've got it all wrong. Money is *never* secondary." Yet a plant that doesn't run, or makes nonmarketable goop, or kills employees is less desirable than one that has even a large cost overrun.

Emphasis on items of secondary importance does untold harm.

When a decision is made to take money from a bank account and purchase equipment, materials, and labor for a project, the project itself becomes more important than the money to finance it. This is so because the act of committing the funds makes it so. If money in the bank account were more valued, it would never be committed to the project. This, in itself, shows where the priorities lie.

Placing more emphasis on capital costs than on project goals is thus a contradiction. This dichotomy is not seen with worldly, knowledgeable, enlightened project people, but it is seen all too frequently, mostly with people having little experience with project work. A poignant example is given in Fig. 4-1.

In looking at capital costs, the most common error in assigning priorities is the assumption that the interest on capital is of supreme importance. This is false. The capital itself is far more important than the interest on it. Fancy maneuvers to maximize interest at the risk of capital are foolhardy. Crazy project schedules fall into this category.

Before we leave the topic of priorities, it is worth considering one that lies directly on the bedrock of all engineering: Between technical skills and liberal arts capabilities, where does the priority belong? Here is the answer: *The top priority must be with technical skills.* Good project work cannot be executed without a thorough recognition of this fact.

---

*Also called the *product specification*. This describes the product to people wishing to buy it. See Chap. 8, *The Mass Balance*.

At the Graduate School of Business

Figure 4-1 At the graduate school of business. (*Danziger in the Christian Science Monitor, copyright 1987, TCSPS.*)

It is true that liberal arts capabilities are important. Also it is fundamental that engineers work in a framework that takes into account the needs of this planet and future generations. Also it is true that engineers must recognize right from wrong. Therefore, the above assertion assumes that the project in question is legal, moral, and beneficial to society as a whole and that the common person (or engineer) would recognize it as such. These things being true, *technical skills* must overshadow liberal arts capabilities. If this were not true, all society would turn upside down. The philosopher would build process facilities, and the project engineer would debate the morality of the politicization of anthropology.

The Hyatt-Regency tragedy in Kansas City* was a horrible, needless occurrence that could have been avoided by better communications†

---

*An elevated walkway collapsed, killing 113 elderly tourists in 1981.

†*Communication* is a technical skill. What is a drawing, if not a form of communication?

and a knowledge of vectors. The teachings of Socrates, the sensibilities of Emerson, and the literature of Chekhov would not have helped a single iota.

Of course, all other things being equal, and maybe even loading things in favor of a good liberal arts background, the engineer with strong liberal arts capabilities will probably prosper more than the "monochrome" engineer, particularly in a corporate environment. The lone innovator, or inventor, will continue marching to his or her own drummer, and some of these remarkable people will have difficulty with liberal arts, while others may have acquired a substantial knowledge of liberal arts. To imply that engineers must be cultured along lines suitable to liberal arts colleges reveals a misunderstanding of priorities.

Engineering work in itself can be highly demanding, so placing a liberal arts, high-culture requirement on the top of everything else is, at best, a distraction. Then, too, some impressionable young engineers think that they will be better engineers or designers by absorbing more culture, whereas in reality there is no shortage of people who can quote several well-known authors, but there are precious few who know how to feed a screw conveyor.

Then ultimately there is the client of the engineer, the person who will pay the bills, and this person could not care less whether the engineer can discuss religions of the world. The client wants good, reliable work at a reasonable price. Anyone who doubts this should just ask the directors of major opera houses and libraries what criteria they use to select engineers. Do not doubt that they select on the basis of value received, *not* an appreciation of arts and letters.

The reader is asked to envision the following scene: A client is out in a drafting "bull pen," looking at a drawing. Nearby, an engineer and a designer (on the client's job) are talking about the opera. Choose one of the following as the client's most likely reaction:

- Pleased to have "cultured" people on the job
- Irritated that they are "wasting" time

Of course, the second reaction is more likely, even if the client is an opera buff. There is a time for work and a time for play, but even outside of work, say at lunch, the client would probably prefer the engineer and the designer to talk about the job at hand instead of the opera.

In spite of this, many influential people have made some very strong statements about how a good engineer is thoroughly versed in the liberal arts. These spokespersons are usually far removed from where the genuine project work takes place. Only occasionally is there a rebuttal from industry, or the engineering profession, probably because a rebuttal would appear boorish. The problem here is that young engineers and students form a highly distorted view of what takes place in the real world where they eventually must function. Too many potentially good engineers become confused on how to get ahead in engineering. They wind up studying nontechnical subjects in night school. Nobody ever told them that for good engineering work, they must constantly practice their mathematics, physics, chemistry, etc. No one ever told them to spend at least an hour a day brushing up on principles and learning new approaches. Sure, they should read history and such, too, but the technical part should take top priority.

—Chapter 5—
Cost and Schedule

SCHEDULE—SOME INTRODUCTORY IDEAS

If a poll were taken among schedulers and project managers, it would probably register a strong predisposition to view the schedule as a tool for shortening project duration. To a lesser extent, the schedule would be viewed as a means of reducing project cost, enhancing the economics of the facility over its life, and achieving higher quality.

In project work today, there exists a strong tendency to favor rapid results over other considerations. Part of this is due to an inborn impatience to which we are all susceptible: "I want it *now*." Some more impatience is hammered into us in the formative years. Even barely past infancy, we learn that being first in a race can leave a bully behind or can lead to compliments or prizes. School exams often put a premium on speed.

This emphasis on schedule shortening is reinforced as we grow. In reading history, one becomes impressed by forced marches to achieve a superior position or a favorable wind that brought a fleet into advantageous position a day in advance: the emphasis is on swiftness. We are told of a relatively modern word, *blitzkrieg*, meaning "lightning war."

In engineering/design the following phrases are heard:

- Time is money.
- Lost sales are costing market share.
- Tying up project money is expensive.

Again, speed is the theme.

In reality, putting all the emphasis on swiftness and shortening the time duration leads to costly results. Projects where the sole consideration is to achieve a result quickly, regardless of cost, are called *all-crash** projects. Two well-known examples are the Manhattan project, where the atom bomb was developed, and Du Pont's smokeless-powder projects during World War I. All-crash programs are the result of emergencies and are special.

Figure 5-1 is the classic schedule compression curve given in texts that cover the critical path method. At the lower right of the curve are easily shortened jobs—schedule can be cut with modest increases in cost. Each increment of compression becomes more costly to compress. Eventually a point is reached where a small shortening of the schedule can double the cost of the project.

---

*The term *all-crash* was coined when the critical path method (CPM) was developed. It means doing all jobs on a project as rapidly as humanly possible. (A sketchy outline of CPM is described below.)

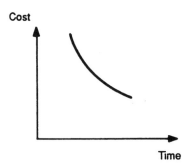

Figure 5-1 Curve showing schedule compression.

At some point, progressing up the curve, lies an optimum. Ideally, the perfect schedule would result in

> Maximum earnings over the life of the facility consistent with quality requirements

This is best understood by examining Fig. 5-2. Cumulative cash flow curves are given for five hypothetical cases:

1. A severely rushed job
2. A rush job
3. A normal job
4. An optimum job
5. A slow job

The numbers at the left, on the vertical scale, are the capital costs for the five cases. For example, a normal job has capital cost C, while a rush job has a capital cost of $1.2C$ (20 percent higher).

For each case, the diagonal line to the left of the knee gives an expenditure rate during design and construction—these cash flows* are negative. To the right of the knee, the cash flows are positive—derived from sales of product after start-up.

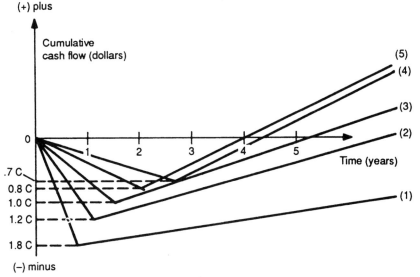

Figure 5-2 Cumulative cash position for five hypothetical schedules.

Cash flow here is defined as after-tax earnings plus depreciation.

The rushed jobs have higher capital costs (Fig. 5-1). Furthermore, their earning capacity is impaired by poorer performance over the lifetime of the facility. This is because such things as maintenance cost, power cost, labor cost, etc., will be higher on those facilities whose design and construction were rushed.

It takes *time* to go over drawings, forming a mental image of how things will work, and then make adjustments when something is seen that will work better. It takes *time* to optimize equipment. It takes *time* to review new developments (control valves versus variable-speed drives, for example). It takes *time* to review unexpected alternative proposals from vendors.

To gain time on a schedule, a designer or an engineer will adopt the *first alternative* that will work. Time will *not* be spent finding cheaper, simpler, or better ways. To gain time on a schedule, equipment selections often will be based on scheduled delivery, while operating advantages will be regarded as secondary in importance.

Summarizing to this point, then, we conclude that a schedule that focuses solely on duration (that is, *time*) raises capital costs and lowers cash flows.

There are two elements that comprise a *good* schedule: performing tasks in the correct sequence and starting each task at the right time. For example, it does not make sense to do underground piping drawings beneath a building until the building (and equipment) foundations are established. As a second example, it does not make sense to start power conduit routings prior to the development of equipment arrangement drawings.

A person should not be started on a job before he or she can be used effectively. If a task is started too early, either the work on it will undergo large changes before it is finished, or the person working on it will be underemployed, that is, working inefficiently while waiting for information. On the other hand, if the task is started too late, this may slow down the whole job. It is on this point that the conflict between *efficiency* (cost) and *time* can be seen. The argument is as follows: The best use of labor is to wait for the appropriate moment for its application. Until the right moment comes, the labor must be used elsewhere (i.e., charged to another job). Then, when the right moment arrives, the labor may not be available immediately, perhaps not for a few days. Thus the new task must await the completion of the previous task. There is nothing wrong with this. It is the economic use of labor.

Owners who demand instant staffing will obtain premature staffing, along with the associated inherent costs.

BASIC CONCEPTS

Before we cover the subject of job sequence, it is necessary to look at a few basic concepts.

The part of scheduling that is its essence is also the part that is most self-evident. Stated simply, some jobs can be done concurrently, and other jobs must be done in sequence. Here are examples:

Concurrent	In sequence
Install siding while sheathing roof.	Install roofing after sheathing roof.
Dig foundation while fabricating steel.	Install siding prior to any major piping installations.
Erect steel while equipment is in fabrication.	Erect steel following building department approval.

In diagram form, the two types of job can be represented as follows:

Concurrent   In sequence

A ——————————————

B ——————————————   A ——— B ——— C ———

C ——————————————

Common parlance often refers to concurrent jobs as *parallel* and jobs done in sequence as *series*. Combinations of parallel and series tasks have been studied and standardized to a great degree. Diagrams that show these combinations are called *network diagrams* (see Fig. 5-3).

The numbered boxes are called *nodes*. The branches are called *activities*. An activity to the right of a node cannot begin until all activities on the left have been completed. Figure 5-3 means that installation of short-run piping must follow installation of long-run piping *and* equipment. Equipment installation follows the installation of equipment foundations. Long-run piping must wait for the installation of pipe racks.

Mathematical methods have been developed to show which tasks and which branches of the network determine the shortest schedule. The route through the network that leads to the shortest schedule is called the *critical path*. This term, as a matter of fact, is the name of a popular method for setting and evaluating schedules: the critical path method, or CPM for short. Another popular method is the program evaluation and resource technique (PERT). CPM and PERT are very similar, but PERT emphasizes achievements, while CPM emphasizes tasks. Both have limitations and have suffered some criticism in the past, but on the whole they are very useful, mostly in establishing a disciplined thought process for schedules. The advent of personal computers has made accessibility to highly evolved network programs a fact. The correct input of information to those programs requires a knowledge of project work, however.

Whereas CPM is widely touted, the Gantt chart is still the workhorse of scheduling and schedule communications. The Gantt chart is more commonly referred to as a *bar chart*. It is most often employed without the formal use of CPM but with knowledge of CPM. Gantt charts are also used to present results of formal CPM calculations. The Gantt chart's wide use is mostly due to the ease with which it can be generated and understood. With a pencil and a paper, the least sophisticated subcontractor can quickly see where he fits into the scheme. He undoubtedly schedules his own activities by using the same charts.

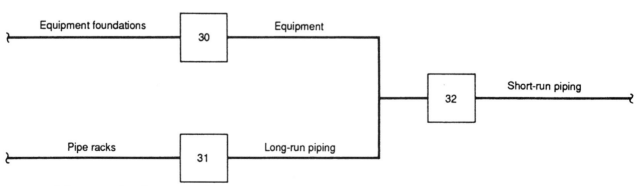

Figure 5-3 A fragment of a job sequence during construction.

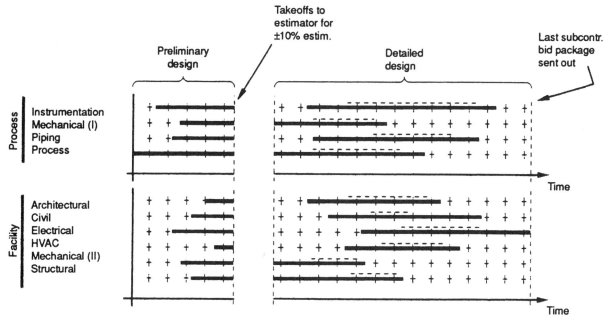

Figure 5-4 Initiation and termination of work on a typical project. Note 1: Solid line shows activity; dashed line above it shows when vendor drawings are being reviewed. Note 2: Mechanical (I)—material handling, rotating equipment, vessels, etc.; Mechanical (II)—utilities and such.

A Gantt chart depicts jobs and their duration along a time scale. Time flows from left to right. Thus Fig. 5-4 shows architectural work starting after structural work in the detailed design phase. Then civil work is shown trailing behind the architectural effort. On a network, the sequence is clearly shown progressing from left to right, and the relationships are shown exactly. On a Gantt chart, any sequences must be inferred. The information contained on the Gantt chart has to do mostly with the timing for each activity.

SEQUENCE

Usually the work of engineering/design is started by the process engineers. There are occasions, however, where the starting group might be architectural or mechanical. The nature of the job will dictate; see Fig. 6-2. The last of the design work is usually done by the electrical group (see Fig. 5-4).

The presumption in the following discussion is that process engineers start the sequence. The terminology used is the author's view of what is most current. Terms such as *preliminary engineering* are often used as though they had a universally accepted definition, whereas much variation exists in their use. Part of the purpose of this discussion is to define terms.

A little further on, we will look at an overall schedule that encompasses a whole venture, from research and development through construction. At this point, we focus attention on engineering/design.

Figure 5-4 shows a typical job sequence for a process-driven project. It shows the usual situation where a fairly good estimate* is needed before detailed design is allowed to proceed in earnest.

---

*Here a ±10 percent estimate is stated. This is either a good *budget* estimate or a so-so *definitive* estimate (see page 64).

The interpretation of Fig. 5-4 is as follows. In the preliminary design phase, the process group takes the lead, and, in particular, the process engineer sets the pace. Once the P&IDs are issued, the instrumentation engineer can begin steady work. Then the piping designer starts sketching possible area layouts and plot plans. The process engineer and the mechanical I engineer write specifications on the major equipment. These are used to obtain quotes on the equipment.

The earliest facility work will probably be done by the electrical engineer, who will begin work on a single-line drawing. The electrical engineer will prepare a general motor specification and specifications for switchgear and motor control centers, plus power transformer specification, if needed. Mechanical II will begin sizing utilities and writing specifications for major pieces.

Structural and civil work should begin after piping and mechanical I and II are able to provide some rough definition for equipment arrangement. Architectural work should begin, once the process platforms have begun to take shape and once the plot plan is able to show the buildings required. Finally rough requirements for HVAC will be established.

Drawings prepared during preliminary design will have two purposes:

- Explore the ramifications of what is implied by the requirements as depicted by the P&IDs, flow diagrams, and scope-of-work documents
- Enable a takeoff of materials for a budget estimate

It is worth emphasizing that finished drawings for the *facility* part of the job should *never* be a purpose of preliminary design. *The main outcome of preliminary design is the budget estimate.* Once the basic design concepts are settled, no more effort should be put into the facility design than is necessary to achieve this end. For this reason Fig. 14-4 shows design-grade drawings for the facility part of the job being developed *after* the budget estimate. This limitation is to minimize expenditures on engineering/design until after the budget estimate. Note that none of the foregoing tasks include process design development, as *that* should have occurred prior to preliminary design (see page 63).

Once a budget estimate has been approved, detailed design can commence (see Fig. 5-4). At that point, the groups that can proceed without restraint are usually process, mechanical I and II, and structural. *These groups are usually on the critical path.* A minor piping effort may be employed, fine-tuning the equipment arrangement and working on long pipe runs; but if not, the piping group can be held back until equipment vendor drawings start to make their appearance.

Because process instruments are rarely on the critical path, the instrumentation group is best held back, to allow as much information as possible to become firm before getting under way. Architectural and civil should be held back for the same reason. However, civil should follow architectural for most jobs, because roadways and underground piping depend on building details. Similar considerations apply to HVAC.

Initiation of the electrical effort should be delayed as much as possible (yet keeping it off the critical path), because of the heavy de-

56   Chapter Five

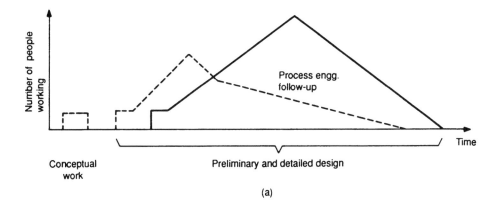

Conceptual
work

Preliminary and detailed design

(a)

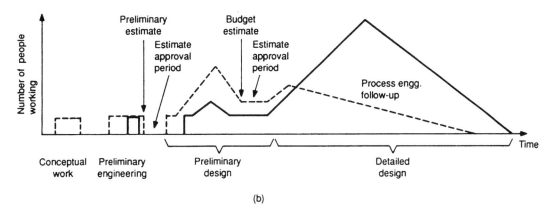

Conceptual
work

Preliminary
engineering

Preliminary
design

Detailed
design

(b)

Figure 5-5 Buildup and decline of workforce during engineering/design. (a) Manloading without estimate approval periods. (b) Manloading with two estimate approval periods. Process effort is shown by dashed line; facilities effort is shown by solid line.

pendence on everyone else. The first job of the electrical group should be to issue construction-grade drawings of underground conduit and grounding. Their work should end last, after the instrumentation group finishes.*

Figure 5-5 shows the increase and decrease of engineering workers during the course of a job. Figure 5-5a shows a case where a budget estimate is not prepared. This is quite rare but is presented as a benchmark. The process effort is shown leading the facilities effort. This is normally the case.

Figure 5-5b shows the effect of preparing estimates, then curtailing effort while the estimate proceeds along the approval process through the owner organization. (More is said on this in Chaps. 3 and 14.) The two types of estimates are reviewed below.

Figure 14-4 should be consulted for further information about the relative timing of tasks.

RESOURCES

A good number of schedule problems are really resource problems. Dates are set down without a clear understanding of what will be needed to meet any one of them. A completely unrealistic schedule

---

*Even though the electrical design group finishes last, their work is usually not on the critical path, because construction must be well advanced before the major electrical work can commence.

can be destructive. An air of scepticism toward the schedule (accompanied by a loss of confidence in management) takes root early. Later, when attempts are made to catch up, responsiveness will be lacking. In such cases, no schedule at all would serve better—an easygoing, cooperative attitude would yield better results. In other words, the very thing the schedule purports to do is subverted and can result in a negative effect, if done improperly.

The failure to consider resources comes mostly from lack of knowledge. An exceedingly optimistic end date is often set on a task by a person who does not understand the work. Many times the person who will do the work is not consulted. The schedule is thus a *wish*, not a sound plan.

During the construction phase, the effect of missing materials is easily evident: no bricks, no wall, for example. In the engineering phase, the missing resources are not so easy to grasp. *Missing information?* What do you mean?

Aside from trivial things like pencils and paper, the two major resources for engineering/design work are

- Information
- Trained, capable people

That people are a resource is generally accepted with ease. However, citing *information* as a resource sometimes causes surprise. A few examples will serve to illustrate.

A soil test is a resource. It is executed by digging up dirt, taking it to a laboratory, and measuring moisture and cohesiveness, among other things. Without the soil test, a foundation cannot be designed.

A certified land surveyor's report is a resource. How else can design personnel decide where different units must be placed, either to comply with code or to make sure something such as the motor control center is not 2 ft lower than the normal flood level?

For understanding lithium salts, solubility data from Russian laboratories is essential. A library that has *Chemical Abstracts* and can access foreign publications is a resource.

A good engineering effort cannot be undertaken without access to good information. Knowing this reveals a subtle means for an owner to evaluate an engineering company:

- How complete is the in-house library?
- How complete is the catalog file?
- Is the type of information germane to the project?
- How good are nearby public and university libraries?

Where do the responsibilities lie in making sure that a project has adequate resources? The generally accepted idea is that the engineering organization will provide trained, qualified people; the owner will provide special trade-secret-type know-how; and both will share in providing less specialized know-how. The sources of know-how are not hard and fast, and it is not unusual for the engineering group to provide special know-how, including their own proprietary trade secrets now and then.

Owners must have their own small project team whom they use to monitor outside engineering work. This team should also be able to do some small projects without outside help. It will be this group that makes the selection when it comes to hiring outside engineering or construction help. This tiny kernel of engineering talent is exceedingly important to an owner. It can make or break projects.

This team is responsible for producing the core of information to be used by the engineers/designers. The information would include such things as

Flow sheets	Project objectives
Process descriptions	Rules for economic studies
Rough mass balances*	Capacity requirements
Uncommon physical/chemical properties	Product specifications
	Maps, plans, drawings
Description of existing operations	Soil reports and surveys
Test and literature data	

Of course, what is shown here is a brief example of what is required. A more complete example is provided in App. A. This project resource should be carefully and thoroughly compiled. It should be issued to the engineering project manager in a three-ring binder (except the drawings). This resource has a name: *design basis.* It can alternately be called *basic data.*

Another resource sometimes provided by the owner team is called the *scope of work.* This document describes who does what. Even though the owner team may (and should) create the original scope document, the engineers/designers will probably rewrite this document for their own use. An example is provided in App. A.

Some people initially experience difficulty distinguishing between *basic data* and *scope of work.* Here is a guide: The former tends toward tabular, numerical information, while the latter is narrative.

For modest operations, where an owner is either too small or simply not organized so as to have a project team, the owner contracts an engineering organization to provide temporary help. Municipalities often work this way. They will advertise, for example, in the *Engineering News Record,* asking for proposals to act as *owner's engineer.* (This is covered at length in Chap. 3 under "Owner's Project Team.")

CASH FLOW

A recurring theme concerning projects is the concern about money not earning interest, tied up as wages and payments before start-up. Until it is spent, capital for the project can be invested in short-term instruments, or it can be borrowed short-term when needed. After the cash is spent, the lost interest should be viewed as secondary in importance (see Chap. 4). *The new capital item* should be the primary concern.†

The term *fast track* came into use about ten years ago. The implication was that a great new way of running projects had been discovered. The idea was to start all jobs at an earlier time to finish earlier. In particular, construction could be started shortly after the start of detailed design—even before vendor information had been incorporated into the design.

Birrell, in the *Journal of Construction, Engineering, and Manage-*

---

*Normally the engineering/design group will provide the firm (or design-grade) mass balances.

†After all, the capital is *principal.*

ment [29], states: "Currently, the supposed advantages of *fast track**
may often be outweighed by its disadvantages . . . the owner can invest his delayed construction cash flow in high-yielding short-term
bonds while design is being completed. This fuller design allows the
owner to achieve a better life-cycle cost profile and higher speed construction."

The *Engineering News Record* of January 20, 1992, cites a major
problem with a project for building a facility designed to process existing chemical warfare munitions for their destruction, that is, the
reverse of manufacturing them. Overruns in the range of $70 million
and schedule delays of a year or so are attributed by many observers
to *fast-track* methods [30].

Less and less is heard of the *fast track* of late. The untold billions in
excessive cost have been another probable cause of the declining fortunes of industry in the United States.

REASONABLE THINGS

Even the most mundane, everyday needs have some surprisingly long
lead times. From the time it is ordered until it is delivered, an ordinary pressure transmitter can easily spend 8 weeks in transit. And
one must exert some follow-up effort to keep from slipping more. This
delivery time applies to the parts and pieces particular to the process
portion of a facility. The common materials, such as welding rod, of
course, are easily available. Naturally, if an emergency exists, a pressure transmitter could be obtained in a few days by paying a premium.

Lead times for fabricated items result from the elements in Table
5-1. The total lead time (approximately 20 weeks) is typical for commonplace items that have electric motors such as agitators and
pumps. On whole projects, where many additional considerations
must be entertained, even more time is needed. The condition of the
soil takes time to evaluate. The availability of construction labor is
another consideration. Flood levels, water resources, and permitting
amenability are still others. The list continues.

Considering all these demands, reasonable project durations are as
follows:

- From the start of conceptual engineering through the end of construction, 28 months

- From the start of preliminary engineering through the end of construction, 20 months

---

*Emphasis added.

TABLE 5-1 Typical Durations That Add Up to Lead Time

Task	Time, weeks
Write specifications, get approval, type purchase documents	2.0
Mail (purchase documents)	0.5
Vendor engineering	5.0
Mail (drawings from vendor)	0.5
Review vendor drawings	2.0
Mail (drawings back to vendor, thus releasing fabrication)	0.5
Fabrication	8.0
Shipping	2.0
Overall lead time	20.5

- From the start of preliminary design through the end of construction, 16 months

These are not hypothetical time frames; they are executable realities by able and willing people.

METHODS

Delivery time in the above example includes time for a vendor to configure equipment for the application at hand (vendor engineering). Time is also included to review the configuration proposed by the vendor. If the review concludes satisfactorily, the vendor is released to commence fabrication. When a process plant is built, almost all equipment is purchased from *vendors.* This vendor equipment is accommodated in the overall scheme by efforts of the project engineers and designers. Here is a key point:

> Project personnel take other peoples' creations and show how these creations are to be installed and meshed together to work correctly.

Only when a store-bought item is unavailable is the design of a special piece carried out. This is done to save time and cost. It doesn't make sense to buy a propeller, a shaft, a gearbox, and a motor when the entire assembly can be purchased from an agitator vendor.

Two concepts from Table 5-1, *vendor engineering* and *fabrication release,* deserve more discussion. First, we examine vendor engineering. This is the engineering/design that a vendor must perform so that his shops may start work on building the assembly to fill an order. Even a simple piece of equipment, such as an agitator, has many different ways of being built; these many possibilities are eliminated in favor of one to suit the need of the moment: a TEFC 440-V motor, agitator must be flange-mounted with a mechanical seal, the gearbox must be a worm-gear right-angle drive (to cut headspace and for economy), etc.

The vendor assembles thousands of components for clients ranging from breweries to municipal waterworks. Each use requires a different assembly. The assembly for a particular job is described in the *vendor drawings* pertaining to that job. For simple rotating equipment it takes 5 weeks, on average, from time of purchase,* to receive these documents for review.

The review is important. Vendor drawings are the hidden secret to success on process plant projects (and even on some so-called facilities projects). How else will the structural engineer know how to size the beams under the compressor? How will the piping designer know that the same compressor needs an 18-in elevation for gravity drainage of a shaft seal?

It is worth knowing that the time to allow for vendor drawings depends on the amount of custom preparation required plus time for doing the paperwork. A pressure gauge, for example, usually requires 2 weeks. This is the time to process the paperwork. Drawings showing gauges already exist when the order is placed.

Pumps and fans would be about the same as for the gauge, but there is a vital difference: the performance curve. Court battles have

---

*Sometimes called *order release.*

been fought over performance curves (pump curves for *that* specie). Thus, although outward dimensions of some pumps and fans have not changed in 70 years, the vendor drawings from pump and fan vendors will take about 5 weeks for preparation. In this case, the vendor isn't so concerned about dimensions; the vendor *is* concerned about materials and performance. As the degree of standardization decreases, the time required for vendor engineering increases. This is no surprise. The following list shows details. The times are averages that can be lengthened by special requirements or shortened by accepting plain vanilla.

Catalog items	2 weeks
Rotating equipment	5 weeks
Pressure vessels	6 weeks
Packaged equipment (complex)	10 weeks
Custom equipment	5 weeks and up

Why go through this? Why go through this vendor engineering step at all? Isn't this just a waste of time? Most vendors have catalogs; why lengthen the process? First, the vendor's catalog is probably out of date before it is published. This is so because vendors are constantly seeking improvements to their products, so their *buyout* components change. Even the same make and model ordered a few months apart can differ in surprising ways. What is shown in a catalog is an *approximation* of reality. Second, *buyers must understand what they are contracting to purchase.*

The second concept from Table 5-1 is *fabrication release.* This occurs when the vendor is asked to start fabrication. This step occurs after the vendor has submitted drawings for approval. Prior to *fabrication release* an engineer or designer may modify a piece of equipment "at cost." For example, nozzles may be relocated for free (as long as they were part of the original vendor proposal). Or a 3-in stainless nozzle can be added for, say, $200, if it is new and did not constitute part of the original quote. Once fabrication has been released, these easy changes start to disappear rapidly. On the third week after fabrication release of a 2000-gal stainless vessel, even the relocation of a planned, known nozzle might cost $600, because that nozzle may have already been installed. A few, early modifications can be tolerated, but that is all. Once in the assembly process, "the piece" is not easy to change.

Figure 5-6 is a Gantt chart showing the limits of engineering/design and some of the components within engineering/design. What is shown is approximate. Variability is included in the activities. In other words, for example, formal equipment inquiries should not start sooner than shortly before 10 percent through completion and should finish no later than shortly before 50 percent completion. If this is not the case, a special reason should be sought; otherwise, comprehension of the whole schedule may be off.

Engineering/design is taken as starting when conceptual engineering ends.

Figure 5-6 contains some very important project concepts. Engineers dedicated to learning project work are advised to study this figure and Fig. 14-4 during the course of a project and to observe how one activity slowly builds up, flourishes, and then fades as other activities take over.

The features shown in Fig. 5-6 can be applied to the great majority

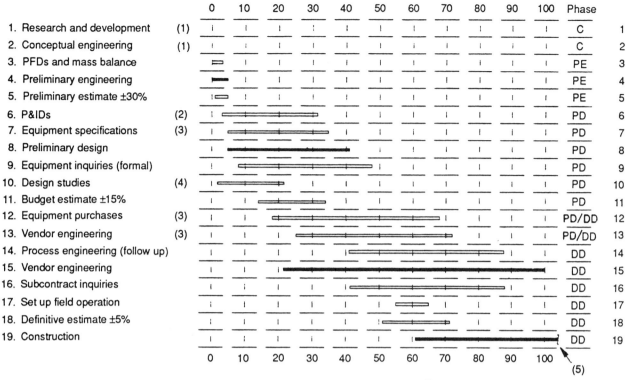

Figure 5-6 Some likely timing to be seen in engineering/design. Filled bars give probable durations of the whole phase. Open bars show probable durations of key activities. Phase abbreviations: C = conceptual, PE = preliminary engineering, PD = preliminary design, DD = detailed design. Notes: (1) These activities should cease at the start of engineering/design. (2) Through design issue. (3) Major and minor equipment. (4) Occurs as part of preliminary engineering and preliminary design. (5) Continues past completion of engineering/design.

of projects. Even so-called unusual schedules can be understood in terms of Fig. 5-6 by using it as a benchmark. What follows is a brief discussion of each activity, telling why it is positioned as shown.

1. Research and development
   1. This is the precursor of all project work.

2. Conceptual engineering
   2. This is used throughout the R&D phase to guide the effort. This is sometimes called *process design*.

3. PFDs and mass balance
   3. This is usually the first activity of formal project work. It is part of preliminary engineering. This work must end before preliminary engineering can be viewed as complete. No process design can take place in this phase (if so, the *real* work is that of activity 2).

4. Preliminary engineering
   4. Preliminary engineering can usually be completed for less than 5 percent of all the engineering, on a few occasions for less than 1 percent. Note that this activity may include some preliminary design (activity 11), but the preliminary *design* does not end until later.

5. Preliminary estimate	5. This is the estimate that invariably is part of the preliminary engineering work. Accuracy is 20 to 40 percent.
6. P&IDs	6. A few, key P&IDs might make their debut in the preliminary engineering phase, but that is all. These few will not have line sizes or instrument numbers. The last task of any significance on the P&IDs will be incorporation of information from the vendor drawings. Figure 5-5 only depicts P&ID work through the heaviest work—the design issue. Small maintenance jobs continue, however, until 80 to 90 percent of the engineering is complete.
7. Equipment specifications	7. Preparation of full-fledged equipment specifications is a key indicator that preliminary design is under way. These specifications will be used in equipment inquiries, activity 9.
8. Preliminary design	8. The start of preliminary design is the preparation of equipment specifications. The end is after P&IDs have been issued for design and vendor drawings on the major pieces of equipment have been reviewed. Process effort will peak prior to the end of preliminary design.
9. Equipment inquiries (formal)	9. These are formal inquiries, based on written (formal) specifications. The replies will be contractual quotes. The quotes will be used for purchasing and to prepare either a good budget estimate or a definitive estimate.
10. Design studies	10. This is the layout work, done by design groups *for evaluation and the budget estimate.* More than likely this work will have to be totally scrapped later, as it is not based on design issue P&IDs and has not benefited from reliable vendor data.
11. Budget estimate	11. This estimate will be in the ±10 to 20 percent range (see "Estimates" below). An estimate of ±10 percent will usually be the last estimate of a project.
12. Equipment purchases	12. This is the watershed for engineering/design work. Once this activity begins, the "real" business of designing a plant can begin. This will occur at about the peak process effort, yet will lead the peak facilities effort. This is the firmest of all reference points during engineering. The *first* purchase may occur after engineering is 15 percent complete and should not occur after engineering is more than 35 percent complete.

13. Vendor engineering	13. After purchase orders are placed, vendors will proceed with *their* engineering work. Their efforts will be shown primarily on their drawings. Said drawings are needed for detailed design.
14. Follow-up engineering (process portion)	14. This consists of following up on what has been done and working with facilities disciplines. The actual process effort will dwindle until one individual, part-time, can move the work along (see Fig. 5-5).
15. Detailed design	15. Except in cases of great urgency, an owner is advised not to authorize detailed design until it becomes obvious that the budget estimate will be approved. Even with this approval, a good deal of the work will depend on vendor information and must wait. Some detailed design jobs, such as grading drawings, concrete specifications, equipment arrangements, buildings, and the like, can be started prior to receipt of vendor drawings, but the majority of this work must wait for vendor drawings—especially in areas where the process has a major presence.
16. Subcontract inquiries	16. The earliest subcontract inquiries (other than for *engineering*) will probably have to do with clearing, grading, or excavation for underground work. Then, not a great deal later, will come steel fabrication. These inquiries will be processed into purchases. Inquiry activity from the home office can cease at some point, as the design effort ends, to be continued out of the field office.
17. Set up field operation	17. This consists of setting up the field office. It should occur about the time inquiries for subcontracts are begun.
18. Definitive estimate*	18. This estimate can be executed after major subcontracts have been established. The accuracy is in the neighborhood of ±5 percent. Rarely is an accuracy of ±5 percent (or better) justified.
19. Construction	19. This is where the greatest part of a capital expenditure occurs. Prior work has a strong effect on these costs.

---

*Here, a *definitive* estimate is defined as one whose accuracy is in the neighborhood of ±5 percent. Some companies refer to a ±10 percent estimate as definitive.

ESTIMATES

As is the case with scheduling, some good computer software exists today that will remove most of the drudgery of estimating. Skill and experience are needed to run this software in a meaningful fashion, however. This author is firmly convinced that the minimum requirement for a junior estimator on process plant jobs should include no less than 2 years' field experience with a mechanical contractor. The estimator must be able to look at drawings and envision craftspeople at work. Computers and software are considerably less important than experience. All the computer can do is help to organize a thought process, eliminate computational errors, and do arithmetic at lightning speed.

The two parts of a process plant (that is, the process part and the facility part) are distinct when it comes to cost estimation. The process part of the estimate depends heavily on equipment, instrumentation, piping, and electrical costs. The facility part of the estimate depends heavily on square footage* and type of construction.

The process part of the estimate requires an estimator with experience in process plant estimating. The facilities part of the estimate can often be done by an estimator with architectural experience. In a good number of cases, however, the facilities estimator must be versed in facilities for process operations.

We take a brief look at how an estimate is prepared.

Figure 5-7 is a worksheet from an estimate showing typical process and facilities portions. The starting point for process equipment is the purchase price of the equipment piece. This is shown in the equipment column of the estimate sheet (see the top part of Fig. 5-7). The next task is to determine the cost to set the item on its foundation. To do this, the estimator is guided by the type of item (whether it is a distillation column, a glass-lined vessel, roof ventilator, pump, etc.), its location (roof, ground, etc.), and its size (where size is usually specified as weight and overall dimensions). On rough estimates and on estimates for small, standard pieces (fans, for example), a percentage of the equipment price is used as the cost for setting the piece. For large or unusual pieces, the required crew (millwrights, crane operators, mechanics, laborers, etc.) and their efforts must be estimated.

In referring to Fig. 5-7, note that the installation cost is broken into *field materials* and *labor.* Field materials include such things as welding rod, shims, grout, nuts and bolts, etc. This figure usually is fairly modest, but on fast-track projects can be large. On such jobs, costly items such as valves and piping are purchased in the field. When this is done via subcontract, the subcontractor's markup must be added.

When a standard percentage is used for equipment installation, the sum is entered in the Total (or Subcontracts) column along with a remark in the Quantity/Reference column signaling that a standard allowance has been used.

The Totals column is employed when the construction effort is done via direct hire. The Subcontracts column is used when the workforce is employed on a subcontract basis (see Chap. 12). Thus the amounts for subcontractor overheads and profits (and other indirect field costs) can be conveniently added separately.

---

*Estimators prefer the term *material quantities* to *square footage. Square footage* is not wholly accurate but conveys the idea readily.

ESTIMATE WORKSHEET
AJAX ENGINEERING, INC.

CLIENT: CENTURY OIL COMPANY

PROJECT NAME: CENTRIFUGE UPGRADE

PROJECT NO.: CF - 121

AREA: LUBRICANT REFINING

DATE: 30 MAR. 1994

MAJOR ACCOUNT: EQUIPMENT

PROJECT LOCATION: LOS ANGELES REFINERY

	I.D. NUMBER	DESCRIPTION	QTY./ REF.#	UNIT PRICE	UNIT	MHRS /UNIT	MAN-HOURS	MTLS. & EQUIPMENT	FIELD MATERIALS	LABOR	SUB-CONTRACTS	$ TOTAL
1												
2	30800	centrifuge, skid mounted, w/ 25 hp motor	std. allow.					53000			2600	55600
3												
11		Description: Slab on grade, 6" th.										
12		Grading	2800		SP	0.010	28			1260		1260
		Excavation	90		CY	0.710	64			2492		2492
13		Fill										
		Formwork	410	1.25	SP	0.230	94		513	3961		4473
14		Re-bar 6x6, W2.9xW2.9, WWF	2800	0.15	SP	0.006	17		420	638		1058
		Concrete	51	60.00	CY	3.540	181		3060	7402		10462
15		Overpour	3	60.00	CY				180			180
		Other:										
16		Description: Ramp										
17		Grading										
		Excavation	23		CY	0.710	16				800	
18		Fill	11		CY	2.850	31				1536	
		Formwork	150	1.25	SP	0.230	35				2000	
19		Re-bar 6x6, W2.9xW2.9, WWF	688	0.15	SP	0.006	4				312	
		Concrete	12	60.00	CY	4.200	50				3362	
20		Overpour										
21		Other:										
		TOTAL THIS PAGE					520		4173	15753	8011	19926

ACCOUNT NO.: 53-4
SHEET NO.: 2 OF: 4

PAGE: 78

Figure 5-7 Estimate sheet showing development of process and facility portion of estimate.

The other components in the *process* part of the job that are associated with the *equipment* are *piping* and *instruments.* Cost estimates of these are team efforts. A purchasing agent verifies prices for the various materials and commodities (piping, conduit, twisted-pair cables, etc.). A piping designer examines his or her drawings and the piping index, then counts required piping materials. An estimator then uses prices and quantities and adds tabulated labor quantities (using the correct productivity factors for the type of construction and working conditions).

The *instrumentation* portion of the estimate is done slightly differently. An instrument list is made up. Known costs of the instruments (from recent projects or from quotes) are given for each item. The cost for *mounting* the instrument in a process line, or on an equipment piece, can be determined by the piping designer, the instrument engineer, or the estimator. For the portion of instruments not mounted on the process but having electrical connections, an electrical designer counts terminal connections, numbers of conductors, junction boxes, etc. This information is then used by the electrical designer (aided by the electrical engineer) to formulate an estimate with little help from the estimator.

The rest of the estimate is for the facility part of the project. Standard methods used in estimating nonprocess facilities are used. For example, a buried fire-water line at an oil refinery is estimated no differently from a buried fire-water line at a shopping center.*

An estimate is usually broken into subunits covering areas or buildings. This makes an estimate easier to understand and easier to check.

A good estimate is impossible without a good understanding of labor costs in the vicinity of the project. A fairly good idea of labor costs can be obtained from *Engineering News Record.* Caution and knowledge must be exercised before the figures in *ENR* can be used, however.

Table 5-2 shows how a fully loaded rate is derived from a bare wage. Further adjustments are needed to account for overtime incentives and differentials between crafts. By using carpenters as the base and assigning to them an index of 1.0, the spread is fairly well covered by roofers at 0.93 and electricians at 1.16.

The usual practice is to estimate an entire craft together; that is, all electrical costs are lumped together in a building, with no distinction between process and facility. This method helps for evaluating subcontract values and cost control during the job. However, it does not promote quality in estimating. If the estimated costs for electrical work on the many different types of equipment were tallied separately (and, on a random-sample basis, monitored separately in the field), a great tool for measuring estimating quality and construction quality would be at hand.

Also the inclusion or excision of equipment (or whole areas) would be greatly facilitated by use of this method.

Ideally, for each piece of equipment, there would be at least one estimate sheet. This estimate sheet would include all the crafts: elec-

---

*Published estimator's guides can be consulted for the usual parts of the facilities portion of the job. Two such guides are *The Richardson Rapid Construction Cost Estimating System* [31] and *Building Construction Cost Data* (commonly referred to as Means) [32]. The Richardson guide also has a large portion devoted to process equipment. Neither guide should be used without instruction.

TABLE 5-2 How a Fully Loaded Labor Rate Is Derived (Union Labor, Subcontract Basis)

	$/h	
Wage (from *ENR*)	25.00	Direct-hire portion
Health and welfare	2.90	
Pension	3.00	
Training	0.15	
Miscellaneous	0.15	
FICA	1.91	
Worker's compensation	0.28	
Overhead (12%)	4.01	Subcontract portion
Profit (10%)	3.34	
	40.74	

TABLE 5-3 A Few Benchmark Quantities for Estimates

	Value to use	Range	Unit
Platforms (light steel)	180	150–300	Dollars/CWT
Building steel (heavy steel)	120	100–240	Dollars/CWT
Stairs (open grating type)	120	100–140	Dollars/LF
Steel from mill	30	27–35	Dollars/CWT
Concrete in place*	260	220–350	Dollars/CY
Electric motor, 5 hp	350	300–600	Dollars
Small agitators†	18	12–30	Dollars/lb
Gasoline engines†	7	5–12	Dollars/lb
Heat exchangers‡	80	30–200	Dollars/SF
Shop-fabricated steel tanks	150	100–300	Dollars/CWT
Field-fabricated steel tanks	160	140–220	Dollars/CWT

CWT = hundred weight, LF = lineal feet, CY = cubic yards, SF = square feet.

*Slab or footing.

†Examples of highly evolved, machined, shop-fabricated equipment.

‡Small (15 to 150 ft^2), 304 stainless, standard design. (This price drops rapidly with larger sizes.)

trical, instruments, piping, structural, etc. Of course, areas and buildings would continue to have their own estimates, as usual.

This approach to estimating is used by some companies. It was the method used by the Du Pont Company some years ago.

On process equipment, there is no single special technique for estimating, but the whole job of estimating process equipment installation is special. The estimator must be aware of special space requirements around the equipment and must understand how the crafts must commence and end their work efficiently. The estimator must know that the difference between a distillation column and a steam boiler is a great one.

For use in quick economic evaluations and to check estimates, it is a good idea to have some rule-of-thumb quantities at hand for the various parts of a process project. A few values that the author keeps are given in Table 5-3. Each project engineer and estimator should maintain individual records of pertinent estimating quantities.

A lean, preengineered, single-story warehouse type of area (including walls, roof, and 4-in slab, but without equipment foundations and without electrical services) can cost in the neighborhood of $20 to $40 dollars per square foot, depending on the types of frills (such as quality of siding and roofing) included.

In the way of contrast, a typical control room, with a rubber-tile floor, air conditioning, soundproofing, plate-glass windows, adequate lighting, etc. (but excluding control panels, instruments, instrument wiring, and so on) can run about $300 per square foot. More complete comparison data can be found in Richardson or in Means.

ESTIMATE ACCURACY

In one way or another, most methods for judging estimate accuracy go back to the methods developed within the Monsanto Chemical Company and published by W. T. Nichols in 1951 [33]. Figure 5-8 has been made up by blending Nichols' approach with what is seen to be common practice in today's world. Variation exists among companies, but the differences are minor. As a benchmark, the requirements for a ±10 percent estimate used by a major chemical company are given in App. K.

As with other project activities, a few simple barometers of progress

1.0	**Conceptual Phase**					
	1.1	Major process steps	C	C	C	C
	1.2	Plant capacity	C	C	C	C
	1.3	Literature search	C	C	C	C
	1.4	Flow diagrams	C^a	C	C	C
	1.5	Mass balance	C^a	C	C	C
	1.6	Equipment list (major items)	C^b	C	C	C
	1.7	Basic data	C(-)	C	C	C
2.0	**Preliminary Engineering Phase**					
	2.1	Conceptual phase	C	C	C	C
	2.2	Flow diagrams	C	C	C	C
	2.3	Mass balance	C	C	C	C
	2.4	Equipment list (major items)	C(-)	C	C	C
3.0	**Preliminary Design Phase**					
	3.1	Process flow diagrams	C	C	C	C
	3.2	Mass balance	C	C	C	C
	3.3	P&IDs	N	C^c	C^d	C
	3.4	Written specifications	N	N	C	C
	3.5	Firm quotes (equipment)	N	N	C^e	C
	3.6	Single line diagrams	N	C(-)	C(-)	C
	3.7	Materials of construction	N	S^f	C(-)	C
	3.8	Temperature and pressure profiles	N	S	C	C
	3.9	Equipment list	C^g	C^g	C	C
	3.10	Instrument list	N	N	C(-)	C
	3.11	Line list, piping	N	N	C(-)	C
	3.12	Plot plans	C^h	C^h	C(-)	C
	3.13	Equipment arrangement drawings	S^i	S	C^h	C
4.0	**Detailed Design Phase**					
	4.1	Buildings and structures	N	S^i	C^h	C
	4.2	List of specialty items	N	N	S	C
	4.3	Order release (major pieces)	N	N	S	C
	4.4	Vendor drawing review	N	N	S	C
	4.5	Facilities arrangement drawings	N	S^i	C^h	C
	4.6	Materials takeoffs	N	N	C(-)	C
	4.7	Subcontract specifications	N	N	N	C
Nominal estimate accuracy			±35%	±25%	±15%	±5%
Range:			30–40	20–30	10–20	0–10

Abbreviations: C = complete; N = not complete; S = started; C(-) = substantially complete.

[a]Eighty percent complete.
[b]Seventy percent complete.
[c]Important sheets started.
[d]Ninety percent complete.
[e]Major equipment.
[f]Unusual materials must be defined.
[g]Major equipment only.
[h]Study grade complete.
[i]Rough sketches only.

Figure 5-8 Project accomplishments versus accuracy of capital cost estimates.

can be examined to establish the reasonable accuracy of estimates. In the very early stages, the existence of a mass balance (items 1.5 and 2.3 in Fig. 5-8) is important. If a good mass balance, along the lines described under "Disciplined Approach" in Chap. 8, exists, then preliminary engineering can be viewed as finished. Thus an estimate in the 20 to 40 percent accuracy range is possible, depending on the amount of effort to be spent. Similarly, if firm quotes (item 3.5 of Fig. 5-8) have been obtained, a budget estimate can reasonably be prepared. A companion indicator to look at is whether vendor drawings have been submitted for review. If *order release* has taken place and if some drawings have been submitted for bona fide review, an estimate tending toward ±10 percent is indicated.

Looking at Fig. 5-8, we see that the difference between a budget estimate (nominally ±15 percent) and a definitive estimate (nominally ±5 percent) is the finishing of design details and completion of subcontract specifications. To go from a ±10 percent estimate to a ±5 percent estimate, it is necessary to perform a formal inquiry of the major subcontracts.

CONTINGENCY

The fundamental reason for a contingency is both to make a provision for items too inconsequential to estimate and to allow for imperfections in estimates.

Engineers/designers and constructors are disposed to view contingencies as necessities. Owner executives often view them with suspicion and even prohibit their use from time to time.

The most common practice is to include contingency as a single line item in an estimate. In this way, the contingency can be seen by one and all—and thus is available for review and discussion. If the use of a contingency is prohibited, it will be buried in many places throughout the estimate, by different parties. This will not be the result of a conspiracy; it is just a fact that numerous, unimportant pieces will not be counted when an estimate is made—so a provision should be included. Each party will thus inflate his or her own estimate slightly to account for this effect. Contingency disseminated and embedded throughout the estimate makes a review or monitoring of an estimate more difficult. It taxes cost control efforts severely.

It is important to note that funds for contingency are slated for expenditure—just as funds for the most important equipment piece are slated for expenditure. The numerous, unimportant pieces will, after all, be purchased and installed.

ECONOMICS

No human endeavor can be repeatedly undertaken unless it fulfills rules of economy. A swimmer of the English Channel has limits of body fat, metabolic rate, and lung capacity that will allow a crossing of the channel in appropriate conditions. Let the water cool a degree or two, or let the tide swing around some, and the crossing cannot be accomplished.

Business ventures are subject to rules of economy, too. Resources can be drawn down over brief periods, but must eventually be replenished. Over the long run, revenues must exceed expenditures.

Even the oldest, most prestigious businesses are not exempt. We all know of at least one old, established business driven into the ground by complacent heirs. Perhaps because of past success, the need to modernize or even replenish is overlooked. Fruits are taken, while nourishment is not forthcoming. The beneficiaries perhaps presume the old firm transmutes air into wealth. And, indeed, living off capital can give this appearance, even for long stretches of time, but eventually the practice must end.

Thoughtful people have observed this phenomenon and have set down methods of evaluating business ventures to not only prevent living off of capital but also build capital in the fastest way possible.

The most common measure of rewards from capital investment is *return on investment,* abbreviated ROI. The most straightforward method of calculating ROI is called *simple* ROI, and it is an excellent tool for quick evaluations during a project. The ROI considered here is for *project* purposes (such as bid analysis), and should not be confused with *corporate* ROI.

Before getting to ROI, we need some basic definitions:

- *Revenues*—money entering the business via sales of products or services
- *Operating expenses*—money paid weekly or monthly for ingredients, wages, electricity, rent, etc.
- *Gross earnings*—revenues less operating expenses
- *Net earnings*—gross earnings less depreciation less taxes
- *Cash flow*—gross earnings less taxes
- *Permanent investment*—money invested for long periods for equipment, buildings, roads, etc.
- *Working capital*—money tied up while in operation, fully recoverable upon liquidation (largely finished goods)

Simple ROI is annual earnings divided by capital, expressed as a percentage. Pretax earnings and total capital are the easiest to use:

$$\text{ROI}(g) = \frac{\text{gross earnings}}{\text{permanent investment} + \text{working capital}} \times 100$$

The *g* in parentheses after ROI signals that it is an ROI based on gross earnings. Two other types of return are discussed here. The first is the return based on after-tax earnings, the *net* ROI:

$$\text{ROI}(n) = \frac{\text{gross earnings} - \text{taxes} - \text{depreciation}}{\text{permanent investment} + \text{working capital}} \times 100$$

The second is the return based on cash flow, the *cash* ROI:

$$\text{ROI}(c) = \frac{\text{gross earnings} - \text{taxes}}{\text{permanent investment} + \text{working capital}} \times 100$$

The last two rates require knowledge of *both* depreciation rates and tax rates (tax calculations require knowledge of depreciation rates).

Any of the three—gross earnings, net earnings, or cash flow—can be used to determine the *rate of return.* The rate basis should be stated, however.

Once tax rates and depreciation rates are known, all three ROIs can be determined. Figure 5-9 shows the relation between the different rates of return for the case where depreciation is 10 percent annually

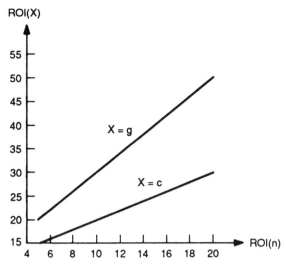

Figure 5-9 ROIs for a depreciation rate of 10 percent accompanied by a tax rate of 50 percent.

and the tax rate is 50 percent, a fairly common approximation for many businesses.

If the required net ROI is 8 percent and taxes and depreciation are about 50 and 10 percent, respectively, then the corresponding gross ROI is about 26 percent and the cash flow ROI is about 16 percent. Due to its simplicity, use of the gross ROI is recommended for journeyman project work. We will use ROI(g) in the examples below.

Note that the rough-and-ready economic exercises during a project are not the same as the corporate economic study upon which the whole project is justified. These latter efforts are performed by corporate accounting people and include a market forecast of product pricing and sales volume.

Probably the most routine ROI calculation employed in project work is the *incremental* ROI, abbreviated IROI, wherein added capital is compared to savings. It is used in selecting the most attractive from among two or more schemes. The IROI is calculated for each alternative, by using the lowest capital cost case as the base case each time:

$$\text{IROI} = \frac{\text{annual savings over base case}}{\text{capital cost} - \text{base case capital cost}}$$

To best see how all this is implemented, two examples, based on actual projects, are presented. In both cases, IROI is used. The first example is for an existing slurry pump that was worn out and had to be replaced. The plant engineer did not know whether to purchase a rubber-lined pump or a refractory-lined pump. The latter is more expensive but would require less attention. Here are the details:

Lining	Flow, gal/min	Head, ft	Capital cost, $	Maintenance cost, $	Power, kW
Refractory	300	120	21,800	2000	11.6
Rubber	300	120	14,900	3300	14.4

The pump was to operate 2600 h/yr. The electric power cost was $0.08/kWh. A full breakdown of costs was not needed for this analysis. Only the parts of capital or operating cost that are not equal are considered. This is because *increments* are compared; therefore, in this example, installation costs were ignored, because the increment between them was nearly zero.

Continuing, then, we have:

	A Power cost, $	B Maintenance cost, $	A+B Operating cost, $	Incremental		
				Operating cost, $	Capital cost, $	Percentage of ROI (g)
Refractory	2413	2000	4413	1882	6900	27.3
Rubber	2995	3300	6295	—	—	—

Case 2 (rubber) was taken as the *base case.*

Reviewing the result, we see that the capital increment earned a return of 27.3 percent. This is a somewhat low return. Within guidelines of company policy, it could be accepted as long as other criteria favor this choice. The dilemma was resolved when the maintenance supervisor pointed out that refractory liners had never failed catastrophically; only rubber liners had, and usually at the worst time [ATD]. The refractory-lined pump was selected.

For most companies, a pretax ROI (also IROI) greater than 25 to 35 percent is acceptable. Company policy on this matter should be stated in the design basis (see App. A for an example). If no company policy is stated, an ROI(g) of 25 percent should be assumed.

As the second example, we have an economic evaluation performed to make a decision during bid analysis.

Competitive bids are received from three vendors for an evaporative crystallizer (Fig. 5-10). A bid analysis indicates they are equivalent except that the condensers differ somewhat in heat transfer area. Reducing the bid summary to bare essentials, we get:

	Area, ft^2	Price, $
Vendor 1	302	45,900
Vendor 2	322	51,000
Vendor 3	316	52,200

One is tempted to dismiss the differences of heat-transfer area and make life simple by awarding the purchase to the low bidder. However, review of the situation indicates that cooling-water use should

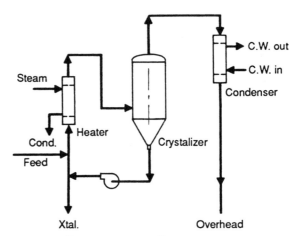

Figure 5-10 Evaporative crystallizer.

decline as the heat-transfer area is increased. Can this possibly justify the greater purchase price?

A review of power costs at the site indicates that cooling-water pumping costs are in the neighborhood of $0.03 per 1000 gal. Furthermore, cooling-water use and costs for each case are estimated as follows:

	Cooling water, ΔT°F	Outlet temp., °F	Cooling-water flow, gal/min	Pumping cost, $	Price, $	Incremental		
						Pumping cost, $	Price, $	ROI(g)
Vendor 1	20	101	485	6310	45,900	—	—	—
Vendor 2	34	115	285	3710	51,000	2600	5100	51.0
Vendor 3	30	111	323	4210	52,200	2100	6300	33.3

The incremental data show that the extra money paid for heat-exchanger surface is worth spending. So, what appeared to be an unjustified cost turned out to be a bonanza [ATD]. It is important to note that an even greater economy would result from more exchanger surface area, but a limit is set on the outlet temperature to prevent excessive mineral deposits. The limit in this case was 115°F.

In these examples, no provision has been made for depreciation or taxes. Nor has discounted cash flow been used. This is because in most cases an evaluation based on pretax earnings is adequate.

The reader is asked to consider what might be gained by including depreciation and taxes in the examples above. Are the results any different if taxes and depreciation are included? Are choices any easier? Is it possible that the return rate is of primary importance and that taxes and depreciation are of secondary importance?

By keeping in mind the needs of project work—not corporate 10-year plans—the same questions can be asked with regard to discounted cash flow. Further, we note that in addition to depreciation rate and tax rate, we must know the project life and salvage value.

If one is not careful, one can be drawn into side issues of little use to the matter at hand. On the typical bid analysis (which an engineer may be expected to perform in one afternoon), the full economic assessment, using discounted cash flow, is not necessary. This type of analysis can be useful for whole projects or complex systems (like nuclear reactors), but is unnecessary during the course of a normal project.

For simplicity and speed, most project economic evaluations should use hurdle rates* based on gross return rates.

To learn more about discounted cash flow analyses and other measures of profitability, the following articles by Ward and Horwitz are recommended:

- "Estimate Profitablity Using Net Return Rate" [34]
- "The Mathematics of Discounted Cash Flow Analysis" [35]

It is interesting to note that Horwitz concludes by saying that discounted cash flow concepts were probably unknown to John D. Rockefeller and J. P. Morgan.

By the application of sound economic analyses during a project, the profitability of the investment will be pushed upward. In so doing,

---

*The rate above which the capital is justified is often called the *hurdle* rate.

available resources will have been employed with care—perhaps even used to maximum effectiveness.

When performing economic studies, one must maintain objectivity. There is a great temptation to inflate cost estimates, because this makes life more comfortable to the person who must carry out the project. The inflated estimate is counterproductive, however, because (1) good, viable projects that should have been done are unreasonably eliminated and (2) a *fat* project squanders resources.

Before we leave this chapter, a review of one more idea is in order: *strategy.* Strategy is most often the purview of the executive, yet it invariably is implemented at all levels in a company.

A good example of a strategic move is when company management selects a low-ROI project over a high-ROI project, because the high-ROI project is tainted with environmental questions.

A successful business requires both things: efficient use of resources and a vision of where to go and what to do in the future. Obviously, the second item is the strategy.

Designers and engineers can do a better job if they are aware of the strategic needs of a project. For example, a misplaced enthusiasm for economy can set back a policy that emphasizes reliability in use, that is, failure-free operation. Designers and engineers should know that some things simply cannot be quantified in economic terms (see Chap. 2 for examples).

For a glimpse behind the scenes at how some CEOs view economic analysis and weigh it against the art of strategy, the reader is directed to a perceptive article in the March 13, 1989, issue of *Fortune* [36]. Among many things, the article states that "Executives are becoming more sophisticated about the budgeting process itself. They are challenging the mechanistic use of the venerable discounted cash-flow model and taking advice on what to buy from managers at all levels. Some are even listening to the people on the factory floor."

Before we end this chapter, note that ROI is only a *measure* of economic worth. Numerous other gauging quantities exist. The true proof of economic viability is whether an activity can persist indefinitely. Thus, even though uncontrolled releases of solids into the atmosphere were viewed as "economic" in the recent past, this activity is now viewed as *uneconomic.* The unsafe working conditions of earlier centuries can be viewed in the same light. With these thoughts in mind, an *economic* activity can be defined as an activity which uses resources effectively compared to alternate activities and which is allowed to persist due to tangible benefits perceived by the general populace. Such an activity will result in a generally improved standard of living.

——Chapter 6——
Project
Organization

A process facility can be viewed as consisting of two parts: the process component and the facility component. Most engineering/design organizations are built up to deal with these two parts. As we shall see, the two parts are heavily dependent on each other; therefore, project leaders have to be conversant with both parts and capable of creating a unified effort.

The process component consists primarily of process equipment, instruments, and piping. The facilities component includes structures, buildings, ventilation, lighting, roads, boilers, etc.

Some process facilities are dominated by the facilities component, others by the process component. Where the dominant part is the facility, one might think of a dairy, a bottling plant, or a candy factory: The buildings dominate the image. Where the process component dominates, one need only think of a petroleum refinery: The buildings and structures pale alongside the columns, vessels, and piping. Both of these are process facilities. And, very pertinently, the two types have their different outward aspects for *process* reasons: Food processes need to keep dirt out, refineries must not trap flammable gases.

As a side note, it is interesting to go through old process buildings that have been gutted of machinery and to look at the odd foundations and ceiling heights. Likewise it is interesting to take a non-process building, say, a warehouse, and fit within it a process. The conclusion one draws in such exercises is that these two intertwined parts affect each other profoundly.

The people who work in these two major areas usually, but *not* always, have different professional backgrounds. Also there probably exists a slight difference in temperament, inclination, and outlook. The facility portion is largely populated by

- Structural engineers*
- Architects*
- Civil engineers*
- Electrical engineers*
- Mechanical (HVAC) engineers*

---

*And designers.

The process portion is heavy with

- Chemical engineers
- Mechanical (vessels and machinery) engineers*
- Metallurgical engineers (or metallurgists)
- Instrumentation engineers*
- Piping designers

It bears emphasis that this division is not hard and fast.

With an experienced team, the two groups have a good understanding of each other's duties and can do limited work in each other's specialty. They will be capable of spotting possible difficulties for each other. A chemical engineer might realize that a fork-lift truck will probably ruin a doorway unless protective posts (bollards) are planted at the sides; the chemical engineer must contact the civil/structural engineer or architect and make sure this possibility has been considered [ATD]. Providence on high does not build process plants. It is people, with their imperfect means of communication, who do.

When the product of a design effort is good, it is because all participants have performed as a team. When a well-coordinated team is at work, the boundary between the facilities and process components goes unnoticed, as it should.

Figure 6-1 shows engineers and designers working on the process and facilities parts of a job side by side. Their efforts are unified by project engineers and the project manager. Figure 6-1 also gives some rough indications of career progression. An entry-level engineer might start out doing material balances, then select and size equipment. Then she or he might generate P&IDs. The engineer who wishes to go farther up the progression must become more and more familiar with facilities tasks, building codes, fire protection, scheduling, cost estimating, job sequences, permits, construction, etc. As this individual acquires broader knowledge, he or she becomes a candidate for the job of project engineer.

The career progression leading to project engineer can start on the facilities side, too. Typically an engineer or architect doing facilities tasks will learn more and more about the process side.

Project managers will be former project engineers who have a very broad understanding of project work and who are comfortable mak-

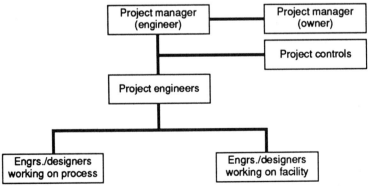

Figure 6-1 Overall outline of the organization for process plant projects.

---

*And designers.

ing decisions and taking initiatives. Ideally, the project manager will also be a leader, that is, a person who can instill a vision in others.

Figure 6-1 shows two project managers: engineering and owner. The engineering project manager is in charge of the design effort. She or he is generally the recipient of and the transmitter of all formal communications, such as letters, periodic reports, periodic forecasts, schedules, change orders, etc. The engineering project manager makes sure resources are available for projects. He or she must discern progress and understand the difficulties well enough to provide remedies before they become serious.

The owner project manager is charged with making sure that work is progressing expeditiously and that the design effort is on target. This person also is the conduit for feeding approval documents back through his or her own organization. During the busiest part of the job, the owner project manager may have a staff of two or three people to provide assistance during the peak effort.

On small projects the roles of engineering project manager and project engineer are combined. On a somewhat larger project, the project manager and a project engineer might share the work. On large projects, multiple project engineers are required, each one being assigned responsibility for geographic *and* functional zones.

It is important that every part or piece of a job, whether it be a brass door handle or a bimetallic thermometer, ultimately tie back to one person with authority and responsibility. This person should be the project engineer.

Where multiple project engineers are required, a clear division of their geographic and functional zones is essential. In setting up these zones it is best to keep geography and function together as much as possible. The engineer with the tank farm also should be responsible for all outdoor work on the project. The engineer with the evaporators, crystallizers, and centrifuges also should be responsible for the building that encloses that equipment. A project engineer's responsibility is pervasive and includes not only the process equipment but also the facilities portion: lighting, motor controls, drinking water—in short, everything that constitutes a functioning whole *area*. This is not to say the project engineer *specifies* brass doorknobs for the rest room. No, it means that the project engineer makes sure an architect reviews the plans. And the project engineer is assured the architect understands the appropriate building codes. The architect, in turn, will call for a bathroom at some location, and a designer will lay it out and choose the hardware for it, including the brass doorknob.

It is the project engineer who initials every drawing and significant document for her or his area. This does not constitute a check (yet the project engineer is advised to review a few key points in his or her expertise), but simply acknowledges responsibility.* When initialing documents, the project engineer should already be thoroughly familiar with what the documents contain.

Refer again to Fig. 6-1, specifically the block labeled *project controls*. This group performs an auditing function for measuring progress and budget. The group watches some key indicators of performance, such as issue dates on drawings and specifications or estimated amounts versus actual amounts for purchase orders, and advises the project manager. They assist the project manager in issuing formal reports. When forecasts do not tally well against perform-

---

*Project managers initial documents only to the extent that they function as project engineers; it is their deputies, the project engineers, who do most of the signing.

TABLE 6-1 Technical Skills for Process Facility Design

 1. Architectural
 2. Civil
 3. Electrical
 4. Heating, ventilating, and air conditioning (HVAC)
 5. Instrumentation
 6. Mechanical*
 7. Piping
 8. Plumbing
 9. Process
10. Specialty†
11. Structural

*Machine design, vessels, rotating equipment, solids handling, etc.

†Corrosion, materials of construction, model making, etc.

ance, deeper investigation is warranted. This is how project controls work. On small projects, the manager or engineer should perform this function without outside help.

The most commonly required technical skills for the design of process facilities are shown in Table 6-1. These are often referred to as *design disciplines.* It is also common to cull out *process* and not refer to it as a discipline; however, this doesn't make sense unless one also culls out piping and instrumentation. Nonprocess jobs are often referred to as "discipline jobs," but it is far better to refer to these as "facilities jobs."

Environmental skills are not included among the technical skills, because the environmental component is more closely allied with interpretation of law, rather than the specification of a design feature. For example, an environmental engineer might conclude that according to the letter of the law, secondary containment is not a requirement, but to be on the safe side, a certain part of the facility should include secondary containment. Then the design disciplines would work as a team to interpret where the boundaries of secondary containment are needed and how best to provide the secondary containment. The environmental engineer would serve as a consultant.

Some projects have a large process component, others have a large facilities component. This has a bearing on the types of skills that need prevail to guide the design effort. In Fig. 6-2 it has been assumed that the guiding forces of a process facility design effort can be resolved into three parts: architectural, mechanical, and process.

Here is how to interpret the charts. The typical facility for producing inorganic chemicals will receive 60 percent of its guidance from process considerations, 30 percent from mechanical considerations, and 10 percent from architectural considerations. The breakdown given in Fig. 6-2 is not the result of an exhaustive survey. It is simply representative of processes with which the author is familiar.

It would be a mistake to suppose that one could build a process facility, just by having the skills listed in Table 6-1. A broad spectrum of capabilities is required in each of the skills listed. It isn't enough to simply know plumbing; something else is needed, too, such as fire sprinklers and codes relating to them.

All technical people in a design organization should be encouraged by their superiors to develop some specialty skills so that the people can be used as consultants in those areas of expertise. For example, a process engineer might decide to become an expert in calculating pressure safety devices and piping. Another process engineer might want to become an expert in heat transfer. At least one mechanical

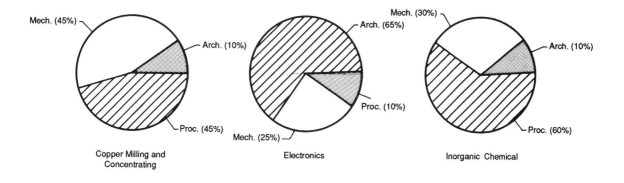

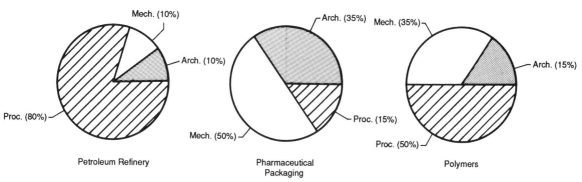

Figure 6-2 Influence upon the facility design.

engineer should become versed in requirements for code vessels. A civil engineer might want to become expert in secondary containment. These efforts lend great flexibility to an organization. Such efforts also give personal satisfaction and raise prestige (and, therefore, pay and job security).

To further understand how process work and facilities work must tie together, we will look at what is required to install a simple centrifugal pump. The need for the pump is first identified by the process engineer (PE). As a reminder not to forget the pump, the PE will mark it on the appropriate P&ID while the P&ID is being developed. At that time, the PE may have a rough idea of what the pumps' flow capacity should be, but will not know nearly as well what the discharge pressure should be—the pressure information must wait until the location of the pump has been established.* On the P&ID, the engineer will also show piping to and from the pump, valves, instruments, and an electric switch for starting and stopping the pump.

Even before the first formal issue of the P&ID, the process engineer may sit down briefly with the instrument engineer to go over possible control requirements. A few things they might talk about include

• What happens if the pump runs dry

• How the flow rate should be adjusted

• Whether any emergency stop conditions are envisioned

Once the P&ID showing the pump is formally issued, the next person to become involved with the pump will be the piping designer. The

---

*For the purpose of preliminary motor sizing, 60 ft of total dynamic head (TDH) is a good, universally applicable number.

designer will have become familiar with the flow sheets* and other available information and may also have some layout sketches showing the larger pieces of equipment. As the designer studies the P&ID showing the pump, he or she will probably have a sketch pad at hand and will be playing around with some rough concepts on equipment arrangement.

Once the designer is sure of having a grasp on what is needed and comes up with a suitable arrangement, she or he will clean up the sketch some and confer with the process engineer to obtain concurrence.

Once the process engineer and the piping designer are in agreement, the designer will issue an equipment arrangement drawing showing the location of the pump. The initial arrangement drawing will simply show the presence of a pump on a short pedestal (occasionally called a plinth). The initial issuance of the equipment arrangement drawing will be to enable an assessment of structural requirements. In the case of this pump, suppose it is located indoors, along a row of heat exchangers and pumps. Leaving room for piping and maintenance access, the pump occupies 9 ft^2 of floor space.

With the equipment arrangement drawing, a good portion of the building size will have been established. A typical manufacturing building will also contain a control room, rest rooms, a motor control room, and other rooms. The architect will work with the piping designer and the project engineer to establish an overall plan for the building. In some cases, it may be decided to use a preengineered building. If so, the architect heads the effort to purchase the building. In the case of a custom building, the architect determines all the architectural details, such as siding, roofing, doors, windows, interior partitions, fire walls, etc. In the second case, the structural engineer designs the structural portion of the building—this is in addition to the normal job of designing supports for equipment, piping, and operating platforms.

As the building plan is being developed, the civil engineer will begin developing plans for underground piping. The electrical engineer will begin thinking about conduit locations and lighting. The HVAC engineer will begin laying out ductwork. The plumbing designer will show potable water piping, drain piping, and sewer piping (aboveground portion).

Once the equipment arrangement has been established, the process engineer can lay out a system curve (see page 154) to determine the required pump discharge pressures under a range of operating conditions.

At the time the P&ID is first issued, the electrical engineer (EE) will become aware of the pump and will note the need for a motor starter on the electrical equipment list. Until the pump has actually been ordered and vendor documents giving pump size are obtained, the electrical engineer will not know exactly what starter to provide. Initially the process engineer will be able to specify, for example, "less than 5 hp." Later, after playing with the system curves, the process engineer might say, "Hydraulic horsepower comes to 1.2, so let's guesstimate 3."

And so it goes, but we won't take this description further, because by now it is evident that the work to install the pump is a team effort. Figure 6-3 shows a typical organization chart for the technical effort.

---

*Formally called *process flow diagrams* (PFDs).

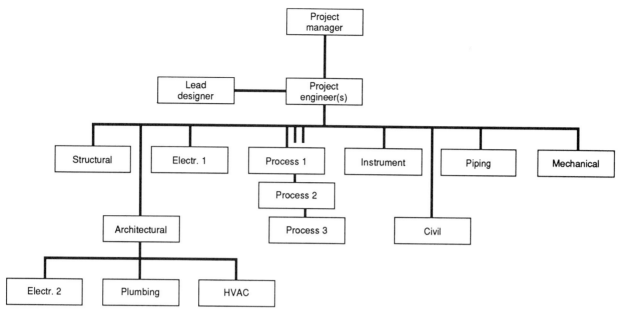

Figure 6-3 Typical organization chart for a process project.

On a larger project, more project engineers with similar organizations under them are required. Two electrical engineers are shown: one for motors, etc., and one for the building.* Many times one engineer does both jobs. The distinction is useful to appreciate the organization, however.

Not all the above personnel will work on the job steadily. Some, like the plumbing designer, may only be on the job for a total of somewhere between 1 week and 1 month. The civil effort may occur in two parts: preliminary work to prepare a budget estimate and detailed design. The first part of civil work might last a week or two. The second part might last from 1 to 3 months. Once the mass balance and process flow sheet have been firmed up, the average process engineer will probably spend 4 to 6 months on the job. The project manager and a key project engineer will be on the job for its duration, but may only be needed part-time toward the end.

For simplicity, Fig. 6-3 addresses only the technical effort. Not shown are a host of service personnel without whom the whole effort would become difficult and costly, if not impossible:

- Secretaries
- Copy and blueprint machine operators
- Mail room personnel
- Clerks
- Telephone operators
- Accountants
- Sales personnel
- High-level executives
- Technical specialists

---

*Even though not shown, there are often two types of mechanical engineer: one for process components, another for utilities components.

- Lawyers
- Estimators
- "Personnel" people

These are the people who help move the paperwork and oversee the strategic needs of the business.

Early in this author's career one of his superiors remarked that the product being made was *paper.* Of course, he did not mean the cellulosic thin sheet; he meant the *information* and how it was packaged. Waving his arm toward a bull pen full of drafting tables, he said, "See all those blueprints. See all these specifications," motioning toward a filling cabinet, "That's what we make. We make paper." How right he was. And how necessary are the support personnel for creating and moving the paper.

To provide a quick glimpse into paper handling requirements, consider the following documents that were prepared to obtain bids for a *minor* piping subcontract (5000 ft of pipe, averaging 3 in in diameter):

- A cover letter (2 pages)
- A scope-of-work document (6 pages)
- A set of bidding instructions (1 page)
- A piping materials specification (43 pages)
- A piping installation specification (28 pages)
- A piping painting specification (14 pages)
- 156 sheets of 11×17 isometric drawings
- 14 sheets of piping orthogonal drawings
- 16 sheets of P&IDs
- A plot plan
- A statement of safety and security rules (7 pages)

This subcontract was worth about $450,000 in 1992. Four companies were originally invited to bid. Each company received a copy of bid documents. Other copies were sent to five destinations within the engineering organization and to three destinations within the client organization. So, for one single initial inquiry, 3504 individual sheets were produced, or about 7284 ft^2 of paper. Revisions to the inquiry and supplemental information during the course of the work added substantially to the final amount of paper produced for this small subcontract.

The support personnel plainly have a considerable job. A well-trained support group is necessary for good communications and, therefore, quality.

No project effort is permanent. It is formed to do a job. For best results, its formation should not be abrupt. It should be staged so that each person coming on the job has information necessary to work effectively. Each will, in turn, generate information for others coming on the job. Finally, as each person completes his or her work, the person will move onto other projects. Eventually, nothing will remain.

A phrase that has been applied to describe this scenario is a *self-destruct* organization.

═══ Chapter 7 ═══
Problem Solving

BACKGROUND

The cornerstone of creativity is problem solving. This is true in art, cuisine, and commerce as well as engineering and science. Furthermore, almost everybody who has reflected on this topic will agree that a key ingredient for solving problems is *simplification.*

Others will go on to say that simplification is greatly helped by breaking the problem into smaller, more manageable parts. The whole scientific method is based on this approach. Chemical engineering itself is often described as being made up, at least in part, of unit operations.

Keith Duckworth [37], automobile engine designer, has said: "There are many complicated solutions to problems, and it is easy to adopt them from the start. But if one thinks harder and more deeply, one frequently can come up with a relatively simple solution, which should always be the one to try."

When it comes to problem solving on process plants, a methodical approach foments quicker, better results. The following five steps can be applied with great effectiveness for understanding all types of phenomena.

- Break into parts.
- Find governing rules for the parts.
- Acquire data.
- Compute.
- Check the results.

BREAK INTO PARTS

The idea here is to sort through the problem, first looking for parts that are familiar. Even one part of a problem recognized as familiar can have a domino effect in showing how to subdivide the rest of the problem.

In this search it may be necessary to put on some rose-colored glasses for a moment or two to simplify—perhaps *oversimplify.* This is fine during the early, brainstorming phase. Later these simplifications must be reviewed.

With the mass balance, converting a process flow diagram to a block flow diagram is a simplification.* Smaller mass balances are then written around each block (see Chap. 8).

FIND GOVERNING RULES

When it has been possible to isolate a part or two for which the rules of operation are known, this can be used to help break apart the

---

*The flow diagram must precede the block diagram, not vice versa.

problem and write rules for other parts. The most common rules are those for conservation of mass, energy, and identity (that is, *calcium balance*). This step will usually culminate in writing out mathematical equations. This step will often require a trip to the library to hunt for a special piece of information.

ACQUIRE DATA

Once the operating rules have been determined, it is a relatively simple matter to review available data, looking for areas where data are not adequate. An equation with two variables requires the determination of one so that the other may be deduced. Tracking down the missing data is often not simple. This step can be lengthy and can involve the intercession of language translators, laboratory personnel, consultants, and far-flung agents.

COMPUTE

Even the average grade-school child can make great headway in this category. Accuracy, of course, is essential—something that the grade-school child will miss out on. The availability of hand-held calculators and mini- and microcomputers renders this the simplest of the five steps. In the old days of the slide rule, this was frequently a difficult task, however.

CHECK THE RESULTS

To the uninitiated, this always poses the great enigma. How does one check her or his own results?

The most usual way is by repetition. If the repetition can be done in a reverse sequence or even by using a different law of physics (or whatever), then the check is better. Perhaps even more important is a straightforward critical overview trying to answer whether the result makes sense. Does it make sense to produce pure water from salt water in an evaporator? Well, yes, if done properly and as long as a tiny amount of salt from entrainment is not objectionable. Does it make sense to expect a product with no salt from such an evaporator? Well, no, but by putting in special demisters and a reflux condenser, one can reasonably design to an acceptably low concentration.*

Checking results requires a good knowledge of the rules that govern. One must understand the points upon which *nature* will become insistent. Experience is important here. Take, for example, a complex mass balance that showed a stream with negative values for water coming out of a reaction step. Everyone was sure there was a problem with some equations or some data. A great effort was mounted to root out the problem—to no avail. Once an overview approach was adopted, it quickly became apparent that the result was correct. The only failure was in the interpretation of the result, namely, that the reaction required water. An equation was altered so that water was taken from a feed stream (something that would actually happen), and the negative flow disappeared.

---

*A philosophical concept arises here: *Zero* is a mathematical entity. A true zero concentration of anything is doubtful—less than 10^{-12} g/L, perhaps, but not zero.

HELPFUL HINTS

Solutions to many problems will often result from pursuing a few simple techniques. The techniques are summarized by the following phrases:

- Definitions of problems and words.
- Who else has had this problem?
- Set condition; examine consequences.

Defining the essence of a problem is a most powerful way of dealing with it, but is sometimes difficult. The techniques for setting priorities (see Chap. 4) are useful in arriving at the essence of a problem. Knowing how to define a word can also be useful: (1) Make a general observation about the word that contains its essence. (2) Give a specific instance. For example, to define the word *brick:* A brick is a building material used for building walls and chimneys. It is made of fired earthen materials. Common U.S. bricks are made of red clay and measure approximately $2.25 \times 3.75 \times 8$ in.

Problem solving is obviously greatly simplified by finding someone who has been faced with a similar problem who is willing to share knowledge about its solution. What is not so evident is where such parties might be and how to locate them. Searches of the literature can be a great help here, and so can conversations with colleagues and equipment vendors. To establish size criteria for an evaporation pond, for example, one should begin by asking which other people would have an interest in evaporation ponds. With a little thought, two come to mind who should be cooperative: U.S. Meteorological Survey and power plants.

Finally, the classic technique of going back to the most ancient philosophers can be employed here. This method requires setting a condition hypothetically, then examining the logical consequences. The Ionian Greeks demonstrated that the square root of 2 was an irrational number by this method. That sonic flow will never develop in a pressure relief line can be determined by showing that energy inputs are too small to develop the necessary upstream pressure.

WHY PROBLEMS PERSIST

Many problems persist long beyond their logical terms of existence. This is evident on plants that have been in operation for long periods. In one case, for example, solid-bowl centrifuges continued to be used for many years after pusher centrifuges became available. The solid-bowl units were hard to clean, ceased functioning without warning, and yielded wet cake. Yet they were used for 15 years more than they should have been, because company management discouraged plant improvement projects.

The author devised Fig. 7-1 about twenty years ago. A copy hangs on the wall of his office as a reminder of the many difficulties encountered in solving problems. It demonstrates, too, that most problems remain unsolved due to poor ordering of priorities.

To begin, one must select problems that are economically* solvable. Thus, impossible-to-solve problems must be excluded from attempts

---

*An *economic* activity is one where labor and capital resources are wisely used. By definition, an economic activity is one that results, generally, in an improved standard of living (see Chap. 5).

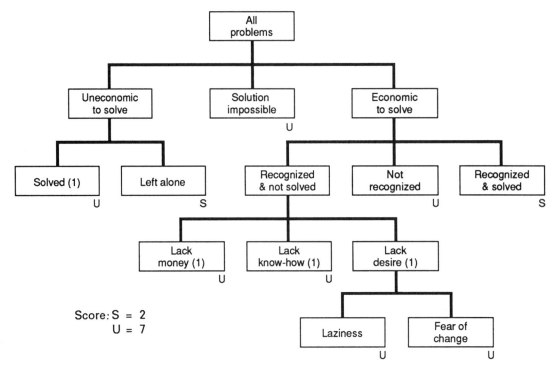

Figure 7-1 Why problems persist. Notes: (1) By virtue of misplaced priority. (2) U and S stand for unsatisfactory and satisfactory results.

at problem solving. The classic example here is the elimination in the last 100 years of any serious pursuit of a perpetual-motion machine.

Ideally, an engineer or a designer or a manager is able to roughly arrange problems in order of economic importance.* Then, with a knowledge of available resources, this person can devote efforts to solving the most important problems. If one of the problems is given undue priority, it can be placed unduly high on the list, and resources can be spent on it that would have been best employed elsewhere—this can result in the solution of an uneconomic-to-solve problem (see left side of Fig. 7-1). Devotion to solving uneconomic problems is often referred to (in the vernacular) as "wasting time."

One method of ranking competing activities is to use the return on investment as the basis for ranking. In theory, this is how a corporation reinvests earnings.

By the same theory, ranking of problems should be dictated by cost-benefit considerations. Sometimes, however, the order is driven by fear, by superstition, by false notions of economy, and by prejudice. The true motivators are shown in the lower half of Fig. 7-1. The most widely used excuses† are

- It can't be done (false claim of impossibility).‡

- We don't have the money (poor understanding of what is economic).

---

*See Chap. 4 for advice on ordering priorities.

†In *Up the Organization* [38], Townsend hit the mark when he said, "It's a poor bureaucrat who can't stall a good idea until even its sponsor is relieved to see it dead and officially buried." Shakespeare's Hamlet was somewhat more lyrical in considering fear of the unknown: "Thus conscience does make cowards of us all; and thus the native hue of resolution is sicklied o'er with the pale cast of thought, and enterprises of great pitch and moment, with this regard, their currents turn awry, and lose the name of action."

‡Assertions of impossibility should always be viewed with suspicion.

━━ Chapter 8 ━━
The Mass Balance

BACKGROUND

The most underrated activity in project work for process plants is the accounting for materials entering and leaving the process. Plainly, whatever enters a process *must* emerge at some point. It will not build up forever.

Today, environmental protection must be built into the design, thus making the mass balance more crucial than ever. The importance of the mass balance is often underrated probably because of at least one of the following:

- The mass balance is humdrum with a tinge of being tedious. (It lacks glamour.)

- Because it is so plain and self-evident, it must not be important.

The casual treatment of the mass balance leads to many design problems. Before we discuss the nature of these, however, an illustration of a simple mass balance is in order.

Imagine a person who has a market for and wishes to make a potassium salt with no more than 0.01% sodium.* Also say that the raw material is a crude potassium salt with 0.64% sodium chloride. Somewhere along the way the excess sodium must be jettisoned via a process operation. This is one way of expressing the requirement:

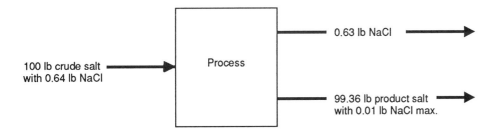

However, if the producer wishes to assure the clients that the maximum sodium chloride they will ever see is 0.01%, then the producer must allow for some process deviations. To compensate for these, the producer may wish to design for an *average* sodium level of 0.008%, or 0.005%, or less, depending on how strongly she or he wants to make the assurance, on the confidence in the process, and other things, such as cost and what the competition is doing. This portion of the basis for design might look like this:

---

*This is one of the criteria of the seller's *product specification.*

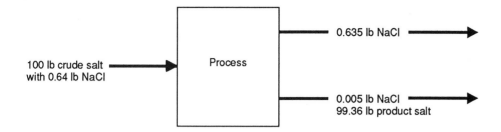

However, such a basis is unrealistic, because perfect separations are never possible. A real-life, practical process might achieve the following result:

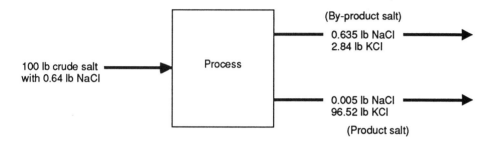

The by-product salt is a subject of concern, since it might be a *waste* if a market cannot be found for it. The by-product stream is often the subject of regulatory requirements.

When a mass balance is treated casually, the following two errors will probably occur: not accounting for *all* substances entering and leaving and not properly accounting for recycle streams. The route leading to these errors is often via a misapplication of two valid techniques for achieving a mass balance:

• Often a quantity can be ignored because it is sufficiently small.

• Often a quantity can be set at some arbitrary value for the sake of argument.

These two techniques are very useful but must be applied with care. No mass balance should be used for design until it has been thoroughly checked by a seasoned professional.

The first approximation above leads to many bizarre abuses. The most notorious runs something like this: A mass balance can be written around the major components while the minor components are equated to zero.

J. F. Carley, professor of chemical engineering at the University of Arizona from 1956 to 1961, used to exclaim, "There are some people who think that, because a quantity is small, it can be ignored. They think that the way to simplify a mass balance is to equate all small quantities to zero!" What Carley was alarmed about continues today. To understand why low concentrations can be important, consider producers of electronic-grade silicon. In this industry the struggle is to achieve parts per *trillion* of some key impurities. To them 0.0001 percent is an astronomical number.

This author recalls all too clearly the client who hoped to make an entry into the electronic-grade silicon market. The client engineers had devised their own material balance for removing phosphorous and other impurities from metallurgical-grade silicon to produce an electronic-grade product. The so-called mass balance was computer-generated and printed on a standard computer printout. The results were neat and orderly, as is the case with computer printouts. These results had been eagerly awaited for several weeks.

Upon receipt, the results were checked by hand calculations and found thoroughly defective within the hour. How? The value of pounds of phosphorous per hour into the process was 0.0169, and that of pounds out was 0.0067. Therefore, what had been presented was a sham. In the succeeding weeks, things did not improve. As a matter of fact, several arbitrary manipulations were made to force the computation to show a false result; these were revealed by repeating the simple tally of incoming and outgoing phosphorous. The rationale, of course, was that the numbers were all small enough to be ignored! But if this were so, then why did their potential buyers bother setting standards in the *parts-per-billion* range? Not only was this sloppy thinking, but also it was unethical comportment.

The same approach is sometimes used to ignore, declare trivial, or fudge recycle streams. Yes, it takes time and patience to work out the simultaneous equations, or the trial-and-error solution, but it is the *only* correct way to deal with a recycle stream. Anything less is not acceptable.

The fact is that, in many cases, values *can* be set to zero and ignored, or fixed at some arbitrary value for the sake of argument. To ignore or not to ignore—*that* is the question. The answer depends on the following:

- Is the component a key component which other lesser components will follow and imitate? For example, in situations where chlorides are predominant, the chloride ion can be taken as the key; then such things as fluorides can often be said to *follow*. A key component must always be tracked.

- Is a component mentioned in the "product specification"? If so, then it must be tracked.

- Is part of the process included specifically to deal with a component? If so, that component must be tracked. For example, if a dryer is included to remove moisture, then water must be included in the mass balance, and its concentrations and flow rates must be tracked (that is, established by valid methods of physics and chemistry).

The point here is that simplifying assumptions can (and often need to) be made, but to do so, they must be proved to be valid. The example given below, under "Disciplined Approach," shows how an assumption regarding entrained ammonium sulfate in the vapor stream from a crystallizer is treated.

Even the most obvious, simple process (or process step) should have its mass balance. Admittedly, it takes discipline to unflaggingly apply this principle. But the rewards it produces and the surprises turned up, even in simple exercises, quickly convince the careful observer of the need for a disciplined approach. The obvious is not always quite so obvious when scrutinized carefully. The disciplined approach is discussed at length below.

Even a simple pipe with water coursing through it can become the subject of an intense mass balance if contaminants begin to leach out of the pipe wall. Any engineer who has designed a system for *water for injection** (WFI) can vouch for this.

PRODUCT SPECIFICATION AND PROCESS RESULT

At the start of this chapter, it was stated that the mass balance is the most underrated activity in project work. *Product specification* and *process result* are the most underrated concepts lying at the heart of the mass balance.

The strange thing is that the sales department of every company making a product for commerce is extremely aware of *product specifications.* Also, in production operations, managers and supervisors are frequently in contact with raw materials suppliers talking about "out-of-spec" material. Why is it that the engineers/designers, almost without exception, have never even heard the term? The communication between sales and engineering could certainly be improved. College faculty can help by introducing the concept. A sample of a current product specification for food-grade phosphoric acid is presented in App. G, courtesy of Monsanto Company.

Here is why product specifications are so important:

> The difference between incoming material and outgoing product defines a process operation. This difference is shown by the respective product specifications.

Raw materials entering a process have *their* specifications. Finished products leaving the operation have *their* specifications. The whole idea of having a process at all is to convert raw materials to *acceptable* products. Whether a product is acceptable depends on whether it meets expectations of the purchaser. These expectations are usually written down. They are called *product specifications.*

Success in business requires not only providing a product, but also making sure it is acceptable. The whole object of process design is to define *exactly* what must be done to a raw material to convert it to a finished product. Finished product does not spring out of the last process step by chance. Its creation is carefully planned for in the design.

The *process result* is what it says. For a drying operation, the process result is the removal of moisture. In a fermenter, it can be the conversion of starch and sugar to ethanol. For a copper electrorefinery, it is the conversion of copper from 98.2 to 99.992 percent pure. In dealing with a process step, or an entire process, the engineer/designer must continually ask, What is the process result we are pursuing here?

PHYSICAL REALITY

A mass balance must describe the process so that harmony with physics and chemistry is preserved. Just as Kanute could not dictate the tides, a process designer cannot make unreasonable demands on

---

*Water for injection is used for production of pharmaceutical products that can be injected into the bloodstream.

the world. The designer must understand what nature requires and make appropriate provisions.

In setting up the mass balance, the designer must know equipment characteristics. Two primary characteristics can be attributed to all equipment: capacity and process result. Here are some examples:

Equipment	Capacity	Result
Pump	Flow rate	Elevation of liquid
Vibratory screen	Flow rate	Separation by size
Chemical reactor	Production rate	Fraction converted
Distillation column	Production rate	Separation
Crystallizer	Production rate	Change of phase
Filter	Flow rate	Separation
Cooling tower	Flow rate	Temperature reduction
Scrubber	Flow rate	Fraction removed
Vacuum pump	Flow rate	Removal of gas or vapor
Flotation cell	Production rate	Separation/recovery

The process result and the capacity are always at odds with each other on a given piece of equipment. For example, a pump delivery rate declines as the elevation (or pressure) at the discharge increases. It will even flow backward (negative flow rate) when the discharge pressure is greater than shutoff.* These phenomena are illustrated by the pump curve in Fig. 8-1. (Most manufacturers' pump curves stop at shutoff, whereas Fig. 8-1 shows some of the reverse-flow characteristic.) As another example, consider Fig. 8-2, which shows the decline in grade from a flotation operation as the production rate is pushed upward.

Every possible aspect of demands made by physics and chemistry must be considered. An example of a common failing is the failure to provide for simple electroneutrality in ionic solutions. This failing is remarkably common.

On one occasion, a Fortune 500 company, on a major contract with the Department of Energy issued the results of a site study to characterize radioactive wastes at a contaminated site. The concentrations

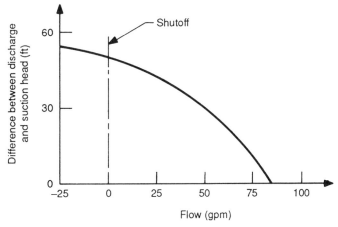

Figure 8-1 Pump curve.

---

*Pump *shutoff* occurs, for example when the discharge is completely blocked. The pressure is referred to as the shutoff pressure. Flow is zero. Although not shown as such, the discharge head can also be less than zero.

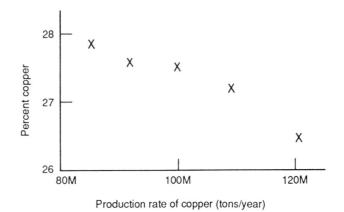

Figure 8-2 Concentrate grade versus production rate.

of all sorts of radionuclides and heavy metals were shown on page after page of data purporting to characterize the wastes. Sulfates and chlorides were given from time to time. One or two measurements of nitrates were shown. No carbonates were shown, or bicarbonates, or fluorides, etc. In short, the anions were relegated to secondary status. The data showed that positive charges outnumbered negative charges by at least 2 to 1 and often by 3 to 1. What made this document all the more remarkable was that it contained several flow sheets for treating the contaminated liquors. Did it not occur to the authors that carbonates behave differently from nitrates, and so on? The whole point of characterization was missed.

Fundamental failings are not the exclusive property of the small and humble.

PROBLEM-SOLVING AIDS

Three simple aids can be a great help in dealing with a mass balance. The first two are concepts; the third is a table on an $8\frac{1}{2} \times 11$ in sheet.

The two concepts are applications of the conservation of mass. First is the idea that a closed curve can be drawn *anywhere* on a flow diagram (or a P&ID) and that mass balance must be conserved for the part of the process within the curve. The curves shown in Fig. 8-3 can be drawn on any flow diagram, in any orientation, and mass in must equal mass out, over the long term—or mass in must equal mass out minus accumulation, over the short term.

A complex process can be carved into tractable pieces by using this method.

The second aid is really an extension of the first. Here the boundary is drawn around the entire plant—not just some areas of a flow diagram. The whole plant is treated as though it were a single process component. This is the treatment given in the example of the potassium chloride producer at the start of this chapter. This second aid is the crucible of fire for looking at by-products and therefore potential wastes.

A good example of how this works is as follows. A pilot operation is being used to develop an aqueous process for making copper metal from the sulfide mineral chalcopyrite (pronounced kal-ko-pie-rite, also known as fool's gold). One of the principal reactions is with ferric chloride:

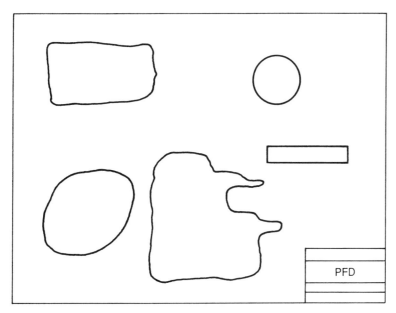

Figure 8-3 Demonstration of closed curves on a process flow diagram

$$CuFeS_2 + 4FeCl_3 \longrightarrow CuCl_2 + 5FeCl_2 + 2S^o$$

The resulting products are cupric chloride, ferrous chloride, and elemental sulfur. Subsequent steps require the regeneration of ferric from the ferrous form, by using oxygen. This also precipitates iron as natrojarosite. Finally aqueous copper is reduced to copper metal by using hydrogen.

Many mass balances are proposed for the process. The majority show as raw materials: ferric chloride, hydrochloric acid, salt, and oxygen. Products are copper, natrojarosite, and sulfur.

All attempts at a mass balance result in nothing useful. Many mass balances are put forward, but can be proved defective within minutes.

The beginning of a meaningful mass balance here starts with the firmest, most believable facts and an imaginary envelope around the entire process:

- Incoming materials are $CuFeS_2$, oxygen, hydrogen, ferric chloride, and salt.
- Impurities, such as SiO_2, called *gangue materials,* are taken as inert for the first approximation.
- Products are copper, natrojarosite, and sulfur.
- The medium is aqueous.
- The anion is chloride.

This question is proposed: Can a process exist whose only process result satisfies the above known facts?

A skeleton chemical equation (not balanced) is written to state the above facts:

$$NaCl + H_2O + O_2 + CuFeS_2 \longrightarrow Cu^o + NaFe_3(SO_4)_2(OH)_6 + S^o + Cl^-$$

After a few false starts, any number of conceptual thoughts, various readjustments, rhetorical questions, and application of chemical equation-balancing methods, this equation emerges:

$$\tfrac{1}{3}NaCl + \tfrac{1}{6}H_2 + H_2O + \tfrac{7}{6}O_2 + CuFeS_2 \longrightarrow$$
$$Cu^0 + \tfrac{1}{3}NaFe_3(SO)_4(OH)_6 + \tfrac{2}{3}S^0 + \tfrac{1}{3}HCl$$

Figure 8-4 shows the ingredients and products plus how the steps fit together. The envelope representing the whole pilot plant is encircled with a closed curve, shown as a dashed line. The envelope cuts only streams that are either ingredients or products—no in-process material streams are cut. Note that apparently ferric chloride is not a required raw material. It is generated and consumed within the process and needs no supplemental amounts added.

Discussions with R&D engineers and chemists reveal that such an equation might describe the pilot operation. It is agreed to run the pilot plant without additions of ferric chloride and hydrochloric acid. Subsequent developments, guided by the results of the "plant equation," lead to modifications of the pilot plant. The modified pilot plant is run for months, thus confirming the concepts of the *plant equation.*

Meanwhile, the mass balance falls neatly into place.

At the start of this section three aids were mentioned. Two have been covered; the third is next. This third aid is a table for keeping orderly records of materials entering and leaving process steps. A full example of the use of this table is given in the next section, but the table itself is introduced here. The table is equally useful at home on a computer or on a plain piece of paper.

The table is called a *mole table* because usually the quantities shown are moles or moles per hour (however, pounds or pounds per hour may also be shown). The organization of the table is such that stream numbers are given along the top while substances of interest are listed along the left side. Table 8-1 is an example. The example is for process step $H^+ + \tfrac{1}{4}O_2 + Fe^{2+} \longrightarrow Fe^{3+} + \tfrac{1}{2}H_2O$, accomplished in a chloride solution having a fairly heavy concentration of zinc. The corresponding block flow diagram is given in Fig. 8-5.

Here is how it works. A ferrous chloride solution is contacted with oxygen after the addition of hydrochloric acid. This converts the ferrous form to the ferric form for use in a subsequent operation. Zinc in

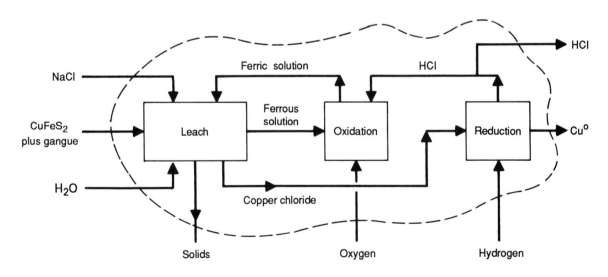

Figure 8-4 Aqueous copper process—plant balance.

TABLE 8-1 Mole Table for an Electrolytic Solution

	Specie	Phase	83	84	85	86	90	104	
					Stream number				
1	H^+	L	9.360	100.939	110.299		9.360		
2	Zn^{2+}	L	119.134		119.134		119.134		
3	Fe^{2+}	L	104.872		104.872		3.933		
4									
5	Fe^{3+}	L	0.000		0.000		100.939		
6									
7									
8									
9									
10	Cl^-	L	435.458	100.939	536.397		536.397		
11	SO_4^{2-}	L	10.957		10.957		10.957		
12									
13	H_2O	L	1,945.278	853.445	2798.723		2,849.193		
14									
15	O_2	G				27.758		2.523	
16	N_2	G				0.416		0.416	CHECK
	Pounds per hour =		65,189.1	19,055.15		899.87	−85,051.7	−92.41	−8.1E−12

charge balance on stream 83:   1.78E−13
                via
          cell formula = $(M21*1 + M22*2 + M23*2 - M30*1 - M31*2)$
                          (plus charges less minus charges)

NOTE: Units are pound-moles.

the solution is not changed but is present and contributes chloride for the formation of complexes.

Table 8-1 illustrates the following points:

- Electroneutrality (or charge balance) is preserved.

- Mass balance is maintained.

- Mole balance is maintained.

The charge balance is performed on stream 83. The quantity of negatively charged ions is subtracted from that of positively charged ions, yielding a difference of 1.78×10^{-13} ions. Given the conditions, this is an adequate reconciliation of positive and negative charges. The charge balance is not carried out on all streams. It is performed only occasionally as a check.

The mass balance is located below the lines at the bottom of the table. Each number is the sum of the mole quantity times the formula weight of the substance. Thus it is the weight of the stream. Entering streams are taken as positive in sign, exiting streams as negative. The sum must approximate zero, which it does: -8.1×10^{-12}.

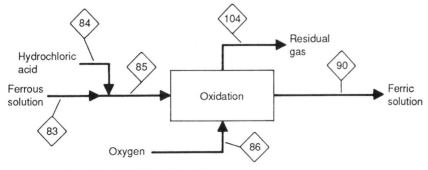

Figure 8-5 Isolated block of block flow diagram.

A simple process may require 6 or so of the mole tables for the whole process. A complex process may require 30 or 40. Having a check (mass balance) along the bottom line for each mole table is a firm assurance of a good, overall mass balance. Such a mass balance is good enough for process design.

Note that the arithmetic of the mole table is the acme of simplicity.* Multiplication and division are usually by whole numbers. A stream is very often derived by simple addition, in spite of chemical reactions and changes of phase. Stream 104, for example, is calculated by subtracting one-fourth of the moles of *ferric* iron in stream 90 from the moles of oxygen in stream 86: $27.758 - 100.939/4 = 2.523$. Nitrogen remains unchanged.

A CRYSTALLIZER-CENTRIFUGE COMBINATION

Now let us look at how to go about achieving a mass balance around a single process step. This example shows how equipment characteristics and principles of physics and chemistry are used to achieve a mass balance.

A disciplined approach is used.

The process in question is for making tungsten metal. One of the intermediate steps requires the crystallization of ammonium paratungstate (APT). The given information is as follows:

- Average production rate, tungsten basis: 373.1 lb/h (515 lb/h APT)
- Feed liquor concentration, tungsten basis: 100 g/L at 100°C
- Liquor compositions:

	Weight percent	
	Feed liquor	**Mother liquor**
APT (anhydrous basis)	9.90	9.74
$(NH_4)_2 \cdot SO_4$	2.71	20.94
NH_3	5.05	3.48
H_2O	82.34	65.84
	100.00	100.00

It is stated that this information comes from pilot data. A specification for a crystallizer is needed. This specification will be used to obtain formal quotes. The crystals will be separated from the mother liquor with a centrifuge. The section of the *flow sheet* applicable to this step is shown in Fig. 8-6. The same operation is shown in Fig. 8-7, but as a block flow diagram.

This example shows how *problem solving* is applied. To begin, the problem is broken into parts, then data are obtained, etc., just as described in Chap. 7. The diagrams help to divide the problem into smaller parts. The two major parts are the crystallizer and the centrifuge. These two parts are then subdivided into smaller parts along lines of physical laws:

Crystallizer	Centrifuge
Solubility	Liquid-solid separation
Vapor-liquid equilibrium	Conservation of mass
Conservation of mass	

---

*When error-free results are a necessity, *simple,* easy-to-check calculations are a great help [ATD].

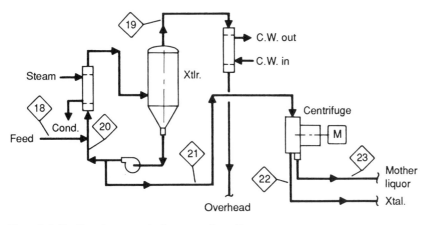

Figure 8-6 Pertinent segment of process flow diagram.

Next comes a review of the data. Do they make sense? A quick review of conveniently available data shows that the stated concentrations of APT and ammonia in the mother liquor are consistent with solubility and vapor pressure information. The sources are Mellor [39] and Chu et al. [40].

Continuing with the accumulation of data, we see that a decision is needed about the design rate to use. In other words, to sustain an average rate of production of 373.1 lb/h, one must be able to operate reliably at a higher rate from time to time. Just as with an automobile, to average 50 mi/h, one must be able to achieve, say, 55 or 60 mi/h from time to time. Another way of thinking about this is to imagine a person driving a car from Muncie, Indiana, to Indianapolis if the absolute top speed of the car is 50 mi/h. Certainly, the person will have the accelerator on the floor most of the time but will be obliged to slow occasionally (due to others on the road). So since the driver is limited to 50 mi/h maximum, the average speed will be less, say, 47 or 43 mi/h or whatever.* Therefore, to average 373.1 lb/h, the *design rate* must be set higher.

In this case, a rate 15 percent higher than the average is prudent, without being overly conservative. For this process step, then, a design rate of $373.1 \times 1.15 = 429.1$ lb/h (tungsten basis) is chosen. This is about 592 lb/h APT. The mass balance is set at this rate.

We also see a need for a law governing liquid-solid separation on

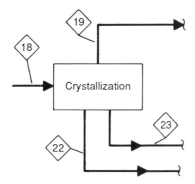

Figure 8-7 Same segment as Fig. 8-6, but shown as a block.

---

*This topic is covered further under "Required Capacity" in Chap. 9.

the centrifuge. A quick search of the literature doesn't reveal very much. Data on flow through porous solids and holdup in beds of solids suggest some theoretical approaches, but obvious rules are not found. Therefore, several centrifuge vendors are consulted by telephone. An engineer with one of these companies states, "A centrifuge is a device governed by volumetric rates, not by mass rates. So in your case, since APT is about 2 times the density of NaCl and you are talking about 600 lb/h APT, then the machine to do the job would be the same one that would process 300 lb/h NaCl. This would be less than 4 ft^3/h of crystal, a very small machine. We could offer our pusher model designed for laboratory use, that is, if the bulk of your crystals are 60-mesh or larger. This machine will produce a cake having a void fraction that itself will be 7 to 17 percent, by volume, mother liquor. Let's say the void fraction is 0.35. Then your liquor retention will be at about 3.7 lb (that is, $0.17 \times 0.35 \times 62.4$) per cubic foot of cake or per 203 lb ($0.65 \times 5 \times 62.4$) of cake. Maximum mother liquor in the centrifuge cake will thus be between 1.5 and 2 percent. Last, but not least, for the pusher type of centrifuge, you must plan on losing about one-quarter of the crystal fraction that is less than 60-mesh to the mother liquor. This is because mother liquor flows out through slots in the basket. These slots will allow passage of particles 60-mesh or less."

A preliminary mass balance is carried out on this basis, and is later confirmed with tests at the vendor's shop.

The identification of rules, or laws, and the accumulation of data can be quite demanding from time to time. A steadfast, wholehearted effort is justified. When in doubt, try a calculation or two to find out where the trails lead. Double back and view results. *Think.* A lack of data can be overcome via calculations or laboratory tests. Only as an act of desperation can you *guess*, and then you must boldly note this fact as an assumption.

Finally, if this assumption becomes a key point, for either economic or safety reasons, call a halt. You must be fully convinced that the proposed activity makes sense. *Never* proceed when an important point is under a cloud. A way must be found to remove the cloud. If necessary, a whole new approach should be tried, one that does not have a cloud hanging over it. A mass balance must be viewed on a par with sizing structural members of a building.

DISCIPLINED APPROACH

For a mass balance, the disciplined approach to the calculation is an absolute necessity. A good way of formalizing mass balances is to *always* use a mole table, that is, a table that lists moles into and out of process steps (see Table 8-2).

It is a good idea to have blank forms of the mole table available. Start out by filling in the specie column, using chemical formulas. Then write down stream numbers for the process block being considered. Include a column describing the phase: vapor, liquid, solid. Without this column, the balance for APT would have been difficult. With this column, it is a simple matter of addition and subtraction.

Table 8-2 is written around the block diagram above. Thus internal streams such as streams 20 and 21 that do not cross the block boundary can be ignored for the moment. Once an integrated, consistent balance for the entire plant has been established, streams 20 and 21 can be dealt with at leisure.

TABLE 8-2 Mole Table for Crystallizer/Centrifuge

			Stream number					
	Specie	Phase	18	19	20	21	22	23
1	$5(NH_4)_2O \cdot 12(WO_3)$	L	0.247598	0	*	*	0.000841	0.030707
2	$(NH_4)_2SO_4$	L	1.562393	0			0.041673	1.520719
3	NH_3	L	22.56773	20.55484			0.053689	1.959205
4	H_2O	L	347.9443	311.9152			0.960994	35.06815
5								
6								
7								
8								
9								
10								
11								
12								
13	$5(NH_4)_2O \cdot 12(WO_3)$	S					0.194444	0.021605
14								
15								
16								CHECK
	Pounds per hour =		7612.347	–5969.22			–617.899	–1025.23	0

Formula weight

$5(NH_4)_2O \cdot 12(WO_3)$	3042.549	(APT, anhydrous)
$(NH_4)_2SO_4$	132.138	
NH_3	17.031	
H_2O	18.015	

NOTE: Units are pound-moles per hour.

*These streams will be determined later.

Each block of a block flow diagram should have its own mole table. This serves to subdivide a problem into smaller parts. While you are doing the calculations, consult a sketch of the process flow diagram pertaining to that block. All three sheets can be stapled together after a block has been calculated [ATD]. Block by block the mass balance is put together for the entire process. At the conclusion, the block flow diagram and the process flow diagram will have been completed.

The procedure was originally developed for hand calculations. It works as well with computer calculations.

When a process does not involve chemical reactions or changes of phase, mass quantities can be used in the table instead of mole quantities.

With each block, begin by filling in the known information. Then employ the clearest and surest concepts, saving the most dubious information for last (sometimes the dubious information need not be used at all, because it turns out to be redundant).

The bottom line of the mole table is in units of weight, not moles. Furthermore, incoming streams are positive; outgoing, negative. The sum of all streams on the bottom line is out to the right by itself and is labeled *check.* This check number is the sum of the bottom line and must *always* equal zero, or a reasonably small number.

Before we leave this example, it is worth noting that the overhead stream (number 19) shows no ammonium sulfate and no APT. Is this true? If it isn't true, can it be justified? The stream, indeed, must contain tiny amounts of ammonium sulfate and APT due to inadvertent carryover of small droplets of solution with the vapor. Just for talking purposes, 200 parts of liquid per million parts of vapor (weight basis) is often used. In this case, the condensed vapor is sent back to the front of the process and mixed with strong concentrations of ammonium sulfate and APT, so declaring them equal to zero is legitimate. If this condensate were to be processed for drinking water, that would be another matter.

What has been said in this chapter with regard to mass balances can also be said about energy balances. The energy balance is equally important. Quite often, large portions of a process do not undergo significant energy changes, so the energy balance is often so simple as to be trivial. It must be *proved* trivial, before it can be treated as such, however.

Chapter 9
Preparation for Understanding Equipment

One of the great challenges encountered on every project is learning about the equipment that is to be installed. Most of the equipment will be familiar to the more experienced project participants. Some of the equipment, however, will be new even to the most experienced engineers and designers.

Before it is possible to look into the operation of specific kinds of equipment, some additional preparation is necessary. This consists of filling some gaps left by traditional courses in unit operations. Typical of these is how to start and stop an electric motor. Six such items are covered. (They are listed at the end of this section.) Note that filling gaps in knowledge is an essential, normal part of understanding equipment. Furthermore, this requires searches of the literature, conversations with others, and measurements in the field or laboratory. It is a perennial task.

Many sketches and drawings are used to help convey the ideas at hand. The reader is asked to note how these sketches simplify the job of communication. When P&IDs are covered (in Chap. 11), the use of sketches to convey ideas is examined in greater depth.

This chapter covers general topics that apply to *many* kinds of equipment. Then in Chap. 10 a few selected pieces of equipment are examined by using some fundamentals from the physical sciences. Many examples from actual projects are given. Thought processes for dealing with equipment are demonstrated.

The single thread that winds its way through these two chapters is summed up in the single word *operate*. It is not enough for an engineer/designer to select a piece of equipment having adequate capacity. *The engineer/designer must be sure that the equipment will operate satisfactorily.* This will require the following:

- The equipment must be suited for its use.
- The equipment must not require inordinate attention, by either an operator or a maintenance mechanic.
- Provisions must be made during the design phase for convenience and safety, both in operation and in maintenance.
- The costs for purchase and operation must be reasonable and acceptable to the owner.

Equipment vendors are a good source of information for their own equipment. This does not relieve the engineer/designer of the need to understand the piece of equipment. Here are some reasons:

1. Knowledge at the disposal of a vendor normally ends where his or her equipment connects to something else.

2. It is the engineer/designer—not the vendor—who is hired expressly for the purpose of integrating many distinct components to make them work as a coordinated whole.

3. Obviously, whoever writes the specification must be impartial. This holds for whoever does the bid analysis; this person must be impartial, too.

4. Now, comes the question of communication. Suppose, for an instant, that knowledge of equipment were not necessary for its purchase. Then all equipment could be purchased by any living (or electronic) thing that could fill out a purchase order. What is missing in this scenario is the interchange of ideas between buyer and seller. Typically the seller will offer some options on the equipment that were not known to the buyer. Furthermore, errors and ambiguities will require clarification. Buyer and seller, communicating with a common understanding of the equipment, stand a much better chance of success than would the seller alone, being guided by a purchase order.

5. Even the mass (and heat) balance depends on an understanding of the equipment. This in turn affects equipment sizing, which has an impact on capital and operating costs.

In short, some of the most profound project questions revolve around *understanding equipment*. The vendor will supply key parts of this understanding, but it is the *duty* of the engineers/designers to also understand the equipment—sometimes even more thoroughly than the vendors.

The starting point should always be a question that arises often as work progresses: *How does this work?* Once reasonable progress has been made on answering this question, the following two related questions require attention:

- What will make this work better?
- What will make this *not* work?

Answers to these two questions will help with the original question.

Answers to more questions are needed, however. These have to do with integrating one piece of equipment with others. Here are some examples:

- Should the start of the motor on this piece of equipment be manual or automatic?
- If a neighboring piece of equipment is stopped, should this one be stopped, too?
- If any valve is inadvertently opened (closed), what will happen?
- Can this unit be stopped in a moment, or must it be coaxed to a halt?
- How can this unit be rendered safe for maintenance?
- If a power failure occurs, what happens?

Then there are the questions to be asked on behalf of the operators and maintenance mechanics. Here are examples:

- Where must the operator stand when the unit is started?
- Where will the operator stand while troubleshooting?
- Where will the electrician stand to check circuits?
- What are the clearances for opening lids and hatches and for removing internal components (tube bundles, impellers, etc.)?
- Will the whole unit ever be pulled from its foundation? If so, how?
- Can this unit be operated outdoors?
- What kind of seals does this unit have? How are they checked and serviced?

Finally come the questions concerning how the unit must be secured in place.

- What kind of foundation or mounting is needed?
- Will special equipment be needed to place the unit on its foundation?
- Will a special job sequence be needed?
- Is secondary containment required?

The whole reason for engineering/design is to *provide features* that will enhance economic performance. The *features* that eventually are provided will come from answers to questions such as those asked above. A haphazard design will result if such questions are *not* asked.

The person most directly responsible for asking questions about equipment will be the process engineer.* This same person will have the main responsibility for the P&ID (or the portion of the P&ID) depicting the unit in question. Although the process engineer has the overall responsibility for a given piece of equipment, the other design disciplines must share in this responsibility to the extent that they must do their own work properly and keep the process engineer informed. For example, the structural engineer must review dynamic loads of rotating equipment.

Other project members who have dealings with a piece of equipment (such as structural engineers, instrument engineers, etc.) must also satisfy themselves that *their* knowledge is adequate.

A process engineer should view operability in the same way as a structural engineer views structural integrity. For the structural engineer, a great concern is that the structure might begin to sag and require reinforcing or that it might simply collapse. For the process engineer or the project engineer, the equivalent situation is *poor operation.* In the extreme, this is a plant that won't run or is dangerous to run. Such a concern is a primary consideration, not a secondary one. To avoid this sort of occurrence, the causes leading up to it must be understood. Let us look at two distinct examples from actual experience and find out what went wrong. First:

> Upon loss of compressed air, all air-operated valves failed in the *open* position, so liquids flowed in any direction, intermingling harmfully, flooding dry equipment, and overflowing small tanks.

---

*Very frequently the process engineer will also be the *sponsor* for all equipment in a process area (see Chap. 14 and App. B).

Here the engineer did not ask "what if" questions during the design. On this job, incidentally, money was "saved" by showing instruments on the flow diagrams to avoid making P&IDs. This plant was never operated successfully.

Second:

> During start-up, the motor of a screw feeder under a bin continually overloaded, shutting down the feed to the entire plant.

Here the engineer did not understand screw conveyors. This problem could have been avoided by asking the vendor to taper the feed section or reduce the screw diameter (or the pitch) in the feed section. Another solution would have been to keep the transport section short, say, less than 3 ft long. However, this latter requirement will not work on spongy or fibrous materials such as polystyrene foam or almond hulls. And, to further complicate matters, if it is *too* short, with a fine granular material, such as refinery catalyst, the screw may not be able to stop a bin of fluidized solids from running through it, like water through a pipe (a phenomenon aptly termed *flushing*).

The remedy chosen above was to cut down the flight diameter in the first two-thirds of the feed section. After this was done, the feed conveyor ran without problems.

These examples show that serious difficulties need not be complex in origin. However, a broad range of knowledge is needed to avoid them. Attention to details is a fundamental necessity [ATD].

Given the almost infinite number of equipment items available, the task of understanding them all seems daunting at first. A good knowledge of some fundamentals, a grasp of physics, a keen sense of observation, a willingness to ask questions, and an understanding of *some* types of equipment greatly simplify the task of learning about a novel piece of equipment. Even more important than this, however, is the curiosity to find out how things work.*

Before we get into understanding equipment, a few words about value engineering are in order. *Value engineering* or *value analysis* provides a formal approach to asking questions and understanding the features of a design. Its greatest use has been with consumer products, but portions of it can be beneficially applied to analyzing equipment and processes. The serious process engineer/designer should become familiar with the *value* approach.† The whole formal approach is probably out of place, given client demands of most process design efforts, but portions of the formal approach such as brainstorming and asking questions about *function* should be a staple of process design work.

The concept of *function* is a key part of value engineering. The function of a pump, for example, is to impart energy to a liquid. The function of the *Mona Lisa*, today, is to amuse, provoke thought, and provide a glimpse into persons and places of long ago. The main functions of a flat washer are to (1) provide an inexpensive, consumable part and (2) spread the load from the head of a bolt or a nut.

In learning about equipment and how to fit it into a process, the engineer/designer must constantly review the *function* of the equip-

---

*Any person who expects to accept responsibilities as a project engineer or process engineer should have a strong desire to know the inner workings of and laws governing the use of all types of equipment, from pneumatic valve actuators to kettle reboilers, by way of continuous stirred tank reactors. Without this desire, the individual will be embarking on a charade that will be of no benefit to himself or herself or the employer.

†A good treatment is given by Theodore Fowler in *Value Analysis in Design* [41].

ment. If a piece is seen to have minor function, the means to eliminate it should be sought.

We now begin with a brief look at six items often encountered in dealing with equipment:

- Required capacity
- Seals
- Bearings
- Start/stop
- Fluid/mechanical energy balance (Bernoulli equation)
- Granular solids

Once these global topics have been covered, in Chap. 10 we will look at examples of real instances of dealings with equipment. The equipment will include

- Pumps
- Ducts, hoods, and fans
- Bins
- Discharge from a dryer
- Valves

This selection is not large and thus permits some depth of exploration. In making the selection, a mix of familiar staples (pumps, fans) and less familiar items (hoods, bins) was chosen.

REQUIRED CAPACITY

Care and consideration should be exercised in determining the plant capacity and the capacity of individual pieces of equipment. Operability and cost are at stake. Rather than apply a multiplying factor (often called the *safety factor*) to nominal capacity, a more rational approach is recommended.

The selection of a safety factor that is too high has two harmful results:

- Good, viable projects can be killed.
- Resources can be tied up uselessly (if the project goes ahead).

In some quarters, there exists the mistaken impression that extra provisions should be included in a project, so that a few minor changes at a later date can be implemented to gain a relatively large increase in capacity. This ties up resources unnecessarily and imperils the viability of the original project. The worst example of this profligacy in the author's experience was a client who wished to be able to operate at twice the nominal capacity and, on top of that, insisted on a safety factor of 2.0. This caused the equipment to be sized at 4 times nominal capacity. The client company went into bankruptcy, partly as a result of this project.

On a $10 million plant, if the overall capacity factor were 1.5 rather than 1.3, the added cost would be $1 million dollars.*

Except under the most unusual circumstances, the greatest provi-

---

*Assuming capital costs can be taken as proportional to capacity to the two-thirds power.

sion for future capabilities should be limited to generous sizing of utilities (air, steam, water, etc.) and generous spacing of equipment.

Just as an automobile is designed for a certain speed, a process is designed to produce a certain amount of product. Furthermore, it is the design limits on equipment within process plants that determine the plants' capacities. To make sure that this limit is reasonable, it must be determined in a rational fashion. To make sure the limits are adhered to and agreed to by all project participants, the development of the design limits should be made known to all personnel. For this purpose, the limits should be included in the basic data (see App. A).

An example will illustrate how equipment capacities should be derived from nominal plant capacities. Say that a new fuel blending facility of 20 million gal/yr is sought. At what rate should blended product enter the product storage tank?

The average flow for an around-the-clock operation comes out to about 38.0 gal/min (using a sidereal year of 8766 h). Obviously, the pump supplying the storage tank must be capable of pumping at a rate above 38 gal/min; otherwise it could not *average* 38 gal/min. Presumably there is a process control somewhere in the blending operation that is trying to maintain a steady blend formulation. This control will drift around the setpoint, and fluctuations in supply flow are to be expected. The pump must be able to handle the flow fluctuations.* These fluctuations have not been measured, but are thought to be no worse than ±10 percent. Lost production time due to scheduled and unscheduled shutdowns also add to the pump's required capacity. Once a month, the blending operation is to be shut off for one shift to carry out scheduled maintenance. Furthermore, an allowance of 4 h/week should be included for unscheduled interruptions. Finally, say that the uncertainty in the pump manufacturer's flow curves can be in error by as much as 5 percent. The situation is summarized as follows:

- Operating hours: $8766 - 12 \times 8 - 52 \times 4 = 8462$

- Therefore, on-stream factor: $\dfrac{8462}{8766} = 0.965$

- Therefore, bare capacity (without contingency):

$$F = \frac{20,000,000}{8462 \times 60 \times 0.90 \times 0.95} = 46.1 \text{ gal/min}$$

Finally, a 15 percent contingency factor is included to provide a degree of comfort in the face of unknown operating difficulties and the inexact approximations used in the calculations. This brings the flow value to 54.2 gal/min (which should be rounded to 54 gal/min). This is known as the *design flow* (or *design capacity*) and should be used for purchasing the pump and sizing the piping.

This flow should not be used as the average rate of flow in the material balance. The *average* rate of flow is 20,000,000/(8462 × 60) = 39.4 gal/min. For equipment having large holdup capacities (compared to process fluctuations), such as storage tanks,† it is best to base the size on the average rate with a provision for contingency only.

---

*This is sometimes called *catch-up* capability.

†With storage vessels, it is also wise to remember that in many cases the vessel should run, on average, half full.

Operating hours can be calculated from the following formula:

$$H = (365.25 - V) \times 24 \times \frac{y}{3} \times \frac{z}{7} - M \quad h$$

where V = days/yr shutdown for vacation or turnaround
  y = shifts/day operating
  z = days/week operating
  M = h/yr shutdown for maintenance

In cases where substandard product is recycled for reprocessing, the capacity must include the recycle quantity:

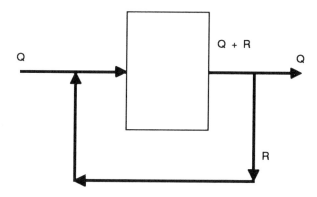

In cases where batch steps are involved, the preparation of a batch sequence table is mandatory. The example given here is of a batch distillation operation.

Step	Description	Time, min
1	Fill reboiler	8
2	Heat up	11
3	Operate	88
4	Hold for analysis	21
5	Cool	9
6	Empty	6
7	Clean up, prepare next	11
8	Idle	20
		174

On more than one occasion, a careless approach to sizing equipment has resulted in batch equipment sized for average flow sheet values. The resulting equipment is so severely undersized as to cause a complete failure of the project.

In today's competitive world, where the stress is on lean, minimum-investment facilities, care should be exercised in setting capacities. Each plant, each operation, and each piece of equipment are worthy of examination. Guidelines for all participants must be established in the basic data (App. A).

SEALS

Without exception, all processes require some form of containment. Even the crudest of beer making, in the remotest jungle on this planet, requires a container, be it a coconut shell, a gourd, a hollowed log, or a clay pot.

Some of the more crucial, practical considerations in process plant projects are centered on sealing off or containment of the process.

Usually, the requirement is couched in a very simple fact: Leaks waste raw materials and products. Containment, therefore, is most often an economic necessity. Three other excellent reasons for containment are (1) to obtain the desired process result (a pressurized reaction, for example), (2) safety, and (3) environmental needs.

Probably the most basic seal is the *static* seal. A good example is the cap on a soda bottle. In this case, carbon dioxide at about 30 lb/in^2 is kept from escaping, and it dictates the majority of the requirements for the seal. The sealing surfaces are the bottle cap and the bottle. A resilient elastomeric compound adhering permanently to the cap serves as the gasket. The seal is classified as *static*, because the two parts that comprise the container (cap and bottle) are fixed to each other.

In general, when two solid surfaces are brought together to make a seal, there will always be small imperfections in matching the two surfaces (see Fig. 9-1). When the two surfaces are pressed together lightly, there are few points where the surfaces actually touch. As greater force is used, more points are brought in contact between the surfaces. On a few, rare occasions, the increase in force is adequate to cause a satisfactory seal. In the vast majority of cases, however, either a gasket must be used, or the gaps must be filled with a liquid that wets both surfaces and then solidifies (or becomes viscous enough to be considered a solid). A gasket will always be softer than either mating surface and will deform enough to block off channels of leakage. Rarely do gaskets (or any seal) stop flow entirely—they simply reduce it to an acceptable level.* Gaskets on water piping improve with age, because as they slowly seep, the water evaporates as it reaches the outer part of the gasket, leaving dissolved silica and carbonates behind. These mineral residues complete the sealing process.

An interesting example of a static seal for rather trying operating conditions is that of the gear pump for metering polymers at 375°C. These pumps are built from ¾-in carbon-steel plates (see Fig. 9-2). These plates are machined with high precision and honed to such a degree that a flatness check, using sodium lamp interference measurements, shows no more deviation from flatness than 2 interference fringes (thus four wavelengths, or a peak-to-valley difference of about 0.0001 in. Thus when these plates are cinched together, the gaps between them are exceedingly small.

In this application, sheets of copper about 0.006 in are placed between the plates as gaskets. Leakage occurs, but it is at an exceedingly low rate (perhaps 1 cm^3 per month?). Furthermore, because the

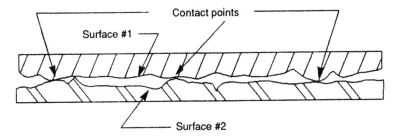

Figure 9-1 Close-up of mating surfaces.

*This level is predictable and controllable, incidentally.

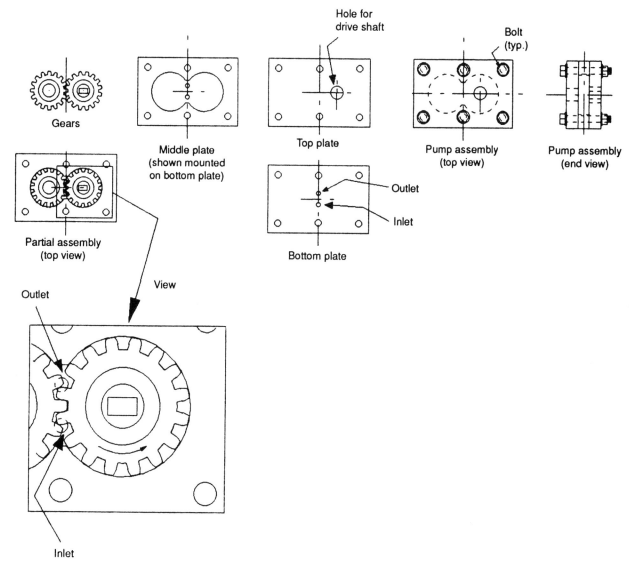

Figure 9-2 Gear pump.

rate is so tiny, the polymer that makes its way into a gap will take a very long time to reach the outside; and with the application at hand, the polymer decomposes, leaving deposits which tend to block off flow even more. This is a good situation for a static seal.

Gaskets are made of all conceivable materials: coated sisal, leather, Teflon, graphite, paper, copper, natural rubber, etc. In many cases, one material will be far superior to other materials. Very frequently, however, almost anything will do.

On an existing operating plant, many gaskets are ordered as parts from an equipment supplier or from companies that supply gaskets. Probably just as many, however, are made on site by the maintenance mechanics.

Gaskets for flanged piping are generally purchased, and not made on site. A common type is depicted in Fig. 9-3. This type of gasket is a carefully engineered composite consisting of two layers of alloy-steel bands separated by a zone of dense, fibrous material. This gasket is used for flat-face and raised-face flanges. When the flanges are bolted

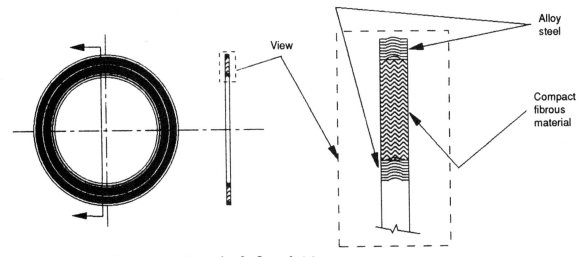

Figure 9-3 Highly evolved compression gasket for flanged piping.

together, the steel bands bend slightly, conforming to the two mating flanges. Because the bands are on edge, they exert high local stresses and cut through dirt or oxides to make metal-to-metal contact with the faces of the mating flanges. The bands are purposely bowed outward for a spring action. The fibrous material experiences much lower stresses, but covers a considerably larger area. This will fill larger defects in the surfaces such as scratches and pockmarks. The combination of the cutting seal and the large area coverage makes for a very effective seal. Furthermore, the metal band eliminates any significant diffusion through the gasket.

DYNAMIC SEALS

A dynamic seal is required when two surfaces forming a part of a containment enclosure move with respect to each other. Most dynamic seals involve a shaft that is either rotating or reciprocating with respect to some container. The substance being contained will invariably be a fluid. At times, this fluid can also carry a solid with it. Here are some examples:

	Moving part	Stationary part	Fluid
Pump	Drive shaft	Housing	Process liquid
Fan	Drive shaft	Housing	Gas
Reciprocating compressor	Piston	Cylinder	Gas and oil
Sliding vane compressor	Vane	Housing	Gas and oil
Sliding vane compressor	Drive shaft	Housing	Gas and oil
Ball valve	Stem	Body	Fluid
Gearbox	Input and output shafts	Housing	Lubricant
Gasoline engine	Piston	Cylinder	Oil and gases

In most respects, dynamic seals are subject to the same requirements as static seals. However, there are two additional considerations: (1) a dynamic seal is subject to wear, and (2) a dynamic seal usually must be lubricated.

Three common types of dynamic seal are shown in Fig. 9-4. The *packed* seal (Fig. 9-4*a*) is very common and is easy to maintain, but has the highest leakage rate and requires the most frequent atten-

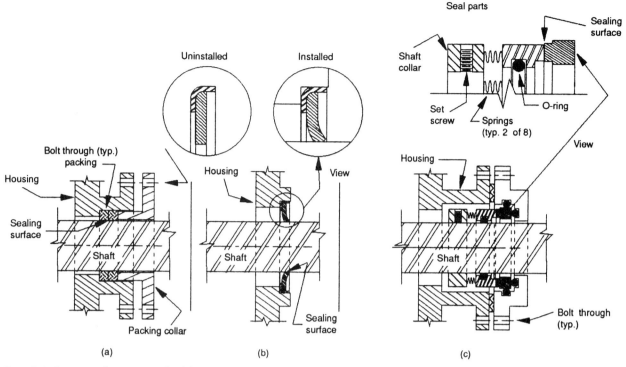

Figure 9-4 Common dynamic seals. (*a*) Packed seal; (*b*) lip seal; (*c*) mechanical seal.

tion. This seal is made by cramming a fibrous material down into the annular space between the shaft and the housing. The material can range from horsehair to shredded linen rags, but these days, in any but the most impoverished operation, it will consist of a specially braided rope, expressly made for the purpose.

The actual seal will occur where the stationary part and the moving part are in closest proximity. They will be touching, or nearly touching but separated by a film of fluid. These *seal surfaces* are shown in Fig. 9-4.

The seal surface of the mechanical seal is highly evolved and carefully controlled. The two mating surfaces are made of special materials, honed to a high degree of flatness, each possessing a small but carefully controlled degree of roughness. When a mechanical seal is installed, the two rings that mate at the sealing surface must be within tolerance limits for being concentric and parallel. Also spring compression must be within stated limits. The care with which mechanical seals must be installed is greater than that for packed seals or lip seals.

The two aforementioned rings are made of dissimilar materials. One is usually graphite or a material high in carbon content. The other is usually a special alloy or a material having the properties of metals and ceramics—a *cermet.*

Examination of Fig. 9-4 also reveals that other sealing surfaces exist; but these are static seals, for example, where the braid of the packed seal pushes against the housing. The lip seal and the mechanical seal also have a static seal against the housing. The mechanical seal, however, has an additional seal on the shaft—note the O-ring on the shaft. Most dynamic seal failures occur at the moving surfaces, aggravated by the effects of wear. Failure of one of the static seals is not all that unusual, however.

Each of these seals has its particular use. The packed seal is preferred where leakage is not important and where low first cost is needed. The lip seal is preferred when pressure differences across the seal are low. The mechanical seal is selected when leakage must be kept low and when frequent service is undesirable. The following table summarizes the situation.

	Packed	Lip	Mechanical
Performance			
Allowable velocity	M	L	H
Allowable pressure difference	M	L	H
Leakage rate	H	H	L
Maintenance characteristics			
Frequency	H	L	L
Duration	L	L	H
Cost of parts	L	L	H
Cost in use	M	L	L

H = high, M = medium, L = low.

Some years back, controversy raged over mechanical and packed seals. The main arguments brought forth by advocates of the packed seal were that mechanical seals were expensive and required special skills to install. Developments since then have brought costs down and have yielded a more user-friendly product. The mechanical seal is now widely accepted. Probably its chief advantage is that it requires little attention once it has been installed.

On some occasions a leakage rate of zero, a negative* leakage rate, or a controlled leak of a compatible fluid becomes a necessity. Here are some examples:

- Lubricating oils associated with agitators for vessels holding pharmaceuticals or fine chemicals

- Corrosive mist and spills in the vicinity of rollers on diverse kinds of equipment

- A hydrogen compressor having its suction at less than atmospheric pressure

Figure 9-5 shows one approach used for the second example. By causing air to flow opposite to the direction in which spills or corrosive mists might flow, the bearing is protected. If the purge air is always turned on when the equipment is operated, the bearings for the rollers should never be exposed to anything except good, clean air.

For the first and third examples, the most likely approach would be to use two seals in series and purge the space between the seals with an acceptable fluid (distilled water and nitrogen, respectively—see Fig. 9-6).

Prior to the application of any piece of equipment or any piping, the engineer/designer must determine that the many different kinds of seals will be satisfactory.

The serious engineer/designer of process plants is advised to spend some time delving into the subject of seals. One starting point, of course, is *Perry's Chemical Engineer's Handbook* [42]. Another highly recommended source is the *Seals and Sealing Handbook* [43]. A good engineering/design firm will have a copy of this handbook in its li-

---

*This is where leakage is caused in a direction opposite to the usual direction.

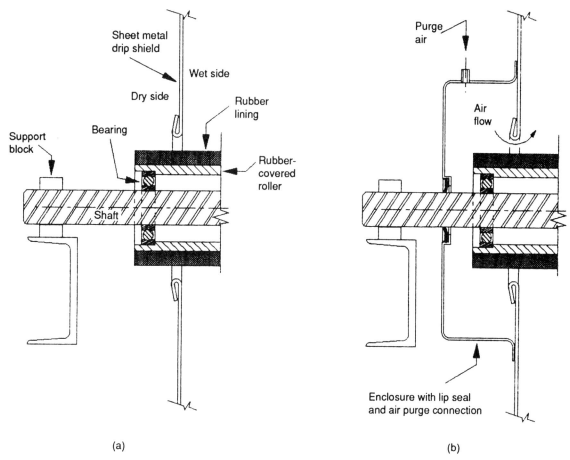

Support
block

Sheet metal
drip shield

Wet side

Dry side

Rubber
lining

Bearing

Rubber-
covered
roller

Shaft

Purge
air

Air
flow

Enclosure with lip seal
and air purge connection

(a)

(b)

Figure 9-5 Purged bearings on rolls. (a) As proposed by vendor. (b) As modified during vendor drawing review.

brary. Finally, the reader is advised to acquire vendor literature on all kinds of different seals.

BEARINGS

Among the greatest unheralded developments of the last 100 years are surely standardized, reliable bearings. This was made possible by truly precise machining capabilities on a large scale, by fabulous alloys and polymers, and by superior lubricating fluids.

When a piece of equipment with moving parts is built and used, a key consideration is the bearings. Project personnel may occasionally become involved in specifying types of bearings or lubrication systems. In any case, project personnel will find themselves engaged in reviewing vendor drawings containing features that pertain to bearings and lubrication. As was true with seals, space does not permit in-depth treatment of this topic. The purpose here is to show the engineer/designer a few basic ideas.

By far the great majority of bearings encountered in industry involve rotating cylindrical shafts, so this discussion is limited to this application.

The purpose of a bearing is to provide support for a moving part. This support must not impede the motion of, nor remove much energy from, the moving part—that is, the support must be low in friction.

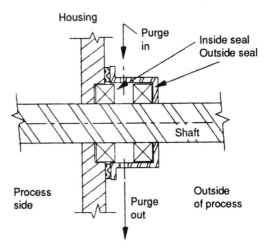

Figure 9-6 Purge between seals.

For radial loads (see below), only two fundamental types of bearing are encountered in virtually every bearing used by industry throughout the world: the journal bearing and the rolling bearing. In one form or another these bearings have served humans for thousands of years. Roman chariots used the journal bearing, sometimes called a *fluid-film bearing*. Some transport of large stone blocks by the ancient Egyptians was done on rollers.

Both these kinds of bearing can be employed without the use of lubricants; however, most industrial bearings require lubricants to reduce wear, and often, but not always, to reduce friction. The majority of bearing applications occur when the major load is more or less perpendicular to the shaft centerline. Loads mostly parallel to the shaft centerline are also encountered, but not frequently. The bearings used for these two kinds of load can be of the fluid-film or rolling type, but must be specifically adapted for the type of load. The two types of bearing are referred to as *radial* and *thrust* (see Fig. 9-7). On many occasions radial and thrust bearings are used together. A good example is found on some kinds of agitators for liquids. The sketch in Fig. 9-8 presents such an application in diagrammatic form. The top bearing counteracts the force of gravity and thrusting forces caused by the propeller. The two lower bearings counteract the bending moments caused by fluctuating forces on the propeller. Both lower bearings are free to move axially. This is an example of the rather rare occurrence of three bearings used together.

Most journal bearings rely on a thin film of lubricant to keep the two moving surfaces from touching. This practically eliminates wear

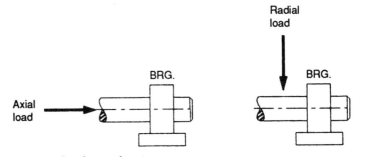

Figure 9-7 Loads on a bearing.

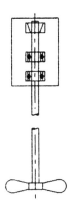

Figure 9-8 Agitator bearings.

and cuts friction drastically. In many small applications the flow of lubricant can be maintained by natural forces such as partial submergence of a part or by wicking through a porous medium. On larger applications, such as the automobile engine and the marine propeller shaft, an external lubricant pump is necessary to "float" the rotating shaft.

The typical representation of a journal bearing depicts a shaft (the journal) riding inside of a cylindrical cavity—the bearing (see Fig. 9-9). The closest point of approach of the surfaces is at an angle downstream (with respect to the flowing film of oil) from where the load vector crosses the oil film. This is because oil is supplied upstream of the load point and leaks out of the sides of the bearing on the way past the load point. In most practical cases, the closest point of approach of the two surfaces must *not* be zero; that is, the two surfaces must not touch.* Wear and the coefficient of friction increase markedly with contact. The three greatest causes of solid-solid contact in a journal bearing are the eccentricity of the cylindrical surfaces, misaligned axes of the two surfaces, and improper application of lubricant.†

Bearings that rely on rolling parts operate quite differently from the

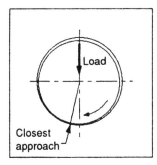

Figure 9-9 Typical representation of journal bearing.

---

*On low-force, low-power applications, the surfaces can, and often do, touch. Usually, this means forces measured in ounces and power dissipation measured in fractions of a watt.

†These three items are usually of little importance on the low-force/low-power applications. An example is a $1/16$-in shaft in a glass-filled fluorocarbon bearing having a power dissipation of 0.01 W.

journal bearing. The most obvious difference is that solid-solid contact of moving surfaces is mandatory. Not so obvious, however, is the fact that the use of lubricants has a somewhat different function: It keeps the wearing surfaces from forming an oxide film. On a microscopic scale, it is true that lubricant allows for minor slippage to accommodate unequal elastic deformation of the contacting surfaces, but its main function is to halt the formation of oxides.

When a rolling bearing that requires lubricant (and there are some that don't) is operated dry, it seems to function well initially, running cool, quietly, and low in friction—really, about all one can ask of a bearing. Before too long, however, such a bearing will become noisy and loose. Examination will reveal galling and pitting at the contact surfaces. Apparently the natural oxides that develop on metal surfaces are dispersed and pulverized when the rolling surfaces come in contact. New oxides are made from fresh metal in the wake of the old oxides. Quickly, good machined metal is eaten away. When an appropriate lubricant is present, the oxides do not form, and the machined surfaces are maintained whole.

New rolling bearings with lubricant generally have a higher frictional dissipation than the dry bearings do.

The actual rolling elements of a rolling bearing come in four shapes: spheres, cylinders, barrels, and tapered cylinders (see Fig. 9-10). The barrel-shaped roller is employed in a variety of bearing called the *spherical roller.* These different types of rolling elements are held by a light retainer, called a *cage,* between the inner and outer races (see Fig. 9-11). The first three types are for mostly radial loads. This means the usual loads should be radial; however, they will accommodate a fair amount of axial loading from time to time. The allowable load rating for the first three progresses from the ball (lightest) through the drum, or spherical roller (heaviest). The tapered cylinder is for combined radial and axial loads.

Care taken to eliminate built-in stresses is one of the keys to low bearing maintenance during the life of a piece of equipment. High stresses can be built in by using undersized bearings. To keep from falling into this trap, particularly on larger pieces of equipment, the engineer should obtain bearing information from equipment vendors when quotes are reviewed, prior to purchase.

Two other causes of built-in stresses are misalignment and lack of provision for thermal expansion. These are both easily understood by realizing that bearings for radial loads are almost exclusively used in pairs. Take the average centrifugal pump as an example (Fig. 9-12). The pump bearings (two) and motor bearings (two) are provided as stated, probably engineered by companies hundreds of miles apart, but quite possibly oceans and languages apart. First is the question of alignment. Each manufacturer must make sure his pair of bearings is aligned correctly. Figure 9-13a depicts such a case. Figure 9-13b shows where this is *not* the case.

A simple way of achieving good alignment is to have both holes in

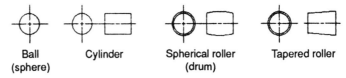

Ball (sphere)   Cylinder   Spherical roller (drum)   Tapered roller

Figure 9-10 Balls and rollers.

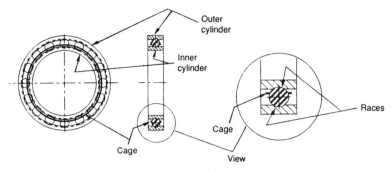

Figure 9-11 A typical ball bearing assembly.

the housing bored on the same pass. This becomes problematic with larger equipment, yet it is precisely with the larger equipment that this feature can reap the largest dividends. On large equipment, it is advisable to become informed about shop techniques during the bidding phase.

Figure 9-13c shows a type of bearing in which the outer ring is segmented at a spherical surface. The outer part is to fit a housing or a pillow block while the inner part is to hold the shaft, as either a journal or a rolling bearing (a ball bearing is shown). The spherical surfaces will move with respect to each other to accommodate a lack of alignment of the borings in the housing. Such bearings are called *self-aligning.*

The second item mentioned above is thermal expansion. If two bearings (a bearing *pair*) are separated by a distance of 18 in, and if the shaft temperature as installed is 60°F, yet its operating temperature is 130°F, then it will try to change 0.008 in in length. If both bearings are held to prevent axial motion, serious damage to them will occur. For this reason, many bearings have a provision that will enable axial movement. Figure 9-14 shows a double cylindrical bearing that can be used in either an expansion or a nonexpansion mode by either removing a ring that holds the outer cylinder or leaving it in place. To accommodate thermal expansion, at least one bearing of a pair must allow axial movement.

Sometimes both bearings are allowed to move, but usually the machine designer has a good reason to hold one of them still, such as at the bearing closest to the pump impeller. This is because exact impeller positioning with respect to the casing can be important for cutting down on unbalanced forces (wear) and improving hydraulic efficiency (lowering power cost).

What happens when two *pairs* of bearings, such as the pump and motor above, must be tied together? A shock-absorbing device called a *coupling* is secured to both shafts, after both shafts have been care-

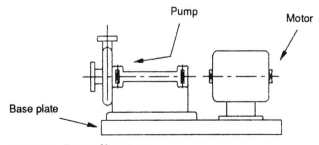

Figure 9-12 Pairs of bearings.

Preparation for Understanding Equipment   119

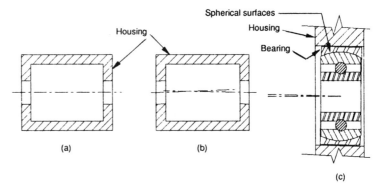

Figure 9-13 Bearing alignment in manufacturing. (*a*) Coaxial; (*b*) skewed axes; (*c*) self-aligning bearing (close-up view).

fully lined up with each other. The usual coupling will be very pliable with regard to axial loads. At the same time, it will be many times stiffer with torsional loads, yet altogether fairly soft. The most common, most pedestrian of all shaft couplings is probably the one that employs a rubber spider between two metal grippers, one attached to each shaft. The reader is referred to the nearest mechanical catalog for an example.

The information given here should help the plant engineer/designer approach the analysis of process equipment with some appreciation for the problems faced by the equipment designer. Being able to straddle the boundary between an equipment supplier and an end user is exceedingly conducive to project success. It makes for teamwork. Teamwork requires the ability to cross boundaries.

During review of vendor drawings, it is the sponsor's* duty to make sure the various reviewers find out how bearings and seals are lubricated and changed. Provisions must be made in the layout to accommodate these service requirements.

ELECTRIC MOTORS AND ELECTRIC CONTROLS

In industry the manner in which an electric motor is started and stopped has no resemblance to the act of throwing a light switch. This fact was among the several interesting surprises the author encoun-

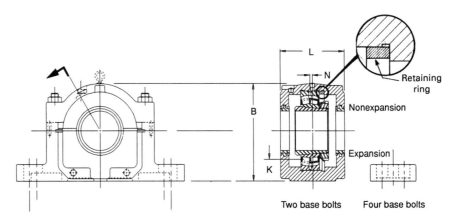

Figure 9-14 Bearing for thermal expansion and self-alignment. (*Courtesy of Emerson Power Transmission Corp.*)

*See App. B for a description of the *sponsor*.

tered in the highly demanding real world of engineering practice. As a matter of fact, in his college career, the author never once heard the following words: interlock, control relay, sealing contact, manual disconnect, lockout, and many more.

The operation of motors is a key part of process control. The competent engineer or designer must become familiar with some of the techniques. As mentioned a little earlier, good teamwork requires that team members be able to see past professional boundaries.

As a bare minimum, a process/project engineer should be able to read a simple ladder diagram (sometimes called an *electrical elementary diagram*), should understand some of the common electrical components, and should clearly see where boolean logic fits into process controls.

Table 9-1 shows a few symbols found on electrical elementary diagrams. Mastery in understanding these few symbols will clear the way for an understanding of most of the symbols.* It is worth noting that these symbols have physical meaning contained in their shapes to help you remember what they stand for. The level switch is made to look like a float. The push buttons look like stylized push buttons in profile. More will be said on this topic in the chapter on P&IDs (Chap. 11).

As a consequence of the Bhopal, India, tragedy in which more than 2500 people died as the result of a poisonous gas release, operating companies throughout the world are examining the inherent safety of their plants. To do this, they have employed outside engineers to prepare P&IDs. This author has had firsthand experience in several cases of this kind. One thing quickly becomes evident: Operating and engineering personnel (including their supervisors) often have no clear notion of how their motors start and stop. This has obviously been relegated to the plant electricians who, in turn, do not understand all the process consequences that result from turning on motors or operating valves. This is not a good situation.

To see how the symbols of Table 9-1 can aid in understanding a process operation or a piece of equipment, a couple of examples are presented. We look at first the starting and stopping of a motor and then the means of adding makeup water to a process.

One minor hurdle to clear away first is the meaning of *normal*, such as with a *normally closed* switch. The best way to determine what is normal is to think of the device as it is shipped when purchased. It will be dry, at room temperature and atmospheric pressure, etc. For example, the switch that turns on the light in a refrigerator is a normally *closed* switch. Almost its entire existence, in use, is as an open switch (while the refrigerator door is shut), yet its *normal* state is closed. It began its existence as a closed switch and did not experience the open state until it was installed during the fabrication of the refrigerator and the door was shut.

Figure 9-15 is an electrical schematic showing the most basic (and probably the most common) form of starting and stopping an electric motor. Included in Fig. 9-15 are three motor protection schemes. The three schemes are the same except for the inclusion of short-circuit protection in two different forms. Included also is a control circuit common to all three kinds of starter.

To understand Fig. 9-15, it is necessary to know the locations of

---

*A good source for a full set of symbols is *Electronic Drafting and Design* [44]. Symbols given in the book are those adopted by the National Machine Tool Builders Association.

TABLE 9-1 Samples of Electrical Components for Process Controls

Electrical schematic symbol	P&ID symbol	Common name(s)	Comments
	HS	Switch, maintained contact (toggle switch)	The common wall switch is of this kind; switch will stay in its last position (open or closed) until changed (by hand)
	HS	Switch, momentary contact (normally open)	Often a push button; a spring holds the switch open
	HS	Switch, momentary contact (normally closed)	Often a push button; a spring holds the switch closed
hand / off / auto	HOA HS	Three-position switch, maintained contact	Similar to the toggle switch above; requires hand actuation
	LS	Level switch, normally open	Symbol depicts a float, but this is just a memory aid; any kind of level sensing can be shown with this symbol
	LS	Level switch, normally closed	Opens when liquid is present
	PS	Pressure switch, normally open	The normally closed switch is just as common
	ZS	Position switch, normally open (also referred to as a *limit* switch)	The normally closed switch is just as common
	TS	Temperature switch, normally closed	The normally open switch is just as common
CR	◇* I	Contacts, normally open (CR means they are part of the control relay)	These contacts stay open until the control relay coil is energized
CR	◇* I	Contacts, normally closed (CR means they are part of the control relay)	These contacts stay closed until the control relay coil is energized
sol	S	Solenoid coil	The P&ID symbol is for a solenoid valve
CR	◇* I	Control relay coil	This is a copper-wire, electromagnetic coil

*The P&ID symbol is for an interlock. Contacts and control relays are *parts* of interlocks.

the components. The motor, of course, will be out in the process area, often called the *field.* The starter will likely be located in a dry, protected, ventilated room called a *motor control center* (MCC). Other starters for other motors will be grouped in the motor control center. The push-button switches in the control circuit can be located either with the motor or the starter or in another place, such as the control

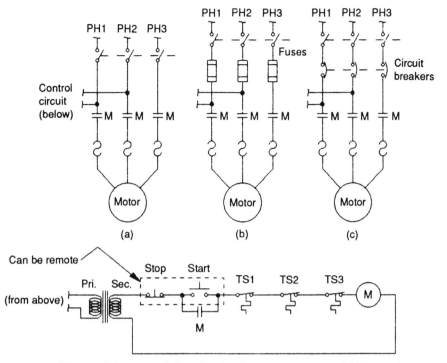

Figure 9-15 Electrical diagram of three kinds of motor protection. (a) Thermal protection; (b) thermal and short-circuit protection; (c) thermal and short-circuit protection.

room. Probably the most common place for a push-button station is close to the motor. Thus an anomaly on starting or stopping can be witnessed by the operator.

In Fig. 9-15a, the starter consists of (from the top down) a manual disconnect (usually a form of knife switch),* transformer taps to the control circuit, power contacts, and heaters. These features are on the *power* side of the starter. A transformer is frequently interposed between power and control for safety's sake—the push-button voltage can be 25 V even if the motor voltage is 480 V. The starter shown in Fig. 9-15a has these features on the *control* side (furthermore, they are *always* on the control side): the secondary coil of the transformer, three temperature switches in series, and a solenoid coil. The push-button station can be part of the combination starter (as shown in Fig. 9-16), or it can be provided separately and mounted anywhere— even alongside the motor. As a matter of fact, the push button *can be* (and often is) replaced by combinations of switches and interlocking logic parts.

Figure 9-16a is a photograph of a combination starter such as that of Fig. 9-15a. The heaters, temperature switches, solenoid coil, and contacts are all combined in close proximity in the assembly at the lower left part of the enclosure. The solenoid coil, labeled *M*, and the four contacts, also labeled *M*, have a special relationship. When energized, the coil pulls an armature connected to one end of each of the four contacts and forces each contact against its mate, closing all four circuits at more or less the same instant. When the coil is deen-

---

*On many starters the disconnect switch is connected to the handle for opening the access door. In this case, when the door is open, the circuits below the disconnect are deenergized.

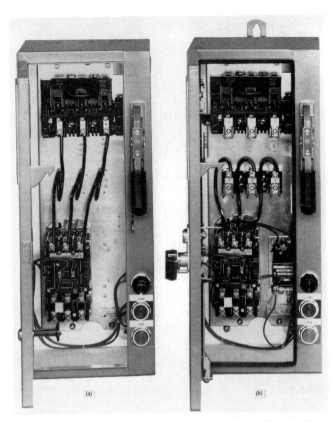

Figure 9-16 (*a*) Combination starter such as that of Fig. 9-15*a*. (*b*) Combination starter with fuse protection. (*Courtesy of Allen-Bradley, Industrial Control Group*.)

ergized, the four circuits are all interrupted more or less simultaneously.

The heaters and the temperature switches also have a special relationship. Each heater has its mating temperature switch. Note that the current for each phase of the motor must pass through a heater on the way to the motor. Should the demands on the motor go beyond its design limit, one or more of the temperature switches will open as a result of the greater heater output. This will deenergize coil *M*. If connected as shown, the motor will not restart on its own when the temperature switch cools off.

A motor can be operated at a power beyond its rated power by installing heaters in the starter that will not put out as much heat. This increases the duty of the motor, but will shorten its life.

Figure 9-15*b* and *c* depicts combination starters with short-circuit protection of two different kinds. Figure 9-16*b* is a photograph of a combination starter with fuse protection (the fuses aren't shown, but the fuse clips are). In the event of a short circuit in a motor winding, the thermal protection will not sense the problem rapidly enough. Fuses or circuit breakers are the answer. An excellent overview of motor protection can be found in the fifth and sixth editions of *Perry's Chemical Engineer's Handbook* [45].

The following is a normal start-stop sequence for a motor. To begin with, the manual disconnect must be closed (Fig. 9-15 shows it open). The normal state for the contacts is open; therefore the normal state for the motor is *off*.* The motor is started by pressing the start button.

---

*Remember what was said earlier about the "normal" state.

This completes an electric circuit in the control loop (see Fig. 9-15). This energizes coil *M*, which, in turn, pulls on the armature and causes the contacts to close. The contact wired in parallel to the start switch is called the *sealing contact*; it keeps the control circuit energized even after the start switch is released.

Any one of four events will stop the motor:

- Actuation of the stop push button
- Overheating (as described above)
- Power failure
- Operation of the disconnect switch

Without any of these events, the motor will run indefinitely. However, once stopped, it will not restart without pressing of the *start* push button. This is because the sealing contact will open regardless of the event that originally stopped the motor. For example, restoration of power after a power failure will bring electricity into the starter, but all four contacts will remain open until the start button is actuated.

This is done for safety reasons and because in a process with 40 or 50 motors, some of the main circuits could be overloaded if all motors were to start simultaneously.

Every motor on a project, whether included as the sole driver of a piece of equipment or as one of many motors provided in a package, must be reviewed for both planned and unplanned starts and stops. It is mainly the joint responsibility of the project engineer and the sponsor* to examine the unplanned stopping of a piece of equipment. The electrical engineer and the instrument engineer will have subsidiary roles, too.

In some cases, safety or economics will require that certain circuits *never* lose power. When this is true, the circuits must be backed up by an uninterruptible power supply (UPS).

Before we leave the topic of motor controls, a quick look at the boolean logic of starting and stopping motors is in order. In its most formal embodiment, boolean logic features all the characteristics of a branch of mathematics (which it is, incidentally). It has functions, operators, identities, postulates, and so on. The rigidity and precision of mathematics can be put to good use by using boolean logic on electric controls. Once the "grammar" is learned, it can be used almost subconsciously, with no formalities, in the more common applications. When the applications become complex, say with more than 10 or 20 electric switches or contacts, it may be necessary to resort to formal methods. In the cases requiring formal study, it is interesting to note the enormous number of unwanted results (that is, motors starting or stopping at the wrong time) compared to the few acceptable results.

Boolean logic relates outputs to inputs. An example of an output is an overhead light in a room. The input is its wall switch. Boolean logic covers only those control circuits which are *two-state*; fortunately, this just about covers all control circuits in the world. The two states can be designated in a variety of ways:

- 0 or 1
- Energized or not energized

*See App. B for a description of the *sponsor*.

- True or false
- Present or absent
- Actuated or not actuated

and there are many more. In the case of industrial controls, the presence or absence of a voltage is the most usual way of signaling status. This is even true of the microprocessor, the key part of the modern computer. The most common control voltages are 110 and 25.*

All logic circuits can be subdivided into three fundamental elements that convert input *information* to output *information:*

- AND
- OR
- NOT

Symbolic representations of these elements and their *truth tables* are presented in Fig. 9-17.† Inputs are shown on the left, outputs on the right. For AND and OR, the minimum number of inputs is two, yet there is no limit on the maximum. The number of outputs is always shown as one; then if this *information* is required in multiple destinations, the branches are shown from this common trunk. The NOT element always has one, and only one, input and output (the output may branch, as before, but the input may not).

The operation of these logic elements is best discerned by an examination of their truth tables. Starting with the AND element, we note that the only case in which an output signal appears is when signals are applied to both inputs. One signal, by itself, is not enough. With the OR element, one signal is enough, and two will work also. The *only* case where the output will lack a signal occurs when neither of the inputs has a signal (there is no signal to relay

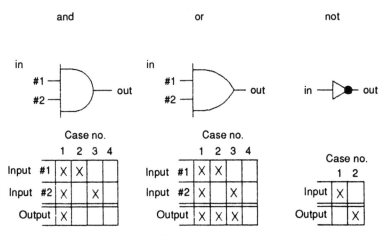

Figure 9-17 Logic elements and their truth tables.

---

*However, neither of these is used by the microprocessor. The microprocessor voltage is less than 5. A typical control voltage in this domain of the universe is around 3.3, the nominal voltage for transistor-transistor logic (TTL) or ceramic metal oxide semiconductor (CMOS) logic.

†The symbols given here may not be those most commonly used by electrical engineers. However, the author believes they might be the symbols most commonly recognized by all disciplines.

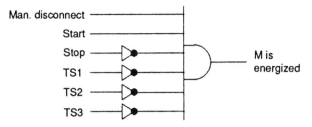

Figure 9-18 Energization of *M*.

onward). The NOT element is easiest to understand: Its output is the inverse of its input.

It was mentioned earlier that AND and OR can have many inputs. The rules are the same as for two inputs. The AND requires signals on all inputs for an output. The OR needs no signals on the inputs to produce no signal on the output.

Figure 9-18 shows an AND element* with six inputs. The diagram represents the boolean logic required to energize the coil (*M*) in Fig. 9-15. Note that *M* is energized only when the start button is actuated (and the other five conditions are met). Releasing the start button deenergizes the solenoid coil.

Figure 9-19 is the same diagram with an OR element (gate) added. Note in this case how the start button and the sealing contact are wired in parallel.† Figure 9-19 is the boolean representation for starting and stopping the motor shown in Fig. 9-15*a*.

Now we have a look at a simple method for adding makeup water to a process. The P&ID representation is illustrated in Fig. 9-20. Conventions for P&IDs require that solid lines stand for piping and equipment, while dashed lines represent electrical connections. The controls of interest are on the left side. The start-stop for the pump (HS-251), its running light (XL-252), and the rotameter (FI-273), all on the right, are shown for realism and to describe the manual part of the operation, but these items are not part of the automatic control scheme.‡ As a matter of fact, this can be discerned from the diagram, as there are no interconnections shown between the instruments on the right and the instruments on the left. The tank supplies water to a process. The process ends with a triple-effect evaporator that returns almost all the water except for that lost due to evaporation from open tanks and that consumed chemically by the process. The loss is small, but steady, and varies with the season and can wax or wane, seemingly without reason.

The only operator intervention is an occasional adjustment to the rotameter (FI-273) by means of the globe valve. The pump runs continuously.

Here is a description of the operation. Say that, at some point, the water level is between the two level switches LSH and LSL. The level is falling due to the steady loss described earlier. When the level reaches the lower switch (LSL), the switch will change state. This will cause the solenoid valve (LCV) in the makeup water line to open. The

---

*In electronic parlance, these are referred to as *gates* rather than *elements*.

†Parallel wiring connections are represented by OR logic. Series wiring connections are represented by AND logic.

‡The reader is referred to App. D and Table 11-2 for nomenclature regarding instruments.

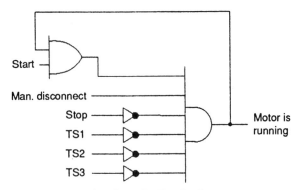

Figure 9-19 Complete logic for Fig. 9-15a.

makeup water flow rate is higher than the loss rate, so the level begins to rise and continues rising until the high-level switch (LSH) is reached. When this switch is reached, it, too, changes state, but now the solenoid valve is caused to close. Once it does, the level will again dwindle downward until it is at the point where it started. This completes a full cycle that will continue indefinitely. What has been described, incidentally, is a very reliable, economic way of adding a consumable ingredient to a process.

The electrical elementary diagram that describes this operation is shown in Fig. 9-21. This unique circuit shows how I-23 on the P&ID is to be implemented. When electric inputs and outputs are used together this way, they are said to be interlocked. The square rotated 45 degrees (see Table 9-1) is a very common way of calling out an interlock.

The process cycle described above can be followed by examining Fig. 9-21. First assume HS-243 is in *auto*. At the beginning, LSH-245 is in its normal state (closed), LSL-246 is actuated (open), LCV-244 is in its normal state (closed—therefore, CR-247 is deenergized). The water level will drop until LSL-246 trips. This will energize CR-247, and both of its contact pairs will close. One pair (CR-247-1) will keep

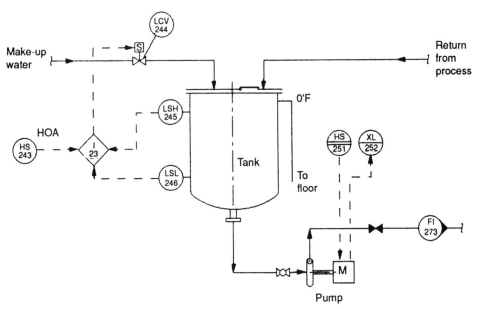

Figure 9-20 P&ID segment for makeup water.

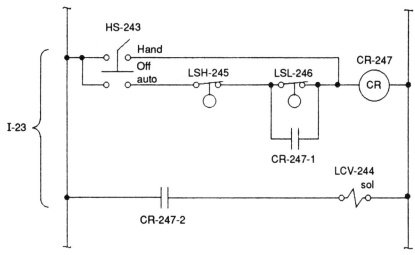

Figure 9-21 Segment of electrical elementary showing I-23.

the relay coil energized, and the other pair (CR-247-2) will energize the solenoid valve.

It is important to note that the low-level switch may not remain in the actuated state very long because of wave action in the tank and because the opening of the solenoid valve is designed to cause an increase in level. The level increase will open LSL-246. When this occurs, the solenoid valve will not be affected, as the control relay is kept energized by the contacts (CR-247-1) wired in parallel to the level switch. The valve will stay open until the high-level switch is tripped. Once *that* occurs, current to CR-247 will be interrupted, the valve will shut, and the system will return to its initial condition.

Standard procedure in reviewing an electric circuit is to ask what happens if a switch closure is noisy. The source of noise in this case would be wave action on the water surface, something that would have a minimum period of, say, 0.1 s. Since the two contact pairs on the control relay can respond in a fraction of that time, neither the relay nor the solenoid valve should chatter or buzz.*

The coverage given here to this fascinating subject is light—just an introduction. The serious process engineer/designer is encouraged to delve further. A suggested starting point is the following set of articles in *Chemical Engineering* magazine:

Ernest M. Cohen and Willi Fehervari, "Sequential Control," Apr. 29, 1985, pp. 61–66.

Edward P. Lynch, "Using Boolean Algebra and Logic Diagrams, I," Aug. 19, 1974, pp. 107–119.

Edward P. Lynch, "Using Boolean Algebra and Logic Diagrams, II," Sept. 16, 1974, pp. 111–118.

Edward P. Lynch, "Using Boolean Algebra and Logic Diagrams, III," Oct. 14, 1974, pp. 101–104.

Texts on this subject can be found under the headings of boolean algebra (pure mathematics), relays (electrical hardware), digital logic (controls), etc. For the novice two texts are recommended that con-

---

*Just imagine CR-247-2 closing immediately, while CR-247-1 takes 5 s to close. The solenoid valve could open and close several times.

nect the physical meaning with the abstractions: *Design of Relay Control Systems* [46] by Polgar and *Electrical Control Systems in Industry* [47] by Siskind.

THE BERNOULLI EQUATION

"In 1738 Daniel Bernoulli, a Swiss mathematician, demonstrated a general theorem in connection with fluid motion, the importance of which cannot be overemphasized. Upon it, as a framework, may be erected the whole structure of fluid motion, and by it, a majority of the problems arising may be completely solved." [48] It was with these words that George E. Russell, renowned professor of hydraulics at the Massachusetts Institute of Technology, introduced, in his book *Hydraulics*, this highly pertinent concept concerning the motion of fluids. Russell was not alone in extolling the usefulness of Bernoulli's work. When Ludvig Prandtl [49] introduced the Bernoulli equation, he stated: "This equation is of the *utmost importance,** in the hydrodynamics of a non viscous fluid. . . . "

From the practicing engineer's standpoint, one of the major beauties of the equation is the ease with which it can be understood and employed. Equation (9-1) is the form of this equation familiar to most engineers. It represents the case where the density of the fluid is invariant.

$$\frac{p}{\rho} + \frac{g}{g_c}Z + \frac{v^2}{2g_c} = \text{constant} \tag{9-1}$$

where p = pressure, lbf/ft^2
 ρ = density, lbm/ft^3
 g = acceleration due to gravity, ft/s^2
 g_c = conversion factor, lbm · ft/(lbf · s^2)
 Z = vertical distance *above* a horizontal reference plane, ft
 v = velocity, ft/s

The overall meaning of the equation is that energy is conserved. The energy can be converted from one form to another—from height to velocity (like the pendulum), from pressure to height, and so on—but it is always there, ready to be converted again. Three memory keys are very helpful in remembering and understanding the equation: (1) All terms are additive, (2) two of the three terms give the rule for hydrostatic pressure ($p = -\rho Z$), and (3) the third term, $v^2/(2g_c)$ is the classic statement for kinetic energy. This third term is called the *velocity head*. It is, incidentally, the velocity that a particle achieves dropping in free fall through the distance Z.

Correct use of the equation requires an understanding of how it is used and the limits on its use. Here are the steps for putting Eq. (9-1) to use:

1. Find a reference plane where pressure, elevation, and velocity are known.

2. Evaluate the value of Eq. (9-1)—this is the reference value.

3. Go to the plane where the unknown condition is sought.

4. Write an expression using Eq. (9-1) at this second plane, and equate the expression to the reference value.

5. Solve the resulting equation.

---

*Emphasis added.

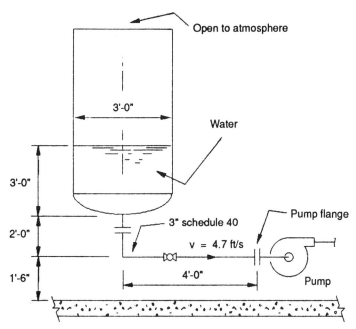

Figure 9-22 Pump suction.

Here is an example. It is desired to know the pressure at the flange on a pump suction. Figure 9-22 shows the situation. (Energy loss due to friction is included later. This is only a rough estimate.) The pump flange can be thought of as defining the second plane. The first plane is at the surface of the liquid in the tank. Note that these two planes are not parallel and, in fact, can be at any angle to each other, as long as the highest and lowest streamlines of a reference plane are not separated by a large vertical distance (leading to significant differences in gravitational energy). It is necessary that each plane be perpendicular to the flow, a condition easily met when the fluid is contained by tanks, piping, and other process equipment.

Equation (9-1) is used to calculate the reference value. The units chosen are feet of fluid (in this case, water). The reference plane is the floor, but any other horizontal plane will do. To be able to use Eq. (9-1) with *feet* as the unit, the equation must be multiplied by g_c/g. Doing so, we get Eq. (9-2):

$$p_f + Z + \frac{v^2}{2g} = \text{constant} \qquad (9\text{-}2)$$

where p_f is in units of feet of fluid (in this case, water). By inspection of Fig. 9-22, values are inserted in Eq. (9-2), and the expression in Eq. (9-3) is evaluated to determine the reference value:

$$0 + 6.5 + \frac{[4.7(3.068/36.00)^2]^2}{2 \times 32.17} = \text{constant} = 6.5 \qquad (9\text{-}3)$$

Use was made of a simple mass balance* to determine the velocity in the tank. It turns out that this velocity head is small enough (0.00002 ft) to be ignored.

Figure 9-22 is inspected, and values are inserted in Eq. (9-2), thereby obtaining Eq. (9-4).

---

*$vA\rho$ = constant, where A is the flow area in a plane perpendicular to the flow.

$$p_f + 1.5 + \frac{4.7^2}{2 \times 32.17} = 6.5 \qquad (9\text{-}4)$$

The pressure p_f is found to equal 4.66 ft of water.

By analyzing the result, the following is noted. The head level in the tank has a direct influence on the pressure at the pump flange. The pump elevation has the same relationship, but opposite in sign. If the pump had been on a platform 10 ft above the floor, p_f would equal −5.34 ft (please note the minus sign).

Also we note that the velocity *decreased* the available head, not due to a friction loss, but because energy was converted from pressure to velocity.

Finally, we see that at 4.7 ft/s the velocity term of Eq. (9-2) is of secondary importance. However, a quick check reveals that the velocity term begins to take on importance at 8 to 10 ft/s. This may be the basis for a rule of thumb that says, for pump suction lines, the velocity should be kept less than 5 ft/s.

The limits imposed so far on the use of the Bernoulli equation are numerous and at first sight seem to be so restrictive as to severely inhibit the use of the equation. In reality, the conditions are readily complied with, at least as an acceptable approximation, so applicability of the equation is extremely broad. This author's experience has been that the equation can easily be used in more than three-quarters of the flow problems found in industry. *By mastering this single equation, engineers/designers put themselves in a commanding position for understanding process situations where flow is a consideration.* What follows is a formal listing of the restrictions:

- Flow rate is constant.
- Density is reasonably constant.*
- The velocity of all fluid elements is constant at the plane where the equation is evaluated.†
- The streamlines are all perpendicular to the plane where the equation is evaluated.
- Mechanical energy and thermal energy are not introduced between the reference point and the second point of interest.
- The effects of gravity, or acceleration, are taken into account [any flow on the earth's surface and not in a rotating or accelerating machine can be evaluated by using Eq. (9-1) without correction].

Clearly the friction losses are not in the above list. This is because in common industrial flow problems, friction *is* important. It has been left out of the discussion up to now to emphasize the interchangeable nature of energy in fluid flow.

Now comes friction. It burns energy, sending it into the night sky, never to be regained. When friction is included, the result is *always* to remove energy. This means that when friction is applied with the

---

*This is easy to check by evaluating the integral of dp/ρ. Under adiabatic conditions this integral turns out to be

$$\left(\frac{k}{k+1}\right) \times \left(\frac{p_1}{w_1}\right) \times \left(1 - \frac{p_2}{p_1}\right)^{(k-1)/k}$$

where $w = \rho(g/g_c)$ and k is the specific heat ratio.

†Maximum error here is one velocity head (laminar flow). In fully developed turbulent flow, the velocity profile is reasonably flat, yet a correction as high as 12 percent may be needed. See Fig. 2-16 by McCabe and Smith [50].

Bernoulli equation, the energy available at the upstream condition is always *reduced* by friction losses. This reduced energy is what remains available downstream.

For the above example, friction effects are incorporated as follows. First Fig. 9-22 is inspected. Four sources of friction are identified: the entrance to the pipe, the elbow, the ball valve, and the pipe. Examination of pages 249 and 257 in *Fluid Mechanics and Hydraulics* [51] turns up the following values for friction losses:

Entrance	0.5 velocity head
Elbow	0.7 velocity head
Ball valve	same as pipe*
Pipe	0.48 velocity head
	1.68 total

The total, multiplied by the velocity head ($1.68 \times 0.35 = 0.59$ ft), is subtracted from the reference value. This leads to a final result of 4.07 ft of water pressure at the pump suction flange.

In this case, note that the entrance loss is for a sharp-edged connection. Also the loss for the elbow is for one having a short radius. A normal welded connection is not sharp and, with a brief note on the fabrication drawing, can be easily rounded during fabrication. This would cut the entrance loss in half at least. A similar reduction in friction could be obtained by using a long-radius elbow. Indeed, many piping specifications call for the use of long-radius elbows in suction lines.

The simplicity and elegance of the basic Bernoulli equation are often hidden by including terms for mechanical energy and heat energy. Here, the recommended practice is to state the problem in such a way that these terms are not needed. Mechanical and heat energy can be incorporated later, just as was done with friction.

One more example of the use of the Bernoulli equation is considered before we look at some specific types of equipment. In this case, it is desired to place a flow distributor inside of an existing crystallizer so that a portion of the incoming fluid will go to a lower level in the crystallizer and the remaining portion will discharge to a higher level. Figure 9-23 shows the situation.

First, the reference plane is established at the liquid level in the distributor. This makes the reference value equal to zero. We note there are two planes where unknowns are sought: at each end of the "downcomer" pipes. For the deep downcomer, we write

$$D - (D + H) + \frac{v^2}{2g} = 0 \qquad \text{(units: feet of fluid)}$$

by using the form of the Bernoulli equation from App. E where units are feet of fluid. For the shallow downcomer, we write

$$S - (S + H) + \frac{u^2}{2g} = 0 \qquad \text{(units: feet of fluid)}$$

Therefore,

$$\frac{u^2}{2g} = \frac{v^2}{2g} = H$$

---

*This is not from the referenced text. It is judged from a knowledge of the geometry of ball valves. A full-port valve is postulated.

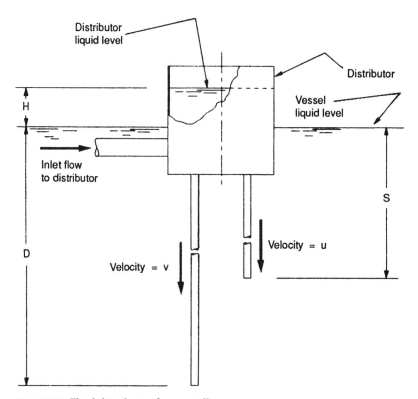

Figure 9-23 Fluid distributor for crystallizer.

It is evident that the velocity in each downcomer will be the same—that is, if friction is of no consequence.

What about friction? We note that entrance and exit losses for the two downcomers will be identical. The only difference is in the lengths. If the downcomer diameters are selected generously, the differences between the downcomers due to friction will be small. In such a case, the proportioning of fluid to high and low levels will depend solely on the diameter selected for each downcomer.

This example illustrates how a thorny problem can be tamed and made comprehensible with the venerable Bernoulli equation. It also illustrates how problem solving requires creativity and judgment on the part of the engineer/designer. No computer in all creation could assimilate the facts and arrive at a *useful* conclusion as directly and rapidly as we have seen in this example. There is no substitute for knowledge.

One more item bears mention. The effects of turbulence in the distributor can have a noticeable effect on flow in the downcomers. To minimize this, the downcomers should be placed side by side, straddling the inlet centerline.

GRANULAR SOLIDS

Prior to looking at equipment for handling granular solids, it is necessary to form a basic understanding about the nature of granular solids. The necessity of dealing with granular solids pervades the whole fabric of engineering/design of processes. From the most high-technology pharmaceutical job to the lowliest sand and gravel operation, granular solids must be accommodated. In some cases, such as major coal handling facilities, the whole job is customized to suit the special requirements of granular solids. Even those bastions of fluid processing, the oil refineries, have their share of solids handling with fluid-bed catalyst, filter aid, and miscellaneous reagents.

Annual capital expenditures, worldwide, for solids handling equipment probably far exceed similar expenditures for distillation equipment. Certainly, the number of instances where solids handling is a consideration far exceeds the number where distillation is a consideration.

To some extent, engineering/design for granular solids is preferentially performed by mechanical engineers. This is mostly by default, for the types of equipment used favor oversight by a person with a mechanical engineering background. It is a mistake, however, for process engineers/designers to think that, because their background is not mechanical, they can ignore granular solids.

The science and engineering relating to this subject are scattered mostly in these disciplines:

- Soil science

- Civil engineering

- Mechanical engineering

However, many other disciplines have made major contributions. Physical chemists have been very influential in characterization of granular solids, and chemical engineers have had a strong influence where fluid beds are concerned. The inclusion of soil science at the top of the list may strike many people as odd. Nonetheless, this science is a basic source of knowledge when it comes to granular solids. This is so because inquiries into the nature of particles often start with questions concerning the very earth we stand on.

Flow from bins, on one hand, and design of building foundations, on the other, have more than a few things in common. This topic will receive more coverage than any of the topics covered so far. Even so, this discussion is limited to

- Individual particles
- Particles in groups

Questions about individual solid particles arise with pneumatic conveyors, fluid beds, crystallizers, mineral concentrators of different types, flash dryers, spray dryers, and kilns, just to name a few types of process equipment. The particle itself is characterized by

- Size
- Shape
- Density
- Surface characteristics
- Chemical composition
- Hardness
- Toughness
- Reactivity

Of course, a particle in a vacuum is rarely a subject of interest in the everyday world of project work. What remains, then, is the fluid in which the lone particle is immersed. The fluid will often have an effect on the chemical composition and/or the reactivity of the particle.

Putting both the particle and the fluid together, probably the most sought-after quantity, in one form or another, is the viscous force exerted by the fluid on the particle. For example, this force will determine whether a particle will be conveyed along with fluid moving upward in a vertical pipe or whether it will move downward, opposite to the flow of fluid.

The historical development for understanding viscous forces on single particles can be traced in large part to the development of ballistics, aeronautics, and particle separation devices used in processing food grains and minerals. This fundamental equation is based mostly on experimental studies:

$$\bar{F}_v = -C_D \rho A \frac{\bar{v}^2}{2g_c} \tag{9-5}$$

where $\bar{F}_v$ = viscous force exerted on particle, lbf, a vector
C_D = drag coefficient (dimensionless), a function of N_R
ρ = density of fluid, lbm/ft^3
A = projected particle area on a plane perpendicular to $\bar{v}$
$\bar{v}$ = velocity of particle relative to fluid, ft/s, a vector
g_c = conversion factor, lbm · ft/(lbf · s^2)

The force exerted on the solid is stated to be proportional to the mass of fluid displaced per unit time ($\rho A v$) times the velocity. The coefficient of proportionality is the drag coefficient.

Note that force and velocity are vectors and always point in opposite directions. The key for being able to use the equation, of course, is to pinpoint a realistic value for the drag coefficient. Data for drag coefficients of spheres were acquired by Lapple and Shepherd [52] from 17 sources. The data were analyzed and unified. Then the drag coefficient was presented as a function of the Reynolds number N_R from creeping flow to sonic flow. The Lapple and Shepherd drag coefficients are widely accepted and can be found in many texts that cover flow around a sphere.

The Lapple and Shepherd coefficients are shown in Fig. 9-24. The sudden decline in coefficient around N_R = 200,000 is where leeward fluid detaches itself from the sphere. From this point and upward, the drag coefficients are of greater interest in ballistics than in the engineering of equipment. Coefficients to the left of this drop are the ones usually needed to understand equipment used in process plants.

The values used by Lapple and Shepherd are given in Table 9-2. The author has developed an equation which can be used to interpolate between the values with good accuracy:

$$C_D = \frac{24}{N_R} + \frac{1}{0.286 N_R^{0.314} + 0.129 N_R^{-1.69}}$$
$$+ \frac{1}{2 + 5720 N_R^{-0.834}} - \frac{0.310 \exp(a N_R) + 0.660}{[\exp(a N_R) + 1]\{\exp[-b(N_R + d)] + 1\}} \tag{9-6}$$

where a = 1.031×10^{-6}
b = 2.83×10^{-5}
d = -2.586×10^5

Values calculated by using the equation are given in Table 9-2 for comparison. The equation can be used in most cases without deviat-

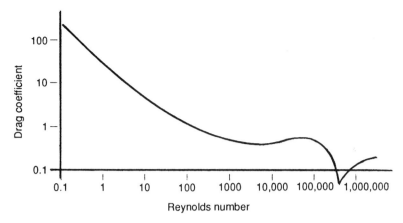

Figure 9-24 The Lapple and Shepherd drag coefficient for spheres.

ing from the data by more than 5 percent. Even in the ballistic region, the equation is within 10 percent of the experimental values. By eliminating the last term of the equation, it is greatly simplified, but values of N_R must not exceed 100,000. The usefulness of the equation is not only for interpolation, but also for inclusion in computer routines for calculating trajectories, terminal velocities, and time required to reach, say, 95 percent of terminal velocity.

An obvious problem here is the fact that most particles are not spherical (although, on occasion, some are). Some particles, such as single, undamaged crystals, are highly regular and symmetric in shape, so models of these shapes could be built and special drag coefficients could be measured. But then what about irregularly shaped particles? In the finest tradition of pragmatism that is required to size equipment and piping, the nonspherical particles are treated as though they were spheres of such a size that viscous forces on the "equivalent sphere" are the same as viscous forces on the particle (see Fig. 9-25). Sometimes the equivalent diameters are actually measured by using a settling test. Usually the particle size distribution

TABLE 9-2   Drag Coefficient Values

N_R	Data	Equation	N_R	Data	Equation
0.1	240.0	240.2	700	0.50	0.519
0.2	120.0	120.5	1,000	0.46	0.473
0.3	80.0	80.8	2,000	0.42	0.416
0.5	49.5	49.5	3,000	0.40	0.399
0.7	36.5	36.3	5,000	0.385	0.395
1.0	26.5	26.4	7,000	0.390	0.400
2.0	14.6	14.5	10,000	0.405	0.411
3.0	10.4	10.4	20,000	0.45	0.444
5.0	6.9	6.87	30,000	0.47	0.465
7.0	5.3	5.31	50,000	0.49	0.488
10	4.1	4.09	70,000	0.50	0.500
20	2.55	2.56	100,000	0.48	0.508
30	2.00	2.00	200,000	0.42	0.452
50	1.50	1.51	300,000	0.20	0.181
70	1.27	1.27	400,000	0.84	0.091
100	1.07	1.07	600,000	0.10	0.100
200	0.77	0.796	1,000,000	0.13	0.130
300	0.65	0.682	3,000,000	0.20	0.202
500	0.55	0.574			

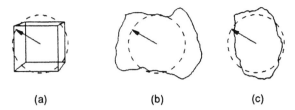

Figure 9-25 Equivalent spheres. (*a*) Cube; (*b*) particle (side view); (*c*) particle (end view).

(PSD, see below) is examined, and a *design particle size* is chosen given knowledge of the desired process result.

Computer programs exist that can calculate the precise drag coefficient for any particle in any orientation, in any fluid, and at any velocity. The problem is that such programs are expensive, not only to buy, but also to learn and to input all the information. Furthermore, the physical meaning is partly obscured from view. Surely 20 or 30 years from now, many of these obstacles will be overcome, but quite likely the concept of equivalent diameter will still be widely used, because of its convenience and ready estimation. Also it is unlikely that the input data (a diameter selected from a PSD) will be any better than they are now.

An important use of Eq. (9-6) is calculation of terminal velocity under the force of gravity at the surface of the earth. At terminal velocity the gravity force will equal the viscous force.

$$V(\rho_P - \rho) = C_D \rho A \frac{v^2}{2g_c} \qquad (9\text{-}7)$$

where V = particle volume
ρ_P = apparent particle density
ρ = fluid density

The particle density can be somewhat deceptive. What is sought is the apparent density of the particle: its actual weight divided by its actual volume. For example, a particle known to be 100 percent reconstituted cellulose does not necessarily have the density of cellulose. Indeed, early synthetic sponges were made by solubilizing cellulose, mixing in rock salt, precipitating the cellulose, and washing out the salt, leaving a porous structure. The resulting mass had a density about 15 percent that of cellulose. *Void fractions of particles* are important to keep in mind. They make unexpected appearances [ATD].

For tiny particles, say those less than 0.010 in in diameter, a common way of measuring density is to take a narrow size fraction, introduce it into a liquid-filled graduated cylinder, and measure the settling rate. This is often more difficult than it sounds. (For one thing, attached air bubbles can complicate matters.) Generally this won't be necessary because a particle or two, say, greater than 0.020 in in diameter can be found (by using a 40X pocket microscope, or a regular stereoscopic microscope, for that matter) and weighed. Large particles around 0.040 in are easy to manipulate with a small, sharp tool, such as a needle. If a stereoscopic microscope with graduated reticle is available, the job of measuring "diameter" is easy. The use of a 40X pocket microscope plus a steel rule having divisions of $\frac{1}{32}$ in will serve almost as well. A small sample is placed on the rule and viewed with the microscope while being prodded with the needle. Smaller particles may require isolation and weighing of a half dozen or so together for a large enough sample weight.

Given the void fraction and bulk density (see below), the particle density can be derived. (However, particle voids must be determined independently of voids inherent with packed beds.)

Before we move on from the lone particle to discuss multiple particles, or groups of particles, some words on *reactivity* are necessary.

Reactivity is important with particles because their nature is to offer large amounts of surface area for chemical reactions to occur. A single, 1-lb piece of steel is, for all practical purposes, nothing to worry about. That very same piece, converted to particles of −200-mesh, can be worse, in the presence of oxygen, than a stick of dynamite. The most universal problem is reactivity with air. Therefore, if reaction with oxygen is thermodynamically possible and air is present, extreme caution is in order.

In the case of the lone particle, the fluid in which it was immersed was also of great interest. In the case of particles grouped together, this is not as true. It is the behavior of the particles in their own company that is of prime interest. Of course, in understanding aggregates of particles, it is necessary to first understand the relationship of lone particles to the fluid in question. As much as anything, this is a way of subdividing a problem into *parts* (see Chap. 7).

The particle size distribution (PSD) probably tells more about granular solids than any other statistic. The two most common ways of stating the PSD are as a table and as a graph on semilog paper. The graph is more useful than the table when it is necessary to make judgments of maximum and minimum size. Table 9-3 and Fig. 9-26 are examples of how PSD data can be presented. For particle sizes larger than 44 μm, standard sieves are usually used to measure PSD. The data for particles smaller than 44 μm can be obtained on devices that measure and analyze reflected laser light. These instruments will measure the larger particle sizes as well.

Some processes use PSD as a control variable, so sampling and sizing tests are performed steadily and automatically. Most sizing tests for design needs are done manually, however.

Occasionally, when sieves are not available or the sample size is quite small, it may be necessary to estimate PSD by using a microscope as described above. The method is a little tedious and cannot be used when a sizable portion of particles is less than about 0.02 in (35-mesh). The method is often useful, however, for choosing maximum particle size, regardless of fines content. The counting method can be used with small particles by taking photographs at large magnifications of carefully prepared samples.

Maximum particle size is often a key parameter for sizing agitators. From Fig. 9-26, if the curve is representative of solids in the process, then 350 μm (45-mesh) would be a reasonable choice for maximum particle size. If the curve represents only a small sample, a larger particle size would be chosen as maximum to allow for inaccuracy in the PSD.

At the other end of the scale, Fig. 9-26 can be consulted to find what the dust loading will be on a dust collector (such as that shown in Fig. 9-27), if the cutoff size for particles carried overhead from a cyclone is 15 μm. Using Fig. 9-26, we see that 8 percent of the solids fed to the cyclone will pass through it. This 8 percent becomes the solids load on the dust collector.

Another important statistic for granular solids is the *bulk density.*

TABLE 9-3 Typical Particle Size Distribution Data

Size, μm	Weight on screen, g	Percent of total	Cumulative percent retained*
250	6	1.0	1.0
149	24	4.0	5.0
88	93	15.5	20.5
44	255	42.5	63.0
30			77.5
15			92.0
10			97.0
Not retained	222	37.0	
	600	100.0	

*Or larger than given size.

This quantity is easy to obtain. A container of known volume is weighed while both empty and full. The weight of the contents divided by the volume gives the bulk density. Care must be exercised in *how* the solids are placed in the container. It is always a good idea to make at least two measurements: with the solids placed loosely in the container and with the solids tamped down tightly.

Process conditions should be reviewed while keeping in mind things that can affect the bulk density (and other properties). For example, the presence or absence of a water of hydration will alter the crystalline state and can have a marked effect on all the properties of a granular solid. On occasion, just a few degrees difference in temperature is all that is required to cause a change of this kind.

At the same time as the bulk density is measured, the void fraction should be measured. For one thing, this will lead to a double-check of particle density. The easiest way to measure the void fraction is by introducing a weighed sample into a graduated cylinder containing a nonsolvent liquid. The change in liquid level should be noted. The

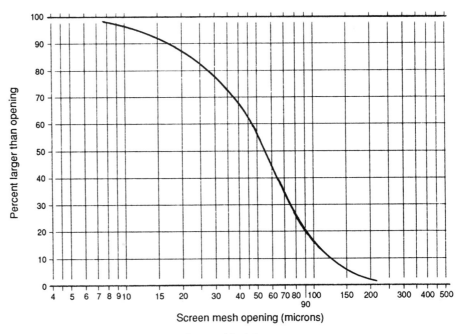

Figure 9-26 Plot of cumulative sizes from Table 9-3.

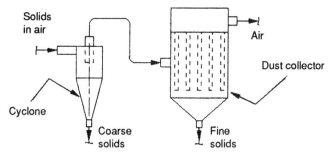

Figure 9-27 Dust going to dust collector.

solids level should also be noted after all the fines have settled.* Some tamping and prodding should be done to ensure that the solids have formed a bed and are not in suspension.

The bulk density and void fraction are needed to calculate

- Volumetric flow rates
- Bin or storage pile sizes
- Flows and pressures of incipient fluidization
- Material balance calculations involving entrained liquids and gases
- Pressure drops across packed beds

In the course of measuring bulk density, care should be taken to observe the cohesive nature of the solids. Do they flow readily? Too readily? Must they be prodded along? Must they be scraped out of containers? Is moisture visible? And so on.

Before discussing the cohesive nature of solids, we take a quick look at how pressure drops across packed beds can be used to estimate some fundamental properties concerning fluid beds. Figure 9-28 shows a typical fluid bed. Granular solids enter from the top and leave from the bottom while gas enters the bottom and leaves from the top. The gas keeps the solids agitated. Often the gas travels

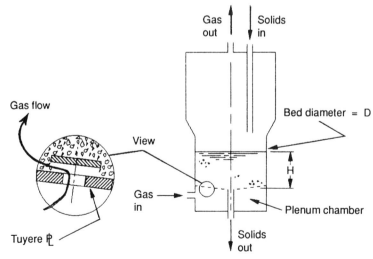

Figure 9-28 Typical fluid bed.

---

*The fines will settle quickly by keeping excess liquid to a minimum, that is, no more than 10 to 20 percent more than the void fraction.

through the bed in bubbles, just as if the bed of solids were a liquid. In the case of a bubbling bed, the bubbles can be observed bursting as they emerge from the surface of the bed. Usually, the reason for employing a fluid bed is to carry out a chemical reaction between the solids and the gas or to induce a physical change. The situation is similar to a stirred-tank reactor for liquids and solids.

The gas enters the vessel under the tuyere plate, into a plenum chamber. To reach the solids, it must first flow through baffled holes in the tuyere plate. The tuyere plate is slightly conical to make the solids tend toward the outlet. The baffles keep the solids from trickling into the plenum when the gas is shut off.

To envision what happens in a fluid bed, one must start with a bed where no solids are added, no solids are withdrawn, and the gas has been shut off. The bed sits in the vessel just as any granular material sits in a storage bin. Once gas flow is begun, the material will offer the flow resistance of a packed bed, which it is. Increasing the flow will cause increased pressure drops across both the tuyere plate and the bed material.

With increased flows, the pressure drop increases until, at some point, the pressure drop across the bed will exert a force equal to the force exerted by gravity (that is, equal to the weight of the bed). This is the point of incipient fluidization (see Fig. 9-29):

$$\Delta PA = W$$

where ΔP = pressure drop across bed
A = cross-sectional area of vessel confining the bed
W = weight of granular material making up bed

Beyond incipient fluidization, increased flows do not greatly change the pressure drop. However, a limit is reached when the bed is lost (that is, conveyed out of the vessel) via entrainment. This phenomenon takes place when the terminal velocity* of even the largest particle is exceeded by the superficial velocity of the fluid.

Once fluidization is achieved, the two-phase mass approximates the behavior of a liquid. The depth of the bed can be inferred by measuring the pressure drop across the *bed*; then knowing an approximate bulk density† at conditions in the bed, the equation for hydrostatic pressure can be employed: $\Delta p = \rho_B L$. This technique can

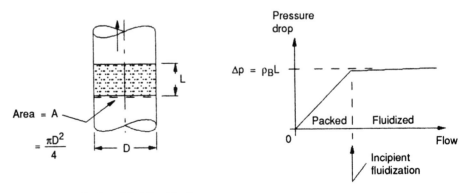

Figure 9-29 Packed and fluidized beds.

---

*That is, terminal settling velocity in a viscous fluid.

†For initial, speculative work, a good *range* for this quantity can be obtained by using a bulk density for *loosely* packed material as the *high* value and a density 10 percent less as a low value.

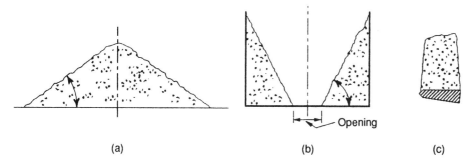

                    (a)   (b)   (c)

Figure 9-30 Some easily measured flow parameters. (*a*) Angle of repose; (*b*) angle of internal friction; (*c*) knife blade.

be used only if the bed is fluidized. Obviously, if the bed has channeled or is slugging severely, this simple rule will not hold.

A common measure of willingness to flow is the angle of repose. Some years ago, the angle of repose was thought to be the best indicator of a granular material's willingness to flow. This angle is the angle at the base of a pile formed by pouring granular material onto a flat surface (see Fig. 9-30). A low angle of repose equates to a free-flowing material.

Today, other indicators, just as simple, have been defined. One is the angle of internal friction. For free-flowing materials, this angle is measured by allowing material to flow out the bottom of a hole in a rectangular box and measuring the slope along the sides of the resulting cavity once flow has stopped (Fig. 9-30*b*). Another indicator results when a knife blade or spatula is slipped into a heap of the material and gently raised through the material. Steep-sloping sides are indicative of a material with a high internal friction.

The angle of repose can be distorted by the effects of aeration.* This problem is only important with small particles, say, less than 40-mesh. The mere act of pouring the sample onto the flat surface through air is sufficient to cause the aeration. The other two simple tests are not immune from this problem either. However, by waiting for a few minutes from the time the sample is placed in position until performing the test, aeration effects can be more or less nullified.

A second problem, however, with angle of repose is that no effects of consolidation with time or bin pressure† are forthcoming. The consolidation phenomena are fairly common, so a measure that excludes them is seriously wanting.

Probably the best all-around indication of the ability of a granular material to flow is its coefficient of friction. By definition, this coefficient is the ratio of the shear force to the normal force. In elementary physics, a dynamic coefficient of friction can be measured by placing two flat objects together and measuring the force to drag one past the other under increasing weights. In Fig. 9-31, the total normal force (load) is taken as the weight of object 2 plus the load weight *W*. An-

---

*Aeration occurs when the particles are kept suspended by entrained air. To experience this in the laboratory, stir up some diatomaceous earth (filter aid) in a beaker with a rod or spatula and notice how, for 20 s or so, the diatomaceous earth will behave as a liquid: Tilting the beaker will result in flow, and the surface will become horizontal, just as with a liquid.

†Bin pressure is the pressure exerted on an element of granular material beneath layers of other granular material in a bin or storage pile. It is similar to hydrostatic pressure under a liquid, but never reaches as high a pressure.

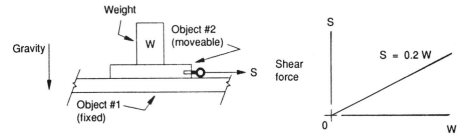

Figure 9-31 Friction by dragging horizontally.

other way of measuring the coefficient of friction is to observe the angle where sliding at constant velocity is sustained down a slope (see Fig. 9-32).

A typical coefficient is 0.30 for smooth, flat solids (wood on wood). Rough surfaces, such as brick on brick, can have coefficients around 0.7. For a sloping surface, where the force is provided by gravity, the slope that corresponds to a 0.30 coefficient of friction is 16.7 degrees (tan 16.7 = 0.3).

Elementary physics distinguishes between a *dynamic* coefficient of friction and a *static* coefficient of friction. So far, this discussion has been limited to the dynamic coefficient. The static coefficient is always the higher of the two. Static coefficients are heavily influenced by two variables: time and normal force.

This is best visualized by considering two waxed pieces of wood, one on top of the other. If the friction test is tried shortly after the pieces are placed together, they will readily slide. After 5 min or so, a noticeable bond between the surfaces will have occurred. The breakaway force to cause motion becomes greater with increasing time and increasing pressure.*

Everything that has been said so far about simple friction between two objects is fully applicable to the friction of granular solids.

For the design of bins, hoppers, and storage piles, and for the design of the equipment drawing granular materials from these bins, hoppers, and storage piles, a knowledge of the friction properties of the solids is essential. Good designs save the owner/operators money year after year. Poor design costs money, a good deal of money, but is rarely recognized as costing anything. Instead, it is simply viewed as being "the way things are." A bulldozer traversing an ore pile is in this category. Equipment depreciation, maintenance, and operating labor for such a situation can easily exceed $150,000 per year. Good design

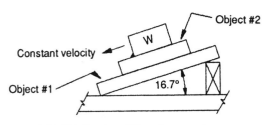

Figure 9-32 Friction by sliding down a slope.

---

*With wax, the temperature is important, too. Up to a point, the stickiness will increase with temperature and/or time, but then it will decrease, as the wax is absorbed or turns to liquid.

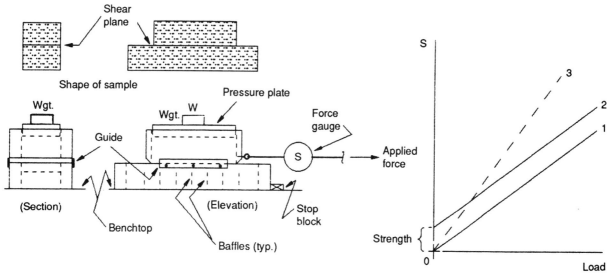

Figure 9-33 Measurement of internal friction.

at the outset might have added half of that amount as a one-time capital expenditure.

With granular solids, there are these measures of friction:

- Dynamic internal friction
- Static internal friction (also called *strength*)
- Dynamic granule-boundary friction
- Static granule-boundary friction

The classic method for measuring dynamic internal friction is an adaptation of the method for measuring friction between monolithic solids described earlier. A sledge containing the solids is dragged across a tray filled with the same solids, and the dragging force is evaluated as a function of the load at the shear plane and perpendicular to it (see Fig. 9-33).

Friction with the bin wall (boundary friction) is measured in a similar fashion. In place of the material in the tray, a sample of the bin wall or hopper wall is used. The sledge (containing granular material) is then dragged across the wall sample.

The lines shown on the cartesian coordinates in Fig. 9-33 give three cases: (1) a free-flowing material of low internal friction, (2) a material that displays strength in spite of a low friction, and (3) a free-flowing material of high internal friction. In the first and third cases, material will not bridge.* That is, it will imitate a liquid in that it will flow through any opening just as if it were a liquid (given limitations mentioned such as the ratio of the particle to the opening). In the third case, the material will not flow as quickly as in the first case. In the second case, the material will be capable of blocking an opening (but it may not do so, if it is not subjected to pressure while at rest—an almost impossible requirement). We revisit this in Chap. 10 under "Bins."

---

*Unless the outlet size is small, say less than 10 to 20 times the particle size.

═Chapter 10═
Equipment Examples

This chapter demonstrates thought processes needed for understanding equipment. Once the technique is grasped, the same kind of thinking can be applied to *all* kinds of equipment.

Recall from Chap. 9 that the whole objective of understanding equipment is to ensure that it will operate properly in the proposed application. Also recall that the analysis is based on asking questions. Recurring throughout is the two-sided question, How does it work? What will keep it from working?

The topics have been selected so that both the commonplace and the unusual are included. Physical sciences and mathematics are used constantly to explore and define. The mathematical treatment is kept simple, consistent with the required result.

The reader should note the extensive use of judgment and of the mind's eye in the following examples.

CENTRIFUGAL PUMPS

The centrifugal pump is a very common piece of equipment on process plants. Its domain does not stop there, however. It can be found in office buildings, hospitals, stone quarries, and even homes. Most automobile engines have one built in.

The centrifugal pump is used to impart energy to a liquid. The Bernoulli equation can be used to determine the need for a pump: If the *required* downstream energy is greater than the *available* upstream energy, a pump is needed to bridge the gap.

The pump alone consists of three main parts: impeller, shaft, and housing. The impeller is flat, has vanes, and attaches to the shaft. The impeller is enclosed in a stationary housing and is made to turn by the shaft, which protrudes through the housing. Bearings are used to support the shaft. Static and dynamic seals are used to contain the liquid.

The inlet to a pump invariably leads to the center (the "eye") of the impeller, and, just as invariably, the outlet from a pump streams from the periphery of the impeller. Velocity, hence energy, is imparted to the liquid as follows. The shaft is forced (by a motor connected to it) to rotate at some speed, say 1750 r/min. From elementary physics (or deductive reasoning) we know that tangential velocity equals angular velocity multiplied by the distance from the axis of rotation:

$$v_t = \omega R$$

where ω is angular velocity in radians per second (see the definition below), and R is the distance from the center of rotation, in feet. For a 6.5-in impeller rotating at 1750 r/min, we have a tangential velocity of 49.6 ft/s at the outer edge. A liquid element traveling from the eye to the edge will find itself moving at an ever-increasing tangential velocity, pushed by an impeller vane (see Fig. 10-1). The housing, being stationary, will act to retard flow, while the impeller will act to promote flow. Most liquid at the periphery will not achieve 49.6 ft/s, but a small portion of the liquid, close to the vanes, will almost achieve this limiting velocity. The effect of the housing can be reduced by attaching a backplate to the vanes. This results in what is called a *semiopen impeller.*

A cover can also be placed over the vanes, becoming part of the impeller. This cover, called the *shroud,* keeps the body of liquid moving through the impeller from being disturbed by the stationary housing. Liquid in a shrouded impeller will achieve a higher tangential velocity than liquid in a nonshrouded impeller.

A shrouded (or *enclosed*) impeller operates with lower friction losses than the impeller with exposed vanes (called the *open impeller*). For all liquids, the shrouded impeller is preferred. For liquids that contain solids, judgment and analysis are required to decide between the higher efficiency of a shrouded impeller and the superior solids-handling capability of the open impeller.

Because the main purpose of this chapter is to illuminate how to analyze equipment operation, we take a brief detour for a look at solids in centrifugal pumps.

Obviously any solid particle larger than the separation between the shroud and the backplate will be caught by a shrouded impeller. It is worth taking into account that even a clean liquid, such as steam condensate, may carry a clump of iron oxide every now and then. In a concentrated slurry, even a pair of particles whose sum of sizes exceeds the separation stands a good chance of meeting, just right, and forming a bridge, which will trap other particles. Use of an open impeller can alleviate the situation some, because it becomes possible to grind a friable particle, enabling it to pass. For shrouded impellers, the particle size limits of one-fifth or one-tenth of the impeller opening may be in order, depending on the solids concentration. For fibrous solids, special semiopen impellers having vanes with rounded edges are needed [ATD].

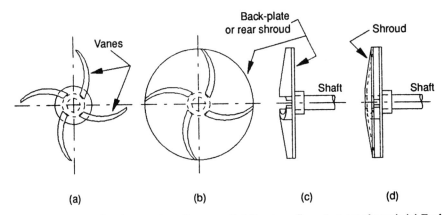

Figure 10-1 Centrifugal pump impellers—radial-flow type (housing not shown). (*a*) End view (open impeller); (*b*) end view (semi-open impeller); (*c*) side view (semi-open impeller); (*d*) side view (enclosed impeller).

These facts are self-evident, once they are considered. It is part of the engineer's/designer's job to consider such possibilities during the course of work. The engineer/designer must constantly ask how a given piece of equipment can be fouled, then ascertain either that the process will never operate in such a mode or that the consequences are tolerable. If fouling is a possibility, these are the ways to remove the cause of fouling:

- Change the process (install a filter, raise temperature, etc.).
- Use a different type of equipment.

Another option is to provide for quick, economic servicing (without shutting down, if possible).

Under no circumstances should a potential fouling problem be ignored.

Now we return to operating principles of centrifugal pumps. If the pump is operating in a shutoff condition (that is, no flow through the pump, just liquid churning around with the impeller), the liquid should achieve a tangential velocity quite close to that of the impeller (assuming a shrouded impeller). Therefore, the shutoff pressure should be approximated by the pressure in a centrifuge full of liquid. This pressure is readily derived from elementary calculus and can be compared to measured values in the vendor literature. Here a derivation along the lines given by McCabe and Smith [53] is presented to show how a fundamental property of pumps can easily be deduced.*

Figure 10-2 shows a centrifuge with an unchanging quantity of liquid and with a vapor space between the centerline and the liquid level. In a pump, this interface would exist only in an abnormal condition. Here it is shown for the purpose of the derivation. It can be made to equal zero by selecting the appropriate constant of integration.

The force needed to restrain a rotating mass is

$$f = m \times r \times \omega^2 \quad \frac{\text{lbm} \cdot \text{ft}}{\text{s}^2} \qquad (10\text{-}1)$$

where m is the mass of the object (lb), r is the distance from the center of rotation (ft), and ω is the angular speed (rad/s).†

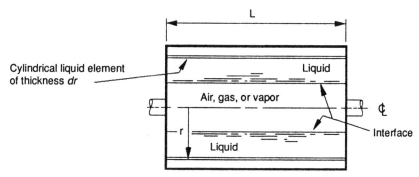

Figure 10-2 Centrifuge.

---

*The McCabe and Smith text is a classic and is a good starting point for learning about many different types of equipment.

†The radian is really a dimensionless unit, since it is the ratio of two lengths: circumferential distance divided by radius (c/r). See the determination of ω below.

In the case of the centrifuge, where a small element of mass is being considered, the equation is written in differential form:

$$df = dm \times r \times \omega^2 \qquad (10\text{-}2)$$

Then noting that

$$dm = \rho L(2\pi r\, dr) \qquad (10\text{-}3)$$

we write

$$df = \rho L(2\pi)\omega^2 r^2\, dr \qquad (10\text{-}4)$$

This element of force is converted to an element of pressure by dividing by the area over which the force is spread: $A = 2\pi rL$. The result is

$$dp' = \rho\omega^2 r\, dr \qquad \frac{\text{lbm}}{\text{ft} \cdot \text{s}^2} \qquad (10\text{-}5)$$

which upon integration gives

$$p' = \frac{1}{2}(\rho\omega^2 r^2) + C \qquad (10\text{-}6)$$

Since we are deriving an expression for shutoff pressure of a pump, and since pump curves are based on a pressure rise across the pump, we set $C = 0$. The result gives the increase in pressure above the inlet pressure as a function of the distance from the center of rotation. Now, inserting the impeller radius R, we have an expression to estimate shutoff pressure:

$$p' = \frac{1}{2}\rho\omega^2 R^2 \qquad (10\text{-}7)$$

This is made more comprehensible and useful by converting the pressure to feet of fluid. Both sides are multiplied by a conversion factor: $1/(\rho g)$. The result is

$$p = \frac{p'}{\rho g} = \frac{\omega^2 R^2}{2g} \qquad \text{ft} \qquad (10\text{-}8)$$

This equation can be prepared for regular use* with commonly encountered dimensions. Expressing rotational velocity in rotations per minute and impeller radius in inches, we finally arrive at

$$p = (1.186 \times 10^{-6})R^2 N^2 \qquad \text{ft} \qquad (10\text{-}9)$$

The test of Eq. (10-9) is presented in Table 10-1. The observed values are for two commercially available pumps, having shrouded impellers, from the Peerless Pump Company [54]. Judging from the ratio of observed to calculated values, our homemade equation for shutoff pressure is a resounding success. One is inclined to attribute deviations to the measured, not the calculated, value.

For open impellers, the observed values are up to 30 percent higher than the calculated values.† This is due to a shearing effect of the vanes, not due to rotational velocity.

---

*Any equation used repeatedly should be reduced to a dimensional form that employs the most readily used dimensions. A list of these readily usable equations should be kept at hand along with an extensive table of conversion factors. Appendix E can be consulted for examples.

†Results not shown here.

TABLE 10-1 Evaluation of Equation for Shutoff Pressure.

Peerless impeller number	R, in	N, r/min	P Calculated, ft	P Observed, ft	Ratio
2689502	4.0	1150	25.1	23.7	0.945
2689502	4.5	1150	31.8	31.7	0.998
2689502	5.0	1150	39.2	38.9	0.992
2689502	4.0	1750	58.1	55.2	0.950
2689502	4.5	1750	73.5	73	0.993
2689502	5.0	1750	90.8	92	1.013
2692719	4.0	1750	58.1	59	1.015
2692719	4.625	1750	77.7	81	1.043
2692719	5.25	1750	100.1	102	1.019
2692719	4.0	3500	232.4	238	1.024
2692719	4.625	3500	310.7	322	1.036
2692719	5.25	3500	400.4	416	1.039

When a centrifugal pump flows, the discharge pressure usually drops off. There may be a part of its operation, near shutoff, where the pressure may be higher than the shutoff pressure (due to the shape and orientation of the vanes), but most of the useful operating range of a pump is where the generated pressure drops as the flow increases (see Fig. 10-3). This drop results from liquid not achieving full rotational speed—and from friction.

Curves 1 and 2 are typical of centrifugal pumps. Curve 1 is meant to represent the same pump as curve 2, but one using a larger impeller or running at a higher speed. Given one curve, the other curve can be derived by using *affinity laws:*

Changing impeller diameter (constant speed):

$$\frac{D_1}{D_2} = \frac{Q_1}{Q_2} = \frac{\sqrt{H_1}}{\sqrt{H_2}} \qquad (10\text{-}10)$$

Changing impeller speed (constant diameter):

$$\frac{N_1}{N_2} = \frac{Q_1}{Q_2} = \frac{\sqrt{H_1}}{\sqrt{H_2}} \qquad (10\text{-}11)$$

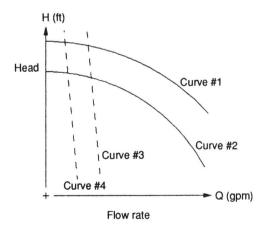

Figure 10-3 Typical pump curves.

When a pump is purchased, the impeller is trimmed on a lathe at the vendor's shop to a diameter large enough to provide the needed capacity, but not so large that excessive power is wasted across a throttling valve [ATD].

New values for brake horsepower can be estimated for small changes in diameter and speed by the following:

Changing impeller diameter (constant speed):

$$\frac{BHP_1}{BHP_2} = \left(\frac{D_1}{D_2}\right)^3 \qquad (10\text{-}12)$$

Changing impeller speed (constant diameter):

$$\frac{BHP_1}{BHP_2} = \left(\frac{N_1}{N_2}\right)^3 \qquad (10\text{-}13)$$

The relations presented here are taken from *Cameron Hydraulic Data* [55]. These relations are kept dimensionless by using numerators and denominators in the same units. The relations are valid only for true centrifugal pumps, that is, those having *radial* flow through the impeller.

For comparison purposes, the "curves" of a positive displacement pump have been included in Fig. 10-3. They are identified as curve 3 and curve 4. Curves 3 and 4 are for the same pump, but curve 3 is for a higher speed. It can be seen that the positive displacement pump has a natural ability for delivering a constant flow, whereas the centrifugal pump displays a tendency to provide constant pressure. This is why centrifugal pumps are usually throttled and positive displacement pumps are rarely throttled. In the near future, the availability of lower-cost, variable-speed motors will result in less throttling of centrifugal pumps, however.

The centrifugal pump is popular not only because it is fairly economical to use, but also because it is easy to apply and remarkably adaptable. Examples of the last two features can be discerned from the curves shown in Fig. 10-3. Ease of application results from the large operating range over which this pump will perform. As long as its pressure-generating capability is not overwhelmed, it is capable of delivering *any* flow rate from its maximum design value to zero. Its adaptability results from being able to change impellers and rotational speeds.

Here is an example of the first feature mentioned above. It is a batch titration of the contents in a stirred tank. The P&ID depicting this activity is shown in Fig. 10-4. After the tank is filled with the batch, a 5% caustic solution is pumped carefully into the tank. Flow is regulated by a control valve and flow sensor working together. Supervising this activity, however, is a microprocessor-based pH controller working in conjunction with a timer. The controller senses pH at a probe in the tank and, via instructions in the controller's memory,* sets the flow rate. The initial flow is set at 15 gal/min. An endpoint at pH = 10.2 is sought. At pH = 9.5, flow is stopped temporarily by shutting the control valve. After a delay of 1 min, flow is restarted at 3 gal/min. At pH = 9.9 the flow is stopped again for 1 min. Thereafter, the valve is opened (full) for decreasing lengths of time (starting at 5 s) and shut for increasing lengths of time until the endpoint is

---

*A digital controller with a programmable read-only memory (PROM).

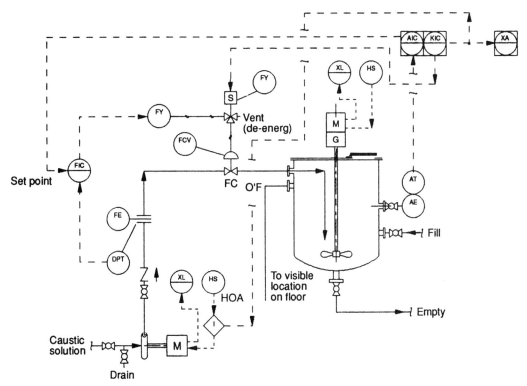

Figure 10-4 P&ID of neutralization tank.

reached. Once the endpoint has been achieved, the pump is shut off and an audible advisory signal is sounded to call the operator.

The pump in this case is being subjected to wildly fluctuating demands, and because it is a centrifugal pump, it can be expected to respond smoothly and reliably, without needing attention by the operator.

The second feature, the adaptability, is equally remarkable. Many years after a pump has been in service, it can be modified for use under wholly different conditions. A larger impeller (and motor) can be installed to accommodate a greater pressure requirement. Or a smaller impeller can be installed, for economy reasons, once the pump's actual operating requirements are better understood. A mechanical seal can frequently be "retrofitted" to replace a packed seal. The pump speed can be changed for reasons of economy, delivery pressure, or delivery rate.

Power (also from *Cameron Hydraulic Data* [56]) is calculated from the following dimensional equation:

$$\text{BHP} = \frac{QHS}{3960E} \qquad (10\text{-}14)$$

where Q = flow rate, gal/min
H = head developed by pump, ft
S = specific gravity
E = pump efficiency

Since a hydraulic efficiency factor is included, the equation gives the actual power required at the *pump* shaft. This is usually fairly close to the output power of the motor, since the remaining losses due to bearings and gears tend to be small. One should not dismiss, offhand, these other losses, however, until they have been reviewed. The

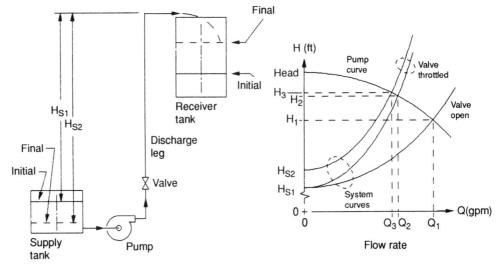

Figure 10-5 Centrifugal pump operating points.

motor finally selected should be the next size larger than the greatest calculated power requirement. The greatest calculated power requirement is sometimes based on the largest impeller that will fit in the pump. Usually such a measure cannot be justified. The best policy is to identify the condition where maximum power draw will occur and add 15 percent for a safety margin. Even if an expansion of plant capacity is anticipated within a couple of years, it is usually wiser to obtain an appropriately sized motor. The greatest power draw will usually occur at the greatest flow rate.

Figure 10-5 shows a very common situation. A pump is used to elevate a liquid from a low tank to a tank at a higher elevation. The curves to the right of the diagram are for the pump (concave down) and for the system (concave up) under three different conditions. The intersection points of the pump curve and the system curves are called *operating points.*

A system curve is the curve that would result from plotting pressure drop versus flow with the pump absent. Imagine Fig. 10-5 without the pump and with the valve wide open. Initially flow would be zero, and the level in the discharge leg would be at the same level as the liquid in the supply tank. If a pressure of magnitude H_{S1} were applied to the liquid surface at the supply tank, the liquid level in the discharge leg would rise to the upper elbow. Once there, it would cease movement. A condition of static equilibrium would exist. This is the point of incipient flow. A slight increase of pressure will result in flow; a decrease in pressure will result in a drop of static level in the discharge leg.

The system curve is generated by starting with the point on the H axis. This is called the *static head* point. Here $Q = 0$, and the friction loss is zero as a consequence. Friction losses (plus the velocity head at the discharge) are then calculated for two or three flows (assuming a wide-open throttle valve), and the results are added to H_{S1}. The resulting points (Q and H) are plotted, generating the lowest system curve.

The middle curve is identical to the lowest curve, with this sole exception: A friction loss due to partial closing of the valve is added. The starting point does not change. All other points do change and must include the higher friction. The highest curve is identical to the middle curve, except that it is moved upward by the difference in initial and final levels.

A simple way of envisioning system curves is to first imagine the pump as being nonexistent and then imagine a flow experiment with different flow rates through the system. Each different flow rate will result in a corresponding pressure drop. Each pair of H,Q points will be a point on the system curve. Such a flow experiment would yield a family of curves: one curve for each control valve position (wide open always being the lowest), another curve for each tank level, etc. It cannot be emphasized strongly enough that it is the duty of the engineering/design professionals to perform analyses similar to those outlined here on every pump* for which they are responsible. Anything less could be construed as nonprofessional performance. This need only be done during vendor print review, but for large pumps a "dry run" prior to inquiry should be considered.

Before we move on to another topic, you are asked to envision yourself operating the system in Fig. 10-5. At first, with the valve wide open, the flow is at its highest (Q_1), and the pump pressure (H_1) is at its lowest. By cutting back on the valve, the flow falls off (Q_2), but the pressure increase across the pump rises (H_2). Finally, when the supply tank is close to empty, the flow is diminished even more (Q_3), and the pump pressure contribution is greater. (Does this agree with common sense?) When the valve is completely shut, flow goes to zero and the pump pressure increase is the greatest. (Does this make sense?)

The technique, just described, of envisioning an operation while watching, manipulating, and asking rhetorical questions is a staple of engineering/design. Even the meteorologist with the greatest computer and the clearest satellite images should peer out the window frequently.

Two more topics of great practical concern for good results in applying centrifugal pumps are NPSH and power dissipation in a shutoff condition. NPSH stands for *net positive suction head.* The *available* NPSH must exceed the NPSH required by the pump manufacturer. The available NPSH is calculated by using the Bernoulli equation. The required NPSH, or NPSHR, is obtained from vendor pump data. The available NPSH, often referred to as NPSHA, is the absolute pressure at the eye of an impeller minus the vapor pressure.† As long as NPSHA is 3 or 4 ft of fluid or more than NPSHR, all is well. If this difference is from 2 to 3 ft of fluid, the situation should be carefully reviewed, probably with the assistance of the pump vendor. If the difference is less than 2 ft, the design should be changed.

Without a sufficient amount of head at the eye of an impeller, the delivery pressure will drop sharply, and the pump will make a rattling sound (cavitation). Both these phenomena are due to the formation and collapse of vapor bubbles in the wake of impeller vanes as they turn. The collapse of the vapor bubbles is similar to tiny explosions repeatedly occurring at the surface of the impeller, and eventually it leads to damage to the impeller.

Often the effects of dissolved gases on vapor pressure are overlooked, yet the flashing of dissolved gas can make or break an appli-

---

*Or, for that matter, on other types of prime movers for liquids, gases, and solids.

†By convention established by pump manufacturers, the absolute pressure at the impeller eye is taken as the pressure at the suction flange *plus* the velocity pressure at the suction flange. In other words, it is supposed that the velocity energy at the pump suction is converted to pressure energy at the impeller.

cation. The key element to watch for is the pumping of a liquid pressurized by a gas or a liquid that may contain dissolved gas, such as a fermentation liquid. Good descriptions of dealing with this problem are given by both Penney [57] and Tsai [58].

The shutoff, or deadheaded, pump can be a problem when the heat generated by the continuous agitation cannot be dissipated adequately. In such a situation, the pump temperature can rise to a point where damage to the pump or degradation of the fluid can occur. With small pumps this problem is not as great as it is for large pumps.

Cameron Hydraulic Data [59] gives the following formula for calculating the temperature rise of a fluid on its passage through a pump:

$$\Delta T = \frac{H(1 - E)}{778E} \tag{10-15}$$

This formula is *not* recommended because it ignores heat capacity and it assumes that none of the viscous heat is lost to the surroundings. As a matter of fact, an infinite temperature rise is predicted at shutoff.

For shutoff, the best way to proceed is to perform a heat balance on the pump by using the brake horsepower at shutoff as the heat input. Then, by assuming surface temperatures on the pump of 15 and 30 degrees higher than ambient, two trial heat losses can be quickly estimated and a decision made as to whether overheating might be a problem. If the pump is rubber-lined, the insulating effect of the lining must be taken into account.

If a deadheaded pump can be avoided, it is best to do so. When it cannot be avoided, a bypass line from the discharge to the tank supplying the suction is often provided. This line is sized to allow a minor amount of fluid to mix back with the feed. The feed, in turn, is a relatively great heat sink.

Other types of pump will impart energy to a liquid. A few common varieties are shown in Table 10-2.

The gear pump, the screw pump, and the progressing cavity pump are all capable of pumping liquids of high viscosity. The screw and the gear pump are known to have been successfully used on liquids having a viscosity of 3×10^6 cP without appearing to have reached a limit. The remaining pumps can be used, with some minor corrections to their performance capabilities, on liquids having viscosities up to about 500 cP. Beyond 500 cP, they can be used, but the equipment vendor should be consulted.

TABLE 10-2 Common Pumps and Usual Conditions for Their Use

Type	Usual capacity range, gal/min		Usual maximum pressure, lb/in²	Solids tolerance	Positive displacement		Relative cost
	Low	High			Smooth	Pulsing	
Centrifugal	5	3,000	100	Yes	NA	NA	Low
Axial	200	30,000	40	Yes	NA	NA	Low
Plunger	5	3,000	500	Yes*		Yes	High
Piston	0.01	3	10,000	No		Yes	High
Diaphragm	0.01	3	3,000	No		Yes	High
Gear	0.001	10	1,000	No	Yes		Low
Screw	0.01	20	1,000	Yes	Yes		High
Progressing cavity	0.2	40	200	Yes	Yes		Medium

*Not normal, but can be accommodated.

HOODS, DUCTS, AND FANS

A good subtitle for this section would be "Pickup of Gas, Vapor, Fume, Mist, and Dust." This section is important because, all too often, air-flows in and around a process are taken for granted, just as we take air for granted while we breathe it. Perhaps there is a subconscious thought in the minds of many engineers/designers causing them to think that air is "natural," and so it can't (or shouldn't) be dominated in the course of process design. Maybe because it can't be seen, it's overlooked (out of sight, out of mind). Whatever the cause, pickup of gases, fumes, etc., does not get the attention it deserves on most projects.

The following example illustrates that *small and detailed* [ATD] does not equate to trivial. It is a good example of how the parts and pieces of some things cost less than the engineering and design effort for conceiving them.

Here is the situation. A specialty liquid polymer product is to be loaded into drums. Oxygen causes cross-linking, so oxygen must be prevented from reaching the polymer. Whatever is to be provided must not interfere with other drum-loading operations for other products. Fume collection is thought to be worthwhile, as some of the raw materials are toxic.

Figure 10-6 shows the final result. The initial problem-solving, conceptual period requires about 20 min. A hand-drawn sketch and a handwritten note for the client require about another 20 min. A review with the client 2 days later requires another 20 min. As a result of this review, a formal memorandum is written, typed, and sent to interested parties. The P&ID is updated to show

- One new nitrogen user
- One new pickup point for the scrubber
- A new rotameter-valve combination
- A short piece of hose or tubing
- Two pipe stubs (closed on top, open on the bottom, and adapted for the hose), a vent, and the polymer line

Detailed descriptions of the last two items are shown by a designer on two 8.5 × 11 in sized drawings as *specialty items.* This requires 2 h.

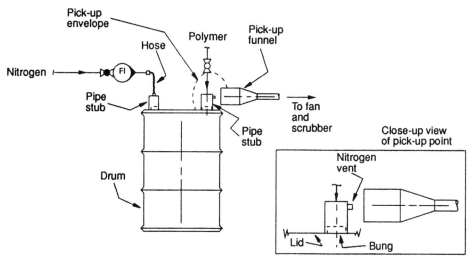

Figure 10-6 Nitrogen purge and vapor pickup.

Another 2 h is needed to show the piping and duct connections. It is estimated that clerical handling and miscellaneous dealings with these parts and pieces require another 2 h of labor during the engineering/design phase.

Here is how the pickup will work. An empty drum (previously purged with nitrogen) will be put in place at the filling spot. A 50 cm^3/min flow will be set on the rotameter. Temporary plastic caps are to be removed from the bungholes, and the pipe stub connected to the nitrogen will be placed on the small bunghole (not screwed, just placed upright). The polymer fill line (with pipe stub welded to it) will be lowered into the large bunghole. Nitrogen will flow through the drum and out the vent in the vicinity of the pickup funnel. Polymer flowing into the drum will displace additional nitrogen.

The pickup funnel will draw air around the pipe stub, ensuring that nitrogen and fumes from the vent will not escape. Presumably any gas-phase element within the pickup envelope would be sucked into the pickup funnel. Elements outside of this envelope might or might not be aspirated.

For this installation, positive measures are taken to ensure that oxygen will not reach the polymer. By these measures, polymer crosslinking will cease to be a quality problem.

This example shows the basic three rules for *pickup*

- Gases, including room air, are guided by means of barriers to acceptable destinations.

- Pickup points are placed close to sources to minimize airflow.

- Gaps between the *process* and the *atmosphere* are kept small.

plus the one overriding rule for all design work:

- Nothing is left to chance.

We will see more of this. Now we go to another example.

A renderer* with four cookers is experiencing complaints from neighbors concerning odors from operations. The renderer has found that the cost of exhausting the whole building, by putting the air through a giant scrubber, will be prohibitive. An analysis of the operation leads to a design which is effective and affordable.

The greatest release of odor occurs when the cookers are opened at the end of the cooking step, after the hot grease is drained off. A cloud of vapor rises to the top of the building and continues to stream out as workers standing on a platform pull the solids from the cooker with long rakes into a screw conveyor. The diagram in Fig. 10-7 roughly shows this part of the operation. The quantity of vapor is estimated by taking notes and recording the sizes and rise rates of vapor clouds. The owner/operator reveals that the cookers can be run so that no more than one would be opened at a time. Also the lids could be eased open, then pulled away slowly, over a period of no less than 5 min, to avoid the great initial vapor rush. From other rendering operations, it is known that the odor can be removed by sending the vapors through a scrubber having a dilute caustic/hypochlorite solution.

---

*Renderers buy fat trimmings and waste from butcher shops, then cook them in their own grease to break them down. The solid product looks like bacon and is used in pet food. The liquid product is sold to soap manufacturers.

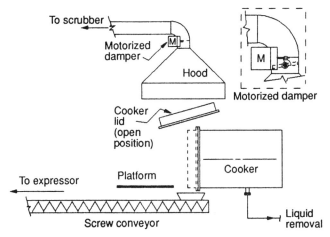

Figure 10-7 Diagram showing cooker and hood.

Required airflows to pick up the fumes are calculated. Initially a uniform face velocity across the hood of 2 ft/s is assumed. However, calculations reveal a fairly large airflow. On the other hand, if only the vapors, undiluted with air, could be sucked into the ducting from the hood, a modest vapor flow would result. As a result, calculations are made while assuming vinyl flaps hanging from the hood to 3 ft above the platform. The envelope separating "process" from "atmosphere" is taken as the open area between the vinyl curtain and the platform. Because the cloud will rise away from this envelope, it was judged that a face velocity at the envelope of 0.5 ft/s will be adequate to keep the fumes headed toward the hood. (This is based solely on the earlier *observations*—not from a text or from theory.) The resulting calculated flows turn out to be acceptable.

Hoods with vinyl-strip curtains are placed over the cookers. The ductwork, fan, and scrubbers are sized for a single cooker being opened (slowly) at any time. Motorized dampers placed in the duct above each hood are interlocked so that only one damper can be opened at once.

After installation, complaints from neighbors ceased.

This example uses all four rules mentioned above.

This work also makes use of measurements. This is often the case. Occasionally, a $1200 anemometer may be needed; if so, it should be purchased or leased. In most cases, a simple smoke test (from a cigarette or a quenched match, or with vapor from ammonia solution mixing with vapor of hydrochloric acid solution) will suffice. Sometimes a pinch of dust dribbled from the fingers, or a fiber from some fabric, can be watched to judge the velocity and size of a gas-phase flow.* When dealing with flow in a duct, the engineer should not hesitate to drill $\frac{1}{8}$-in holes in the duct (with the owner's permission and knowing that a dangerous condition will not ensue) to take pressure readings. Pressure measurement, of course, will require a manometer (something easy to acquire, or one can be made from clear tubing and a piece of cardboard in a half-hour or so). A simple, single-leg Pitot tube can easily be fashioned from $\frac{1}{8}$- to $\frac{1}{4}$-in metal tubing. Orifice plates can be quickly cut from cardboard, sheet metal, plywood,

---

*The great, and practical, Enrico Fermi is reported to have judged the energy of the first atomic bomb by dropping scraps of paper and measuring their horizontal travel when the shock wave was felt at that 1945 test blast in New Mexico [60].

acrylic sheet, etc. When a measurement is needed, there is no excuse for not making it.

The work described above also makes use of knowledge regarding fluids and the gas phase in particular. Continual observations of all sorts of phenomena, from fog swirling around the back end of the garage on a cool evening to vapor rising off the surface of a bowl of soup, are important. Visualization of streamlines and potential lines is important. In this regard, the results of conformal mapping for basic flow phenomena (the corner, the open tube, the cylinder, the flat blade, etc.) are quite useful. (Figure 10-8 gives flowlines and constant-velocity lines at the entrance of a cylindrical duct.)

Finally, the energy balance (that is, the Bernoulli equation) requires understanding and application.

Before we go on to the next topic, we take a look at another industrial operation for pickup of an airborne material. In this case, the sought material is generated during the final stages in the manufacture of lithium hydroxide monohydrate ($LiOH \cdot H_2O$). See Fig. 10-9. The capture of this material is important not only for environmental and economic reasons but also because a small droplet or fine particle, when caught in the mucous membranes of the nose or throat, causes an extremely strong choking sensation. No person can stand

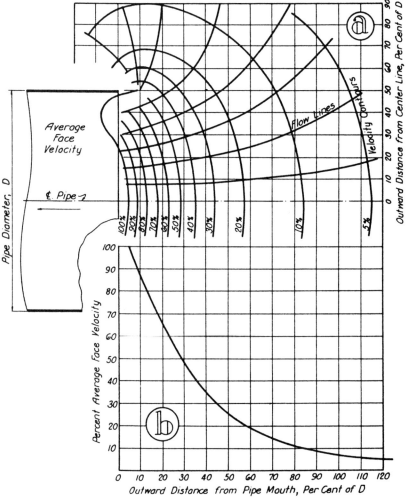

Figure 10-8 Streamlines and constant-velocity lines close to the end of a cylindrical intake. (*Design of Industrial Exhaust Systems [61], with permission.*)

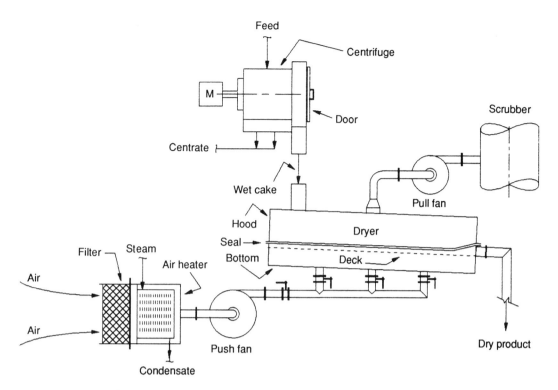

Figure 10-9 Process for drying lithium hydroxide.

more than a few micrometer-sized droplets or crystals before deciding to evacuate the area. Tolerating fugitive emissions from this equipment is out of the question.

The process consists of a centrifuge that takes a crystallizer slurry and spins off the great majority of the mother liquor (aqueous LiOH). This liquor is shown leaving the centrifuge as "centrate." The crystalline monohydrate, with residues of mother liquor clinging to it, is flung down a chute into a shallow-bed, vibrating, fluid-bed dryer. Wet masses of particles spread their liquid as a thin surface coating to dry material in the bed. Hot air blown into the bottom of the bed drives off liquid-phase water, but temperatures are kept low enough to leave the water of hydration intact.

During operation, the door of the centrifuge is opened for inspection (and to obtain samples) at least twice per shift. About once every 2 weeks, the operation is stopped for the purpose of removing solids accumulations. The centrifuge feed is stopped. The fans, dryer, etc., are turned off. The clamps holding the dryer hood to the body are removed, and the hood is raised about 2 ft to expose the inside. This seal between the hood and the body has the potential of leaking great amounts of fluidized material.

Under the circumstances just described, the only way of keeping the mist and dust from escaping is to make sure that leakage always occurs from the atmosphere *into* the process, *never* the other way around.

The scheme shown in Fig. 10-9 shows a push-pull design with two fans.

A single fan alone could probably never be made to work, because the fan would, of necessity, be placed as a *pull* fan. In that position, opening of the centrifuge door could not be tolerated (flow through the heater, and bed, would be lost). As a matter of fact, as we will see, with a pull fan alone, the centrifuge door would be hard to open, due to the atmosphere pushing it closed. The approach* to this design problem will be as follows: (1) Establish a reasonable airflow rate for moisture removal. (2) Using this flow rate, calculate pressure drops, assuming all dampers are wide open. (3) Choose a somewhat lower flow rate, and recalculate pressure drops. (4) Compare the two cases and see what conclusions can be drawn.

The process requires that 80 lb/h of free water be removed from the product on its way through the dryer. To avoid running the risk of losing the water of hydration, the solids must not reach a temperature higher than 200°F. Some bench tests by the dryer manufacturer suggest using an incoming air temperature of 250°F. The dryer manufacturer also suggests limiting the airflow so that the moist air leaving the dryer is at 140°F. This will result in a solids temperature close to 140°F, a good safe margin from the 200°F.

To find the amount of air needed, we go to a humidity chart, such as that shown in Fig. 10-10. Air taken into the heater from the atmosphere will already contain moisture. For our purposes, we will take as a worst condition 100°F and 100 percent relative humidity (RH). In Fig. 10-10 this is the point on the 100 percent RH curve directly above the 100°F temperature. The scale at the right indicates that the moisture content of such air is 0.043 lb of water per pound of dry air.

Two possibilities are examined in Fig. 10-10. The first, denoted *a*, represents the manufacturer's suggestions. The heating/evaporation cycle would be as follows: Entering air would be heated to 250°F, and air and water would be brought together where adiabatic evaporation

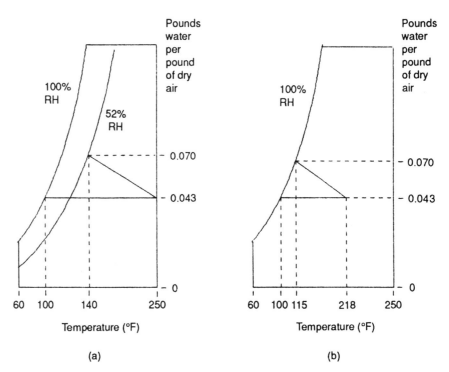

Figure 10-10 Humidity curves for air at 1-atm pressure. (*a*) Temperature with allowance for flexibility. (*b*) Minimum air temperature.

*The reader is asked to observe that a very common tactic is being employed here: A condition is set. Calculations are performed. Results are examined.

would occur. The final vapor would be at 140°F and would contain 0.070 lb water per pound of dry air. Its relative humidity would be about 50 percent. The second possibility, denoted *b*, has a cycle that ends on the 100 percent RH curve. The air is heated to 218°F. This is somewhat more energy-efficient, but will be difficult to operate, because of condensation in the ductwork and because control flexibility is absent.*

We note that the manufacturer's recommendation (scheme *a*) includes a margin for control flexibility. In either case, the amount of air is the same and is calculated as follows:

$$\frac{80}{0.070 - 0.043} = 3000 \text{ lb/h dry air}$$

This is roughly 980 acfm (at 250°F and 1 atm) and 860 acfm (at 140°F and 1 atm).

Table 10-3 lists friction losses based on the above flows. The losses are grouped together as five major "resistances," designated by *R* with an appropriate subscript. These resistances are shown in an abbreviated† diagram of the situation in Fig. 10-11. Velocity head has been subtracted in the suction line of the push fan.

The calculated friction losses alone are not enough to define pressures throughout the system. One additional condition is needed.

---

*When a minor process fluctuation cannot be corrected, *control flexibility* is said to be absent. The most usual example is a control valve that is wide open. If a signal is sent to open wider, it can't do it. Furthermore, it is no longer controlling. In the case of the dryer, if the air is leaving at 100 percent RH, carrying away 80 lb/h water, any increase in feed moisture will not be carried away in the air; it will go on through as an increase in product moisture.

†The ability to abbreviate and retain the essence of the subject at hand is of *primary* importance to problem solving and understanding equipment.

TABLE 10-3 Friction Losses in the Equipment and Ductwork of Fig. 10-9*

Equipment and ductwork	Loss, inches WC	
Filter	0.25	
Heater	0.30	$R_1 = 0.60$
Entrance	0.02	
Suction (push fan)	0.03	
Duct	0.06	
Elbows	0.23	$R_2 = 0.29$
Damper	0	
Exit	0.15	
Deck	8.0	$R_3 = 12.15$
Bed	4.0	
Entrance	0.01	
Duct (pull fan)	0.03	$R_4 = 0.04$
Duct	0.06	
Discharge	0.12	$R_5 = 0.48$
Scrubber	0.30	

*Losses are listed in the same sequence as they occur.

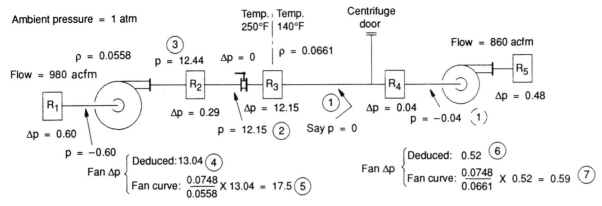

Figure 10-11 Abbreviated diagram—maximum-flow case.

What is finally chosen is shown in Fig. 10-11 (keyed by the numeral 1 in a solid circle). We say for the sake of argument that the pressure in the hood area of the dryer is equal to zero; that is, it is at atmospheric pressure. This does not represent a true design condition, but is adopted briefly for the sake of argument. If, indeed, such a condition were to be maintained during operation, some dust would surely escape from the hood because of turbulence. Nonetheless, it is a good limiting case to examine.

From this condition, we are able to deduce pressures throughout the system. The sequence of calculation is given by the remaining circled numerals. Two of the deduced numbers are required pressure increases across the two fans. These deduced fan pressures must be converted to equivalent fan performance at 70°F before further evaluation can continue. A review of the results turns up no anomalies.

The calculated fan operating points are marked (as solid circles) on their fan curves, shown in Fig. 10-12.

This maximum flow case is a limiting case. In practice, a plant would not operate in this fashion, because the operation would lack

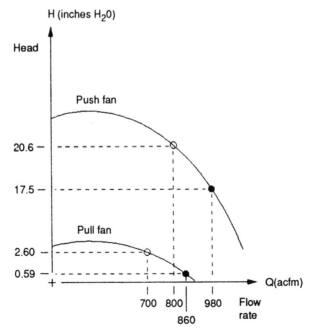

Figure 10-12 Fan curves and operating points. Conditions: air at 70°F, 1 atm.

the control flexibility mentioned above. Therefore, the next step is to calculate pressures at some reduced flow. The chosen flow is 800 acfm at the push fan.

Individual resistance pressure drops are scaled down from the original pressure drops by a factor of $(800/980)^2 = 0.67$. The new set of friction losses is written down on the flow diagram of Fig. 10-13. New pressure contributions from the fans are obtained from Fig. 10-12 (open circles). The fan curves are corrected to actual operating conditions. As above, the sequence of the final calculations is shown by the numbers in the circles in Fig. 10-13, the last one (8) being the pressure drop required across the damper.

A review of the pressures and pressure drops reveals that cutting back flow with the damper will result in a negative pressure (with respect to the atmosphere) under the dryer hood. This was the hoped for, and suspected, result. The calculated negative pressure, almost 2 inches WC, is too much for practice, but represents a limit: In reality the damper(s) would be set to maintain say −0.25 inches WC. Here we see control flexibility is available. If a fan impeller erodes or a duct starts plugging up, the damper(s) can be adjusted to compensate.

Throughout this exercise, air has been treated as incompressible. Since, at most, we are seeing pressure changes of 20 inches WC and because our reference pressure is about 34 ft WC, the volume changes are less than 5 percent. Thus the results are acceptable even for fairly exacting work.

Now, for the sake of curiosity, we'll estimate the force required to open the door of the centrifuge if the pressure at that point is −0.25 inches WC. We'll say the door has a 14-in diameter. The result is 0.7 lb. If only a pull fan had been employed and the hood pressure were −18 inches WC, a 50-lb tug would have been needed. The average operator would run the risk of injury in trying to open the centrifuge door! This is a perfect example of why calculations are needed for process project work [ATD].

Before going on to bins, we look back briefly and note that we have used elementary physics, some simple measurements, some elementary mathematics, and vendor information of different kinds to deal with hoods, ducts, and fans. The results have not been compromised by debilitating suppositions. The results could be used (and actually *were* used) to build parts of real process plants.

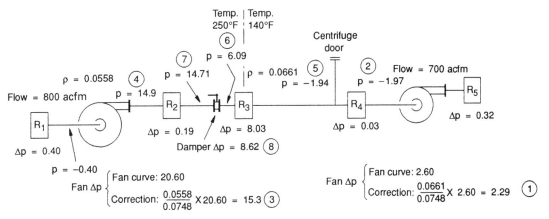

Figure 10-13 Abbreviated diagram—low-flow case.

BINS

In Chap. 9, under "Granular Solids," we noted that some granular solids possess cohesive strength. As a matter of fact, curve 2 on Fig. 9-33 was pointed to as an example of a granular solid having cohesive strength.

The bridge, or arch, that stops flow is aptly named. The principles which guide the construction of structural arches for gateways and bridges come about naturally with cohesive particles. The science of designing bin openings, hoppers, and reclaim schemes from piles is the science of providing for stresses that exceed the rupture stress. In general, this science is not simple and involves a good deal of testing and a sound capability in stress calculations. The brute-force approach of vibrating and pounding on the outside of a chute or bin bottom is often counterproductive in that it only serves as a gentle stimulus to compact the materials to a greater degree.

If a material displays strength, most usually called *cohesiveness*, careful attention should be given to bridging. The simplest test for cohesiveness is to grab a sample in the palm of a hand, squeeze hard, and observe whether a clump emerges. Of course, if the whole handful stays together, showing finger grooves and all, the material obviously displays cohesiveness. If only a tiny clump makes an appearance every now and then, a minor amount of cohesiveness is displayed. It is this quality that makes bridges. Cohesiveness can be evaluated quantitatively by measuring static friction by using the shear test device. This is shown in Fig. 9-33 as a displacement from the origin, labeled strength. It is also measured by forming a test cylinder and compressing it to fracture, just as with concrete test cylinders.

The distinction between free-flowing solids, on one hand, and cohesive solids, on the other hand, is an important one.

Cohesiveness, when it is present, should be evaluated under the whole range of process conditions to be expected. Bin pressures, humidities, temperatures, times of storage, contaminants—all these and more—can impact heavily on cohesiveness.

A rough idea of how the hopper opening can affect bridging is given here. Figure 10-14 shows $D_2 > D_1$; therefore, three factors will cause higher stresses in the bridge across D_2 which will foster its failure: (1) this larger arch will not be as thick, (2) the span will be greater, and (3) the shear forces at the hopper wall will be greater.

For a bin of a given diameter and height, the size of the hole in the bottom is probably the most important variable available for manipulation during the design of the bin.

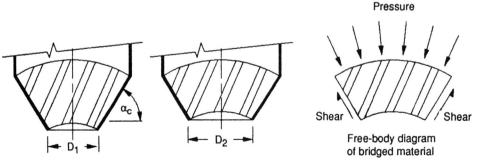

Figure 10-14 Cohesive dome in a bin.

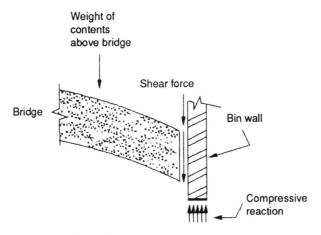

Figure 10-15 Bin wall compression.

The next most important variable is the slope of the hopper—generally, steeper slopes make solids flow better. This is often perceived as adding some height, and therefore cost, but the actual cost in terms of dollars per *active* cubic foot of bin volume may indeed be lower.

Other design features such as coatings on the inside walls, or heaters outside the walls (to prevent freezing or condensation), or aeration devices, can be used to promote flow also. However, the hopper opening and slope should be the starting point with any design.

Two cautions are worth emphasizing here concerning bridging across the whole bin and forces resulting from air injection. In the case of bridging, the entire weight of material above the bridge is supported by the bridge and, in turn, by the bin wall under the outside of the bridge. This can put a compressive stress in a place where it was never planned* and can lead to buckling of the bin wall (Fig. 10-15). In the case of air injection, a similar situation can arise in that stresses unknown to the bin designer can suddenly be imposed with unforeseen catastrophic effects.

With the two basic types of solids (free-flowing or cohesive) the most commonly encountered flow situations are

- Funnel flow (free-flowing material only†)
- Mass flow (free-flowing material only†)
- Intermittent bridging (external stimulus required)
- Rathole flow
- Fluidized flow

Figure 10-16 illustrates three of the flow types. The following discussion is limited to situations where flow is from a point beneath the center of a bin or pile.

Funnel flow is the type of flow that occurs in an hourglass. The core

---

*In almost all cases, bin wall strength calculations are done by the bin vendor to accommodate proprietary features. In general, a bin wall will be sized for tension to contain bin pressure, plus a combination of tension and compression for wind loads on the exterior, plus seismic accelerations.

†Actually, a cohesive material will flow in funnel or mass modes as long as cohesion limits of time and pressure are not exceeded. When the limits are exceeded, either a plugged bin or a rathole is the result.

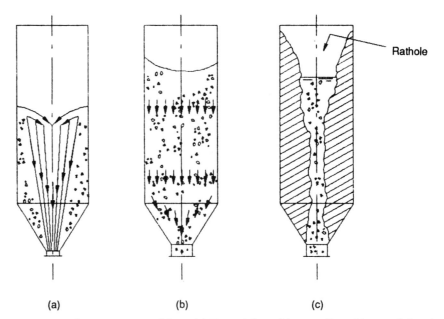

Rathole

Figure 10-16 Common types of flow. (*a*) Funnel flow; (*b*) mass flow; (*c*) consolidated material around a rathole.

of material directly over the outlet is most disposed to flow. The material against the walls is least disposed to flow. The material moves down the core at a rate so fast that surrounding material slides into the resulting void, becoming new core material. The angle that the upper surface makes with the horizontal closely approximates the angle of repose. Funnel flow is often depicted with a cylindrical core over the outlet. With low-friction materials, the cylinder is more like a steep cone. This suggests acceleration of the particles as they descend toward the opening.

Mass flow is similar to funnel flow except that the flowing material occupies the whole bin, not just the central shaft. Mass flow is desirable because the material along the walls and in the corners does not stagnate. This cuts down on the opportunity for consolidation and plugging. If mass flow can be achieved conveniently, it is usually the most desirable kind of flow for most purposes. A funnel flow bin can be converted to a mass flow bin by

- Enlarging the opening
- Making the hopper steeper
- Reducing internal friction
- Employing a low-friction wall material

Johanson [62] gives as criteria for mass flow from cylindrical hoppers

$$\alpha_c < 38 + 1.39\phi'$$

where α_c is the angle between the hopper wall and the horizontal (see Fig. 10-14) and ϕ' is the angle of friction between the solids and the hopper wall. This condition states that the slope of the hopper wall must be greater than 38 degrees, plus a factor for the friction between the solid and the hopper wall.

Apparently this criterion covers all reasonable conditions for flow such as opening size, internal friction, etc. The rule is generally regarded as a good one, but it should be tested over the range of expected process conditions before being used. A few early, simple sliding friction tests can be used to provide guidance for more exacting work at a later date. These early tests, in fact, may show that mass flow without external stimulation is not possible. Having this single piece of information can be exceedingly useful.

Probably the most common form of granular flow encountered in industry is where external energy is provided to promote flow when it is needed. For the engineer, this is a safe way to proceed as long as the flow promotion devices are not too costly. See Fig. 10-17.

The external energy is usually provided by a slowly rotating agitator placed where a bridge is most likely to occur. Alternately, the energy can be injected via air (or inert gas), or by using the hopper bottom as a conveyor. When such measures are taken, most arches are broken as they are formed.

The *agitator* (not shown here) is commonly seen on small feeders for powders. Air injectors are usually seen on larger installations, mostly for powders. The moving bottom, in one form or another, is seen on all kinds of installations.*

Figure 10-17 shows three distinct types of moving bottom. The table feeder and the multiple screw are used for exceedingly cohesive

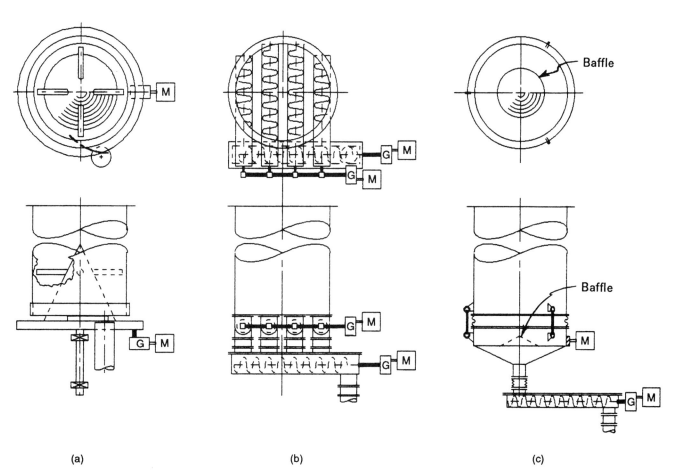

(a)   (b)   (c)

Figure 10-17 Three types of moving bottom. (*a*) Table feeder; (*b*) multiple screw; (*c*) live bottom.

---

*The bin vibrator is still to be seen. However, its use has declined as operators and engineers have become aware of its effects as a *compactor*. Where the solids loading is light, the vibrator can be used to *convey* the solids toward a desirable location.

materials, including wet filter cakes, iron oxide pigment, starch, etc. The live bottom is used on somewhat cohesive materials, but not as cohesive as the types just mentioned. The live bottom is used much more than the other two kinds of devices and possibly may be specified on more than 10 percent of the storage bins installed today. It is ubiquitous.

With a very sticky material, two commonsense rules are worth observing:

- Always* keep the material moving.
- Never provide more than a bare minimum of storage volume.

This latter rule explains why table feeders and multiple screws are generally applied on small bins. On the other hand, the live bottom is used on both large and small bins.

On all three of these feeders the basis of operation is removal of material by means of a conveying device. This is fairly evident with the table feeder and the multiple screw. With the live bottom, a bridge is formed between the baffle and the shallow conical bottom, but this bridge is broken by the oscillatory motion of the bottom. A common amplitude of motion is from 0.5 to 1 in. This motion not only breaks bridges as they form, but also conveys material down the shallow cone to the outlet. The live bottom differs from the common bin vibrator in three respects:

- Much higher power
- Large amplitudes of motion
- The flexible connector between the bottom and the bin

With respect to this last feature, note that the bottom is free to move horizontally, because its only support is from three swinging links. In cases where the bridge between the baffle and the bottom cone is sufficiently strong, flow from a bin having a live bottom can be started and stopped simply by turning the motor on or off. This isn't always the case, however. In Fig. 10-17c a screw conveyor is depicted under the live bottom. This feature is used when the material in the bin is mostly free-flowing in nature and so will have a tendency to keep flowing once it gets started. In such a case, both motors are stopped to halt flow. In such a case, the live bottom serves to get flow started, and the screw conveyor is provided to make sure flow stops when required. Many other configurations are possible.

The screw conveyor can often be used as a coarse regulator of flow rate (say ± 2 percent by weight) by providing it with a variable-speed motor.†

A small snip of *value analysis* is worth introducing at this point. We ask what we're trying to accomplish (that is, the *function*) with solids storage and recovery. Almost invariably the answer is the provision of surge capacity. One piece of equipment might run fast for brief periods (such as a briquetter). The feed to this piece might be from a slower device that operates for longer periods (such as a paddle mixer). Surge capacity (in this case, provided by the paddle mixer it-

---

*Or to the extent practical.

†Flow control accuracies 10 times better (± 0.2 percent) can be achieved by use of a weigh-belt feeder or a loss-of-weight feeder.

self) is needed.* More than likely, a list of required features will look similar to this:

- No bridging
- No stagnation points
- Adequate capacity
- Low wear and low care
- Reasonable cost†

For the most part, the live bottom satisfies these requirements. Also, in passing, note that the devices in Fig. 10-17 all have the ability to *gather* material from a large area and transport it to a relatively small area (from the bin as a whole, to a chute).

The flow rates of the devices in Fig. 10-17a and b can be estimated by using a fraction‡ of the displaced volumes. The flow rate of the device in Fig. 10-17c can be estimated by using the formula for free flow of solids through an opening:

$$W_S{}^2 = \frac{g\rho_B h(\rho_B - \rho_f)}{\tan \alpha} \tag{10-16}$$

where W_S = mass flux, lb/(s · ft^2)
      g = acceleration due to gravity, ft/s^2
     ρ_B = bulk density of solids, lbm/ft^2
     ρ_f = density of fluid, lbm/ft^2
     h = short side of rectangular opening (ft), or diameter for circular opening
     α = angle of internal friction

This formula was obtained by Zenz and Zenz [63, 64] as a result of working with a refinery catalyst.§ Zenz and Zenz recommend limiting its use to cases where the largest particle is smaller than $\frac{1}{16} h$.

A FINAL EXAMPLE CONCERNING SOLIDS

The reason for covering granular solids so extensively here is to give the reader an idea of the level of detail required to deal with real, live issues and to cover a subject that has (probably) not been presented in college coursework. Thus, this subject is tinged with the uncertainty that figures into most work encountered in designing and building process facilities. Problem identification and problem solving are shown. Many times the solution is not by calculation, but by observation of what works. This way, the reader can appreciate the degree of judgment often needed.

It is hoped that the reader will see that in today's world (where it may seem that few unexplored areas exist) here is an area (among

---

*See Fig. 11-4 for a diagram of this setup. The reader is requested to note whether Fig. 11-4 is any help in understanding the description of the paddle mixer/briquetter. This is meant as an example of how the understanding of concepts is aided by the use of symbols and visual stimulus.

†Not only by itself, but also installed and operating.

‡Determined by experience, or provided by a vendor.

§Its applicability, however, is quite general. By calculating the flow rate (lb/s) through a given opening and using appropriate dimensions, it can be seen that the formula is similar to, and in some respects more general than, the formula on page 764 of *Unit Operations of Chemical Engineering* by McCabe et al. [65].

scores more, really) that still requires extensive work. The field of granular solids handling is ripe for a period of development.

Finally, part of the idea of this chapter is to show the reader examples of thought processes, so that the reader can pattern thought processes along similar lines. Two messages are underscored here:

- Take nothing for granted (if data are missing, get them; take measurements, when necessary).

- Ask questions as you proceed, with the most frequent one being, How does it work?

In the way of a final statement, before we leave the subject of granular solids, a pernicious pitfall clamors for mention: *removal from a dryer*. This is a quintessential example of how the design thought process must lead to examining a process step, spotting a problem, and solving it.

In the normal course of events, the identification of the pitfall starts with a question: As the solids are removed from a drying step, what happens to the gases that accompany them?* Obviously, the withdrawal of solids will be accompanied by moist air that probably has a composition similar to the air ducted away from the air outlet (see the following block flow diagram).

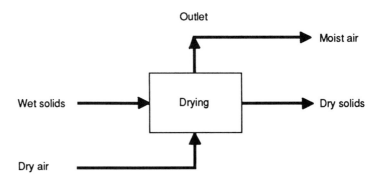

Generally, the solids leaving a dryer will fall through some sort of air lock, such as a rotary valve, to keep the dryer gas from blowing out of the solids discharge port. A typical situation is shown in Fig. 10-18.

The problem arises after the solids cool down and the moisture condenses from the air that fills the interstices of the bed of granular solids. This coats the particles with a thin film of water which can greatly affect flow characteristics (internal friction). In cases where the solid is soluble, recrystallization due to diurnal and seasonal temperature cycles will bond particle to particle, making a monolith. This is commonly called *caking*, and it is often seen with granular products in bags and drums. When a whole bin of granular material cakes up, a huge mess ensues. Not only can production be halted, but also equipment can be damaged and quantities of waste material can rise sharply.

The solution to the problem is exceedingly simple: Dry air (sometimes *instrument* air) is blown up through the leg that leads to the air lock, as shown in Fig. 10-18. This drives away almost all the moist

---

*The author has never seen this question addressed in a college text, vendor literature, or any treatise on the topic. It is a good illustration of how the engineer/designer must use imagination to spot a potential problem.

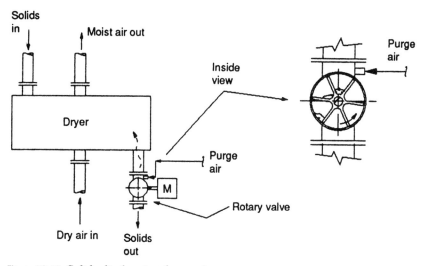

Figure 10-18 Solids discharging from a dryer.

air. Some rotary valves are provided with ports for introducing flush gases. This is depicted in Fig. 10-18. By asking questions and using the mind's eye, a serious problem is averted [ATD].

VALVES

This is the last topic before Chap. 11, which is devoted to P&IDs. When P&IDs are discussed, some idea of the different types of valves will be needed.

Most valves are employed primarily for one of two reasons (functions): blocking and throttling. A block valve enables or prevents flow; the action is *on* or *off*. A throttling valve *regulates* flow. Here are a couple of quick examples: (1) block: gate or ball and (2) throttle: globe. It is not unusual to employ the two kinds of valve in close proximity (or even back to back), as depicted in Fig. 10-19. To understand how this arrangement is useful, imagine an operator who must turn off the wash when the filter is stopped and who must start the wash again when the filter is restarted. Presumably the production rate settings will not change, so the wash setting should be the same. This is done with the globe valve. The on/off function is accomplished by the ball valve.

Actually, a ball valve serves fairly well as a throttle valve in some cases. Let there be no doubt, however: In the situation described in the sketch, the globe valve is so superior for fine-tuning as to leave no doubt regarding the distinction between "block" and "throttle." The

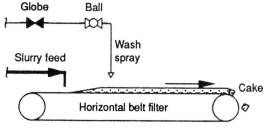

Figure 10-19 Two valves together.

operator will attempt to cover the filter cake with as much liquid as possible. During throttling with the globe valve, adjustments will be continuous and steady. With the ball valve, they may seem continuous to the touch, but when viewed on the filter cake, the adjustments will be seen as discontinuous—really, a series of small jerks. Once the globe valve is set, it can be ignored except for the occasional tweak. Start/stop of the filter is handled with a thoughtless, ham-handed sweep of the ball valve [ATD].

Table 10-4 names some common types of valves, shows some often used P&ID symbols for them, and briefly outlines areas of application. The designations shown in the table are brief guidelines for first-cut thinking. For example, pinch valves are designated as block valves. However, in cases where nothing else worked, pinch valves have been used as throttle valves. The reader is encouraged to look through valve catalogs and talk to maintenance mechanics and operators to appreciate sound practice in the use of valves.

A valve that becomes stuck is exasperating in the best of circumstances. This happens when a crystallizing or polymerizing material can bond the two sealing surfaces on a valve. Gate valves and plug valves are adapted, by virtue of their design, to minimize this prob-

TABLE 10-4 Common Process Valves

	Initial cost	Maintenance	Chemical resistance	Usual function	Robustness	Niche	P&ID symbol
Ball	Moderate	Moderate	Mostly limited by alloy	Block	Good	Might be most widely used today	
Gate	Moderate	Moderate	Mostly limited by alloy	Block	Good	Most widely used in the past	
Globe	Moderate	More than ball or gate	Mostly limited by alloy	Throttle	Good	Most common valve for throttling	
Plug	High	Low	Mostly limited by alloy	Block	Best	Best overall reliability	
Three-way plug	High	Moderate	Mostly limited by alloy	Block	Good	Special applications only	
Four-way plug	High	Moderate	Mostly limited by alloy	Block	Good	Special applications only	
Butterfly	Low	High	Limited by elastomer	Block	Weak	Where a tight seal is not high priority	
Pinch	Low, moderate	Moderate, high	Versatile at low temperatures	Block	Weak	Good with slurries	
Diaphragm	Moderate	Moderate	Versatile at low temperatures	Mostly block, some throttle	Moderate	Good in corrosive service	

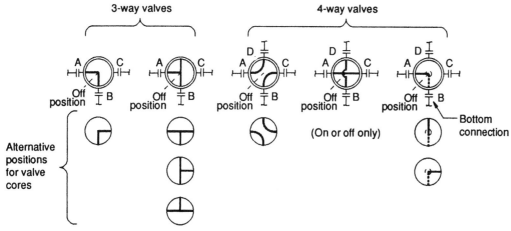

Figure 10-20 Some common configurations of three- and four-way valves.

lem. Even so, special models are available to go one step further and lever the operator off the seat, if necessary. When one of these truly* nonstick valves is put into service after a sticky valve has been causing trouble, it seems like a deliverance.

When thinking about valves, the engineer/designer should have *seals* at a high level of consciousness in the thought process. The places where the process and the atmosphere meet should be scrutinized. These are the places with a high potential for trouble.

Before we move on to the next chapter, a word of caution regarding three-way and four-way valves is appropriate: There is no way that the P&ID symbols for these valves can convey their characteristics. Figure 10-20 shows two types of three-way valves, so one symbol can represent two possibilities. Three possibilities are available with four-way valves. Therefore, whenever a three-way or four-way valve is shown on a P&ID, a notation with a subsidiary diagram showing the actual operation should be given among the notes on the P&ID. The alternative is to abandon the simple three-, four-way symbol and replace it with the symbol used in the notes.

Figure 10-21 shows an application of a three-way valve for feeding a centrifuge. The possible configurations are noted off to one side. The pump feeding the centrifuge is a positive displacement, flexible-vane unit. The feed rate is governed by using speed control on the pump. A good, steady feed to the centrifuge is important and is obtained as shown. Line plugging is avoided by keeping the slurry in motion, by keeping stagnant zones small, and by providing for natural drainage, when flow is stopped.

Here is how the equipment of Fig. 10-21 works. The three-way valve is mounted directly on the tank flange. Normal flow is straight through the valve, into the pump; this occurs with the valve in position 1. When the valve is shifted, the pump draws water from a funnel for a short time and then is shut off. This clears the pump and the line to the centrifuge. The only stagnant region is in the tank nozzle and the valve nozzle when the valve is in position 2. This is only a few inches long and does not cause plugging.

Two limit switches are shown on the valve. Switch 2 stops the

---

*As with most things: *almost.*

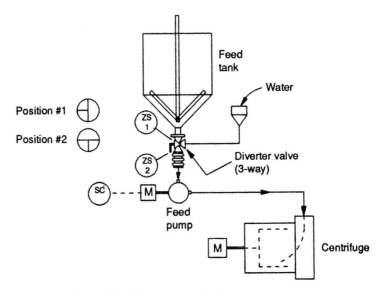

Figure 10-21 Example of three-way valve in use.

pump after a time delay (not shown)* when position 2 is achieved. Switch 1 starts the pump immediately when position 1 is achieved.

---

*Time delays are usually not shown on P&IDs. Occasionally the process engineer will call some out in the notes on the P&ID to make sure they aren't missed. They are always shown on electrical elementary diagrams.

Chapter 11
P&IDs

OVERVIEW

Most of us can probably relate to a childhood experience in which a friend draws a diagram in the dirt or on a piece of paper describing a football play, or describing a place where something is hidden. These diagrammatic sketches come from us with great ease. The hieroglyphs on rocks dating to ancient primitive people are often explained as maps, or diagrams, for locating game or gold or whatever. It takes very little imagination to envision a group of hunters returning from a hunt and pausing to record, on a prominent rock, a few images, putting down a memory key or two for future sojourns in the area.

The P&ID is in keeping with these types of diagrams. As a matter of fact, its two primary purposes have just been mentioned: It is a communication tool and a record to assist memory.

The acronym P&ID stands for *piping and instrument diagram*. Occasionally the letters P or M are used ahead of P&ID to distinguish between *process* and *mechanical* varieties: *process piping and instrument diagram* (PP&ID) or *mechanical piping and instrument diagram* (MP&ID). Mostly, however, the term *P&ID* is generally used without further distinction. If HVAC equipment is shown, it is undoubtedly a mechanical-type P&ID. If process equipment is shown, it is a process P&ID. On projects where slurry handling or pneumatic transport is in evidence, the distinctions between mechanical and process fade away.

The P&ID is undoubtedly an extension of the flow diagram, examples of which can be seen in treatises on mineral processing of more than a century ago. In the flow diagram, process steps are shown connected by lines with arrows. Thus the sequence of processing is established. Figure 11-1 shows the process for gold recovery using mercury amalgamation. This particular type of diagram is called a *block flow diagram*. Process steps are shown, but the type of equipment is not shown. Energy inducers such as pumps and fans are not shown.

The interpretation of the diagram is that first the ore is crushed. Then the ore is screened, or somehow sized, so that insufficiently ground particles are returned to the crushing step. The crushed particles are carried by sluice water over a sloping copper plate containing a coating of mercury stuck to the upper surface. Free gold will stick to the film of mercury while gangue material will roll along on top of the film, unhindered, and will follow the sluice water out of the amalgamation zone.

Once a shift or once a day, depending on design considerations and ore grade, the operation is stopped while an operator scrapes the amalgam into a container for squeezing and cooking. Fresh mercury is then poured onto the copper plate to form a new coating. This coating is held in place on the copper plate by a copper-mercury amalgam. Occasionally, the bonding surface between copper and mercury

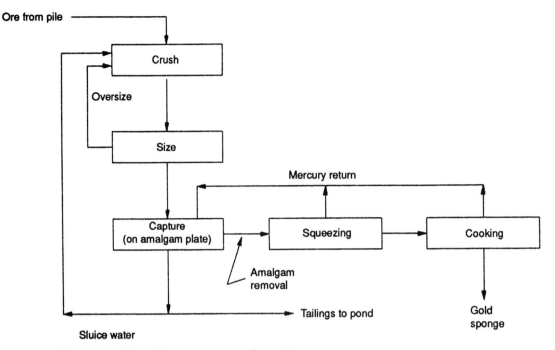

Figure 11-1 Flow diagram for gold recovery via amalgamation.

becomes poisoned. When this happens, the plate is pulled and a new one, with an untarnished coating of mercury, is installed. The old plate is cleaned, etched with acid, and reamalgamated with mercury for further service.

The amalgam scrapings are first poured onto a chamois skin lining a container (see Fig. 11-2). The corners of the skin are raised and twisted together so that the mercury and its contents are trapped and completely surrounded by the chamois. The twisting operation is continued (see Fig. 11-2). This forces mercury out through the pores of the chamois. Eventually a point is reached where further twisting and squeezing produce little mercury. A solid lump of gold-mercury amalgam, saturated with mercury, is what remains in the chamois. This is removed and placed in a small retort where the mercury is driven off at 1200 to 1400°F. Mercury from squeezing and cooking is returned to the copper plate.

The process just described was the traditional one used in the

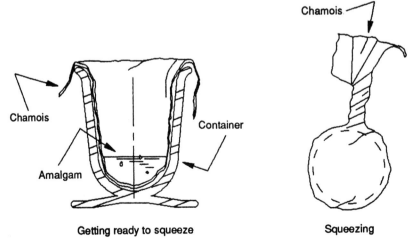

Getting ready to squeeze

Squeezing

Figure 11-2 Detail of squeezing step.

United States until just a few years ago. As it was practiced, it lead to mercury contamination, and operators were exposed to mercury poisoning. For use today, the process would require additional safeguards.

The reader is asked to note how the use of the diagram and the sketch of the squeezing step have aided the description of the amalgamation process.

The block flow diagram is a most useful diagram, because it helps keep the focus on process sequence and mass-balance requirements without excessive involvement in equipment considerations. The block flow diagram is limited, however, because equipment selections are needed to carry out a complete mass balance. Also equipment selections are needed to build the plant. Thus, the next step toward P&IDs is the *flow diagram,* or *flow sheet.* Here the equipment is shown. Typically, symbols that can be understood by a fairly diverse audience are used. Classic symbols for a pump and a stirred tank are shown in Fig. 11-3. Lists of symbols are presented in many publications. No list can ever be complete. A list presented in *Chemical Engineering* a number of years ago is reproduced in App. F. Note that these symbols are for flow sheets and generally *not* for P&IDs. The reasons are explained later.

If a standard symbol cannot be found, one must be invented.* Usually this is not a difficult task. However, some engineers, with little artistic talent, have felt uncomfortable performing such a task. In such a case, consultations with colleagues is the answer.

For the most part, valves are not shown. Here and there, a key valve for safety or for determining capacity might be shown, but that is all. Perhaps only one-third of the pumps (fans, etc.) will be shown. This is because, largely, their inclusion in a flow sheet is not necessary. Furthermore, elevations and therefore pumping requirements are usually hard to define early in the project—precisely when the flow sheet is being developed. Also it is understood that whatever it takes to get a stream from point *A* to point *B,* will eventually be provided. In general, motors will not be shown on a flow diagram. However, they should be shown when doing so helps to describe the nature of the equipment. Neither the pump nor the agitator in Fig. 11-3 shows a motor. It is not needed to aid in understanding. Figure 11-4 shows motors on the unfamiliar symbols for the paddle mixer and briquetter (because the motor aids in understanding the symbol). A motor is not shown on the conveyor because it is a familiar symbol. The slide gate is included to remind the reader of the separation of the processes: batch mixing and batch briquetting.

A more complete example of a flow diagram is given in Fig. 11-5. Here a thermoplastic scrap is processed for reuse. Diverse forms of

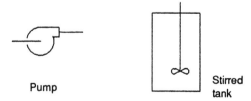

Pump

Stirred tank

Figure 11-3 Two classic symbols.

---

*For example, what should the symbol be for a dissolved air flotation unit on a petroleum refinery?

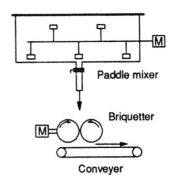

Figure 11-4 Paddle mixer feeding a briquetter.

scrap, from plastic cups to rejects from a ball-point pen manufacturer, are brought together and disintegrated in a hogging machine. This is done to make the job of feeding the extruder easier. The resulting flakes and chips are fed to an extruder along with a small number of chips of similar material, containing a high concentration of pigment.* The combined materials are melted down and blended in the extruder. The melt emerges from the die as ⅛-in strands. These are solidified in a quench bath. The strands are chopped in the dicer and packaged for sale in large, heavy cloth bags.

The flow diagram shows process sequence and pertinent equipment pieces. Streams are numbered. Large engineering companies often refer to the flow diagram as the *PFD*, that is, the *process flow diagram*. Flow information for each stream can be obtained from a table such as Table 11-1.

Often, the table showing the streams is incorporated into the flow diagram† along the bottom. Less often, the table is presented sepa-

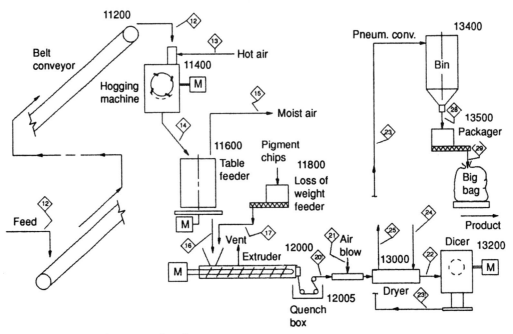

Figure 11-5 Thermoplastic recycling line.

---

*Most of the feed is limited to colorless or white material, with small portions of pastel colors permitted. The pigment masks the off-color quality caused by dirt and by the light colors. The resulting product is light gray.

†As used here, *flow diagram* and *PFD* are different names for the same thing.

TABLE 11-1 Stream Descriptions for Fig. 11-5

	⟨12⟩ hogger feed		⟨13⟩ drying air		⟨14⟩ hogger discharge		⟨15⟩ moist air		⟨16⟩ extruder feed		⟨17⟩ pigment chips	
	average rate	design rate	average rate	design rate	average rate	design rate	average rate	design rate	average rate	design rate	average rate	design rate
polymer	1050	1260			1050	1260			1050	1260	26	34
pigment											4.1	6.3
dirt	2.6	5.2			2.6	5.2			2.6	5.2		
other #1	2.1	2.5			nil	.1			nil	.1		
name #1	water	water			water	water			water	water		
other #2												
name #2												
water			5	18	7.1	20.5	7.1	20.5				
air			450	900	450	900	450	900				
temperature			130	150	130	150	130	150				
pressure			~atm.	~atm.								

	⟨18⟩ [unused]		⟨19⟩ [unused]		⟨20⟩ extrudate		⟨21⟩ blow air		⟨22⟩ dicer feed		⟨23⟩ dicer output	
	average rate	design rate	average rate	design rate	average rate	design rate	average rate	design rate	average rate	design rate	average rate	design rate
polymer					1076	1294			1076	1294	1076	1294
pigment					4.1	6.3			4.1	6.3	4.1	6.3
dirt					2.6	5.2			2.6	5.2	2.6	5.2
other #1					11	13	n/a	n/a	nil	.5	nil	.5
name #1					water	water						
other #2												
name #2												
water												
air							22.4	25.8				
temperature												
pressure												

rately on 8.5 × 11 in sheets. This latter method makes the use of computer printout, which is convenient for directly presenting stream information. This saves time and eliminates transcription errors. Some companies like the added security this approach provides: The tables showing stream names and compositions can be kept in the hands of project leaders, while the PFDs are distributed more widely.

Table 11-1 shows streams 18 and 19 as not being used. This is a recommended approach to numbering streams. The initial numbering should leave two or three unused numbers for every five or so assigned numbers. This allows streams to be added while taking on a number that is close to neighboring streams.

The values for average rate are factored directly from the mole tables (see Chap. 8, *The Mass Balance*). Often the mole table is set up to coincide with plant production capacity, in which case the factor is 1.000. Sometimes mole tables are set up on bases different from plant production (on the basis of 100 mol of the key product, with no time base stated, for example). This latter type of mole table requires a multiplying factor in order to obtain meaningful rates in pounds per hour. The values for the design rate are derived from the average rate by the method described under "Capacity" in Chap. 9.

A common practice among large engineering companies is to include names and numbers of all the equipment shown on PFDs as legends above the top of the diagram, under the margin. The author does not subscribe to this practice, as it takes precious time and requires continual updating later in the project, when full attention should be focused on the P&IDs. Furthermore, since only part of the equipment is shown, the format is wrong.

The purpose of a PFD is to define the process and aid in the production of heat and mass balances. The inclusion of legends that constantly require revision has a great tendency to become a distraction.

Figure 11-5 gives an example of the recommended practice. Numbers and text are included in the diagram close to the pieces with which they are associated. The text is descriptive and does not constitute an actual equipment *name*.* The best format for assigning equipment names is the P&ID. Should legends and equipment names be required for *PFD*s, the information should not be added until the last possible moment.

Occasionally a kind of PFD is developed to show as much equipment as possible. This is done to prepare an order-of-magnitude estimate without going so far as to prepare P&IDs. In such a case, the PFDs will be used not only to show how the process works but also to identify pieces of equipment. This is good for the sake of efficiency, but it must not be lost from sight that the product is neither fish nor fowl—that is, the product of such an effort is neither a PFD nor a P&ID.

Although effort on the flow diagrams should not be deflected by naming equipment, time *should* be spent in assigning equipment numbers. Equipment numbers *do* belong on the flow diagrams in close proximity to the equipment symbol they label.

The equipment list should be started at the time numbers are put on the flow diagram. In the earliest stages, this list may contain some names, some descriptions, and some blanks. Often the specific type of equipment is not defined, so a good name cannot be chosen. Final names are often established when the first issue of a P&ID is developed.

Once the flow diagrams begin to take on a firm nature, work on the P&IDs should begin (see Fig. 14-4).

It is possible to do a P&ID without doing a block flow diagram or a flow diagram, but it is usually best to do some hand sketches of a flow diagram before launching into the production of a P&ID.

Small modifications to an ongoing process should include a P&ID, even if it is on an 8.5×11 in sheet of paper. For example, the addition of a temperature switch in the discharge of a compressor merits its own P&ID (on an 8.5×11 in sheet).

---

*A *name* differs from a *description* in that the name is more specific. For example, the extruder in Fig. 11-5 might be given the name *4-in extruder,* to distinguish it from other nearby extruders on other production lines (not shown).

The evolution of the P&ID from the flow diagram is easy to envision. As a matter of fact, every engineer in the business has probably been tempted from time to time to convert a PFD to a P&ID simply by adding instruments. Those of us who have attempted this know what folly it is.

Here is a comparison that shows the differences between a PFD and a P&ID:

	PFD	P&ID
Used during construction?	No	Yes*
Shows *all* process and service piping?	No	Yes
Indicates presence of *all* controls?	No	Yes
Shows all motors?	No	Yes
Shows thermal insulation?	No	Yes
Shows major equipment?	Yes	Yes
Shows flow quantities?	Yes	No
Shows stream compositions?	Yes	No

*This is the most revealing distinction. The P&ID on a job site is probably one of the most used documents. Everyone working on piping has one in pocket, and it is constantly spread out during discussions. PFDs, on the other hand, are never seen on a job site. They are available, in the files, but not used.

The PFD is a drawing needed early in the project. Indeed, the PFD is the *most* important drawing while the mass balance is being prepared. Later, the PFD guides the preparation of the P&ID. Finally the P&ID supplants the PFD, totally eclipsing it.

Both PFDs and P&IDs can be characterized as

- Communication tools

- Records

- Aids to thought processes

but the P&ID is done in much greater depths, where what is shown can reach as far as sight and smell, and can delve into speculation as to the mathematical abilities that will be required of the graveyard shift operator.*

In terms of value analysis, the above three items are called functions (see Chap. 9, *Preparation for Understanding Equipment*). It is a good idea to memorize these three functions, to see how they work, as this chapter develops. The first two functions are readily appreciated and were mentioned at the beginning of the chapter. The third function is best appreciated via the following example.

Figure 11-6 shows a segment of a P&ID in which a tank receives liquid from part of the process. On the discharge from the tank there is a level control and a flow control. As an aid to thought processes, the P&ID is used as follows. First, imagine that flow into the tank is steady. Next, imagine what happens when pressure P_1 in the incoming line declines and flow drops off by, say, 10 percent. The level valve will respond by cutting the outflow to maintain the level. At the same time, the flow valve will open to maintain flow. This latter action will be countered by a further cutback by the level valve. In its final state, the result will be a fully open (and, therefore, useless) flow valve and a level valve doing all the work. Such a situation is unsatisfactory.

Simple relocation of the flow valve to the inlet side of the tank, as shown in Fig. 11-7, enables a reasonable operation. Here is how the

---

*To provide useful leadership on process projects, all project leaders should possess a fair ability for reading P&IDs.

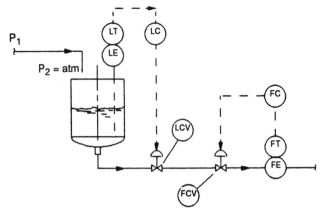

Figure 11-6 Conflict between flow and level controls.

situation is analyzed. As before, imagine a steady flow into and out of the tank. Next, say the available pressure declines in the inlet line. This would result in a drop in flow (and, therefore, tank level) except for the correction of the flow control. It opens the valve to compensate for loss in upstream pressure. While this is happening, the level valve should experience only minor adjustments. The level valve will follow the flow valve when changes in flow are made. For example, if the operator changes the set point on the flow, cutting back by 10 percent, the level control will quickly sense this and also cut itself back 10 percent to maintain the level.

The above description shows how the P&ID is a great aid in the thinking that accompanies process design. The mental, query-answer format used in examining a P&ID often leads to the *gedanken* experiment. The example we just reviewed was *gedanken* at work. More on this topic follows shortly.

Note that the level can be raised or lowered at will, but if downstream equipment is impacted by the corresponding surges in flow rate, care should be exercised in level adjustments.

A typical use of the storage capability is as follows. Say that a heat exchanger downstream must be shut down for 4 h to inspect for leaks (and to plug leaking tubes, if leaks are found). The upstream process is difficult to stabilize, so interruption is to be avoided, if possible. Operations personnel take note of process rate settings. The level control

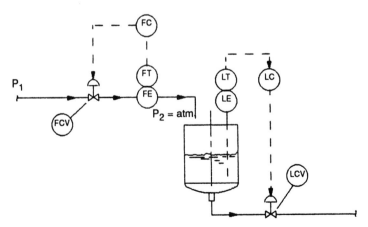

Figure 11-7 Flow and level controls in harmony.

will be set on *manual operation* at a valve setting 10 percent greater*
than the stable operating point. This will draw down the level in the
tank while imposing a minor imposition on downstream operations.

Once the level in the tank has reached a minimum value, the plan
requires that flow *from* the tank be cut off. Meanwhile flow into the
tank will continue without change, or it can be curtailed by an acceptable amount. In this way, the exchanger can be serviced without
affecting the upstream process. After work on the exchanger is finished, the level in the tank will presumably be high, but, via opera-
tional maneuvers, will be worked back to a normal state.†

These examples show how the P&ID is an aid to the thought process. This concept is important and will be repeated.

The P&ID is a relatively modern document on process projects.
While an employee with Du Pont, the author was privileged to examine the original P&ID for the first nylon production facility in the
world (built at Seaford, Delaware). The P&ID was dated in or around
the year 1937. It was an ink drawing on linen, measuring about 34 ×
44 in. The linen was completely devoid of the original varnish, used to
give it a stiff consistency. It was completely limp, like an unstarched
handkerchief.

This document was *not* a modern P&ID in many respects. For one
thing, the entire process, from polymerization through spinning, was
crowded onto the single sheet. Today, the practice is to limit what is
shown on a single sheet to three to five major items or four to eight
minor items (see below for the distinction between major and minor
items). Another difference was that the symbols were not uniform in
size, apparently the later additions being accorded less space. Pumps
from the early part of the job were shown at $\frac{3}{8}$ in while later additions were squeezed down to $\frac{1}{8}$ in. Lettering suffered the same treatment. The one single impression that remains after all these years is
one of a vastly overcrowded drawing. It would be possible to focus
attention on a 6 × 6 in segment for at least ten minutes to gain a
rudimentary feel for the contained message.

The instruments were not shown with Instrument Society of America symbols. In many cases the operation of the instruments was not
obvious from the diagram. Some were drawn without showing connections. Evidently, an instrument installation drawing was relied
upon to convey further information about the operation. Yet, this
drawing was without doubt a P&ID. It had the attributes listed above
for P&IDs.

P&ID SYMBOLS

In the masterpiece of written communication entitled *The Elements of
Style* [66], a reader is characterized as in serious trouble most of the
time: " . . . a man floundering in a swamp, and it [is] the duty of anyone attempting to write English to drain this swamp quickly and get
this man on dry ground, or at least throw him a rope." The same can
be said about readers of P&IDs: Most of the time they are in trouble
and need help.

Good symbols are essential to helping the reader of a P&ID.

Hubert G. Alexander, professor of philosophy at the University of

---

*This is equivalent to replacing the control valve with a manual valve and then
setting the flow at 10 percent greater than the stable operating point.

†Half full for most tanks.

New Mexico, stated [67], "The ease with which a thought process is carried on depends very greatly upon the nature of the symbol system. In fact, without symbols, thinking would limp along on one cylinder, if it could go at all." A little further along, Alexander points out that Cassirer [68] asserts "the discovery, or invention, of symbols is the greatest of all human discoveries, ranking on a par with, or ahead of, the domestication of fire and animals."

A logical question at this point is, What is a symbol? In philosophy a symbol can be defined in a number of ways. For our purposes, the definition given by Alexander [69] is appropriate: A symbol expresses or suggests an idea by *standing for it.*

In terms of a P&ID, the symbol for a pump replaces the pump itself on the drawing. Thus, when reading a P&ID and thinking about starting a pump, the reader should be able to envision a pump as it quickly winds up to speed, almost before the operator has removed his finger from the start button. Furthermore, the reader who is thinking about the possibility of cavitation should easily conjure sounds of cavitation, just as he or she should smell oil while thinking about a mechanic pulling an oil seal. The symbol should, indeed, stand for the real thing.

To aid this, the P&ID symbol is usually more elaborate than the flow sheet symbol. It is developed to allow more features to be shown. The centrifugal pump is an ideal example. Figure 11-8 shows two common symbols for a centrifugal pump. The classic symbol is probably the most widely recognized process symbol in the world today. A good amount of meaning is embedded in the symbol. Furthermore, it is easily distinguished from other symbols. However, it labors under a shortcoming: It does not adapt naturally to showing associated parts and pieces. The motor is awkward to include, so in past years it was generally omitted. Its presence had to be assumed. Instruments and seal purges seemed to connect to the pump casing (see Fig. 11-9). The new symbol corrects these deficiencies. On P&IDs the new symbol is slowly (but surely) replacing the classic pump symbol. On flow diagrams, the classic symbol reigns, and will continue to do so.

As a further illustration of the versatility provided by the new symbol, consider Fig. 11-10, which shows the inclusion of a speed switch. The symbol allows the reader to form an idea as to whether the switch is located outboard of the motor or between the motor and the pump. Admittedly, this is not a great advantage, but many small advantages often serve more than a single great advantage.

The pump symbol is somewhat exceptional in that it enjoys a high degree of uniformity. Most P&ID symbols tend to be customized for a particular situation. Figure 11-11 is an example of how the symbol for a deep-well pump is developed, given that the pump is a series of centrifugal pumps ganged together on a common shaft. Such a symbol conveys to the reader some of the ideas that have to be kept in mind when such a pump is contemplated:

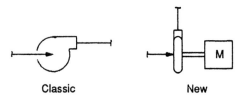

Classic   New

Figure 11-8 Two centrifugal pump symbols.

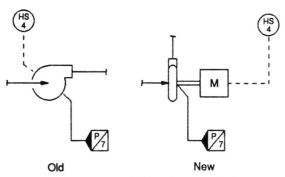

Old   New

Figure 11-9 Comparison of old and new symbols.

- The pump is long and slender.
- Pressure is obtained by multiple stages (as many as 20 stages are common).
- Radial support is necessary.
- When such a pump is inserted down a long hole, it is necessary to assemble the pump in the field.
- Shaft bearings will be needed every 10 ft or so; they must not fail by running dry (30 such bearings might be needed for a deep-well installation).
- A medium-sized rock caught in the suction would require pulling the whole pump and reinstalling it; strainers, or screens, are used to keep rocks from getting to the pump.

The standard symbol for a pump is wholly inadequate for triggering the thought processes needed to successfully employ such a pump. The standard symbol would be misleading.

The time required to create such a symbol is not easy to forecast. A few symbols can be created from scratch in a matter of minutes. Others seem to require some soul-searching, false starts, and consultations with colleagues before a suitable one is found. A great number of symbols can be adapted from previous work or from "standard" symbols such as those of App. F. Some symbols seem to arise naturally as one reads the vendor literature.

In general, no symbol should be composed of anything more than

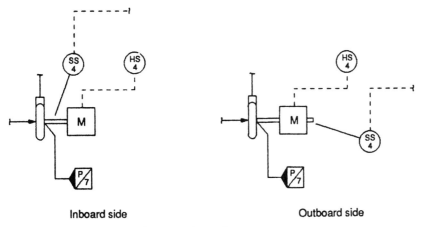

Inboard side   Outboard side

Figure 11-10 Two locations for a speed switch.

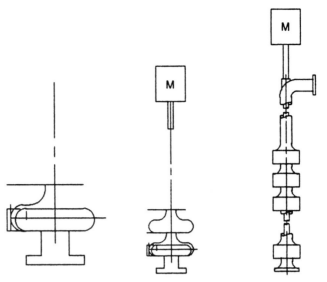

Figure 11-11 Development of a symbol for a deep-well, or staged, pump.

- Lines
- Circles or circular arcs
- Ellipses or elliptical arcs
- Polygons of fewer than seven sides

The development of CADD (computer-aided design and drafting) in the last few years makes it easy to repeat features (such as the stages in the deep-well pump) and move symbols with ease. Thus the mechanical generation of the symbols has been made simpler. In spite of the power available by using CADD, it is probably wise to limit symbol generation to the use of the four geometric shapes mentioned above.

Without CADD the following four drafting tools are all that is needed to manually generate top-grade symbols (and P&IDs):

- Drafting triangle
- Combination template (circles, squares, triangles, and hexagons)
- Ellipse template
- Compass

In the layout of a symbol, the very first step is often the establishment of a line of symmetry, or centerline. This is true with CADD as well as manual drafting. Often the centerline should be included as part of the symbol, because it aids the eye in appreciating what is shown. Also the centerline can be used to assist minor adjustments at a later date—a symbol often evolves as information develops.

Figure 11-12 shows symbols representing basic shapes of tanks and pressure vessels. Orientation and even some hints as to function are enhanced by the use of the centerline [ATD].

The development of a P&ID symbol from scratch for a thorny application can be appreciated by the following example. Here, a compressor for pumping a mixture of hydrogen bromide and hydrogen gas is needed. Significant quantities of silicon tetrabromide can be present. This mixture is poisonous, reactive with the atmosphere, and corro-

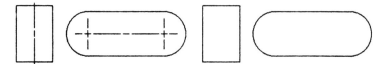

Figure 11-12 Use of centerline with symbol.

sive. The best piece of equipment for the circumstances is a diaphragm compressor.

The symbol used on the flow diagram (the PFD) is shown in Fig. 11-13. This is based on catalog information from Fluitron (see Fig. 11-14) and the use of a diaphragm compressor in the pilot plant—thus the pilot unit has been seen in a state of disassembly. A search through personal files and old project P&IDs does not yield a symbol for a diaphragm compressor. The starting point is primarily the vendor catalog, but includes perceptions gathered in many different places, including the maintenance shop and physics courses from bygone years.

The first sketch, done by hand (not shown), is very close to Fig. 11-14. It takes up an $8\frac{1}{2} \times 11$ in sheet and obviously is too elaborate to use. The question in mind at this time is, Where is the essence? The answer is that it lies in

- The shape
- The process interface*
- The operator interface
- The maintenance interface
- Gravity

The first sketch is discarded.

The thought process is aimed at the first two "essences": *shape* and *process interface.* Thus the symbol shown in Fig. 11-15 is developed. This has a good feel to it. The flywheel and diaphragm are represented. A gravity vector (never represented, but always understood to point downward), conjured in the reader's mind, makes sense. For example, oil entering the symbol will flow *down.*

More sketching and experimenting lead to the symbol shown in Fig. 11-16. The features added to this symbol are as follows:

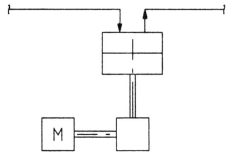

Figure 11-13 Flow diagram symbol for diaphragm compressor.

Interface is where two disciplines meet or, as here, where the engineers' design meshes with the vendor's design.

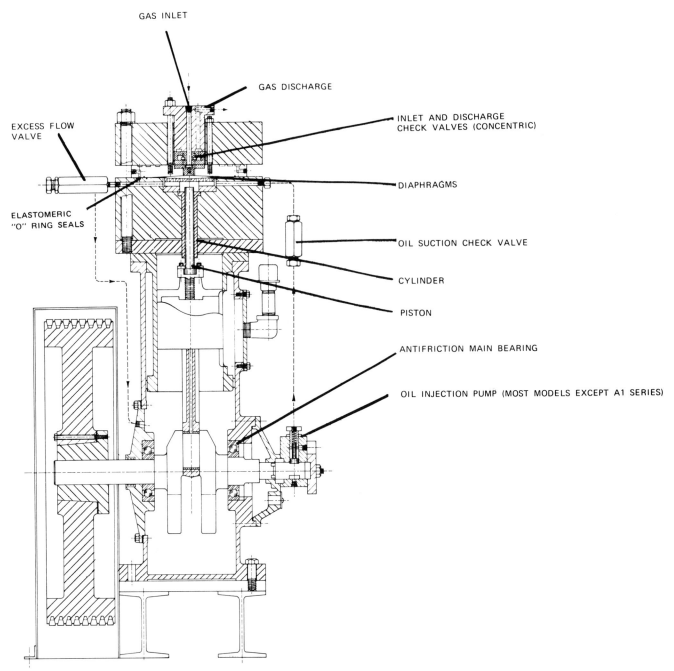

GAS INLET

GAS DISCHARGE

EXCESS FLOW VALVE

INLET AND DISCHARGE CHECK VALVES (CONCENTRIC)

ELASTOMERIC "O" RING SEALS

DIAPHRAGMS

OIL SUCTION CHECK VALVE

CYLINDER

PISTON

ANTIFRICTION MAIN BEARING

OIL INJECTION PUMP (MOST MODELS EXCEPT A1 SERIES)

Figure 11-14 Sectional view of compressor from Fluitron catalog. (*Courtesy of Fluitron, Inc.*)

- Oil loop (with pump)
- Slider-crank mechanism plus piston
- Diaphragm and cavity
- I-beam supports

The last feature has only a communication function. It makes the symbol more recognizable to people working with catalog drawings (see Fig. 11-14).

The first three features are important for defining the process, operation, and maintenance interfaces. To appreciate this, Fig. 11-17 must be studied. The two logic blocks for OR in Fig. 11-17 illustrate how the P&ID shows interfaces. The OR at the right has an asterisk,

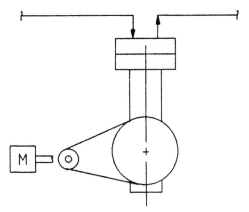

Figure 11-15 Symbol that captures the essence.

indicating that it will be provided by the vendor. The OR at the left will be provided as part of software logic in a microprocessor domain. It will be defined by the engineers, not the vendors. This is a crucial point. One of the signals leading to shutdown comes from a reactor pressure switch of which the compressor vendor has no knowledge.

Further examination of Fig. 11-17 shows that the speed control loop (loop 167) for the motor is to be provided by using parts specified and purchased by the engineering group, not by the vendor (note the lack of asterisks). Originally the vendor had planned to supply these parts. However, the engineers removed such a provision during the bidding on the compressors because the engineers knew they would provide a microprocessor-based environment (MBE)* that would service the whole process, not just the compressor. There was some debate among the engineers as to who would provide the speed sensor (denoted SE 167) to detect shaft speed. Because eventual interfacing with the MBE would be easier to do, the engineers decided to provide the sensor.† The power supply was also discussed, but it was

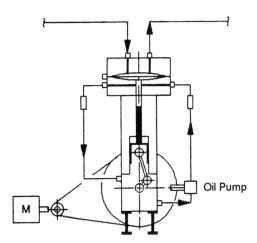

Figure 11-16 Fully developed symbol.

---

*Instrument functions are performed via software in a microprocessor-based environment that may be configured as a programmable logic controller (PLC), distributed control system (DCS), a hybrid of the two, or some other customized form (also see Table 11-2).

†This later resulted in a request to the vendor for fabrication drawings showing the motor mount.

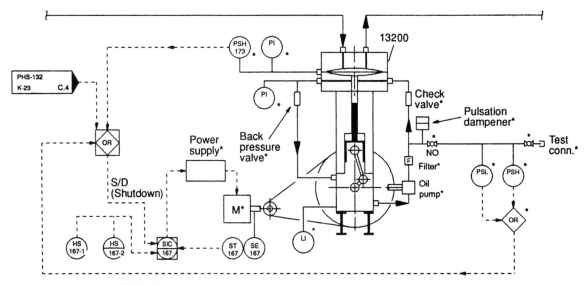

Figure 11-17 Portion of P&ID showing diaphragm compressor.

quickly decided that the compressor vendor would be in a better position to specify and purchase this item.

Before we move on to the next section, some other features of Fig. 11-17 bear mention:

- The ball valves on the oil-loop branch are used to isolate the pressure switches, so that their trip points can be calibrated.

- Shafts of the motor and oil pump are shown broken; then each is shown rotated 90 degrees to enable depiction.

- Vendor-supplied check valves and such are shown as boxes because their nature is uncertain—this is a flag to the reader to go to the vendor drawings for further information.

- This is the case for the power supply, too.

- Pressure in the hollow diaphragm is sensed and is used to initiate an emergency shutdown.

This last feature is unique and special. When highly toxic gases are pumped, the hollow diaphragm can provide a good deal of security. A close-up of a segment of a hollow diaphragm is shown in Fig. 11-18. This diaphragm is perhaps 0.02 in in overall thickness. It is a metallic sandwich with a porous, flexible, solid core. The core is under a full vacuum. The core is connected to an absolute pressure gauge and absolute pressure switch. When a leak occurs in either layer, the pressure devices react, notifying the operators and shutting down the compressor, thus avoiding further damage to the diaphragm. This also keeps a leak from entering the oil system.

In Fig. 11-17, note that, in general, numbers are not used for vendor-supplied instruments. Vendor instruments are numbered at an interface, however (PSH 173, for example).

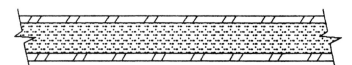

Figure 11-18 Close-up of hollow diaphragm.

A P&ID symbol must convey meaning to many different readers for many years. During the design phase, the readers will be colleagues, owners/clients, vendors, etc. During construction, the readers will be craftsmen, bosses, suppliers, etc. During the life of the plant, the readers will be operators, supervisors, training personnel, maintenance people, etc. Care in the creation of the symbol will pay ample rewards.

CONVENTIONS

The purpose of a convention is to help the reader decipher a message. English grammar is a convention. German grammar is another convention. A reader in either language has a good idea of when a verb may be approaching by knowing the grammar. German and English have different conventions for placement of a verb. Either language functions equally well.

The same can be said for P&ID conventions. Any convention can be adopted as long as the convention is not changed unexpectedly.

In *Grammatical Man,* Campbell [70] says:

> Grammar is an antichance device, keeping sentences regular and law-abiding. It is a systematic code applied at the message source. But there are millions of possible grammars, all different from one another, that could have been selected by the learner of the language. These other grammars, if chosen, would lead to error and confusion, because they would not coincide with grammars possessed by other speakers.

Like it or not, the "grammar" for making and reading P&IDs is not uniform and standard; that is, conventions for making P&IDs vary. A practice viewed dimly by one client may be highly prized by another. Fads come and go.

Some conventions are obviously helpful and are widely employed. The convention assuming that gravity will pull down, from the top of the P&ID to the bottom, is an example. Occasionally this convention cannot be adhered to, so a note is included to help the reader (see Fig. 11-19). Another popular convention is to lay out the P&ID so that the major process flow moves generally from left to right. This convention is subject to exceptions, too.

Some conventions were originally derived for a particular need, but are seen to be cumbersome if used in different circumstances. This is the case for showing all pumps along a single line at the bottom of the P&ID. It is fine where all the equipment is mounted on grade, but becomes awkward and misleading for equipment such as filter precoat pumps and venturi scrubber pumps, often mounted on elevated

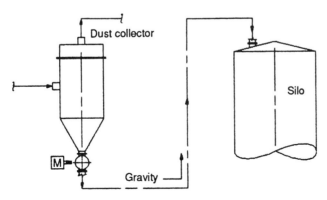

Figure 11-19 Direction of gravity.

platforms. This convention should be used only when it makes sense to do so.

Lines going from one P&ID to another are usually terminated by a special delimiter such as an arrow-box (see Table 11-2). The commodity contained in the line is given inside the box, along with the connecting P&ID and the grid coordinates of the mating P&ID. One end of the box terminates in a blunt arrow point, showing the direction of flow.

Line delimiters vary from company to company and even from job to job within the same company. Shapes, styles, and sizes all vary. The delimiter shown in Table 11-2 can quickly be drawn by hand, and because the arrow tip is filled (that is, solid black), the delimiter is easier to spot.

One convention requires that the line delimiters be taken to the right and left borders of the drawing. With this practice it is supposed that a line can be located on a mating P&ID with ease. In reality, it is insufficient help. Also it can result in needless line routing problems and the waste of valuable space on the P&ID.

Having match lines for putting P&IDs side by side, sheet after sheet, adds another dimension to needless problem-solving and real estate waste. To be entirely consistent, some P&IDs will have a line that enters one side and leaves the opposite side without connecting to anything—and sometimes this can continue for two or three sheets.

The coordinate method is far better. The reader can go directly to the sheet needed. Each sheet is subdivided into smaller sections. Each section has its own coordinates. These are given along the upper and left-hand margins.

A short form of the delimiter is shown for instrument air, purge connections, and so on. Details are then given on numbered detail sheets.

Some companies, including one or two major oil companies, favor the scroll P&ID. This P&ID is typically 30 in high by perhaps 1200 in (100 ft) long. The only delimiters are for utility connections. To use such a P&ID, one needs a special crank handle device to reel the P&ID back and forth. Meetings of more than three or four people to look over the P&ID together are impractical. When two items are being reviewed for mutual interaction and they are far apart, it is difficult to keep a thought process fired up while cranking back and forth. Much inconvenience is borne to avoid looking for a line delimiter on a mating P&ID. This approach is not recommended.

The most common convention for showing instrumentation is to use the Instrument Society of America (ISA) symbols (see App. D). The most common conventions and symbols are shown in Table 11-2.

Of course, all piping, including piping for natural gas or even potable water, must be shown *when it connects to the process.* Thus the drinking fountain in the control room is *not* shown on the P&ID, but everything else is. Not only is the piping shown, but so are the reducers.* Furthermore, the reducers are shown in the correct sequential position along the path of flow. In other words, if a reducer should go downstream of a certain branch, *that* is where it must be shown, not upstream (see Fig. 11-20).

---

*The inclusion of reducers almost never occurs while the P&ID is being developed, yet should be done as soon as the need is identified. This is mostly done when lines are numbered and sized. Final determination of reducers occurs during piping design, by piping designers. These are marked in red pencil on the P&ID by the designer for review and incorporation by the engineer.

TABLE 11-2 Examples of Common Symbols Found on P&IDs

Lines and Connections

Common line for depicting a piping connection, or for tracing the outline of an equipment symbol. Arrow shows direction of flow. Often a heavy line is used to represent piping, while equipment is outlined with a normal line thickness. Major engineering companies do this. Equal line weights for the two are not uncommon, however.

Tilde (~) means line is continued farther along the same trajectory. Occasionally it is used to show the end of a line. The symbol is meant to show a slight tear in the drawing whereby the line continues unimpeded under the paper.

Mostly means electrical connection, but can be hidden line.

Multipurpose. Perhaps most commonly a hidden line.

Instrument capillary.

Instrument air.

Hydraulic, power and/or control.

Multisignal.

Class break.

Duct.

Elephant trunk or flexible duct.

Hose.

Insulated line.

Parts and Pieces

Piping reducers (eccentric on the left, concentric on the right).

This symbol flags items included with other components.

Steam trap assembly—type 4.

Specialty item—sketch 23 shows the details.

Instrument function performed via software in a programmable logic controller or a micro/mini computer (also referred to as MBE; see p. 191). Control room mounted.

Same function in a stand-alone unit.

Air-operated control valve. Internals are the globe valve type— even though symbol is for a gate valve—by convention.

Solenoid valve.

Three-way solenoid valve.

Check valve.

Air set, instrument air—type 8.

Line delimiter. Equipment at destination is given. The continuing P&ID and pertinent coordinates are given.

Eq.No. K-89   B,4

Electric motor and electric motor with integral speed reducer (gear motor).

Gearbox.

Common field-mounted instrument.† This instance shows a manually operated switch.

Rotameter.†

Interlock—interlock 9.

Purge connection—type 6.

Connection at battery limit.

Shutdown.

*For common valve symbols, see Table 10-4.

†For Instrument Society of America terminology, see App. D.

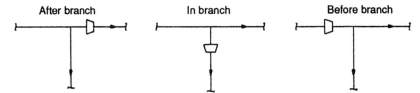

Figure 11-20 Nonidentical reducers at a branch.

Many times it makes no difference where the reducer goes. Every now and then it does. Thus the convention is to respect the sequence. Obviously a piping designer who can see a way to save money by relocating a reducer should check with the engineer. The answer will more than likely be yes—then the P&ID must be changed to match the piping design.

A convention that leads to great simplification is to show utility distribution on its own P&ID (or P&IDs, if more than one). Thus headers for air, water, nitrogen, steam, condensate, etc. do not add to the clutter on P&IDs, which generally are full enough in any case. The utility distribution P&ID is the link between the boiler and the evaporator, for example (see Fig. 11-21). Of course, the distribution P&ID also shows branches to other steam users, such as dryers and steam jets on their respective P&IDs, but these are not shown—to keep things simple.

By this convention, a boiler is shown on its P&ID, an evaporator is shown on *its* P&ID, and the tortuous route between them is shown on the *distribution* P&ID.

A few more simple, useful conventions are as follows:

- Almost always, piping and instrument lines should be either horizontal or vertical.
- Horizontal lines have the right-of-way.
- Equipment numbers should be placed near the upper right-hand corner of the equipment.
- Crooks should be placed in lines that point. They must also be kept from being horizontal or vertical (this helps distinguish them from piping).
- A P&ID should be oriented so that its position for reading is with the longest edges at the top and bottom

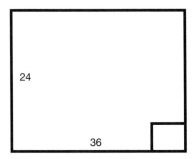

and the title block in the lower right-hand corner.

In general, P&IDs should not be bogged down with great numbers of conventions. In practice, a *good* P&ID will sparkle with ideas and

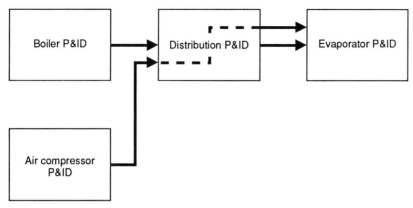

Figure 11-21 Use of a utility distribution P&ID.

statements. It is not a format in which conventions are supreme. It is a format for communication and invention. The creator of the P&ID should constantly keep in mind what the eventual reader will gather from what is put on the P&ID.

DEVELOPMENT

Development of a P&ID is best understood by standing on the sidelines, watching as one is developed. Figure 11-26 is the P&ID which we will follow. The equipment shown on this P&ID is listed in Fig. 11-27.

The process requirement is to provide humidity-controlled air for a coating operation. Temperature control is provided coincidentally. The coating is cellulose-based and requires humidity control for reproducible results. The coating operation takes place in the coatings room (in the upper, right-hand part of the P&ID). The rest of the P&ID shows how the constant-humidity, constant-temperature air is made. The design criteria require a temperature in the range of 75 ± 2°F and a relative humidity (RH) no greater than 30 percent. Extremes of atmospheric conditions in which these criteria must be met are as follows:

- Summer: temperature 90°F
             humidity 100 percent
- Winter: temperature 5°F
             humidity 0 percent

This P&ID is in a fairly advanced state, but is not yet ready to issue for design, because the line numbers and instrument numbers have not been added yet. In this case, the P&ID has undergone internal review and has also been approved by the client, thus the P&ID is ready to receive line numbers and instrument numbers. It is close to being good enough to issue for design work. It is good enough to issue for a ±15 percent estimate.

What is the origin of this P&ID? Where is the germ of this origin?

It so happens that, here, the origin lies with the mass balance and the PFD. This is often—but by no means always—the case. Many times, the start of a P&ID might be a crucial design detail, or a piece of equipment, or some other physical thing or abstract concept. There is no firm rule on where a P&ID gets its start.

Here the germ of its origin lies with the review of a psychrometric chart to envision how the demands of physics affect the desired process requirement. Examination of the chart (see Fig. 11-22) shows that

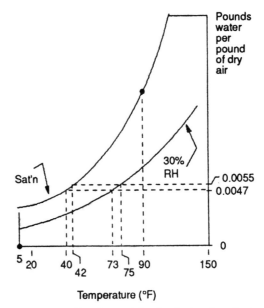

Figure 11-22 Psychrometric chart showing design parameters.

at a room temperature of 75°F, the moisture content is about 0.0055 lb water/lb air. Furthermore, such air would begin to condense water if cooled to about 42°F (its dew point). This is the germ of the design concept, namely, air with 0.0055 lb water/lb air can be obtained by saturating air at 42°F and then heating to 75°F.

Once the criteria for summer and winter extremes have been marked on the humidity chart (solid circles in Fig. 11-22), it is clear that there will be three modes of operation: (1) in the summer when moisture must be removed, and the temperature lowered, (2) in the winter when moisture must be added and the temperature raised, and (3) the occasional time (regardless of season) when the moisture swings from surplus to deficit.

The germ of the design concept is quickly jotted down in the form of the sketch shown in Fig. 11-23. The circles with arrows represent two forms of heat transfer: cooling (arrow down) and heating (arrow up). The box with water coming into it is just that, an undecided piece of equipment that adds water to air. A series of thought experiments, called *gedanken* experiments, are reviewed by looking at the humidity chart and at the sketch. The conclusion is that *basically the concept is sound, and what is needed is to work out the details* [ATD].

The next step is to replace the box with a known entity. How about just a box with a spray nozzle? This would work, but too much spray would be carried over with the air. Furthermore, in winter, the water

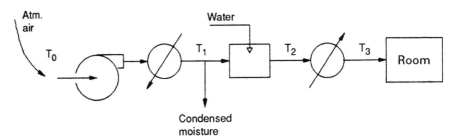

Figure 11-23 Germ of the concept.

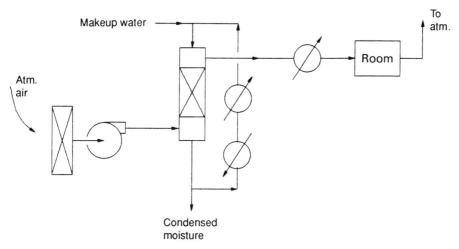

Figure 11-24 Sketch showing development of basic concept.

flow should be cut back. The spray nozzle pattern will then change—one more unnecessary variable. Also the nozzle would tend to clog, as nozzles are wont to do.

Far better would be a low-velocity flow over a solid medium that would spread the fluid across the whole gas stream. This is a classic application for a packed bed. This is shown in Fig. 11-24, which is a precursor of the process flow diagram (PFD). A recirculating loop around the packed bed provides good contact between the air and the water. This also is a conduit for heat addition or removal.

A good understanding of the process is needed before any effort is committed to this particular P&ID. There are some problems to be solved.

- Is the 30 percent relative humidity achievable over the course of a whole year?
- How does one decide when to add makeup water?
- How does one ensure that the heat addition for winter service does not fight the heat removal for summer service? How are these two started and stopped?
- How is the coatings room kept under a slight positive pressure (to prevent uncontrolled air from leaking in)?

To answer the first three questions, four rough mass balances are prepared.* They cover the following conditions for incoming air:

Temperature, °F	5	45	75	90
Relative humidity, %	0	0	30	100

These mass balances reveal the amounts of moisture added and removed. The humidity chart facilitates calculation of the energy re-

---

*The initial balances will be speculative, assuming end conditions, such as given here (below) with "not unreasonable" temperature profiles. Eventually, however, complete mass and heat balances are performed on the column, and the heater, for all four cases. None of this is shown. Along the way, it is concluded that the heater in the recirculation loop is somewhat awkward, so it is moved to the air inlet line (see the P&ID).

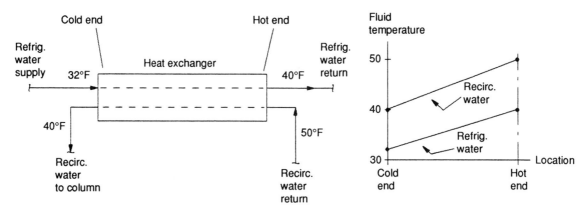

Figure 11-25 Examination of heat exchanger.

quirements. These calculations bring to light the existence of a process limit that has serious implications: How cold can the chiller go before the formation of ice at the heat-transfer surface begins to limit performance?

This latter problem runs as follows. For the recirculation water to enter the top of the packed bed at 40°F, heat must be removed by the refrigerated water (actually a glycol-water mixture) at, say, 32°F. For the sake of argument, if a counterflow exchanger were used, a temperature profile as shown in Fig. 11-25 would be achievable, and not unreasonable. This does not mean the exchanger will turn out to be true counterflow (it does not); it is a test hypothesis to check for "reasonableness."

Note that if the refrigerated water were lower than 32°F, a film of ice could build up (on the recirculation side, at the cold end). This is the limit referred to above. One result is that lower relative humidities are not easy to achieve by using the above scheme, because the heat exchanger will grow in size as the available temperature difference shrinks. Ultimately, this means that a relative humidity of say 20 percent is *not* achievable with the proposed design. The size of the exchanger becomes ridiculous.

The fourth question above, about room pressurization, is answered by determining that the minimum required pressure is 0.25 in WC. Pressure control is not needed. Pressure is achieved by sizing the exhaust duct to yield the desired result.

Thus the germ of the idea is developed by using laws of conservation, basic physics, and qualitative arguments. Note that the early parts of the conceptual work require a good general feel for basic physics: humidity, condensation, latent heat, etc. Later, the emphasis centers on basic mechanical or chemical engineering: mass transfer, heat transfer, equipment selection, flow diagrams, etc.

Once a good, solid feel for the process has been established via calculations and understanding of fundamentals, the work on the actual P&IDs can commence. In other words, the process should be firmed up before the P&IDs are begun. If commenced earlier, the result will be wasted effort with attendant undue costs.

As a P&ID is developed, it goes through stages. In order of development, the stages are as follows:

1. Conception (development of the germ)

2. Process definition (with unequivocal choices of equipment and process conditions)

3. Choosing what equipment to show on a single sheet

4. Selection and development of symbols

5. Deciding in which quadrant of the drawing to place the symbols (that is, deciding the *layout* of the P&ID)

6. Drafting

7. In-house reviews

8. Client reviews (including "hazmat")

9. Numbering equipment (usually partially completed already on the PFD)

10. Numbering instruments

11. Numbering lines (the design issue)

12. Incorporation of vendor's drawings (the construction issue)

Stages 1 and 2: The first two stages are usually termed *preliminary engineering* or *putting together the process package.* Sometimes these steps are done under a separate contract, prior to starting work on the P&IDs, so the connection with the P&IDs is not clear to all participants on the job. This can lead to the view that P&IDs can be developed without any process work (in the eyes of those who come on board the project without knowledge of the preliminary work). There is the rare occasion, mostly with a purely mechanical P&ID, when this is the case, but it is the exception.

Stage 3: The choice of what to show on a single sheet* is not an easy one. The rule of thumb is two or three major pieces of equipment or four to six minor pieces of equipment.† Initially, Fig. 11-26 was laid out with the supposition that, because simple air handling was involved, instrumentation would be minimal and perhaps up to eight equipment pieces might be accommodated. This supposition turns out to be wrong. Before line sizes can be added, the P&ID must be broken into two separate drawings. This drawing is obviously too crowded.

What is major and what is minor? Here is a short snippet for guidance. As usual, the rules are not hard and fast; judgment is required.

Major	Minor
Distillation column	Pump
Fired equipment	Fan
Fermentation vessel	Small tank (less than 2000 gal)
Agitator (40 hp)	Agitator (10 hp)
Cyanidation vat	100 gal/min cooling tower
Motor control center‡	Item costing less than $5000 that uses less than 60 ft² floor space
Reaction vessel	

Stage 4: The selection and development of the symbols have already been discussed above.

Stages 5 and 6: Layout and drafting can occasionally be left entirely in the hands of an experienced designer. This is not true with a

---

*Here, as elsewhere, the standard drawing being discussed is the D size, measuring 24 × 36 in.

†However, a *single* polyethylene extruder, in a high-production, highly automated environment, will quite likely require *two* P&IDs, and the same holds with a horizontal belt filter.

‡This is not shown per se on P&IDs, but is an example of a major piece of equipment.

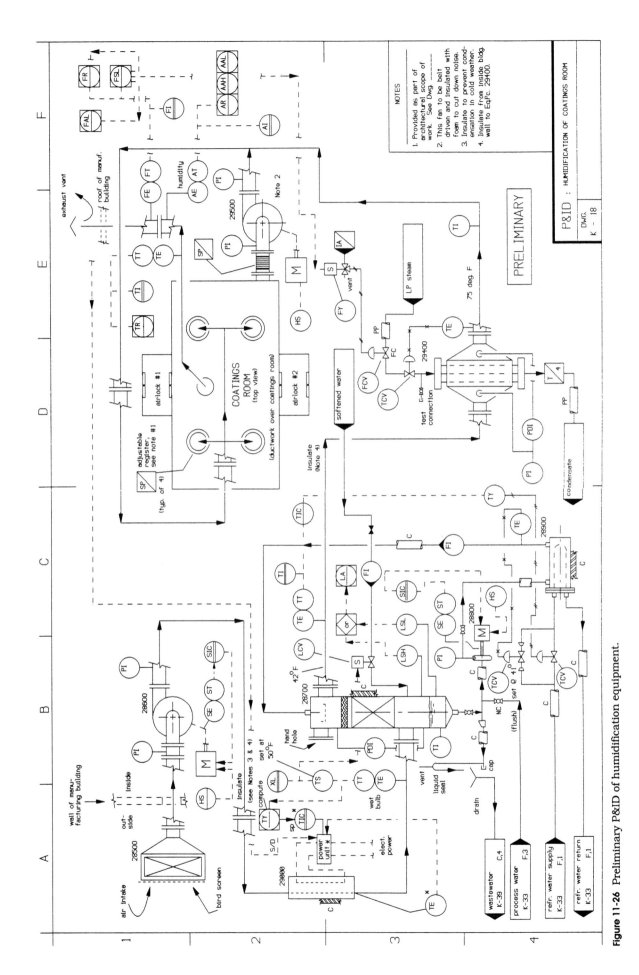

Figure 11-26 Preliminary P&ID of humidification equipment.

junior designer. A good knowledge of equipment operation is required for good layout of the P&ID. It is not unusual for an engineer to get hung up on some part of P&ID layout. Discussions with senior designers can be a great help in such a case. In all cases the designers should be consulted about the P&IDs to develop a good, readable product through *teamwork*. The project engineer is ultimately the responsible party who must foster a team effort.

Stage 7: In-house reviews are needed to coordinate the design effort. These reviews also stimulate some clear thinking among the engineers/designers working with the P&ID (having to present ideas has a way of making them clearer to the presenter). The reviews also place the P&IDs in the view of more senior engineers and designers.

The in-house review often keeps silly mistakes from being presented to the clients, thus avoiding embarrassment. The format of all reviews is largely as follows: (1) Review copies are sent to reviewers. (2) After reviewers have had a few days for review, the review meeting is held. (3) Copies of the P&IDs are spread out and discussed. (4) Comments are marked on a set of copies and/or noted on paper or in a recording machine. (5) Appropriate changes are made to the drawings.

Stage 8. Client reviews are carried out in the same way. Very often client reviewers are scattered across countries and continents, so more planning is needed and the review process might take longer. A major element of any review, past or present, has always been a focus on safety. Today, this aspect has been formalized somewhat by legal requirements aimed at preventing a Bhopal-type incident. A *hazmat review* (hazardous materials review) is mandatory.

Stages 9, 10, and 11: Equipment numbering usually begins with the PFDs and continues heavily as the P&IDs are developed. Instrument numbering and line numbering are done only after a P&ID has been subjected to both reviews. At the time when lines are numbered, they should also be sized. A quick, reliable way of numbering and sizing lines is to use spreadsheet software that employs macros to do the sizing calculations and size selections. A flow and a fluid commodity are entered for a line (see Fig. 11-33), then the macro does the rest.

While the P&IDs are being developed, and on through the construction issue, job progress can be monitored reliably by reviewing the P&IDs. Whether lines have been numbered (and therefore sized) is more or less a watershed, just as receipt of vendor drawings is a watershed for a project as a whole.

Stage 12: The last formal issue of the P&ID is the construction issue. This issue should not occur until after almost all pertinent vendor information has been incorporated into the drawing. Issues subsequent to the construction issue are not unusual. They usually contain tiny changes that result from the generation of design details. Often the author of the change is a designer.

It is important to note that while *preliminary engineering* occurs in stages 1 and 2, *preliminary P&IDs* don't come along until much later—steps 6, 7, and 8. This often causes confusion.

To get the maximum use out of P&IDs as they are being developed, the following advice is offered:

> When you think of something, put it on the P&ID immediately. Don't wait. It is better to erase later than to forget.

This is a good reason for including elementary forms of boolean logic on P&IDs. This should not be overdone, however.

It is a good idea to sketch or write proposed additions in red and simulated erasures and notes that need not be transferred (for the information of the annotator only) in blue. The P&ID thus functions as a notepad.

In Fig. 11-26 an eccentric reducer in the line going to the drain has been shown by the process engineer even though lines have not been sized. The engineer just "knows" it will be needed, owing to a familiarity with the mass balance.

As mentioned earlier, Fig. 11-26 is a P&ID in a fairly advanced state of development. From the time a sheet was spread out and the crude sketches of equipment were made until its present state, it has undergone about 68 h of development work, including 23 h of effort expended by the client. By the time all work on the drawing ceases, another 40 h or so will be spent by the engineering/design team, plus 4 h or so by the client engineers. See Table 11-3.

In reaching its present state, the drawing has undergone numerous alterations, each time to remove a flaw or a doubt. The original concept, no matter how good, will always have a few problems. These problems must be eliminated. It is doubtful that a *perfect* P&ID (one that has undergone *no* changes) has ever been produced.

The following statement, albeit somewhat graphic, can be made about the design process in general, and applies very much to P&IDs:

> Progress is proportional to the depth of the eraser crumbs around the drafting tables and desks. No eraser crumbs is equivalent to no progress.

It is far cheaper (and results in a vastly superior design) to make changes on paper instead of trying strange things with steel in the field. The above statement is made in reference to normal design development, *not rework* caused by errors and false starts.

In the course of preparing the P&ID shown in Fig. 11-26 and the list in Fig. 11-27, quite a few alterations took place. Some changes were even changed back to their original states. In the next few pages some of these changes are discussed, but by no means all.

Figure 11-28 shows the original concept for adding water to the scrubber. This arrangement is simple and cheap. Here is how it works. A drainage rate (or *bleed* rate) is established by adjusting flow

TABLE 11-3 Hours Expended on P&ID in Fig. 11-26

Layout and symbols		1
Hand sketching		6
CADD drafting, 1st		8
Gedanken experiments and revisions		4
Review by instrumentation department		8
CADD update		2
In-house reviews		9
Incorporation of review information		2
CADD update		1
Client reviews		(15)
Miscellaneous client input		(8)
Incorporation of review information		3
CADD update		1
	Total	45
	(Total including client)	(68)

```
                        EQUIPMENT / COMMODITIES      LIST
       Customer: Aegean Pharmaceutical                          Proj:    BZ - 112
       Location: Ontario, CA                                    Date:    8-SEP-93

                              Process Group
```

	area	tag number	pr	quantity	name	spec.# inqy.#	PO # VP #	diag # OD #	motor HP(1)	description
1	6	28500	L		inlet filter	S- 64 Q-	P- V-	K- 18		similar to unit at the boiler, see K-32
2	6	28600	M		inlet fan	S- 43 Q- 30	P- V-	K- 18	3.0'	900 cfm
3	6	28700	M		saturator	S- 36 Q- 18	P- V-	K- 18		fiber glass
4	6	28800	M		saturator pump	S- 52 Q- 39	P- V-	K- 18	0.5'	carbon steel
5	6	28900	M		saturator chiller	S- 35 Q- 23	P- V-	K- 18		carbon steel
6	6	29000	M		air heater	S- 46 Q- 33	P- V-	K- 18		electric, unit to include power + controls
7	6	29400	M		air reheater	S- 51 Q- 38	P- V-	K- 18		finned coils, steam servic
8	6	29500	M		coatings room recirculation fan	S- 43 Q- 30	P- V-	K- 18	1.5'	1,600 cfm
9										
10										
11										
12										
13										
14										
15										
16										

```
      Notes:    1. Apostrophe on motor size means: estimated, otherwise per vendor.      p. 4  of 7
                2.
                3.
                                                                              Form 123
```

Figure 11-27 Equipment/commodities list corresponding to P&ID of Fig. 11-26.

to the drain (by observing the flow rate on the rotameter—the FI—and adjusting the globe valve appropriately). The bleed rate is set to accommodate the worst, most humid summer day, and more. Even during periods when atmospheric water enters torrentially, makeup water is added. The makeup water starts on a signal from a low-level switch (LSL) and stops on a signal from a high-level switch (LSH). This design will work beautifully, but it is wasteful and can be costly (if the wastewater must be regarded as contaminated in some way).

To minimize waste, the scheme shown in Fig. 11-26 has been adopted. Water is added only when the wet-bulb temperature of incoming air drops below 50°F. Level is maintained effectively and cheaply with the liquid seal. Extra storage capacity for water is not regarded as necessary, so the reservoir at the bottom of the vessel is eliminated.

The next sketch (Fig. 11-29) shows one of the original ideas for

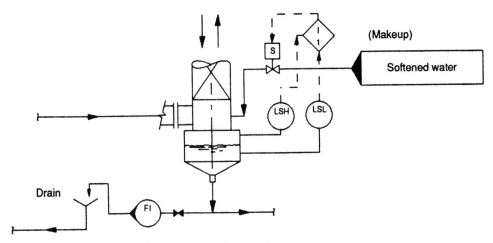

Figure 11-28 Original concept for adding makeup water.

achieving the goal of 0.0055 lb water/lb air. This sketch is illustrative in that it shows how good, basic concepts must give way to commanding realities. Here is how. The sketch shows the original design concept. It is lean. Control loops are simple. Flow control is manual, and temperature controls are self-contained, without reset or derivative features (plain proportional control)—a good starting point for analysis.

A *gedanken* experiment is used. What is described below is based on judgment, not calculation. Perhaps 15 min of deep thought is required.

Say air into the system experiences a temperature change from 80 to 70°F instantly. What will happen?

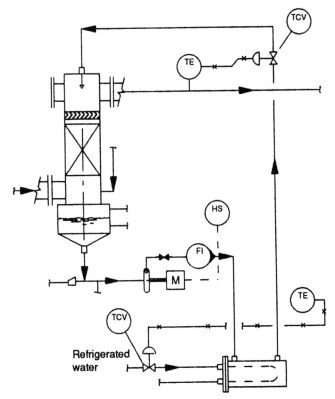

Figure 11-29 Sketch used to judge dynamic response.

Air leaving the saturator will drop rapidly in temperature. By how much? We can't say, but it is important and detectable. The sensor in the outlet duct will sense this and cut back on the control valve in a few seconds (less than 3 s). Down below, at the exchanger, the sensor will begin to see a low temperature after a few seconds, due to the cut in recirculation. This will initiate curtailment of flow of the refrigerated water supply. The initial actions occur in a few seconds, but recovery to stable operation will take much longer, because the mass of water already in the reservoir must arrive at a new temperature. If the holdup time in the reservoir is 60 s, a new, stable control point on the valves may take 3 min to achieve.*

On pure proportional control, the correction will never be fully compensatory; but often, in spite of the bias it produces, it is acceptable. We ignore this for the moment, but make a note to examine this question at another time.

Where are we? We have response times on two control loops of a few seconds and a thermal capacitance effect lasting a few minutes in response to a hypothetical, instantaneous step change of $-10°F$ in the incoming air.

Continuing the experiment, we observe: Even during a summer storm, the most rapid temperature change might be 10°F in 30 min or so. Therefore, our control scheme, even though sluggish, can certainly keep pace. In terms of heat balance, we note that the 10°F drop will result in a rather small change in the heat removal rate, say, less than 5 percent of the design maximum. The final position of the valve will be slightly closed, compared to the initial state. This is acceptable. The system passes the first test of the "thought experiment."

Another question in this process is posed as follows. What happens from day to night? During a normal day, the temperature and relative humidity might be 80°F and 40 percent. At night, 12 h later, they might be 50°F and 80 percent relative humidity. How will the proposed control scheme respond?

Obviously the dynamic problems will be minimal, since the rate of change of heat load is not as high as in the previous analysis. What about the final conditions? Here we find a fatal difficulty. Comparing heat removal demands, we see that the control valves will be, for all intents and purposes, in a shutoff state at night—hence there will be no control at night. The scheme will not work.

It is always a bitter pill to swallow when one must leave simplicity and move toward the more complex. At this point the *gedanken* experiment analysis is temporarily suspended.

A phase is entered in which many sketches of different control schemes are made while heat and mass balances on the saturator column are calculated. The heat and mass balances are exploratory, not definitive, and full of speculations and assumptions. It is known that once a good prospect makes its appearance, the assumptions will be checked out.

In this case, about six flawed designs are tested over a period of about 4 h. Finally one is hit that leaves a warm, comfortable feeling.† Here the assumptions are reviewed from a process standpoint and are found acceptable. There are some minor doubts, however, and

---

*All this is judgmentally stated, without a calculation. This is *gedanken*. The judgments are of variable accuracy, but are regarded as realistic.

†In testing a series of ideas on paper, this should be the goal: a warm, comfortable feeling.

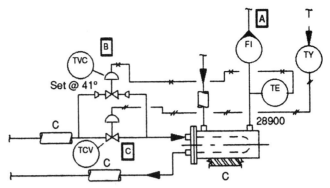

Figure 11-30 Two-mode control.

these are written in a brief handwritten memo* to the instrument engineer (these are covered later).

The seventh scheme is given in Fig. 11-30. Here is what is shown. The saturator chiller (equipment piece 28900) is operated in two modes. Loosely stated, these modes are daytime and nighttime. A different control scheme is associated with each mode.

In the six flawed attempts (not shown), the *gedanken* experiment technique was used briefly from time to time. Now it is resumed fully from where it was dropped earlier.

The thinking proceeds as follows for three cases:

- On a hot summer day, the temperature at *A* might be as low as 39°F. This still leaves a 3°F (42 – 39) approach at the top of the column. So *B* will be shut off, since it is set at 41°F. Therefore, *C* will be in full control.

- Later, at night, the heat removal rate drops markedly. The temperature at *A* begins to rise; *B* gains control while *C* hovers at shutoff.

- Minimum heat removal will occur in the winter or on cool nights. When the enthalpy of the entering air is less than the enthalpy of saturated air at 42°F (that is, 16.2 Btu/lb of air), the heater (equipment piece 29000) must add heat so that *B* will control; this is OK.

The first case has already been discussed.

In the second case, the heat removal rate is a small fraction of the design limit. Therefore, temperature approaches of less than 1°F are possible. For example, air entering at 50°F and 50 percent relative humidity, with the heater off, will impose no load on the cooling system. The adiabatic cooling line can be followed on the psychrometric chart straight to 42°F and 100 percent RH. This means that the heat required to evaporate water to saturate the air is matched by the heat obtained by cooling the air from 50 to 40°F.

We now look at the third case, which is crucial and can only be worked out by the process engineer. The instrument engineer, in this case, has an electrical engineering background and is only faintly aware of psychrometric charts, enthalpies, etc.

Here is how this last case works (see Fig. 11-26). Just before air enters the saturator, it passes over a sensor that detects the wet-bulb

---

*During project work, short, handwritten memos should pass back and forth between project team members routinely. Verbal communications are great for most matters, but when a key question is at hand, the memo is best [ATD].

temperature. The signal from this sensor is used to compute a set point for the air heater. The proposed equation is $t_S = -0.325t_W + 63$, where t_W is the wet-bulb temperature. When the computed set point is lower than the dry-bulb temperature, the heater will stay turned off naturally,* without operator intervention. This is good.

When the computed set point is higher than the dry-bulb temperature, the heater will add a small amount of heat—just enough to keep the recirculation loop at about 42°F. The heat addition is needed on cold winter nights. It not only will keep the saturator from freezing, but also will allow the refrigeration system to maintain temperature *control*. In the case of the air entering at 50°F and 50 percent RH, the computed set point is 52.6°F. This should put a small load on the refrigeration system and enable temperature control.

Along the way, an additional change, having only secondary effects on the control of humidity, is introduced. This is the speed control on the pump, along with the elimination of the throttling valve—this is due solely to economics, not for process reasons.

Before we discuss the P&ID further, we pause to take a quick look at the roles of the process engineer and the instrument engineer. It is at the interface of these two disciplines that great amounts of overlap are needed. The process engineer must have a good knowledge of instrumentation. The instrument engineer must have a good knowledge of process principles. The process engineer and the instrument engineer must work together as a team. The P&ID is where the team effort is most in evidence. The project engineer makes a contribution, too, by fostering a harmonious effort. As a senior staff member, the project engineer will have valuable contributions to make to the P&ID.

In the memo to the instrument engineer, the process engineer explains the workings described above and includes flow data for the different cases. From this, the instrument engineer should be able to size the control valves. The process engineer mentions concerns about overlap in the operation of valves *B* and *C* as hypothesized. The process engineer concludes by asking that the instrument engineer provide a minimum controllable flow for valve *B*. With this minimum flow, the process engineer can check the equation for the computed set point.

With regard to the above sketches, note that some of the lines end in a tilde. On a P&ID, tildes are allowed in pairs (see above, "P&ID Symbols"), but not singly. No line on a P&ID (or PFD) should have an undefined origin or destination. Even fans drawing air from or discharging air into the atmosphere should show by notes what is going on (see Fig. 11-26). This is a key point for sound environmental design [ATD].

In the case of this P&ID, the process design was fairly demanding and required a good deal of attention. There are other things that require attention, too, however:

- Noisy fans can make a workplace uncomfortable (hence note 2).
- Closed-pore insulating material (designated *C* for *cold*) should be used to keep moisture from condensing on the outside and causing rust or moisture damage on everything below. If the material is not closed-pore, the result is soggy insulation in addition to the other problems [ATD].

---

*A natural result is always preferred to a guided result. This is the basis for failsafe design.

- Since this unit is to be installed in a region where dissolved solids are somewhat high, the use of softened water is deemed necessary to prevent solids buildup in the saturator.

- The mass balances were performed to account for dissolved solids in the makeup water—if softened water is used, no further treatment is necessary.

These are typical, peripheral issues that crop up and are dealt with along the way. There are many more, not discussed here for brevity's sake.

All questions that arise must be dealt with and resolved. An unanswered question on a construction-grade P&ID is normally not permitted. (How does a craftsperson install a line whose diameter is unknown?) Questions should be answered at the earliest possible time. On a rare occasion, a small piece of information might be missing from a vendor drawing. If so, the affected area on the P&ID is outlined in pencil with a "cloud," and the notation *HOLD* is made. Design disciplines and field craftsmen will wait before going further. This practice can cost more money than is commonly imagined. When this practice is used, alarm bells should sound in the minds of all project team members, particularly client team members. The astute manager should seek ways to minimize future occurrences.

INFORMATION ON P&IDs

The information content of a P&ID is usually much higher than an initial glance would suggest. It has been this author's experience that (in a simple case) an acceptable process can be built from P&IDs, without arrangement drawings. The reverse, however, is a doomed effort. Attempts to put processes together with arrangement drawings fail. This is because necessary piping connections are missed and because motor controls are almost impossible to work up without a P&ID.

In the paragraphs that follow, part of the contents of Fig. 11-26 is examined.

Returning to the humidification P&ID, we note that some instrument functions are performed via software in a microprocessor-based environment (MBE).* These instrument balloons are framed in a box. This means they are MBE types. The single horizontal line inside the balloons indicates that the instrument is located on the main control panel of the coatings operation. Other instrument functions are performed in the "field" (that is, in the general vicinity of the equipment). Part of this latter instrumentation is mounted on a small control panel located near the equipment. This latter case is denoted by balloons with double horizontal lines. In the case of the humidification operation, it has been decided that things that can affect the process in the coatings room should be handled in the MBE. For this reason, temperature, flow, and relative humidity of air leaving the coatings room are in the MBE (along with the scrubber-level alarm). However, the day-to-day monitoring and maintenance should not be the concern of the coatings personnel. This order of priorities ensures that the coating operation is stopped if the humidity goes out of control, but does not distract attention from the coatings operation. Also,

---

*See footnote on page 191.

when the mechanic checks the humidification system, she or he will not have to enter the coatings area.

All motor-driven equipment is shown with a start-stop switch (HS) mounted in the field. This is done so that the operator, or mechanic, will be close to the motor as it is energized and thus can spot any anomalies immediately. A bad seal often makes its presence known upon starting or stopping, for example. The first clue to a problem is often an unusual noise. This noise is easiest to detect on start-up or shutdown. After a while, it may blend in with other sounds.

The air reheater (equipment piece 29400) contains a few features that can pass unnoticed. The temperature control is straight proportional, because the load should be quite steady. Grid E3 contains a solenoid valve that will shut off steam flow if airflow is lost for any reason, including a power failure. Without this provision, the control valve would open wide in an attempt to heat the still air surrounding the sensor in the duct. On the other hand, in the reheater, the stagnant air would circulate by convection within the heater, possibly overheating it and perhaps making the surfaces hot enough to cause a burn if touched. The *FC* notation on the steam valve stands for *fail closed.*

The test connection on the steam line is to measure the steam pressure in the event that the reheater shows signs of trouble. This possibility is presumed to be remote and not worth the price of a pressure gauge, that eventually, when needed, will be so old that it may not work or at least will be viewed with a great deal of suspicion and will be changed.*

Before we leave the reheater, note that two pressure sensors are provided: The PDI is used for looking at the pressure difference across the unit, and the PI is used in conjunction with other pressure indicators all the way along the air path for troubleshooting. By keeping records, acquired only once every month or two, it is possible to see a problem developing. Thus maintenance can be scheduled before a problem causes a shutdown—this is preventive maintenance.

On the entire P&ID there is not a single spare to be found. No controls are duplicated. Control valves are not bypassed. This is not an oversight. It is intentionally lean design. Equipment in the coatings room can be out of service for 2 or 3 h/day while undergoing cleaning and maintenance. If a piece of equipment on the humidification side goes down for a while, the coatings side will take the opportunity to do repairs at the same time.†

We now shift our attention to the heater (equipment piece 29000). The heater is depicted as a box because, at this point, a choice has not been made regarding its configuration. Once a vendor is selected and the type of heater is known, the symbol may or may not have to be changed so that a clear message can be conveyed to the reader.‡

The asterisks on the P&ID show that the power unit and the controls are purchased, along with the heater, from a single supplier. In a case like this, the heater supplier is in a better position to provide

---

*The idea here is to think ahead, be practical, be thrifty [ATD]. The P&ID is the medium in which to do this.

†Blind, unthinking inclusion of spares and bypasses adds untold amounts needlessly to project costs and gives project engineers/designers a bad reputation for guilding lilies.

‡This is in contrast to the chiller, which the process engineer has already decided will be a U-tube type of exchanger.

the power supply. As a matter of fact, the heater was probably designed by the vendor with a power supply in mind. On simple economic bases, it is best to accept the recommended power supply rather than reengineer it.

This isn't always the case, however. How much of the engineering should be provided by the vendor? In reality, there is no pat answer, because the answer depends on the knowledge of the different parties, what is needed, and who volunteers to take a leadership role.

The simple case of a fan is illustrative. In most cases, fans are thoroughly preengineered. One would not dream of intruding on a standard design, right? But wait, didn't we just see a case where a belt-driven design was called out? Such modest modifications are barely intrusions on standard designs. However, the modifications often extend to calling out bearings by name and model. Finally, in the extreme, diatomaceous earth manufacturers are known to go to a fan company with drawings and tell the fan company what to build. These manufacturers have heavily modified their fans to accommodate heavy solids loadings down through the years and know what they want.

In the case of the air heater above, the only feature that appears to require some customization is the controller. Here the requirement for a remote set point may—or may not—be viewed as a custom feature by the heater vendor. Once the unit has been purchased and vendor drawings are in the review process, other customized features may be seen to be desirable.

CONSTRUCTION-GRADE P&ID

Figure 11-31 is an example of a construction-grade P&ID. Careful examination will reveal that every piece is identified, whether equipment or commodity. For example, the hose from the drum to the reactor is identified as piping specialty item 57. Also the removable hopper is given an equipment number: 22002. The instruments have numbers, and so do branches of piping. Valves are not numbered individually, but are numbered by type.*

Once numbers have been established, it is possible to provide a history for each component. Thus, if a line size comes under question at some point, the calculation pinpointing its size can easily be found. This is true whether the calculations are done by hand (and the sheets have been filled out by hand) or within a spreadsheet via a computer program. If the question should arise of whether all the globe valves of type V5 have been put on order, it is possible to find out within a matter of minutes.

What is the NEMA classification of LSH-289 (E4)? The answer is obtained in a few short minutes by looking on the instrument list, finding a specification number, and pulling the specification from the file.

Eventually, every nut, bolt, and washer could be counted if the need arose. In practice, only the expensive ones are counted, and an allowance is made for the cheaper ones. However, where flanged connections are involved, all nuts, bolts, and washers must be counted, and provided at the jobsite before needed, lest the job be held up.

To appreciate the construction-grade P&ID, one has to envision

---

*A valve type usually is very specific: a particular valve made by a named manufacturer, or equal. The V5 (on cooling water bypass, at B3 to B4) is a Walworth 606F, 607F, or equal.

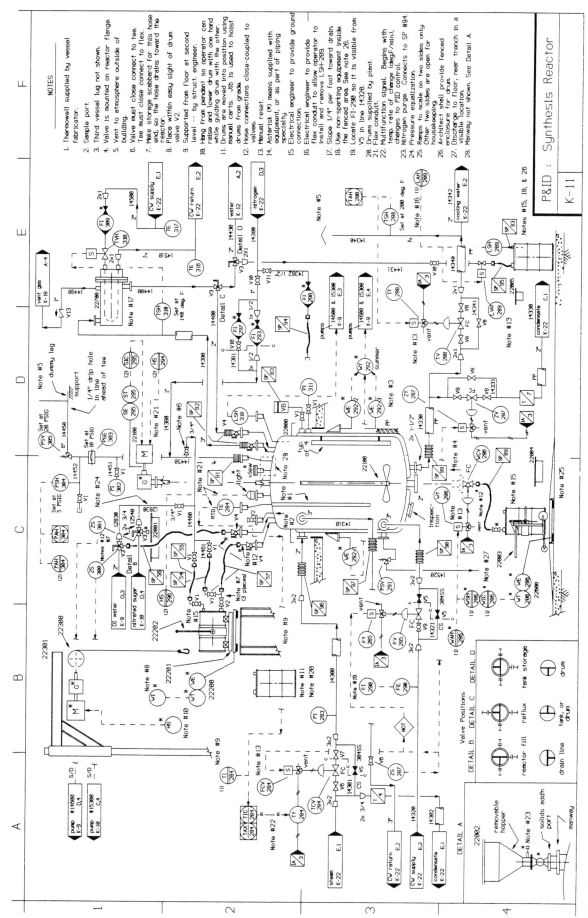

Figure 11-31 Construction grade P&ID of synthesis reactor.

how this document is used in the necessarily pragmatic art of construction.

Here is how line 14300 is erected. For weeks, the piping superintendent has waited to begin piping the synthesis reactor. Process and utility headers on a nearby piperack have been coming along well. To avoid stalling the piping crew, they have been moved onto other jobs while waiting for delivery of the reactor. Finally, on March 12, 1994, the reactor arrives. It takes half a day to get it off the truck. It takes another 2 days to check it out and schedule the work crews for its installation. Only 1 day is required for setting, leveling, and securing in place.

After the reactor has been installed, the piping superintendent gives the order to install "the hookup piping* to reactor 22000." The clerk in the pipe trailer sees that line 14300 is among those that must be installed. She looks on a list of spools and notes that this line is 150 lb/in^2 class, flanged, carbon-steel pipe. Two major lengths have been prefabricated and are marked with spool numbers. (The spool number is a number assigned by the fabricator.)

The clerk then reads a material takeoff list that accompanies the fabrication drawings (also called *spool drawings*—see below). She fills a burlap sack with materials that will be needed by the piping mechanic: nuts, bolts, washers, and manual valves, still in their boxes. She attaches a heavy cardboard tag to the sack and sets it aside for the piping mechanic. A note on the tag gives the two spool numbers.

A few more background details are noteworthy. Spool drawings are prepared by the piping fabricator. Normally they are based on isometric drawings, which were prepared from P&IDs, and piping orthogonal drawings. The sequence is as follows:

$$\begin{matrix} \text{P\&IDs} \\ + \\ \text{piping} \\ \text{orthogonal} \\ \text{drawings} \end{matrix} \longrightarrow \text{isometric drawings} \longrightarrow \text{spool drawings}$$

Not all lines will have isometric drawings prepared for them. Small, screwed lines will be prepared from orthogonal drawings and sometimes lesser drawings, such as modified equipment arrangement drawings. Table 11-4 gives a rough breakdown of the types of drawings generated for piping fabrication. Exceptions to what is shown in the table abound. Practice varies greatly depending on the industry, the end use, and the owner company standards.

Returning to line 14300, we see that on the day that it is installed, the piping mechanic and his apprentice will pick up the burlap sack from the clerk in the storage trailer. By reading the tag, they will note that two spools and two 20-ft lengths (sometimes called *sticks*) must be picked up from the storage yard. The clerk will obtain their signatures for receipt of these materials.

Retrieval of the control valve from stores may be put off until shortly before it is to be installed. Otherwise, it is a heavy, somewhat delicate device that can be in the way. In this case, the piping mechanic sends the apprentice over to the supply shed later in the day to obtain TCV-284.

Hookup piping is the relatively short piping that runs from the header to the equipment piece. This piping is installed after the equipment is in place and after the header piping is in place.

TABLE 11-4 Drawings Required for Piping Fabrication

Size and type of fabrication, in	Drawings				Shop fabrication
	P&ID	Orthogonal	Isometric	Spool	
0.5–2 screwed	X	X*			No
2.5–4 screwed	X	X	X		Sometimes
1–3 welded	X	X	X	X†	Sometimes
4+ welded	X	X	X	X	Yes

*For a simple modification of an existing operation, sometimes dimensions are not given, allowing the installer to determine the exact location.

†Some fabrication drawings are made of the more complex pieces.

Installation of the cooling water line (14500 in E1) is different. The location of the line is given on the orthogonal drawings, but installation details are worked out by the piping mechanic. Isometric and fabrication drawings are not prepared. The piping mechanic makes his own installation sketch and submits a bill-of-material order for sticks, fittings, valves, etc. As before, when the materials are dispensed for line 14500, the clerk notes this fact in a log.

In these instances, the P&ID has functioned as a *record* and a *communication tool.* It is a source of indisputable labels: the numbers. These numbers are used for filing, labeling, and clarifying ideas. The numbers are used in lists that contain cross-references and further information. Two lists included here are presented as Figs. 11-32 and 11-33.

There are other lists associated with P&IDs. Two that are on a par with the two presented are the instrument list and the specialty items list. These additional lists are not presented. The point is that the P&ID is a source of numbers for the many lists prepared by the many disciplines.

The equipment list is discussed in App. C.

A few words concerning the pipe list (Fig. 11-33) need to be mentioned here. First, is the coding of the pipe number. As shown in Fig. 11-33, the line referred to as *line 14342* is designated as

$$14342 - I - C8 - LC - 2$$

The segments of the line number are understood as follows:

14342 = identifying number
     I = thermal provision [that is, hot insulation; others are
        cold insulation (C), tracing (TR)]
  C8 = piping commodity code (that is, 304 stainless)
  LC = fluid commodity code (that is, low-pressure condensate)
    2 = nominal size (that is, 2-in USP)

The first issue of the pipe list is the responsibility of the process engineer. Subsequent issues are the responsibility of the piping designer. The existence or nonexistence of a pipe list is a key indicator of true project progress (see Fig. 14-4).

The overall operation shown in Fig. 11-31 is described as follows. A nitrated sugar compound is delivered to a reactor by pumping from bulk storage. The degree of nitration is quite low, so the compound is not considered explosive, or highly energetic. A series of homologous derivatives are synthesized by alterations of the nitrate group. Addi-

```
 ----------------------------------------------------------------------------------
:                          EQUIPMENT / COMMODITIES   LIST                          :
:           Customer: Synthesis, Inc                          Proj:   AS - 43      :
:           Location: Esterville, Iowa                        Date:   6-SEP-95     :
:                                                                                  :
:                                   Process Group                                  :
 ----------------------------------------------------------------------------------
:   :    : tag    :  :quan:       name        :spec.#: PO #:diag #:motor:          :
:   :area:number :pr:tity:                    :inqy.#: VP #:  --  : HP  :description:
 ---:----:--------:--:----:------------------ :------:-----:------:-----:-----------:
1  : 4  : 22000 :H :    :Synthesis Reactor   :S- 11:P-  6:Fig. :     :           :
   :    :       :  :    :                    :Q-  8:V-  3:11-31:     :           :
2  : 4  : 22001 :L :    :Upper Drip Pan      :S-   :P-   :  "  :     :           :
   :    :       :  :    :                    :Q-   :V-   :     :     :           :
3  : 4  : 22002 :L :    :Removable Hopper    :S-   :P-   :  "  :     :           :
   :    :       :  :    :                    :Q-   :V-   :     :     :           :
4  : 4  : 22003 :L :    :Drum Dolly          :S-   :P-   :  "  :     :           :
   :    :       :  :    :                    :Q-   :V-   :     :     :           :
5  : 4  : 22004 :L :    :Lower Drip Pan      :S-   :P-   :  "  :     :           :
   :    :       :  :    :                    :Q-   :V-   :     :     :           :
6  : 4  : 22005 :L :    :Drum Drip Pan       :S-   :P-   :  "  :     :           :
   :    :       :  :    :                    :Q-   :V-   :     :     :           :
7  : 4  : 22100 :H :    :Reactor Agitator    :S- 11:P-  6:  "  : 50  :           :
   :    :       :  :    :                    :Q-  8:V-  3:     :     :           :
8  : 4  : 22200 :M :    :Feed Weigh Scale    :S- 43:P- 14:  "  :     :           :
   :    :       :  :    :                    :Q- 30:V- 12:     :     :           :
9  : 4  : 22201 :L :    :Drum Cradle         :S-   :P-   :  "  :     :           :
   :    :       :  :    :                    :Q-   :V-   :     :     :           :
10 : 4  : 22202 :L :    :Drum Clamp          :S-   :P-   :  "  :     :           :
   :    :       :  :    :                    :Q-   :V-   :     :     :           :
11 : 4  : 22300 :M :    :Drum Hoist          :S- 62:P-   :  "  :.75*:           :
   :    :       :  :    :                    :Q- 47:V-   :     :     :           :
12 : 4  : 22301 :M :    :Jib                 :S- 71:P-   :  "  :     :           :
   :    :       :  :    :                    :Q- 53:V-   :     :     :           :
13 : 4  : 22600 :M :    :Product Weigh Scale :S- 43:P- 14:  "  :     :           :
   :    :       :  :    :                    :Q- 30:V- 12:     :     :           :
14 : 4  : 22700 :M :    :Reflux Condenser    :S- 36:P- 11:  "  :     :           :
   :    :       :  :    :                    :Q- 22:V-  8:     :     :           :
15 :    :       :  :    :                    :     :     :     :     :           :
   :    :       :  :    :                    :     :     :     :     :           :
16 :    :       :  :    :                    :     :     :     :     :           :
   :    :       :  :    :                    :     :     :     :     :           :
 ----------------------------------------------------------------------------------
       Notes:     1. Asterisk (*) on motor horsepower means estimated.    page 5 of 12
                  2.
                  3.
                                                                          Form 123
```

Figure 11-32 Equipment/commodities list.

tives are poured into the reactor from drums. However, there is one product where the additive is a solid.

No gaseous products are released in the synthesis. Liquid products and by-products are compatible with the end use and are not separated. Dilution water sometimes must be added and removed. Small quantities of catalyst dissolved in methanol are added. A rough methanol separation is carried out at the end of the synthesis by boiling a small fraction off into drums, which are shipped back to a specialty supplier who distills the methanol and makes up new batches of catalyst.

The reaction is carried out at temperatures ranging from 180° to 220°F.

Heating begins after the nitro sugar has been added. The heating cycle begins with a jacket that has been drained of water. The jacket is filled mostly with air at the start of the heating cycle. Say the initial temperature is close to room temperature. The heating sequence goes as follows:

• The sequence starts with the reactor jacket filled with air and vented to the atmosphere through TV-288 (D3 to D4).

```
Project No. AR-336                                                           Date: 12 Nov. 1994
Project Name: Nitro Sugar Reactor
                                         PIPE LIST
```

	Number	From	To	Temp. (deg.F) Oper.	Design	Press. (psig) Oper.	Design	(ft/sec) Veloc.	(psi) PD/100'	(1) Flow	P&ID No.
1											Fig.
2	14300 - I -C3 -LS - 3	11500	E22000	300	450	10	100	125	1.1	1800 P	11-31
3											
4	14301 - I -C3 -LS - 2	14300	14300	300	450	10	100	280	6.5	1800 P	"
5											
6	14302 - I -C3 -LC -0.7	14300	11620	220	300	10	100	1.1	0.4	1.8 G	"
7											
8	14310 - N -E2 -CW - 3	E22000	11980	100	200	10	50	7.8	3.2	180 G	"
9											
10	14320 - N -E2 -CW - 3	11990	E22000	80	120	10	50	7.8	3.2	180 G	"
11											
12	14321 - N -E2 -CW - 2	14320	14320	80	120	10	50	17	23.5	180 G	"
13											
14	14330 - I -C8 -LC - 2	E22000	11620	220	300	10	100	2.4	0.6	22 G	"
15											
16	14331 - I -C8 -LC - 2	14330	14330	220	300	10	100	2.4	0.6	22 G	"
17											
18	14340 - I -C8 -LC - 2	14330	11980	220	300	10	100	7	negl.	600 C	"
19											
20	14341 - I -C8 -LC - 1	14340	14340	220	300	10	100	28	negl.	600 C	"
21											
22	14342 - I -C8 -LC - 2	14340	11980	220	300	10	100	7	negl.	600 C	"
23											
24	14380 - N -E6 -N2 - 1	15110	14450	90	120	0	100	55	0.3	1100 C	"
25											
26	14381 - N -E6 -N2 - 1	14380	14380	90	120	0	100	55	0.3	1100 C	"
27											
28	14382 - N -E6 -N2 -0.5	14380	SP94	90	120	0	100	82	0.6	300 C	"
29											
30	14390 - I -U11-ME - 3	E22000	E22700	200	300	0	100	70	0.4	600 P	"
31											
32	14400 - N -U11-ME - 2	E22700	E22000	200	300	0	100	>1	negl.	1.2 G	"
33											
34	- - - -										
35											
36	- - - -										
37											
38	- - - -										
39											
40	- - - -										

Notes: 1. Flow units: G = gpm; C = acfm; P = lbs/hr

page: 4
of: 12

Figure 11-33 Pipe list.

- Steam valve controller TIC-284 (A2) is set on manual control to open the valve by 10 percent; this is a preliminary step to the actual opening of the valve, because FCV-284 blocks the signal from TIC-284 to TCV-284 until the next two steps are accomplished.

- Block valve V6 (A3) in the cooling water return line is closed, actuating limit switch ZS-287, causing two things to occur automatically: the cooling water supply valve FV-285 shuts, and condensate valve ZV-287 is opened.

- When solenoid valve FCV-284 is reset, TCV-284 takes control.

- Initially, the steam entering the jacket will meet a great cold sink and will quickly condense; in a few minutes, however, the reactor wall will begin to heat, and steam entering the reactor will reach lower levels in the jacket, driving out air as it goes.

- The air will flow mostly through line 14340, which is expressly provided for air venting.

- Condensate will flow down line 14330. Initially it will be cold, accompanied by much air; it will flow partly into line 14340, too, where eventually it will go via line 14342 to become cooling water makeup.

- Once air is displaced, temperatures will begin to climb, and steam will blow through line 14340. This will cause TSH-288 to change state and will result in TV-288's closing.

- The end result is that the trap (shown on detail drawing T-7) in line 14330 will take over for the rest of the cycle.

- When the change in mode occurs, an audible message is sounded (via TAH-288) to prompt the operator.

- The controller (TIC-284) is then set at a heating rate of 1.33°F/min with a software trip point that will switch control to plain temperature control at 220°F (or some other reaction temperature).

At this point, additives are fed into the reactor from drums. Finally, the catalyst is added. While additives and catalyst are being added and while the reaction is occurring, condensate from the vent condenser is returned to the reactor.

Once the reaction is complete, the valves shown in details C and D are reset so that condensate is diverted to either drums or an accumulation tank. Once the methanol-water boil-off is complete, the cooling sequence can be started.

- The initiation of the cooling cycle occurs when the valve (V6) in the cooling water return is opened; this actuates ZS-287, which opens FV-285, starting cooling water flow.

- Note that the cooling water flow rate is manually modulated.* The previous activities merely turn it on or off (the reader's attention is called to globe valve V5 downstream of FV-285).

- Cooling water entering the jacket will cause water vapor (from the heating cycle) to condense; this will create a vacuum, causing the vacuum breaker (SP-83) to allow air into the jacket.

- As the water level in the jacket rises, a point will be reached where no more significant condensation is taking place. The vacuum breaker will close; shortly thereafter the whole jacket will be full of cooling water, and the reactor will be in the cooling mode.

- Opening valve V6 has caused ZV-287 to shut; this keeps cooling water out of the condensate.

- Also while cooling, TY-288 continues vented to the atmosphere; thus TV-288 has failed closed.† This ensures that the entire jacket is full of cooling water, not just the bottom.

---

*When controls are discussed, *modulation* is exemplified by the action of the globe valve. *On-off* (or discrete) is exemplified by ZS-287, FY-285, and FV-285. The discrete controls enable the modulators.

†The reader is referred to catalogs showing control valves and actuators to understand the mechanics of a *fail-closed* valve. The simplest form of such a valve is one having a strong spring that *normally* keeps it closed. Upon application of air pressure, the valve is *forced open.*

- The end of the cooling cycle is terminated manually* by closing ball valve V6 in the cooling water return line, deactuating ZS-287 and causing VF-285 to close.
- The last step consists of draining the jacket; this occurs when TY-288 (D3, E3) is manually reset and leads to the opening of TV-288.
- As the water drains, air will enter the jacket in the place of the water through the vacuum breaker.
- The system thus returns to its initial state.

Figure 11-31 contains many practical details [ATD]. The following list covers salient points. Each comment is preceded by an approximate grid location.

A1	Signals to pumps 146 and 153 (shorthand notation used for equipment numbers) ensure that they will start only when the three-way valve is in the correct position.
A3	Trap assembly T-4 is to carry away condensate drips, so that when TCV-284 is opened, slugs of condensate will not impede steam flow or cause hammering.
A3	In the event of a power failure, FCV-284 will vent the actuator on TCV-284, stopping the flow of steam. This is a safe mode of failure. Upon regaining power, FCV-284 continues to vent the actuator until reset by hand. This, too, is prudent.
A3	Line delimiters refer to P&ID K22. This is a utility distribution P&ID (see above, under "Conventions").
B1	Jib hoists are useful, economical, handy items.
B2	Equipment piece 22201 is a simple oak cradle (built in a local carpenter's shop) without which this operation would not function reliably or safely [ATD].
B2	The structure associated with note 9 need not be shown, but it helps communications measurably.
B3	Simple is better than complex. Full automation of cooling water flow is not needed. See description above.
B4	Instruments provided by the vendor for the weigh scale are numbered because they are integrated with two other items: the local panel and solenoid valve WY-286. Note that this is not the case with the weigh scale in grid B2 (equipment piece 22200).
C1	The pressure relief valve (PSV-305) is kept hermetic by the rupture disk PSE-303. Sticking or corrosion will be eliminated.
C1	If PSE-303 should develop a leak, the central alarm and the field alarm will both be sounded.
C1	The drip pan (equipment piece 22001) is provided to keep the floor from getting messy from dripping hose connections [ATD].

---

*The product can be drummed out at 120°F or less. The operator will be watching the temperature on TI-284 as he or she sets the drums in position for the packaging part of the operation. A rough economic study shows that a grossly careless operator might waste 100,000 gal of cooling water per year by not automating this operation. At a pumping cost of 6 cents per 1000 gal, no automatic shutoff can be justified.

C2   All connections to the reactor head are flexible to minimize force distortions on the weighing instruments (load cells WE-292.1, WE-292.2, and WE-292.3).

C2   On the P&ID this zone appears crowded. The reality in the
+   field is that, indeed, it is crowded. This is a busy place. If the
D2   operator could stand where the agitator flange is located, he or she could probably reach and touch 40 percent of what is shown.

C3   Flexible connections are provided to minimize force distortions, as above.

C3   A brief showing of the approximate location of the floor at the second level is very helpful. The antidrip ring shown in the floor around the reactor is a good memory key. Will it be included on the structural drawings? The P&ID will serve as a reminder to check. Over the years, that simple concrete embedment will prove extremely profitable. It will improve quality. It will improve employee morale. It will greatly limit maintenance. It will improve housekeeping and make a safer workplace. This simple drip ring can thus be seen as something of immeasurable worth. If a return on investment could be measured (which it cannot), this simple embedment might tip the scale at 1000, or 10,000 [ATD!]. The effort to show it on the P&ID is negligible. The *knowledge* needed to show it is not great, but is certainly significant—the kind that comes from using trained, experienced personnel.

C4   The operator wheels an empty drum into position on the weigh scale. He then pushes a button on WIC-286, causing it to record a tare weight. He then pushes a start-sequence button, and walks away to do other things. Once the (previously entered) fill weight is achieved, valve WCV-286 is shut automatically, and the operator is notified via WAH-286. He repeats this until the reactor is empty.

C4   There are two field panels associated with the reactor. One is at ground level; the other is mounted at the second level. Instruments mounted in the field panel at ground level are preceded by the numeral 1 enclosed in parentheses: (1).

C4   Note drip pan (equipment piece 22004). This helps housekeeping and minimizes waste. Other drip pans are called out at other locations on the P&ID.

D1   Too often the support under a relief point has been ignored. By calling this out on the P&ID, this requirement is kept in view.

D1   Instruments mounted in the field panel at the second level are preceded by the numeral 2 enclosed in parentheses: (2).

D2   The rotameters (FI-297 and FI-293) are set up for two different purging modes: (1) a high purge rate to rid the reactor of air once it has been opened, or if the manway should be opened for some reason when a batch is present, and (2) a normal, low rate to make sure nitrogen is always present. The change from one mode to the other is accomplished quickly and surely with the ball valves. The globe valves are available to adjust flow rates, but are rarely touched.

D2   The point where this nitrogen is introduced is at the relief line, under the rupture disk. This is so that the rupture disk will see a clean environment and the relief line will be clean [ATD].

D2   LSH-318 will stop pump 146 or 153 from overfilling the reactor.

D3   Signals from load cells under vessel supports are added (summed). The resulting signal, representing the vessel weight, is sent to a controller (shown on P&ID K9). The controller is set to stop pumps 146 and 153 once preset quantities of nitrated sugar and DI water have been added to the reactor. The controller is programmed to reject weights that could lead to overfilling. This means that LSH-318 (above) is redundant. It is thought that the redundant control is justified because of the possibility of a load cell malfunction.

D4   *Question:* In place of the pneumatically operated valve (ZV-287), why not use a solenoid valve directly in the condensate line? *Answer:* This would work well for a while, but eventually would run into trouble, because a reasonably sized solenoid cannot exert the kind of force needed to overcome increased friction as sliding, mating surfaces become rough, pitted, and scaled up in this kind of service. The first 6 months are a breeze, but the engineer/designer must think ahead for the next 10 or 20 years.

D4   Valve V8, bypassing TV-288, is not a globe valve. This is because modulating control is not desired. On-off control is desired. The same is true with the ZV-287 bypass.

E1   The reflux condenser cooling water (CW) flow is set manually, because automatic controls are not justified. The basis for the flow setting is a 5 to 10°F rise from CW supply to CW return. This setting will be adjusted infrequently, perhaps weekly or monthly. However, per procedure, perhaps once a shift, the temperatures of TI-309 and TI-308 will be recorded on the operator's log sheet. TVH-310 (in conjunction with its temperature switch) will shut off cooling water when hot vapors fail to reach up into line 14390. Conversely, cooling water will automatically be restarted when hot vapors return to line 14390 and cause TSH-310 to change state.

E4   Two drums of water-methanol are filled for each drum of catalyst added.

Where bypasses have been included, it is usually in rather severe service, such as steam and condensate. A bypass has been included in the jacket for cooling water because it is important to cool off the reaction mass once the reaction has been completed. The reaction mass can be spoiled if held too long at reaction temperature.

A bypass is not provided on the reflux condenser because the service is not severe and because a problem such as a stuck solenoid valve can quickly be resolved.

Before we leave this chapter, we repeat the following observations:

> The P&ID is the place where a good deal of inventing and problem solving will take place. Use the P&ID for that purpose. Do not become hidebound by conventions and symbols, yet be consistent.

═══Chapter 12═══
Procurement

INTRODUCTION

Procurement can be subdivided into two broad areas: goods and services. Typical goods are pumps, tanks, reinforcing rod, concrete, and paint; typical services are secretarial work, bricklaying, engineering, site grading, and painting.

The procurement activity on a project brings together purchasing agents, owners, engineers, designers, fabricators, vendors, and contractors. A typical job ranging from $5 to $20 million can result in the following purchases of goods and services:

Description	Number of purchase orders
Engineering, design, procurement, and construction management	1
Major equipment	12
Minor equipment and commodity items	30
Instruments	30
Major subcontracts	5
Minor subcontracts	25
	103

Most owners are not set up to execute large numbers of complicated purchase orders with multiple bids. Therefore, they hire the engineering contractor to do this. Thus, from the above list, the owner issues one purchase order (the one at the top of the list), and the engineering contractor issues the remaining 102 purchase orders. The hiring of the engineering contractor is covered in Chap. 13, *Hiring the Engineers.*

When the engineers are hired to do procurement for the owner, there are two basic kinds of arrangement: Engineers work as agents for the owner or as outright purchasers. In the first case, it is the owner who is executing the purchase contract with the vendor; the engineers are simply representing the owner. In the second case, the engineers sign the purchase contracts on their own recognizance. Technically, the engineers have some rights to the equipment until reimbursed by the owner. The second arrangement is usually preferred, because the owner's accounts payable staff often is not prepared to handle some of the questions that arise.

The goods and services mentioned at the beginning of this section deserve more attention. The goods are generally divided into the following three groups: equipment, commodities, and materials. The best way to appreciate the distinction among them is via a comparative listing:

Equipment	Commodities	Materials
Thickener rake	Doors for building	Concrete block
Filter press	Pressure transmitters	Welding rod
Compressor	Ductwork*	Conduit
Switchgear	Piping	8-gauge copper cable
Motor control center	Valves	Nails
Pressure vessel	Mirror for bathroom	Thermal insulation
Room exhaust fan	Steam traps	Wooden forms

*Without fail, this is called "duck-work" at the job site.

The above distinctions are useful because differing amounts of effort are required for their procurement and because they can be procured in different fashions. The equipment is almost always purchased from the home office. The materials are purchased either from the field or via *inclusion* in a subcontract. Commodities can come from either source. The above terminology is not hard and fast. It varies from company to company, industry to industry, and even job to job.

A subcontract usually includes commodities and materials plus a very important third item: labor. Inquiry work and procurement work are almost always done from the home office. However, modifications during the job mostly originate in the field, and when the paper hits the purchasing department in the home office, many times the modification has been finished, and purchasing just formalizes an accomplished fact.

Some subcontracts include fabrication of equipment. This is how large field-erected tanks, which are too big to transport from a shop to the field, are provided.

SUBCONTRACTS

Contract, subcontract, and *direct hire* are terms encountered often on a project. Here is an example of what these terms mean. You hire a *contractor* to redo your kitchen who, in turn, *subcontracts* the tile portion of the job. You could have elected to *hire* a handyman, a laborer, and a tile setter *directly,* but you made your life easier by *not* acting as your own *general contractor.*

In a situation where many contractors are involved, the one who leads and has major responsibilities is called the *general* contractor.* On many construction sites, the general contractor provides managerial and clerical services only, with the actual labor all being performed by subcontractors. The contractor in such a position is called the *construction manager* (CM).

Theoretically, the construction manager doesn't cinch down a single bolt or even brush dust off of a pressure gauge. In reality the CM will pitch in and run an errand or two for the subcontractors or act as helper, if requested and if time permits. Typically, the construction management team is busy coordinating the efforts of the many subcontractors. Timing of execution is one of their main tasks. For example, the subcontract on piping must wait for the installation of corrugated sheet- metal siding, since it is far easier to punch holes in corrugated sheet metal, already in place, than it is to fit an 18 × 12 ft

---

*The term *general* is used exclusively in construction, whereas *prime* is often used when several firms are involved in a joint engineering effort.

sheet-metal panel around even one stick of pipe, much less a half dozen or so.

As nerve center, the construction management team also

- Keeps daily records of all site activities, noting which tasks were performed, which subcontractors were present, and every single person who set foot on the site from company executives to delivery people
- Maintains receiving reports for materials and equipment
- Leads site security
- Leads site safety and keeps records of safety meetings
- Communicates with the owner and the engineer for interpretation of project needs
- Keeps drawing files, purchase order files, specification files, vendor print files, etc.
- Posts construction permits and hosts inspectors
- Negotiates, authorizes, and records changes on subcontract work

In this discussion, it is assumed that the construction management team* is already in place. Therefore, discussion of procurement activities is limited to subcontracts. The construction management team may have come on board as an adjunct of the engineering effort; it may have been selected on merit or from past experience; or it may simply be part of the owner's permanent staff.

The procurement of a subcontract requires clear job definition, just as described in Chap. 13, *Hiring the Engineers.* The responsibility for achieving this job definition for the construction effort rests squarely on the engineers. It was for just for this purpose that they were hired.

The usual subcontract will be based on competitive bidding among four to six subcontractors—more is unfair, fewer is risky. An award strictly on the basis of low bid is not recommended. As much as anything, the bid should be viewed as a window into the soul of the subcontractor. Too low a bid might mean that the contractor fails to understand the job . . . or she or he may have a new approach to the job that is impossible to beat, and justifiably attractive. Interviews with the major subcontractors are indispensable. Proposed job supervisors and managers *must* be present during such interviews. Visits to the contractor's offices and shops are highly recommended.

The following example illustrates how contract execution, and the subsequent costs, can differ from contractor to contractor.

Two kilns side by side were put up for sale at a defunct spodumene calcining plant. The kilns were identical: 10 ft in diameter by 120 ft long. One kiln was sold immediately. The buyer hired a local contractor to cut it up and ship it to a new location. The crew who did the work were about 20 strong and took about 2 weeks. They removed the brick and cut the shell in 20-ft lengths. A crane was on the site the last 5 days of the job.

The second kiln was not sold until about 6 months later. The crew who took it apart were specialists. There were four of them. They had

---

*For a job ranging from $5 to $20 million, this will consist of a site manager, a clerk or two, and a part-time secretary. The home office will provide engineering and scheduling support as needed, and during major subcontracts, such as piping and electrical, some backup from construction specialists in those crafts will be needed.

a 1-ton truck with a small hoist. A load of timber was dropped off a week before they arrived. Two worked in the kiln, removing rings of brick every 20 feet while the other two hoisted cribbing into place from the outside. On the third day a carbon-rod (arc) cutter was mounted at one of the 20-ft prepared segments and set to work, slicing through the 1-in wall. On the fourth day a crane and two "lowboys" came in. The lowboys left loaded. On the fifth day three lowboys were loaded. On the sixth day, the job was completed, and everyone went home. A few days later the cribbing lumber was picked up.

No doubt, the second kiln was cheaper to take out and easier to put back in service than the first. No doubt, *knowledge* has merits.

The most common *construction* subcontracts are

Piping*	Paving
Electrical*	Fire sprinklers
Mechanical*	Plumbing
Concrete*	Grading and site preparation
Steel (fabrication)*	Masonry
Steel (erection)*	Insulation (thermal)
Painting	HVAC
Ductwork	Siding and roofing
Fireproofing (steel)	Instrument calibration
Sewer	Excavation
Temporary electrical	Shoring
Temporary water	Sheet metal
Architectural	

Others, such as carpentry and scaffolding, are included in concrete and masonry. There are still others such as trailer rental, office equipment rental, port-a-potty rental, etc., which are also common, but don't add greatly to expenditures.

Depending on the size of the job, some of the above can be further subdivided into more specialized subcontracts, for example, underground piping and aboveground piping. Usually the opposite approach, however, yields better results: combining masonry with concrete, for example, or excavation with shoring. Choosing what to include in a subcontract is an exercise requiring careful attention. The capability of the subcontractor, not on jobs in the past but *at the moment*, merits the closest attention.

In addition to construction subcontracts, there are engineering subcontracts, performed mostly prior to construction. Some are

- Surveys
- Soil tests
- Model making
- Special stress computations

SPECIFICATIONS

A specification is a written description of what is required. In a letter to Santa a child describes what he or she wants—a red three-wheeler, for example. Even for informal quotes, an engineer must write down what he or she had in mind when the quote was asked for. Sometimes

---

*These are usually the *major* subcontracts.

it can be months between the time an informal quote is sought and the final quote is hammered together. The original basis will be lost if not put in writing.

When a potential procurement starts to become a reality, a formal specification becomes a necessity. (For an example of a formal equipment specification, see App. H.) This will occur fairly early in the project, usually when preliminary engineering has finished, and when firm quotes are needed for the budget estimate. The specification serves these ends:

- It is a record of ideas.

- It communicates these ideas to a broad audience.

- It is a gauge for taking the measure of suppliers and contractors.

There have been occasions when purchases have been made on a very informal basis and almost no written description was provided. Neither the owner nor the provider (vendor of subcontractor) is well served in such a case. An engineer who obtains quotes on or procures a good or service without a written specification* commits a professional error and opens the door to accusations of negligence. Such action puts the employer in a delicate situation and may cause problems for suppliers or contractors who are dealing in good faith.

The three broad classifications for specifications are (1) standard specifications, (2) custom specifications, and (3) contract (or subcontract) specifications.

Standard specifications vary little from job to job or from year to year. Typical examples are concrete, orifice meters, bimetal thermometers, shop-fabricated tanks, and so on. In general, one can take a standard specification, read through it, make a few minor changes, add a sketch or two, and send it on its way. Standard specifications can take from 2 to 10 h of *engineering*† to review and update for purchasing requirements.

Custom specifications are for very well-defined requirements, where one particular configuration of parts and pieces will serve the need, and no other will. Even here, other specifications are built upon to create the new specification. The genesis of a custom specification probably will be another custom specification that is related in some way. A large Dowtherm heating system might be revised for a proposed small Multitherm system, for example. In a case like this, a considerable amount of effort is needed to create the new specification. This kind of specification can take from 20 to 60 h of multidiscipline *engineering* to create. This includes calculations, reviews, conversations with vendors, literature searches, etc. In no way is the 60-h figure a limit. Where very unusual requirements occur, the 60-h figure will easily be exceeded.

Writing a specification from scratch should be avoided strenuously. For standard specifications, many sources can be tapped. One can even purchase specifications, in electronic data format, developed for U.S. government projects.‡

For custom specifications of equipment, some source can usually

---

*This is not to say that a full specification (such as given in App. H) is always needed. Many times the *specification* consists of notes on drawings or statements on a Requisition.

†When the word *engineering* is italicized, reference is only to engineering, not engineering/design.

‡One source is the National Institute of Building Standards, Washington, D.C.

```
┌─────────────────────────────────────────────────────────────┐
│  1.0   General Description                                    │
│  2.0   Codes, Standards, and Other Specifications            │
│  3.0   Operating Conditions                                  │
│        3.1   Capacity                                        │
│        3.2   Feed                                           │
│        3.3   Intermediates                                   │
│        3.4   Product(s)                                      │
│        3.5   Available utilities                             │
│        3.6   Special physical/chemical properties           │
│        3.7   Atmospheric conditions                          │
│  4.0   Equipment                                            │
│        4.1   Process components                              │
│        4.2   Instruments                                    │
│        4.3   Electrical components                           │
│        4.4   Arrangement                                     │
│  5.0   Design Requirements                                   │
│        5.1   Equipment                                      │
│        5.2   Appurtenances                                   │
│        5.3   Materials of construction                       │
│        5.4   Provisions for corrosion                        │
│        5.5   Operation and maintenance                       │
│  6.0   Degree of Assembly                                    │
│  7.0   Drawings and Documents for Approval                   │
│  8.0   Testing                                              │
│  9.0   Surface Finishes                                      │
│ 10.0   Cleaning                                             │
│ 11.0   Responsibilities and Guarantees                      │
│ 12.0   Shipping                                            │
│ 13.0   Installation and Start-up Assistance                 │
└─────────────────────────────────────────────────────────────┘
```

Figure 12-1 Equipment specifications, general outline.

be found, whether it be by querying colleagues or trade organizations or piecing a specification together from multiple specifications of components. Therefore, the outline of specification headings in Fig. 12-1 is not meant to be used to write a specification from scratch, but is meant to serve as a memory aid for pulling together diverse ideas for an equipment specification.

Contract specifications can be either standard or custom. The diversity of contract conditions is far greater than that for equipment, so it is not unusual to compose a contract specification from scratch. Undesirable as this is, it is better than trying the obverse, that is, forcing a contractor to follow a poorly adapted specification from some other job.

Contract specifications have a huge range of size and complexity. On the small end, there is the contract with the company that supplies drinking water at the jobsite: typically to two or three locations, three or four times per week. Then there is the mechanical contract for setting equipment, aligning it, grouting under it, piping it, leak-testing it, painting parts of it, mounting some of the instruments, and operating it during water tests. This portion of work can sometimes account for more than one-third of the field effort. Also it can be so diverse as to include thermal insulation, small equipment foundations, process ductwork, HVAC ductwork, and building air conditioning.

Locale is very important on contracts. What you might be able to pull off beautifully in Kingsport, Tennessee, using the local contractor who specializes in comfort air conditioning and does plant construction as a sideline, can fail olympically if attempted with some other firm 200 mi to the north.

The contract specification must consider from where the labor forces will be obtained. Construction forces, labor and supervision, are quite mobile. One year, some top-flight millwrights might be in Gillette, Wyoming, and the next year they might be in Cameron, Louisiana. Therefore, what might be easy to do in year 1 in Gillette, becomes more problematic in year 2.

When a specification is written for custom contract work, it must be reviewed by experienced field personnel prior to being issued for bid. This simple provision will save large amounts of time and money.

THE PROCUREMENT PROCESS

Most equipment procurement occurs in the following sequence:

1. Inquiry
2. Bid analysis
3. Purchase order
4. Drawing approval
5. Fabrication
6. Delivery

Subcontract procurement is similar, but step 4 is often not included (when it is not needed), and the delivery step occurs prior to erection (fabrication):

1. Inquiry
2. Bid analysis
3. Purchase order
4. Drawing approval
5. Delivery
6. Permitting
7. Erection

Note also that permits must be obtained prior to erection, something not needed for equipment fabrication.

Because procurement entails expenditures of money and involves contractual obligations, it requires a degree of formality one step higher than that for most project work. Communication via the written word, a good idea at any time, must be exercised without fail on matters involving procurement. This is true for communications internal to the engineering (or construction) organization and even more so with external communications with vendors and contractors.

This, then, is the backdrop for a procurement maxim:

> Any alteration to the status quo that affects a procurement must always be recorded and disseminated via a requisition.

The ultimate change in status quo, of course, is placement of the purchase order, and in this case the need for a requisition will not likely be overlooked. The need for a requisition to initiate inquiry is fairly obvious, too. Some other, not so obvious, cases of a change in status quo are these:

- One bidder is granted a 1-week extension on the due date; the other bidders must be granted the same extension.
- A mistake is corrected on one page of a specification after the specification has been sent out for inquiry; there is some chance this might affect bid prices.*
- An extra pair of contacts is marked onto the control diagram by the electrical engineer during vendor drawing review.†

However, there are some things that, at first glance, appear to merit a requisition, but on further examination can be seen to be manageable without a requisition. For example, a bidder calls to say that her model of ball valve employs Viton O-rings as a standard feature, and can these be used instead of the butyl ones called for in the specification? Since for the proposed use the Viton is superior, it is an acceptable alternative, but not a requirement. The other bidders should be allowed to bid per the specification. The superior feature by the one vendor should be noted in the bid analysis.

The initiation of the procurement process occurs with the creation of the inquiry requisition. Subsequent steps are as shown in the two numbered lists above. In addition to the inquiry requisition, at least two more requisitions are needed for equipment: purchase and return of approval drawings. (For a subcontract, only the purchase requisition will be needed if no drawings are involved.) Of course, other requisitions might be needed to comply with the procurement maxim.

Before we move to the next topic, it is worth noting that the requisition is a formal internal memorandum, directed *always* to the purchasing agent and having, for the most part, a fixed distribution. It should be composed carefully, so that it is brief, clear, and complete. The requisition should not repeat what is covered by the specification unless there is a key point for the purchasing agent to call out in the cover letter. All attachments, whether standard or not, must be called out in the requisition. This is not a task that the purchasing agent can execute alone. Specifications and drawings that are not standard must, of course, also be listed in the requisition. Required bid or delivery dates must be called out. Bidding instructions and a list of bidders can be included in the body of the requisition or attached.

On a new project, it is a good idea for the project engineer to review the first few inquiry packages that are sent out to make sure something hasn't been omitted or that something sensitive (such as the bidder's list) hasn't inadvertently made its way into the package.

BID ANALYSIS

This is a procedure for comparing bids. It culminates in the selection of a single favored bidder. One will win, while the others will not. In

---

*If there is no chance that bid prices can be affected, a requisition is not needed, but the change should be called to the attention of the successful bidder when the order is placed.

†A requisition should accompany any set of marked-up drawings being returned to a vendor (see App. B, under "Routing"). To determine whether to flag a potential price change for the purchasing agent, the vendor should be consulted. If the vendor says the additional contacts will change the price or schedule, this should be duly noted on the vendor drawing route slip (Form 137, App. C) and on the requisition. Negotiation of the actual price increase should be left to the purchasing agent.

approaching a bid analysis, the engineer should fix two thoughts in mind:

- What I am about to do must be fair and unbiased.
- My own company is a bidder in other markets, so I will use this thought to maintain a balanced perspective.

The most common way of carrying out a bid analysis is on a sheet of paper having lines and columns (see Fig. 12-2). The most convenient sheet is 11×17 in. Distinct features being compared are annotated as a paragraph number from the specification and/or a description of the feature. The responses of the different bidders are noted in the different columns.

A bid analysis should be as short as possible. Ideally, the only annotations should be those where the quote differs from the specification or where quotes differ from each other. Critical features should be included to make sure they are reviewed. A long list of secondary features common to all bidders is not necessary.

A bid analysis should answer these questions:

- Is the specification adhered to? If not, in what way?
- What features differentiate the different bidders?
- How do operating costs compare?
- How do selling prices compare?
- Will vendor drawings be a problem?
- What are the promised deliveries?

Engineers doing the bid analysis must put themselves in the shoes of several people while engaged in this activity:

- The owner, who will pay the initial investment and subsequent operating costs
- The operator, who will make the unit perform over the years
- The maintenance mechanic, who will have to keep it running and fix it

These are the people who must live with the unit after it is purchased. A bid analysis that addresses only selling price is seriously deficient.

The following letter, published by *Chemical Engineering* magazine [71], gives a view from the vendor's side.

> Sir:
>   I read your October reader-interaction survey with great interest. Although the respondents claimed to put performance and reliability first when making purchase decisions, my experience working for an equipment vendor tells me that often these criteria are put in third and fourth place behind price and delivery. This makes it hard for a high quality vendor to compete with the cats and dogs and yet make a decent profit. In the end, if users are not willing to pay a higher price for better equipment, they will not get it. The result will be loss of productivity for the entire chemical process industries, and for the U.S. economy as a whole. Therefore, I would like to share my thoughts on what the correct hierarchy of purchase decisions should be, from most important to least.
>
> (1) Process performance. If the equipment fails to do what it was bought for, productivity and product quality suffer. A unit that does not perform the required task is not a bargain at any price.

SPEC. NO. 24 TAG NO. 18100

BID ANALYSIS DETAILS

Customer: Old Soldier
Location: Elko, NV

Instrument Air Compressor

Proj. CU-850
Date 12JUL94

	Paragraph	Description	Vendor #1	Vendor #2	Vendor #3				
1	3.1	Capacity 120 SCFM	157	111	117				
2		@ 125 PSIG	125	125	125				
3									
4	4.1	Screw type	Y	Y	Y				
5		INCL FILTER	Y	Y	Y				
6		DRYER	Y	Y	Y				
7		RECEIVER	80 gal	50 gal	45 gal				
8									
9	4.3	High Eff. Motor	Y	Y	Y				
10		Motor HP	40	30	30				
11	4.3	Local Panel	Y	Y	Y				
12									
13	6.0	Assembly	complete on skid	complete on skid	complete on skid				
14									
15	7.0	Approval Docs.	Y 4 ARO	Y 3 ARO	Y 4-5 ARO				
16									
17	Price		25,200	24,000	23,100				
18	Terms	(1)	20:70:10	15:75:10	20:70:10				
19									

Notes: 1. a: b: c where a = percent due upon receipt of drawings
~~2.~~ b = percent due upon " " equipment
~~3.~~ c = percent due 90 days after receipt of equipment

Form 142

Figure 12-2 Bid analysis details.

(2) Reliability. Forced shutdowns cost productivity, as well as in-process material losses. These costs dwarf any differential in equipment price.

(3) Operating cost (including energy cost). This also dwarfs equipment-price differentials. However, the desire to save energy should never lead one to use marginally designed equipment.

(4) Maintainability (including ready availability of parts). Given that all equipment must be maintained or rebuilt eventually, preference should go to equipment that can return to service in the shortest time.

(5) Vendor support services (process and mechanical technology, troubleshooting, maintenance seminars, etc.). These capabilities cost money, and many vendors lack them. But it is less expensive to buy from vendors who have these services than to create a cadre of in-house specialists for all conceivable types of equipment.

(6) Delivery. Delays in startup cost a great deal of money. However, the project engineer should always seek vendor delivery input early, so that he or she can properly plan for the delivery. If equipment delivery becomes an issue, the buyer may be forced to buy something that is not optimal in other respects. Good scheduling can forestall this.

(7) Price. If two or more vendors are equal in all other respects, then and only then should the decision be made on price. However, this is so rare that it might be better to make the purchase decision "price unseen" in most cases.

All in all, initial purchase price is by far the smallest cost associated with the buying and operating of a piece of equipment for its useful design life.

I hope your readers agree with this listing. Perhaps they can use it to help redirect the priorities of those who hold the purse strings at their facilities.

> Gregory Benz
> Chemineer, Inc.
> Dayton, Ohio

In theory, the use of qualified bidders should level out differences in categories 1, 2, 4, and 5. In practice, this is not easy to do, much less prior to asking for quotes. In some cases, previous experience with a vendor might date back several years, and believe it or not, things can change radically in a matter of several years.* In other cases, a vendor's shop might be swamped with work, so the attention given to the item in question will be minimal. Thus, when an inquiry process begins, the bidders are thought to be equal, but in the best of cases, this will only be approximately true. For this reason only part of the inquiry process is to ascertain price. The other part deals with such things as current capabilities and value while in service.

Placing purchase orders strictly on the basis of bid price is wrong. Upper management must transfer some responsibility to and put faith in their engineers. A good way to do this is to allow acceptance of a bid based on criteria other than the lowest price—within limits, that is. Here is how it works. Here are the bids:

---

*Even in fairly substantial organizations, much of the leadership and inspiration can be traced to a single individual. When this individual goes, some profound changes will follow unless there is a capable, trained successor.

	Bid*
Bidder 1	102
Bidder 2	85
Bidder 3	108
Bidder 4	115

Say company policy allows selection of a bidder within 7 percent of the low bidder, also say that, as a result of bid analyses, and examination of credit ratings, it appears that bidder 2 is undergoing some difficulties. Generally accepted policy is that an unqualified bidder may be eliminated from the bid list. If this is done, bidder 1 becomes the low bidder. If management were to allow engineering discretion for bids within 7 percent, then bidder 3 would be in the running. By allowing the 7 percent discretionary option, the owner's company management is signaling concurrence with *quality*.

A FINAL REMINDER

Without other instructions, a vendor typically will provide a certified overall dimensioned assembly drawing plus a parts list and a maintenance manual (all a few weeks prior to shipment). There will be no approval drawings. This is usually *not* acceptable.

The request for vendor drawings must be made clear at the time of inquiry. After bidding, and especially after the order is placed, if drawing approval has not been prearranged, a meaningful drawing submittal becomes unlikely.

This subject is covered more at length in Chap. 14, *Paper*, and in App. B.

---

*Bid price here is given when operating costs for all bidders are the same. When operating costs differ, a review of *incremental rate of return* is recommended; see Chap. 5, *Cost and Schedule*.

—Chapter 13—
Hiring the Engineers

Except in controlled economies, prices are ultimately determined by bargaining between two parties. The profound sameness of goals, stratagems, and emotions on the floor of the New York Stock Exchange and the pig market in Chichicastenango, Guatemala, is striking. The holder of the goods always wants more cash, and the offerer of the cash always wants to pay less. First there is the offer, often followed quickly by a sometimes haughty refusal. Then comes a new offer, but the second refusal often will be not made so quickly and will be a little gentler, too. Maybe after some conversation about the weather will come the offer that is finally accepted. Quite likely both parties will show countenances that signal defeat or resignation, as though each has given away too much. The variations on this basic theme are interminable. Sometimes, even the first offer is accepted without hesitation. In that case, the offerer is sure to feel he or she has blundered.

In most cases, both parties are on an equal footing. Indeed, both may feel they have been unduly generous, but the bargain they struck was fairly made. From time to time unscrupulous or unethical people have tried to use the bargaining process for unfair gain. This has generally led to intervention by authorities to preserve the peace. Some of the earliest writings deal with adjudications concerning bargains. Thus the bargaining process has been examined at length from a legal standpoint. It is not unusual for the average college course in business law to dwell at least a couple of weeks on the topics of *offer* and *acceptance.* The extent of legal writings on these two topics has probably never been measured, but the weight of the paper upon which they are written must be measured in tons, not pounds. The part covering winks, ear pulls, and head scratching at cattle auctions might make a fairly hefty bundle by itself.

Projects start, flourish, and finish with the bargaining process. Long after the plant has started up, change orders are under review for settling final payments. Dickering over warranties can go on for years.

JOB DEFINITION

An inherent element in any bargaining process is the object in question. For a camel merchant, the beast on the hoof is the object. For a civil engineer asked to propose her firm's ability to engineer a river crossing, it is where the crossing is to take place and whether it is for automobiles or trains via solid roadway or ferry boat, and so on. For a pressure gauge supplier, it is a description of the service conditions.

Successful projects begin with clear, thorough job definitions, in writing. This forms the basis for bargaining, serves as a record of what was bargained, and informs participants in the project about the tasks expected of them. Once bargaining has concluded and project work is begun, the different tasks are easy to understand. Progress is measurable. Teamwork comes naturally. False starts are avoided.

Without good job definition, the project is being entrusted to chance. Lawyers love projects with poor job definition.

The evolutionary sequence for a project is from a developmental stage (also termed the *conceptual* stage), through various stages of preliminary engineering and design, then procurement, detailed design, and finally construction (see Fig. 5-6). Development is usually performed by the owner/operator. Sometimes the owner/operator will do the preliminary engineering, too, but often it will be farmed out to an engineering firm. This is usually to acquire a second-party opinion and to employ the greater resources generally obtainable from the engineering firm. The culmination of this step will usually be an estimate.

The transition from when work is being done by the owner/operator to when it is in the hands of the engineering organization is important. In some respects, this is the birth of the project. This is when its existence as a hypothesis starts to give way to its existence as substance. Here, care in preparing a good job definition will pay manyfold rewards.

This point is important enough to merit a little more probing. Suppose 6 months and $100,000 have been spent looking at a way to raise the molecular weight of a urethane polyol. How much time and effort are justified in organizing available information for an outside engineering firm? One hour? One week? There is no pat answer, of course, but it definitely is more than 1 h, and let there be no doubts: 1 week's preparation would pay handsomely. Yet, the reality of the situation these days is that most development work of the magnitude described is followed up with *no* formal definition in writing or as drawings. Fleeting conversations with the developers are more than likely the sum total of substance available at the start of preliminary engineering. In fact, the developers sometimes are distracted by new assignments. Multimillion-dollar plans are literally transmitted on the backs of envelopes, and used ones at that.

The paucity of information is sometimes further compounded by questions of confidentiality. It is as though the engineering firm were expected to read the mind of the owner/operator as part of the contract requirement. Sometimes the origin of this approach to projects can be traced to an owner who believes that engineers/designers are all-seeing and all-knowing. Therefore, they don't need additional information. Often, during sales presentations, the engineers/designers do their best to appear all-seeing and all-knowing—this does not help. The fact is that an owner must describe to the engineers/designers what he or she needs.

SCOPE AND BASIS

The written word and drawings are needed to transmit job descriptions. The spoken word is not good enough, *no matter how small the job.*

The job description for a process plant project is most often called the *scope of work*. It gives the what, when, where, who, and why concerning the job. For small jobs or small parts of big jobs, the scope will be short. A sample scope-of-work document for a small job is presented in App. A.

All scopes of work must include the following at a minimum:

- A written description of the process
- Pertinent scientific facts (such as pertinent chemistry)
- A process flow diagram
- A rough (but carefully documented) mass balance
- A rough location drawing
- Required amenities: telephones, outdoor lighting, intercom system, etc.
- Statements describing what is required of the engineering firm
- A description of project timing
- Need for emergency power
- Need for field-mounted instrument panels
- Need for special rooms: process control, laboratory, shop
- Need (or lack thereof) for lightning protection
- A list of exclusions
- A brief description of new utilities
- Design basis (basic data)

The last item, *design basis,* is also referred to variously as *basic data* or *basis for design.* This item, in turn, should contain as a minimum:

- Design temperatures and pressures
- Design live loads for platforms
- Site surveys and soil bearing data
- Physical and chemical properties* of (1) raw materials, (2) in-process materials, and (3) finished products
- Product specifications for both raw materials and products (see Chap. 8 and App. G)
- A derivation of annual capacity
- A derivation of maximum operating rate for key equipment pieces
- A derivation of operating hours per year
- Sizing criteria for tanks, pumps, heat exchangers, etc.
- Dirt factors for heat exchangers
- Allowances for future expansion on new air compressors, cooling towers, electrical transformers, etc.
- Safety considerations
- Corrosion allowances
- Special materials of construction

---

*That is, viscosities, densities, specific heats, and such, not readily obtainable in the literature.

- Special equipment (including used equipment)
- Governing standards and specifications (owner or engineer?)
- Instructions regarding installed spares (yes/no, which items?)
- Available utilities and a brief description of them
- Location of "tie-ins" (utilities and process)
- Conventions: drawing sizes, units, drawing scales, numbering schemes (of drawings, equipment, etc.)
- Altitude above sea level
- Weather conditions: lows and highs for dry- and wet-bulb temperatures, wind, relative humidity, etc.
- Earthquake zone
- Jurisdiction: city, county, state, regulatory

A sample design basis is given in App. A.

Not all this information will be available at the time outside engineers are brought in. Furthermore, in discussions with the outside engineers, some issues may resolve themselves, or the engineers might be in a position to help fill in some of the blanks. Work should not be stopped due to a few loose ends, but definite steps must be taken to acquire all the named items, plus others that will be evident as the job is thought through.

OBTAINING ENGINEERING SERVICES

Almost without fail, the earliest participation by an engineering company on a project is seen in the preparation of a proposal or a bid. Very often the first inkling such a company has that a project is at hand is the receipt of a brown, manila envelope containing drawings and some form of a job description. The cover letter is likely to use the term *request for proposal* or *request for quote.* Sometimes the abbreviations *RFP* or *RFQ* are used.

The request for proposal asks the engineers to propose a course of action to achieve some goal or set of goals. For example, the request may ask what it will take to prepare an estimate with an accuracy of ±30 percent—what kind of work will be done, who will do it, what their qualifications are, and how long it will take.

A request for a quote usually asks the recipient to provide a quoted price in addition to the proposal. The request can be for a list of reimbursable charges plus other charges and fees, or it might be for a lump-sum amount. Examples of the two kinds of quotes are given in Table 13-1.

Payments can be on a periodic basis or according to accomplishments (sometimes called *milestones*). For example, the lump-sum

TABLE 13-1 Examples of Reimbursable (Cost Plus) and Lump-Sum Quotes

	Reimbursable (cost plus)	Lump sum
Labor	$30.50/man-hour	$42,000
Benefits	30 percent	
Overhead	40 percent	
Expenses	At cost	
Fee	1.5 percent	

quote above may specify a payment of $30,000 upon submittal of the estimate, then the balance upon submittal of all deliverables. Compensations based on a reimbursable basis or as a lump sum probably constitute more than three-fourths of the engineering contracts in force at this time. There are many other forms of compensation, however. Here is an abbreviated list, including the two already mentioned:

Cost plus percent fee	Costs plus other charges plus a percentage for profit
Cost plus fixed fee	Costs plus other charges plus a fixed amount for profit
Unit price	Payment per document issued
Lump sum	An agreed amount, no more and no less
Not to exceed without prior agreement	Cost plus with a limit that can be moved up, if agreed
Guaranteed maximum	Cost plus with a limit that can be moved down, but not up
Convertible	Start out at cost plus; convert to lump sum after an agreed milestone event is reached

Except for very brief projects, payments are in installments. Sometimes incentives and penalties are inserted into the different forms of compensation.

From a contractor's standpoint, the first option—cost plus percent fee—is the most desirable. From the owner's standpoint, the third option—lump sum—seems to offer a good deal of security. In reality, both parties can benefit from one approach or the other when the circumstances are right. The reality, too, is that neither type of arrangement is all that it seems to be. Listening to staunch advocates of either arrangement can make one wonder just what kind of experience they may have had with the other kind—perhaps none at all?

The obvious peril of cost plus is that it can easily become a featherbed. With no incentives to maintain an intensive work pattern, the contractor can get sloppy and inefficient. And what is worse, this is to *the contractor's* benefit. If the job takes longer, great.

The dispute over cost plus and lump sum will not end soon. Over 70 years ago Mead [72] wrote that with cost plus "the owner can secure [the contractor's] services, with the advantages of his skill and experience for the lowest practicable amount." Then, a little later on, he reverses himself by saying, "Experience shows it is almost or quite impossible to secure efficient working conditions under the cost plus percentage arrangement."

Nonetheless, this can be the most economic approach to project work because

• The owner and the engineer have common objectives.
• The owner can stick his or her nose into the project work, calling the shots as desired.
• The owner can (and should) be present in the work area, watching how money is being spent.
• The work will be done without having a contingency tacked on.

On the other hand, under lump-sum conditions, the engineer can politely inform the owner that the bid was not based on a mutually common objective, but on a certain number of things that were to be done. In other words, the owner's advice is not needed. Stay out of the kitchen until the cooking is finished.

The owner must judge progress from documents submitted. He or she will not see a design as it unfolds and may be shocked when this finally happens. The owner can, of course, request to become involved in the design, but will be opening the door to *change orders.*

Under lump-sum conditions, the owner will not see labor reports and so will have little idea what the actual cost of the job was. The owner may have paid dearly, but will never know. The labor reports also give a good indication of progress; without the reports a job can fall silently behind. Lump-sum work has a reputation for running late.

Probably the greatest motive for seeking lump-sum work is to "put a lid on project costs." For an owner, the open-checkbook* approach of cost plus is unsettling.

Strangely enough, the lump-sum approach may put on less of a lid than is commonly imagined. As mentioned earlier, both lump-sum and cost-plus approaches have preferred niches in the world. For the lump-sum method, it is well-defined, repeat jobs. For cost plus, it is the opposite: ill-defined pioneering efforts of amorphous character. An owner who absolutely insists on lump sum for the second kind of job may be accommodated with a bid restricted to known tasks. Then as the job progresses, *change orders* to cover the rest of the job start to make their appearance. The owner is bound to feel alarmed and betrayed (in spite of having been warned about poor job definition) as the job undergoes a metamorphosis, so that to complete it, it must become a sort of cost plus job without a lid—just what the owner was striving to avoid. This, without the clout of a cost-plus contract!

Another reason for requesting lump-sum bids is to use the bids in a competitive comparison to achieve "lowest cost." Competitive bidding for professional services rarely yields lowest cost. The reasons have been well articulated by Jacobs [73]. Here are some paraphrased excerpts:

- Who absorbs the costs of multiple bidding? Remember there are no free lunches.
- Who absorbs the losses on an underbid job?
- What losses accrue when the principals are adversaries?
- What happens to creativity and the free exchange of ideas when an inflexible limit is imposed? Is the engineer asked to quit thinking as the limit approaches?

Knowledgeable professionals generally concede that competitive bidding for engineering services is wrong. The rhetorical question always asked is, Would you seek bids on open-heart surgery—or on a physical checkup, for that matter? Why should the health of a going concern be worth any less than one's own health? After all, many peoples' well-being is probably tied to the well-being of the firm for which they work.

In the *War Prayer,* by Samuel Clemens (AKA Mark Twain), a

---

*Of course, it is "open checkbook" only if the owner is incapable of evaluating the performance of the engineers/designers *and* the engineers/designers are unscrupulous.

stranger stands before a crowd who have recently prayed for victory. He states that the prayer will be answered, but first he must explain the unmentioned results that will inevitably come from this victory. He then describes that this means tearing others to bloody shreds, covering fields with their dead, and leaving small children roofless to wander a desolated land.

In a similar fashion, a company that performs bid analyses strictly on price is also asking for unmentioned results:

- That the cheapest labor be hired

- That companies who keep good libraries, historical files, training sessions, participation in conferences, etc., need not apply, because their overhead costs will be too high

- That the bidders cut their benefits, so that the young, energetic, next generation will not find engineering an attractive profession

By basing procurement decisions solely on price, a company is making a derogatory statement about itself. It is entering into associations with companies that are destined to fail. It is also associating with companies whose level of professionalism *cannot* be great. Furthermore, this company fosters the growth of incompetence, while taking a slap at professional pride. Its actions are selfish and shortsighted.

Many companies understand the destructiveness of this situation and will not permit competitive bidding for professional services, but some do. In general, the federal government prohibits competitive bidding not only when it does the contracting, but also as subcontracts through its contractors. Many states have gone the same route. Typical is Nevada which passed a law, NRS 625.530(3), for public works projects in excess of $35,000. The law states that selection of a registered engineer, land surveyor, or architect must be made on the basis of competence and qualifications and not on the basis of competitive bids.

Many people are apt to think that without competitive bidding a valuable market function is being bypassed. To understand that this is *not* so, and to appreciate how wild profligacy will not result from selection based on qualifications, the following selection procedure is presented. Many other procedures are possible.

- A *scope of work* and *basis for design* should be drawn up.

- An RFP should be drawn up; it should request a written response that must contain as a minimum a description of how the bidder proposes to carry out the work, a list of documents to be prepared during the work, a work schedule, an organization chart, resumés of key people, and descriptions of pertinent experience.

- Three or four qualified bidders should be identified.

- The scope, basis, and RFP should be sent to the selected bidders.

- Responses should be ranked in order of qualifications.

- The top firm should then be invited to sit down and negotiate contract terms.*

---

*Which can be cost-plus, lump-sum, or some other arrangement.

- If a satisfactory arrangement cannot be found with the top firm, the procedure should be repeated with the next firm, and so on.

In going through this procedure, the negotiators (owners and engineers alike) will be forced to clear up their thinking regarding the job. This will have a remarkably salubrious effect on the outcome.

Before we leave the topics of cost-plus and lump-sum approaches, one more concept is worth a brief glance: the *convertible contract.* This approach combines cost-plus and lump-sum methods. It is seen more and more these days. It is a contract that begins as cost plus, while job definition is still fuzzy, and is converted to lump sum once job definition has become clear. The usual break point is where *design* development has ceased, perhaps at the conclusion of preliminary *design* (see Fig. 5-6). Under this scheme, about 10 to 40 percent of the engineering will be cost plus while the balance will be lump sum.

The *not-to-exceed** contract gives the impression of being cost plus, but it really isn't. Extra recordkeeping and forecasting are required to give proper notification in a timely fashion to abide by contract requirements. This means adding accountants to the staff and increasing review efforts, something few owners are willing to pay for. Furthermore, the costs early in the project are not thoroughly scrutinized (because the limit is so far away), and the later costs take all the pressure for being cut. Who is to say that a problem late in the design effort should undergo more cost pressure than one early in the design effort? After all, the early fix-ups are cheap, it is the later ones that cost big money.

Of the other kinds of contract mentioned, the only one meriting further explanation is the *guaranteed maximum.* With this contract, the engineer has everything to lose and nothing to gain. It is like striking a bargain with a taxi driver to take you to some destination for the lesser of either the agreed amount or the eventual amount on the meter. The taxi driver is better off seeking another fare. Most engineers will not enter into such a contract. If one does, you are advised to make a quick trip to your stock broker to make a *short* sale in that engineer's stock—and your own, if you should choose this type of a contract.

---

*The full description of this contract is *not to exceed without prior authorization,* which is too much of a mouthful; thus the shortened, somewhat misleading phrase is used. This is also called an *NTE* contract.

Projects are first built on paper in a well-illuminated, comfortable environment. Later, they are built for real, in the field, under varying atmospheric conditions. The answer to those who ask how the marvelous pyramids of antiquity were built is: by following images and records plotted on soft clay, on hides (vellums), or papyrus. Quarry block by quarry block the pieces were cut, measured, trimmed, marked, transported, and fitted into place. Geometry and computational abilities were drawn upon. A whole description of how this work was carried out has been lost, but enough remains to surmise what was done.

In more recent times, the use of drawings for planning and executing the construction of the modern world is well documented, but largely unappreciated by the general public—even by the engineering profession. How many of us are aware that some of the first railroad engines were laid out on paper or linen at full scale, with drafters scampering about in stocking feet over drawings that were the size of a barn?

If an army marches on its stomach,* then a project can be said to march on its brain, that is, its collective memory bank and information processing ability. This memory bank comprises the project files and the personal files of the project team. Duplicates of many parts of these files are moved to the field at the start of construction.

It is clear that any project of worth is not built without drawings. Because engineering is most commonly thought of as the profession of having things built, it is amazing that drafting was removed from the curriculum of many engineering disciplines at colleges about 30 years ago. Yet, for the most part, it was. Surely, the great Ramses engineers are spinning in their sarcophagi!

FILES AND FILING

As a young engineer on his first assignment in a cellophane plant, this author's first impression on the job was one of being intimidated by the paperwork. In all the years of college study there was not the slightest hint that filing would be a key requirement in the sink-or-swim world of practical engineering. This requirement continues in prominence today and continues to be handled in a catch-as-catch-can fashion. Bitterness and pain resulted from attempts to let secretaries do the filing on technical matters. More than once, the ironic comment about filing has come to mind: "Filing is easy. It's the *finding* that is challenging."

On that first job, there were the normal demands of *the assignment:* to improve plant yield by achieving better thickness control in the casting machines. Some subjects of interest were xanthation chemistry, rheology, acid-bath coagulation, and cellulose chemistry. There

---

*This statement is usually attributed to Napoleon Bonaparte.

also were the drawings on the casting heads, the rolls, the drives for the rolls, the speed control schematics, and so on. Apart from "the assignment," however, there were safety messages, production statistics, weekly reports, credit union statements, laboratory reports, test program reports, minutes of the plant manager's weekly production meeting, press notices, and so on.

The need for a good filing system was evident. The senses were alerted. Attention was paid to this neglected art. What is presented here is the result of almost 30 years of observations. It is not general, but is focused specifically on project work. It is not comprehensive, but it goes to the essence.

The rest of this section is devoted to the *project file.** The reader is cautioned that this description of the project file is not complete; it is a starting point for all project files. Comments and observations on personal files are found in App. J, *Personal Files.*

First is the goal of the filing system: A current document in a project file must be accessed within 1 minute after the index is consulted. A document 6 months old, or older, on an active job, must be accessed within 2 minutes. This kind of access should be available to all project team members, not just the curators of the file.

Second is advice about indexes and logs: Be generous with them. Make them available, publish them. Hone and polish them.

To create a file index, treat the whole of the subject matter as a term paper. Then what would be the outline becomes the file index.

Subdivisions (file folders) should be created so that they contain from 20 to 100 items. If there are too few, a merge should be considered; if too many, another division is needed. Of course, adjustments should be made while the files are growing, so that these are the file sizes at maturity. Sometimes a numerical subdivision (part 2, part 3, etc.) is the only sensible way out, but this should be avoided in favor of some memory key that truly characterizes a logical subdivision.

Subdivisions should be set up with the idea of scooping a few folders out of a file drawer to attend a quick meeting. If digging and sorting or taking 10 folders is necessary to cover a topic, chances are that some reorganization is warranted.

Next are a few simple mechanical requirements:

- With only the rare exception, everything must fit the $8\frac{1}{2} \times 11$ format. Legal or European sizes must be folded or trimmed to fit.

- A file subdivision can be delimited by a single folder (or envelope), a divider, or a binder of some sort.

- The contents of each subdivision should be maintained in approximate chronological order, with the most recent items coming to view when the file is opened.

The physical location and format of the files are also important. To begin with, space and furnishings are needed. A table, no less than 3 × 4 ft, and four to seven four-drawer filing cabinets will require about 90 ft^2 of office area. This space should not be farther than 80 ft or so from the project engineers, the lead designer, and the project secretary.

Table 14-1 gives details on storage of documents. Again, please note that the files discussed here are the *project* files. Purchasing will

---

*This is the file that serves all project members. It is located in an area easily accessed by all disciplines and by the client, probably no more than thirty paces from the project secretary.

TABLE 14-1 Custody and Organization of Project Files (ATD)

Document	Type of file	File location
Original tracings	Spring-loaded vertical	Copy room
Original specification and revisions	Filing cabinet	Near secretary
Owner drawings	11 × 14 in manila envelopes	Book shelves
Vendor drawings	11 × 14 in manila envelopes	Book shelves
Logbooks*	Three-ring binders	Secretaries' desk
Inquiry file†	Vertical file cabinet	Near secretary
Purchase file†	Vertical file cabinet	Near secretary
Copies of active‡ drawings (master copies)	Vertical file cabinet	Near lead designer
Archive copies of drawings	Vertical file cabinet	Near secretary

*Duplicate-drawing log is in copy room.

†These are duplicates; the originals are in the purchasing area.

‡Latest revision is the active one. The word MASTER is stamped or written prominently on the document. Previous revisions are archive copies, marked VOID and filed elsewhere.

have its files. Engineers and designers will have their personal files, too.

Two items in Table 14-1 deserve further explanation: the filing of the tracings and the use of the manila envelopes on bookshelves. The tracings should be kept in the copy room in special vertical files having spring-loaded folders. The reason for keeping the tracings in the file room is to establish custody over them (even the sponsor or designer must check them out) and to simplify (plus accelerate) issuance. Tracings will spend most of their existence in the luxury of the vertical files, and when they are not, a paper trail will lead to them. The next section will expand on this.

These vertical files are a great advance in project work. The tracings are stored vertically and are accessed within seconds, not like a flat file where tracings must often be removed in layers (as though on an archaeological dig) and replaced with a sliding motion that folds or crinkles sheets almost without exception. The vertically stored drawings contain the file number in the upper right-hand corner,* so that almost with a sweep of the hand the numbers can be flipped through [ATD]. Vertical storage costs somewhat more at the outset, but the savings over the long run are handsome. Among other things, the vertical storage requires less floor area. An example of a vertical file is given in Fig. 14-1. Many different makes and models are available.

The second item from above concerns the manila envelopes. These are used to group and store the owner drawings and the vendor drawings.† This is done to accommodate the diverse drawing sizes and methods of folding and to simplify filing by *logical grouping.* Obviously a skid-mounted air compressor drawing has meaning only when it is in the company of drawings of the other items on the skid, such as the lubrication system, the filter, the dryer, the receiver, plus drawings on pressure switches, control schematics, electric power schematics, etc. A single drawing won't do; it is the *group* of drawings, sometimes called *the drawing package,* that is important. This drawing group must be kept together. The 11 × 14 in manila envelope is

*Stamps 19 and 20 (Fig. 14-6) are for the purpose of putting an identifying number *any place* on a drawing, including $8^{1}/_{2}$ in up from the right lower corner to aid in finding folded drawings.

†Furthermore, each sheet in a grouping is marked, so it can be used and easily returned to its correct group. The marking is guided by stamps 22 and 23 (see Fig. 14-6).

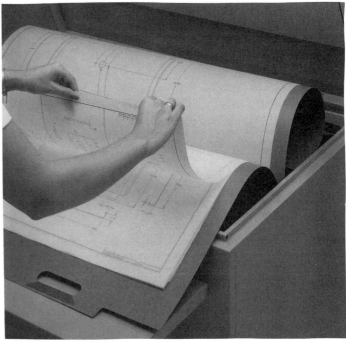

Figure 14-1 Example of the vertical file for storing tracings. (*Courtesy of Plan Hold Corporation, Irvine, Calif.*)

the answer. The way to file these envelopes is on an ordinary bookshelf, vertically, long side up, held by bookends, with the file number on a corner where it can be seen [ATD].

The file headings for the project file at the outset of a job can be something of a mystery, as peculiar requirements might take a while to surface. However, Fig. 14-2 is a fair starting point for any project.

This presentation shows one of many ways of organizing files. There are other ways, a few perhaps a little better. The point here is to give guidelines and reveal the level of detail necessary to ensure a smooth operation. In parting, this concept is offered: The heart of a good filing system is logical thought, but constancy in using the numbering system will overcome many lapses in logic.

INFORMATION FLOW

The best way to appreciate information flow is to follow a couple of documents from their conception and throughout their use on a project. This will be done for two documents: an equipment arrangement drawing and a specification for a cooling tower. The two great documents on a project are the drawings and the specifications. Thus the examples are pertinent.

First, we'll follow the arrangement drawing though its history. Then we'll follow the specification. Before we do, we need some definitions, however.

- *Tracing:* This is the original drawing. It is not a copy.
- *Vellum:* This is a blank sheet upon which a tracing is made. The most common materials are paper, polyester film, and treated linen. The word *vellum* is often used generically to speak of either a tracing or a blank sheet.
- *Blueprint:* Until about 1955 or so, most copies were this kind. The background was dark blue, and the markings on the tracing came

```
FILE CABINETS
(in project secretary area)
  1.0  Project Organization
        1.1  Organization chart
        1.2  Distribution list
        1.3  Instructions and
             procedures
        1.4  Blank forms
  2.0  Contract
  3.0  Business File
        3.1  Invoices to client
        3.2  Labor reports
        3.3  Reimbursable charges
        3.4  Financial statements
        3.5  Specification approval
             copies
        3.6  Drawing approval copies
  4.0  Communications File
       (filed by number)*
        4.1  Project memos
        4.2  Project letters
        4.3  Transmittal letters
        4.4  Internal memos
        4.5  Correspondence from
             client
  5.0  Schedules and Status Reports
        5.1  Inquiry schedule
        5.2  Drawing schedule
        5.3  Permit schedule
        5.4  Project schedule
        5.5  Purchasing report
        5.6  Cost report
        5.7  Monthly report
  6.0  Estimates
        6.1  Capital and operating costs
        6.2  Engineering labor hours
  7.0  Permits
  8.0  Technical Information
        8.1  Calculations
        8.2  Material balance
        8.3  Equipment/commodities list

        8.4  Line list
        8.5  Soil reports
        8.6  Surveys
        8.7  Plot plans
        8.8  Owner data
        8.9  Vendor information
  9.0  Meeting Notes and Agendas
 10.0  Construction
 11.0  Environmental
        11.1  Air
        11.2  Water
        11.3  Solids disposal
 12.0  Specifications File
 13.0  Drawing Archives† (first by file
        number, second by revision
        number)
 14.0  Inquiry File‡
 15.0  Purchase File‡


THREE-RING BINDERS
(within reach of secretary)
Book 1
   Basic Data
   Scope of Work
Book 2
   Project Letter Log
   Project Memo Log
   Client Correspondence Log
   Transmittal Letter Log
   Specifications Log
   Inquiry Log
   Purchase Order Log
   Owner Drawing Log
   Vendor Data Log
   Standard Attachment§
Book 3
   Requisitions
Book 4 (by purchase order number)
   Invoices Pending Approval¶
   Approved Invoices
```

*Logs are located in book 2 on secretary's desk.

†Master copies are in a cabinet near the lead designer.

‡One folder per file number [ATD].

§These are added by purchasing to inquiries and purchase orders.

¶Photocopy of principal page only. Whole document is in the purchasing file (15). This is a handy reference only.

Figure 14-2 Proposed project file subdivisions at the start of a job.

through as white (the blueprint is a negative of the tracing). This kind of copy is rare today.

- *Blueline:* This kind of copy is the most common today. The blueline is a positive of the tracing. Markings on the tracing show as blue on the copy. The background is white.

- *Bond:* This kind of copy is seen more and more. The image on the tracing is transferred onto ordinary (bond) paper via a xerographic process. The line color is black.

The equipment arrangement drawing consists of four stages of stirred-tank reactors, with agitators on a concrete pad with a sump and a sump pump.* The agitators will be supported from the tank walls. A segment of the review issue of the drawing is shown in Fig. 14-4.

The need for this drawing will probably be formally recognized for the first time during the preparation of the preliminary estimate, when the first reliable man-hour estimate is made for the engineering portion of the job. At that time, the staged reactors will appear on a plot plan, but the arrangement drawing itself, even though its need might be recognized, must await the next phase of work—that which will culminate in the budget estimate. Of course, sketches of possible arrangements will be done while the plot plan is put together, but most of these will be discarded as flawed ideas.

Equipment arrangement drawings will be started after the plot plan is started and after a budget-grade estimate has been authorized (see Fig. 14-4). The purpose of an equipment arrangement drawing is to show where to locate equipment, not only in a north-south, east-west sense, but also in elevation. An equipment arrangement drawing gives dimensions to show location. The dimensions are usually referred to a pair of perpendicular grid lines and a horizontal datum point. The equipment arrangement drawings are prepared by either piping designers or mechanical designers, depending on the nature of the job. Other design groups use these drawings to develop their own drawings for pinpointing the locations of foundations, structures, piping, and conduit.

The start of our drawing will be when the lead designer fills out a copy room work order (see Form 136, App. C) and requests a new blank vellum. After receiving the vellum, the designer fills out drawing log P, and then consults the drawing list and fills out the title block on the drawing. Next the lead designer turns the blank vellum over to the piping designer assigned to work in that area of the plant. At this time the lead designer will brief the piping designer on the operation of the tanks and the sump and will inform him or her of others assigned to work on that portion of the project.

The designer will study the P&ID, the plot plan, the equipment list, and any other information available. He or she will discuss this portion of the job with the project engineer and the process engineer.

In the earliest stages, the process engineer will provide most of the information: tank dimensions,† agitator size and model,‡ elevation differences from tank to tank, elevation of at least one tank, etc.

The designer will probably begin by doing some sketches and perhaps by cutting out some cardboard pieces in the shape of the cross section (or silhouette) of individual equipment pieces. The pieces of cardboard can be moved and contemplated while the designer is thinking about such things as piping simplifications, maintenance access, operator convenience, avoidance of line plugging, safety, constructability, waste minimization, etc. Once the designer hits upon a scheme that seems meritorious, he or she will develop these sketches to a greater level of detail.

---

*Note that equipment locations and structural features are given. Piping is not shown on this type of drawing. Piping is shown on a piping arrangement drawing.

†All dimensional information is only approximate until vendor drawings are approved.

‡Equipment models are speculative until purchases are executed.

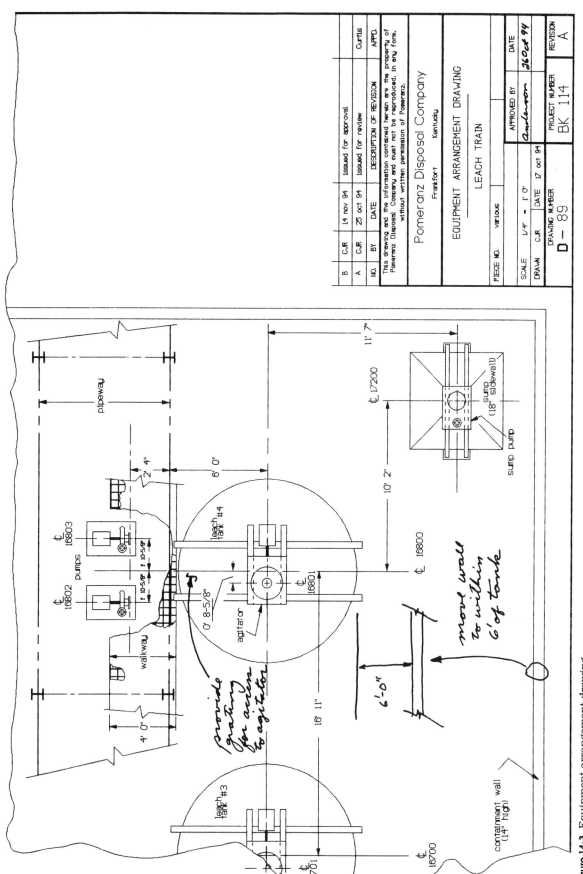

Figure 14-3 Equipment arrangement drawing.

At some point this person will sit with the lead designer and the process engineer to see whether they will go along with the plan. In all likelihood, at this point, the vellum still has yet to pick up its first line. Once the basic concepts of the equipment arrangement have been more or less agreed upon by the principal project powers, the piping designer will unroll the vellum and in a short time turn it into a tracing. On it the piping designer will show the spatial arrangement of the tanks and the sump as well as spaces where pipe racks and service areas are best located.

This drawing will make its debut after the designer fills out Form 136 and sends the tracing to the copy room for formal issue. The debut issue is the *in-house review*. Copy room personnel will not only make copies but also put the copies into the distribution network,* make the appropriate log entries (Forms 138 and 139), and file the tracing in the copy room. The designer will receive two copies: one for the file as the *master*, the other for a personal copy, just like everyone else. The master will be used for accumulating markings and comments. The tracing will stay in the copy room file until the next issue (presumably the approval issue) is prepared.

The designer will have a date for moving this drawing onward, toward approval. To meet this date, comments from the design team are solicited. In this example, the comments are fairly minor. In general, there is agreement as to the layout and location of the pipe rack. When the piping designer decides to incorporate the suggestions from the internal review, he or she will use Form 136 to gain custody of the tracing. Once comments have been transferred from the master† onto the tracing and the designer is sure the drawing is ready for the next step (approval), he or she again fills out Form 136 and sends the tracing along with the form back to the copy room. The copy room personnel do what they did earlier: They copy and distribute. The tracing stays in the copy room in the vertical file, as usual.

CADD does not change this situation. Only one vellum should be printed of each revision, just as with hand-drawn tracings. The CADD-generated tracings should be stored with hand-drawn tracings in the copy room. These are the *official* records of a revision. Any project participant should be able to obtain a true copy of the latest revision, CADD or no CADD. When a new revision is generated, it must be issued by sending it to the copy room with a work order (Form 136). The copy room personnel are responsible for marking the old tracing VOID and returning it to the designer. The designer has the choice of filing the tracing or destroying it.‡ The new tracing replaces the old one in the copy room vertical file.

While a drawing is being reviewed by the client for approval, the design groups can be using it to make preliminary sketches and take-offs for the budget estimate. The structural engineer, for example, can start to explore tank foundation designs and platform supports.

Other people can get in the act, too. The electrical engineer now can begin to locate the motor control center since he has a better idea of where the agitators will be located and, knowing where the pipe rack

---

*Whether it be by mail or, if urgency is justified, hand delivery.

†The designer, like anyone else, should note developments on his or her personal copy or on the master. These developments are transferred to the vellum only when a formal issue of the drawing is required.

‡Destruction is recommended. Copies already exist for documentation purposes.

is, from which side the conduit will be run. Another piping designer, working in the adjacent area, can determine exactly how he will bring in the line that will feed his equipment.

During the review of the drawings, the client makes a note that the slab on the south side must be shortened (brought closer to the tanks) to allow a boom truck access to pull any agitator, should it become necessary. The client also comments that all the tank manways should face south. This latter comment is referred to the process engineer, who makes a note of it on the data sheet of the tank specification. This comment is not shown on the equipment arrangement drawing (although it could have been).

The client signs the marked-up copy and returns it to the project engineer. The project engineer files that copy along with other approval copies in the project file, under file heading 3.6 (see Fig. 14-2).

At this point the engineering design should be around 10 to 20 percent complete. Quotes on the tanks might not have been formally obtained yet, but certainly their specifications will have been written and the tank diameters and side lengths will be known to within an inch or so. For the budget estimate, study drawings on the piping will be under way. These developments can be seen by examining Fig. 14-4 in the area between 10 and 20 percent of completion.

The next issue of the equipment arrangement drawings for the cascaded reactors should be the design issue. In the example given here, this should not occur until after the P&IDs have been issued for design and quotes have been requested on the major equipment pieces. For equipment such as tanks, the engineers have total control over equipment size and configuration, so a design issue can occur prior to the acquisition of vendor data. The agitators and sump pump, however, are another matter; their dimensions will not be fully defined until after vendor drawings are received. In the example, the arrangement drawing could be issued for design with hold balloons encircling the dimensions that locate the agitators and the sump pump. This limited issue for design would allow the structural group to begin its design issues for the tank foundations and the slab.* The actual issue would be handled in the same way as before, by using Form 136 and the services of the copy room.

The next step on the odyssey of our drawing is the issue for construction. This should occur after the P&IDs are issued for construction *and*† after *certified* vendor drawings have been received and accepted. The dimensions given on the vendor drawings are used for calling out dimensions on the equipment arrangement drawing. These later dimensions, in turn, will be used to finish the structural drawings (in this case, the platforms, the sump, and the sump pump support).

Subsequent issues for minor revisions can occur after the issue for construction, but these should be minor, some requiring only a few minutes to carry out.

When the time comes to include this drawing in subcontract bid packages, it will be convenient to do so, as the tracing will be convenient to the copy equipment in the copy room. Designers need not

---

*This is not an efficient way to proceed, however. It is best to await vendor drawing submittals except in case of dire necessity.

†This is a boolean AND.

mount a search/find effort to gather tracings from different file locations (in spite of the task force approach) for an issue.

Now let's have a look at a specification for a cooling tower. To begin, some rough sizing information and perhaps some construction details might have been worked out during preliminary engineering. In all likelihood, however, the early work went far enough to put together an estimate, but no more. Therefore, a full-scale investigation is warranted. This investigation should reveal the following:

- Average cooling loads in winter and summer
- Design load condition
- Atmospheric design conditions: temperatures, relative humidities, etc.
- Makeup water assays
- Blowdown disposal: location, allowable concentrations
- Common practices for operation of other cooling towers in the area
- Treatment procedures for makeup and blowdown
- Specifications for cooling towers of similar size and construction
- Likely vendors of the kind of tower needed

A complete heat and material balance should be done. This should include treatment chemicals and inputs from the process (where process vapors are quenched by cooling water in direct-contact condensers, for example).

Conversations with other cooling tower operators in the neighborhood, such as power plants, will give a good feel for the allowable concentration ratio. Vendors of treatment chemicals are good sources of information, too.

Once the above steps have been taken, there should be not the slightest doubt as to the size of cooling tower and its type. There should also be no doubt as to the correct method for controlling the water chemistry of the tower.

The appropriate occasion for writing a specification for a formal inquiry is when an estimate ±15 percent accuracy, or better, is needed, that is, when a firm price with a contractual obligation is needed. Formal specifications and quotes on estimates of lesser accuracy are a waste of resources for the client, engineer, and vendor.

If an appropriate specification can be found, it should be edited to conform to the conditions at hand. If not, a new specification must be written (see Chap. 12, *Procurement*). The person who writes the specification should be the process engineer who performed the background investigation described above. As with the case of the drawing, the specification will make its debut as an internal review issue after the engineer submits the original to the copy room.

After copies have been made and distributed, the original will be returned to the requestor for storage in the project file (under heading 12, Fig. 14-2).

Form 140 in App. C is an example of a cover sheet for a specification. By examining it, one can see some of the history of a specification. The stages of development in the example are as follows: internal review, approval, inquiry, and purchase. These are fairly typical. When the specification is issued in the latter two cases, a requisition (Form 124) must accompany the copy room work order (Form 136).

When the purchasing department receives its copies, it will attach a cover letter and append some standard attachments that go out with inquiries and purchases. Copies of purchasing information are maintained in the project file. While in the inquiry stage, this information is kept under heading 14 (Fig. 14-2). Once the purchase order is placed, however, the destination for project copies is heading 15. The *standard attachments* are not included with the project file copy for each inquiry or purchase order, since this would be redundant and wasteful; one copy of each is kept in book 2 of the three-ring binders (Fig. 14-2).

DOCUMENT SCHEDULE

Figure 14-4 displays some of the key project documents and gives the approximate timing for their production. The horizontal axis is the completion percentage of engineering/design.*

With this document schedule, it is assumed that engineering, design, and construction are executed in an overlapping fashion, without pause:

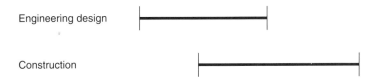

The way to interpret Fig. 14-4 is best understood by the use of examples:

- If the mass balance is still being worked on, the completion percentage on engineering/design is probably less than 5 percent.

- If study-grade layouts are under way and material takeoffs are being prepared for the estimator, the estimate accuracy will be in the ±10 to 20 percent range.

- If the building foundation drawings have all been released for construction, the completion percentage is probably greater than 60 percent.

A pivotal point built into Fig. 14-4 is that design-grade work cannot be produced by the design disciplines until vendor drawings are obtained. This is why the period for vendor drawings has been marked as a gray bar at line 8.1. Note that this applies to *design* work, and *not* to process flow diagrams, mass balances, and P&IDs. These latter documents generally achieve *design* status prior to receipt of vendor information.

In the case of the electrical single-line (*design* grade), work is shown ending after architectural work is finished; this allows inclusion of lighting panels in the design issue. The same has been done with the construction issue.

The last of the construction issues will usually be by the electrical and instrument groups at about 90 percent completion. The last 10

---

*Please recall that engineering/design usually includes procurement.

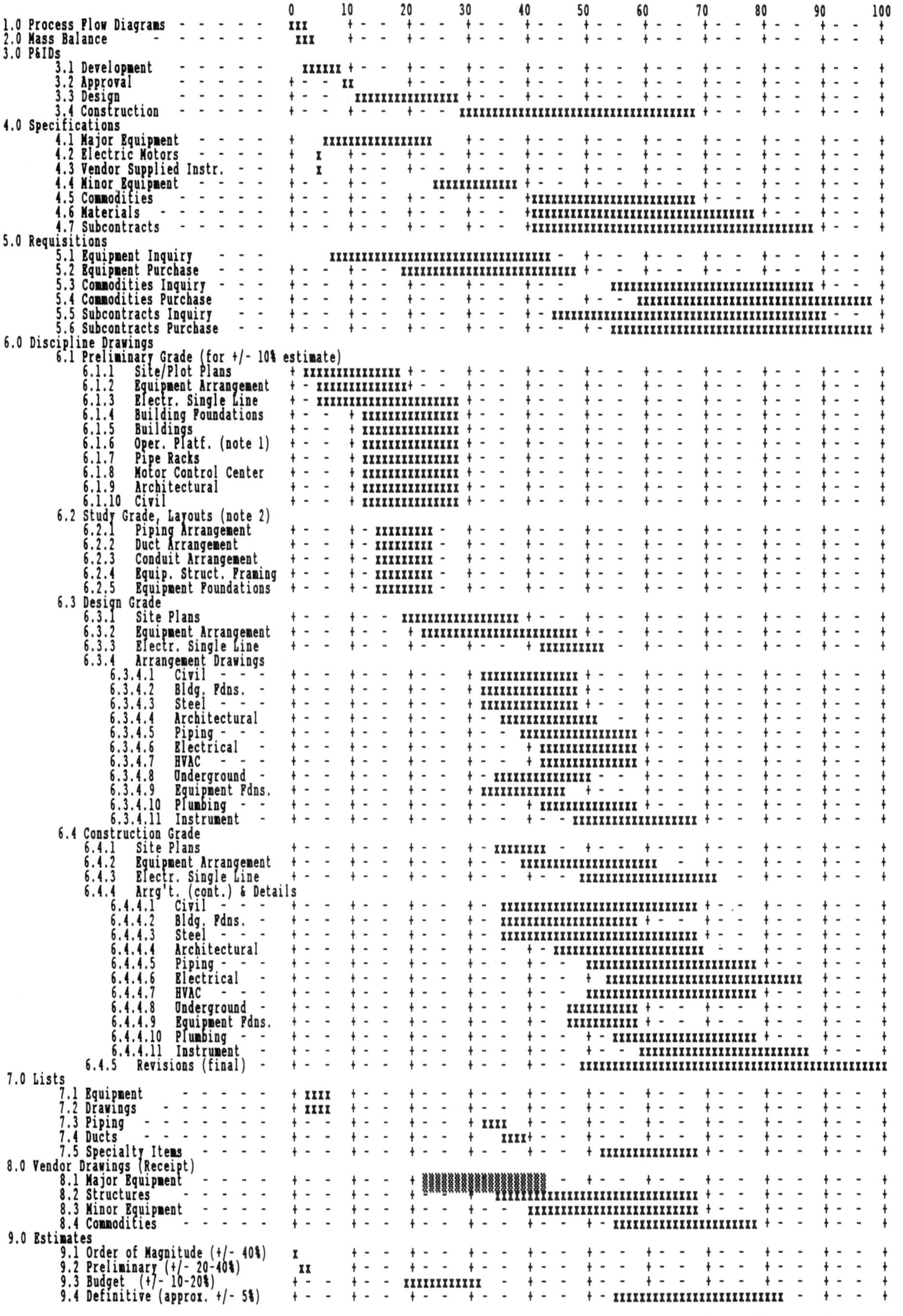

```
                                        0    10    20    30    40    50    60    70    80    90   100
1.0 Process Flow Diagrams  - - - - -   XXX  +  -  +  -  +  -  +  -  +  -  +  -  +  -  +  -  +  -  +
2.0 Mass Balance           - - - - -   XXX  +  -  +  -  +  -  +  -  +  -  +  -  +  -  +  -  +  -  +
3.0 P&IDs
    3.1 Development         - - - -     XXXXXX +  -  +  -  +  -  +  -  +  -  +  -  +  -  +  -  +  -  +
    3.2 Approval            - - - -     +  -  - XX  +  -  +  -  +  -  +  -  +  -  +  -  +  -  +  -  +
    3.3 Design              - - - -     +  -  + XXXXXXXXXXXXXXXX +  -  +  -  +  -  +  -  +  -  +  -  +
    3.4 Construction        - - - -     +  -  +  -  + XXXXXXXXXXXXXXXXXXXXXXXXXX +  -  +  -  +  -  +
4.0 Specifications
    4.1 Major Equipment     - - - -     +  XXXXXXXXXXXXXXXX -  +  -  +  -  +  -  +  -  +  -  +  -  +
    4.2 Electric Motors     - - - -     +  X  +  -  +  -  +  -  +  -  +  -  +  -  +  -  +  -  +  -  +
    4.3 Vendor Supplied Instr. - - -    +  X  +  -  +  -  +  -  +  -  +  -  +  -  +  -  +  -  +  -  +
    4.4 Minor Equipment     - - - -     +  -  +  -  + XXXXXXXXXXXX +  -  +  -  +  -  +  -  +  -  +
    4.5 Commodities         - - - -     +  -  +  -  +  -  +XXXXXXXXXXXXXXXXXXXX +  -  +  -  +  -  +
    4.6 Materials  - - - -  - - - -     +  -  +  -  +  -  +XXXXXXXXXXXXXXXXXXXXXXXXXXXXXXX +  -  +
    4.7 Subcontracts        - - - -     +  -  +  -  +  -  +XXXXXXXXXXXXXXXXXXXXXXXXXXXXXXXXX +  -  +
5.0 Requisitions
    5.1 Equipment Inquiry   - - -       +  XXXXXXXXXXXXXXXXXXXXXXXXXXXXXXX -  +  -  +  -  +  -  +
    5.2 Equipment Purchase  - - -       +  -  + XXXXXXXXXXXXXXXXXXXXXXXX +  -  +  -  +  -  +  -  +
    5.3 Commodities Inquiry - - -       +  -  +  -  +  -  + XXXXXXXXXXXXXXXXXXXXXXXXX +  -  +  -  +
    5.4 Commodities Purchase  - -       +  -  +  -  +  -  +  -  + XXXXXXXXXXXXXXXXXXXXXXXXXXXXX +
    5.5 Subcontracts Inquiry  - -       +  -  +  -  +  -  + XXXXXXXXXXXXXXXXXXXXXXXXX -  -  +
    5.6 Subcontracts Purchase - -       +  -  +  -  +  -  +  - XXXXXXXXXXXXXXXXXXXXXXXXXXXXXXX +
6.0 Discipline Drawings
    6.1 Preliminary Grade (for +/- 10% estimate)
        6.1.1  Site/Plot Plans         +XXXXXXXXXXXXX +  -  +  -  +  -  +  -  +  -  +  -  +  -  +
        6.1.2  Equipment Arrangement    + - XXXXXXXXXXXX+  -  +  -  +  -  +  -  +  -  +  -  +  -  +
        6.1.3  Electr. Single Line      + XXXXXXXXXXXXXXXXXXXX +  -  +  -  +  -  +  -  +  -  +  -  +
        6.1.4  Building Foundations     + -  + XXXXXXXXXXXXXX +  -  +  -  +  -  +  -  +  -  +  -  +
        6.1.5  Buildings                + -  + XXXXXXXXXXXXXX +  -  +  -  +  -  +  -  +  -  +  -  +
        6.1.6  Oper. Platf. (note 1)    + -  +XXXXXXXXXXXXXX +  -  +  -  +  -  +  -  +  -  +  -  +
        6.1.7  Pipe Racks               + -  + XXXXXXXXXXXXXX +  -  +  -  +  -  +  -  +  -  +  -  +
        6.1.8  Motor Control Center     + -  + XXXXXXXXXXXXXX +  -  +  -  +  -  +  -  +  -  +  -  +
        6.1.9  Architectural            + -  + XXXXXXXXXXXXXX +  -  +  -  +  -  +  -  +  -  +  -  +
        6.1.10 Civil                    + -  + XXXXXXXXXXXXXX +  -  +  -  +  -  +  -  +  -  +  -  +
    6.2 Study Grade, Layouts (note 2)
        6.2.1  Piping Arrangement       + -  + - XXXXXXXXX -  +  -  +  -  +  -  +  -  +  -  +  -  +
        6.2.2  Duct Arrangement         + -  + - XXXXXXXXX -  +  -  +  -  +  -  +  -  +  -  +  -  +
        6.2.3  Conduit Arrangement      + -  + - XXXXXXXXX -  +  -  +  -  +  -  +  -  +  -  +  -  +
        6.2.4  Equip. Struct. Framing   + -  + - XXXXXXXXX -  +  -  +  -  +  -  +  -  +  -  +  -  +
        6.2.5  Equipment Foundations    + -  + - XXXXXXXXX -  +  -  +  -  +  -  +  -  +  -  +  -  +
    6.3 Design Grade
        6.3.1  Site Plans               + -  + - XXXXXXXXXXXXXXXXX + -  +  -  +  -  +  -  +  -  +
        6.3.2  Equipment Arrangement    + -  + -  + XXXXXXXXXXXXXXXXXXXXXX +  -  +  -  +  -  +  -  +
        6.3.3  Electr. Single Line      + -  + -  +  -  + XXXXXXXXXX +  -  +  -  +  -  +  -  +  -  +
        6.3.4  Arrangement Drawings
           6.3.4.1  Civil - - -         + -  + -  + XXXXXXXXXXXXXXXX + -  +  -  +  -  +  -  +  -  +
           6.3.4.2  Bldg. Fdns. -       + -  + -  + XXXXXXXXXXXXXX + -  +  -  +  -  +  -  +  -  +
           6.3.4.3  Steel -             + -  + -  + XXXXXXXXXXXXXX + -  +  -  +  -  +  -  +  -  +
           6.3.4.4  Architectural       + -  + -  + - XXXXXXXXXXXXX -  + -  +  -  +  -  +  -  +
           6.3.4.5  Piping - -          + -  + -  +  - XXXXXXXXXXXXXXXX +  -  +  -  +  -  +  -  +
           6.3.4.6  Electrical -        + -  + -  +  -  + XXXXXXXXXXXX +  -  +  -  +  -  +  -  +
           6.3.4.7  HVAC - -            + -  + -  +  -  + XXXXXXXXXXXX +  -  +  -  +  -  +  -  +
           6.3.4.8  Underground         + -  + -  + - XXXXXXXXXX -  -  +  -  +  -  +  -  +  -  +
           6.3.4.9  Equipment Fdns.     + -  + -  + XXXXXXXXXXXX -  +  -  +  -  +  -  +  -  +  -  +
           6.3.4.10 Plumbing -          + -  + -  +  - XXXXXXXXXXXXXX + -  +  -  +  -  +  -  +  -  +
           6.3.4.11 Instrument          + -  + -  +  -  + XXXXXXXXXXXXXXXX + -  +  -  +  -  +  -  +
    6.4 Construction Grade
        6.4.1  Site Plans               + -  + -  +  - XXXXXXXX -  + -  +  -  +  -  +  -  +  -  +
        6.4.2  Equipment Arrangement    + -  + -  +  - XXXXXXXXXXXXXXXXXX -  + -  +  -  +  -  +  -  +
        6.4.3  Electr. Single Line      + -  + -  +  -  + XXXXXXXXXXXXXXXX + -  +  -  +  -  +  -  +
        6.4.4  Arr't. (cont.) & Details
           6.4.4.1  Civil - - -         + -  + -  +  - XXXXXXXXXXXXXXXXXXXXXX +  -.  +  -  +  -  +
           6.4.4.2  Bldg. Fdns. -       + -  + -  +  - XXXXXXXXXXXXXXXXXXX + -  +  -  +  -  +  -  +
           6.4.4.3  Steel -             + -  + -  +  - XXXXXXXXXXXXXXXXXXX + -  +  -  +  -  +  -  +
           6.4.4.4  Architectural       + -  + -  +  -  + - XXXXXXXXXXXXXXXXX -  + -  +  -  +  -  +
           6.4.4.5  Piping - -          + -  + -  +  -  + XXXXXXXXXXXXXXXXXX + -  +  -  +  -  +  -  +
           6.4.4.6  Electrical -        + -  + -  +  -  + XXXXXXXXXXXXXXXXXXXXXXXXX +  -  +  -  +
           6.4.4.7  HVAC - -            + -  + -  +  -  + XXXXXXXXXXXXXXXXXXXXX + -  +  -  +  -  +
           6.4.4.8  Underground         + -  + -  +  -  + XXXXXXXXXX + -  +  -  +  -  +  -  +  -  +
           6.4.4.9  Equipment Fdns.     + -  + -  +  -  + XXXXXXXXXX - -  +  -  +  -  +  -  +  -  +
           6.4.4.10 Plumbing -          + -  + -  +  -  + - XXXXXXXXXXXXXXXXX + -  +  -  +  -  +  -  +
           6.4.4.11 Instrument          + -  + -  +  -  + - XXXXXXXXXXXXXXXXXXXX + -  +  -  +  -  +
        6.4.5  Revisions (final) -      + -  + -  +  -  + XXXXXXXXXXXXXXXXXXXXXXXXXXXXXXXXXXXXXXXXXX
7.0 Lists
    7.1 Equipment     - - - - -         + XXXX +  -  +  -  +  -  +  -  +  -  +  -  +  -  +  -  +  -  +
    7.2 Drawings  - - - - -             + XXXX +  -  +  -  +  -  +  -  +  -  +  -  +  -  +  -  +  -  +
    7.3 Piping  - - - - -               + -  + -  +  -  + XXXX +  -  +  -  +  -  +  -  +  -  +  -  +
    7.4 Ducts - - - - -                 + -  + -  +  -  + XXXX+  -  +  -  +  -  +  -  +  -  +  -  +
    7.5 Specialty Items - - -           + -  + -  +  -  + XXXXXXXXXXXXX +  -  +  -  +  -  +  -  +
8.0 Vendor Drawings (Receipt)
    8.1 Major Equipment - - - -         + -  + -  + ▓▓▓▓▓▓▓▓▓▓▓▓▓▓▓▓▓▓▓ -  +  -  +  -  +  -  +
    8.2 Structures    - - - -           + -  + -  +  - XXXXXXXXXXXX +  -  +  -  +  -  +  -  +  -  +
    8.3 Minor Equipment - - -           + -  + -  +  -  + XXXXXXXXXXXXXXXXXX +  -  +  -  +  -  +
    8.4 Commodities   - - - -           + -  + -  +  -  +  - XXXXXXXXXXXXXXXX +  -  +  -  +  -  +
9.0 Estimates
    9.1 Order of Magnitude (+/- 40%)    X  + -  + -  +  -  +  -  +  -  +  -  +  -  +  -  +  -  +
    9.2 Preliminary (+/- 20-40%)        XX + -  + -  +  -  +  -  +  -  +  -  +  -  +  -  +  -  +
    9.3 Budget  (+/- 10-20%)            + -  + - XXXXXXXXXXX -  + -  +  -  +  -  +  -  +  -  +
    9.4 Definitive (approx. +/- 5%)     + -  + -  +  -  + XXXXXXXXXXXXXXXXXXXXXXXX - +  -  +

                                        0    10    20    30    40    50    60    70    80    90   100
```

Notes: 1. Without equipment framing and supports.   Percent Completion of Engineering/Design
       2. This designation is used instead of "preliminary" because some study drawings
           will be completely scrapped, whereas a preliminary drawing will undergo further
           development, finally reaching design grade. These are many times hand
           sketches, their only purpose being to take-off materials for a +/-10% estimate.

Figure 14-4 Document timing chart.

percent of the home office effort will consist of minor revisions and support work. All significant design effort should have ended before the construction effort reaches its peak. There may be design follow-up, but typically this should only consist of a half-dozen telephone calls a day from the construction site to the engineering/design office. A visit to the jobsite by engineers/designers should not be necessary. The information for construction must be contained in the drawings and specifications.

As a general measure of progress, the P&IDs are very useful:

- If instrument balloons and piping are being added regularly, the P&IDs are still in development.

- If instrument balloons and piping are only changing slightly, the P&IDs have been approved by the client, line sizes and numbers are included, and instrument numbers have been added, then the P&IDs are probably ready for design issue.

- If the P&IDs have been revised to show features on vendor drawings, plus other details such as drains and vents, then the P&IDs are construction-grade.

THE NEED FOR VENDOR DATA

Without vendor data, it would not be possible to make a meaningful design drawing. How would the foundation be sized otherwise? How would the bolts be embedded in the concrete to secure the piece without vendor drawings? Typical information to be found in vendor data includes the following:

- Overall dimensions and weights
- Accurate identification and clear labeling of all process and utility connections
- Bolt-hole locations
- Location of access ports
- Required clearances for removal of internal parts
- Need for massive foundations or vibration isolators
- Sizes and features of motors
- Exact nature of auxiliary systems, including parts lists (such as lubrication systems, hydraulic controls, etc.)
- Cross-sectional views through all seals, dynamic and static, with parts lists
- Performance curves for centrifugal pumps and fans
- Power curves for agitators

In the design phase of a project, drawings of equipment are more important than the equipment itself. To appreciate this, imagine a project in which an existing piece of equipment is to be put into service, say a large vessel. If drawings of the vessel exist, these can be used to lay out a structure in which to house the vessel or to lay out piping connections to the nozzles. If vessel drawings do not exist, then they must be made. After all, it would be impractical to bring the vessel into the project area so that the designers could make measurements as they prepare their drawings. This example reveals one of the problems associated with incorporating used equipment in a project.

Imagine also a large piece of rotating equipment requiring air purges on the seals, hooked up and operated for 10 h, when suddenly the bearings start smoking because the seals had not been purged. The air purges for the seals were not hooked up, because it was impossible to know by inspecting the machine that the seals required an air purge. Only a drawing can convey that kind of information; the same holds for clearances for removing tube bundles, impellers, and the like.

The need for vendor drawings first becomes apparent after the P&IDs have been issued for design. At that point it is obvious that to finish the P&IDs (issue them for construction), the vendor drawings are needed. The need also becomes evident as the equipment arrangement drawings are developed. By examining Fig. 14-4, we see that all this is happening when the engineering is 15 to 30 percent complete. By having scheduled it that way, this also coincides with the approval of the budget estimate. This is because reliable vendor data are usually not available until after a purchase order is placed, and on many occasions, purchases are not allowed until *after* the budget estimate is approved.

If a delay should occur in obtaining vendor information at this point, the delay will carry right on through to the finish date. With only the very rarest of exceptions, the receipt of vendor data is squarely in the middle of the critical path on project schedules. Furthermore, any delays at this time will result in increases in engineering costs, due to interruptions in the work flow.

There are two basic ways of avoiding these problems associated with delays in budget approval:*

- Make funds available for cancellation charges on major pieces of equipment.
- Provide authorization to proceed† as long as the budget estimate is no greater than some tolerance limit over the preliminary estimate, say, +20 percent.

The first option might require setting aside 2 to 6 percent of the project cost, so that vendor engineering can proceed while the budget estimate is being authorized. If the project is canceled, this money will be lost, but as venture capital, it will have a sizable return, since it will maintain the project schedule while holding down engineering costs. If the project is not canceled, this is money that would have been spent anyway.

The second option should be instituted by *all* operating companies. It is a low-risk and high-return option.

To understand the consequences of making no provision along these lines, consider Fig. 14-5.‡ Figure 14-5a shows how project staffing is maintained on the increase prior to peaking out. From then on it decreases. This is the case when funds are set aside for cancellation charges or the project achieves an automatic go-ahead, as de-

---

*These and some additional thoughts are covered in Chap. 3, *For Company Executives.*

†In every respect, including the issuance of major purchase orders.

‡Some of these ideas are covered with a slightly different emphasis in Chap. 5, *Cost and Schedule.*

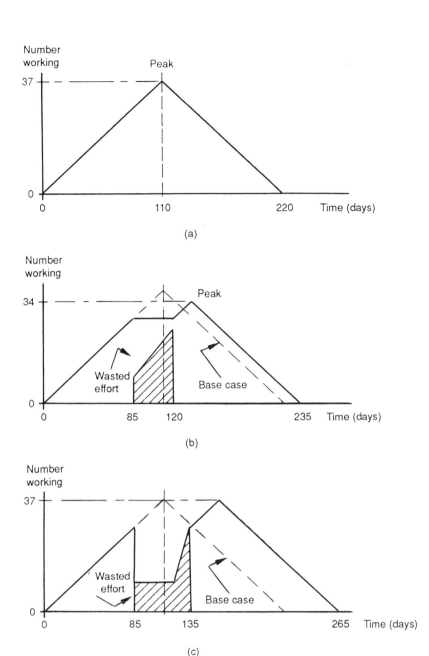

Figure 14-5 Effect of interruptions on project timing and staffing. (a) Uninterrupted staffing, uninterrupted information (base case). (b) Uninterrupted staffing, interrupted information. (c) Interrupted staffing, interrupted information.

scribed earlier. The next example, Fig. 14-5b, shows a case where crucial information (the vendor data) is being withheld while the staffing is kept in a holding pattern. Some less important tasks can be taken care of while in the holding pattern, so the peak won't be quite as high once things get moving again; but for the most part, the efforts of the holding operation will be wasted (crosshatched area). Finally in Fig. 14-5c, we see the effects of cutting back on staffing while waiting for authorization. Here people are lost to other projects, so some progress that was made prior to the cutback is lost. A reduced staff is kept during the cutback. Presumably a workforce buildup can occur more rapidly than the original mobilization, because the tasks are clearly carved out, sitting there, ready for some attention. In reality, this may not happen (the former case is shown in Fig. 14-5c). Demobilization of a project never works well. The mere psychology of it is detrimental. How does one credibly press for urgency once the project has been remobilized? Also, in addition to wasted engineering/design efforts there might be another cost: Some engineering contracts have penalty charges for remobilizing.

Clearly, vendor drawings are crucial to engineering/design.

Vendor drawings are needed during construction, too. On one job, a large dust collector was due for installation on top of some storage silos. To begin, the area construction superintendent and the mechanical supervisor looked through the open crates containing dust collector parts; they realized right away that more help was required—some parts seemed to be missing. Together with the site engineer, a receiving clerk, the vendor, a P&ID, and a sketchy arrangement drawing, plus 2 days of their time, they were able to discern that the dust collector was being provided *as a package* in the following manner:

Component	Origin	Shipping container	Accompanying enclosures
Collector housing	Michigan	Three wooden crates	A bag of bolts and washers in one crate
Bags, bag cages, clips, gaskets	Michigan	One wooden crate	A bill of lading
A structural frame of 4-in angle iron, in assembled parts	Maryland	One wooden crate	A drawing showing the dust collector on this frame
Electrical panel	New Jersey	One small crate	With control relays from Spain
Dwyer pressure gauges and switches	New Jersey	One cardboard box	Data sheets
Asco solenoid valves	Kansas	One small crate	A bill of lading

The solenoid valves were not known to be part of this order and were found in surplus inventory, labeled as spare parts, at the end of the job. Meanwhile, because this was not known, replacement valves were ordered and installed. Because vendor prints had not been asked for, they had not been provided. The field effort was further thwarted, however, because, without vendor information, the P&IDs were inaccurate; as a matter of fact, they were *false.* The P&IDs were the imaginings of some poor soul, toiling in a vacuum, on some cloud. No one had ever told this poor soul that good, solid data were available. One simply must make provisions to obtain them. There is no need (and no excuse) for guessing. Yet, in his brief career this process engineer had seen guessing institutionalized. Furthermore, he had never experienced a well-executed job, so how could he know better? The people who were to have trained him had gone into retirement years earlier.

In this case, the design effort, not performed under good working conditions, by trained individuals at drafting tables, was performed on the top of a silo, by four craftsmen and two supervisors, with a crane costing $750 per day (including the operator) sitting dutifully below, while some trial-and-error construction was carried out.

The saga of wiring and instrumentation on this same unit was equally noteworthy.

The value of the vendor data does not end at installation, however. It continues throughout the life of the plant. Maintenance is greatly simplified when vendor data are available.

How can a maintenance mechanic troubleshoot a noisy and leaky drum dryer gearbox without vendor information? Just to open it up for a look entails consulting the drawings to learn the types of gearing, bearings, and seals. Then, after the look, if the mechanic has the drawings, he or she can put some parts on order. If not, well then, good luck.

With older equipment this can be crucial. The parts are usually fairly standard, but not easy to identify without the drawings. Perhaps the drum dryer company has folded, but the gearbox supplier and/or at least suppliers of standard parts for the gearbox are far more likely to continue in business.

The need for these drawings (and data sheets, like pump curves) extends beyond the life of the operation on which they were originally employed. Used equipment gains currency and value when it is accompanied by vendor drawings.

So far the benefits from vendor drawings have been shown accruing to the owner. Benefits also accrue to engineering firms that recognize the crucial nature of these documents. They will gain in stature and run smooth jobs. Repeat business will be automatic when the competitors are firms that have *not* learned how to acquire and handle vendor data.

ACQUISITION OF VENDOR DATA

The major stumbling block in acquiring vendor data is poor communication. The solution to this problem is easy: Make your need known during inquiry. Surprisingly enough, when there is a problem with vendor drawings, mostly it can be traced to this.

The next major stumbling block is failure to select qualified bidders (see Chap. 12, *Procurement*). An unqualified bidder, attempting to enter the game, may try to appear cost-attractive by cutting all things out of the bid except for the most obvious necessities. Drawings are always excised early, as their absence is not noticed by the unskilled. In a situation like this, an unscrupulous vendor will attempt to pass off catalog pages, advertising matter, or maintenance brochures as though they were approvable items. The *last* thing an unqualified vendor wants the buyer to see is a clear description of what has been bought. As a matter of fact, this is a clear indicator of inferior performance as a whole, and such a vendor should be excluded from future bids—as long as you are sure your requests were clear and fair.

Another reason for having problems with vendor drawings is due to lodging the request in the wrong place. Sometimes local representatives will take it upon themselves to provide, in a bona fide fashion, technical information, as though they were the inventor, fabricator, and principal. In this surreal but all too common situation, local representatives have been known to sidetrack many a request for vendor information. The solution here is to make sure the contact for technical information (not commercial information) leads directly to the engineering department of the *fabricator*. This must be established before the order is placed. *Nothing else will do.*

Still another problem arises from unthinking (and occasionally unethical) treatment at the hands of the owners and the engineers/designers. Here the culprits completely overlook the effort required to put together a set of drawings that are meaningful. There are no free lunches. Engineers and owners tend to abuse the soft sales side of the equipment vendors, making demands for catalogs, quotes, drawings, estimates, presentations, and lessons in physics as though these provisions were without cost. Then there is the despicable practice of trying to have a vendor violate ethics by revealing secrets about an owner's competitor. Is it any wonder that a vendor wants to have a secure contract in pocket before going to the trouble of putting together a custom drawing submittal?

Last, and most important from the vendors' standpoint, is the question of confidentiality. Here they are in a bind. They clearly want to do all in their power to make their equipment function perfectly, and they know that releasing the drawings will serve this end. Vendors also know that imitators of their product might benefit from seeing their drawings. Thus when vendors' drawings are sent out, it is with the provision that

- The drawings be recognized as the vendors' property
- They are not to be copied
- They are to be returned upon request

When the company requesting vendor drawings has proved itself to be a well-run, professional organization, capable of complying with these provisions, it will not encounter obstacles of distrust.

The best way of asking for vendor data is to include the request in the body of the specification. To include this request in a lesser place is to suggest that it merits less attention than the equipment, and this just is not so. For an example, see Exhibit D (App. B).

A project team that understands the benefits of good vendor document information, and the procedures to acquire it, can bridge communication gaps with vendors. To make sure that the project team appreciates the utility of vendor data and to ensure that they know how to handle vendor data, copies of a procedure for handling vendor documents should be issued to all engineers, designers, clerks, etc. A sample is given in App. B.

To ensure that the vendor understands the need for drawings, a copy of Exhibit C (see App. B) should be attached to the inquiry. When the inquiry is handled through a representative, the inquiry cover letter should specifically state that the principal must be advised that drawings are needed and that a copy of Exhibit C must be forwarded along with a copy of the specification.

A good way of securing the vendor's cooperation in the quest for drawings is to offer partial payment (typically 10 to 20 percent) for approval copies. This is the money for which the purchaser becomes indebted anyhow, within a month or two from when the order is placed—one should just as well obtain some benefit from it.

HANDLING OF VENDOR DATA

Receipt of submittal documents and return of the same should be handled by the purchasing department. Once in-house, a submittal must be examined for completeness and pertinence. Then, because three copies are requested for approval, the sheets must be collated into three piles: two for temporary safekeeping and one for circulation. The in-house handling is done by three project people: a document clerk, the lead designer, and the sponsor.

The document clerk on a project in the $5 to $20 million range is usually a junior designer or drafter who can do other things when not tracking vendor drawings. For larger projects, the duties as clerk can be full-time at the peak design effort. Part of what the clerk must do is log in submittals and check the log to identify those that are taking excessive time for approval. An important part of the clerk's job is to break the submittal into logical groups that will each have a separate identity and thus a separate vendor print number. Each logical group should be capable of being reviewed and approved on its own. One sheet showing all the details of a tank constitutes a logical group. Nine sheets* showing a skid-mounted air compressor constitute a logical group.

For each one of these groups, the clerk must make the appropriate entries in the vendor data log (Form 132, App. C). Each group of drawings is kept together in an 11 × 14 in manila envelope with the "V-" number (vendor print number) clearly written or stamped in the upper right-hand corner.

The clerk must mark each sheet of a package with stamps 18 and 23 (see Fig. 14-6). Each sheet must be numbered, and the number must be written in the appropriate box on stamp 23. The remaining information must also be written into the stamp 23 box for each drawing. With the assistance of the lead designer and the project engineer, the clerk will determine the sponsor and the reviewers for the document package and will fill out Form 137 (the vendor data routing

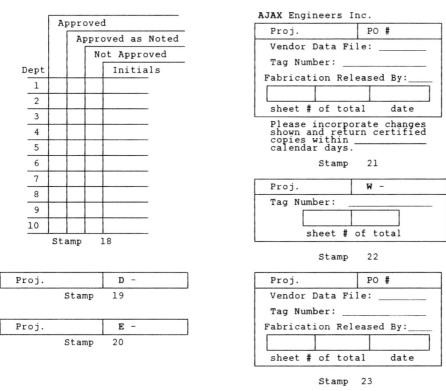

Figure 14-6 Document stamps.

---

*The sheets are as follows: compressor, filter, dryer, receiver, panel, electrical elementary, starter, process diagram, overall assembly.

sheet). In this way, each sheet of a vendor submittal, including the "buyouts" (parts purchased from others), is uniquely identified and kept together with other pertinent information. This approach saves enormous amounts of time and greatly reduces the confusion associated with handling vendor documents.

The clerk's duties temporarily end when he or she turns collated, labeled groups of vendor documents over to the lead designer. The clerk's duties resume after the documents have been reviewed. At that point, the clerk will probably be designated to transfer markings and comments over to a clean set of drawings for return to the vendor.* Once this is done, the clerk will once again update the vendor data log and take the return marked submittal back to the purchasing department for return to the vendor.

The lead designer coaches the document clerk and reviews his or her work. The lead designer, with the concurrence of the project engineer, also names the sponsor and the reviewers for the vendor drawing package. The lead designer reviews markings and comments once the package has made the rounds. Finally the lead designer selects a drafter or junior designer to copy the review markings and comments onto a duplicate set.

The sponsor is the person most directly tied to the success or failure of the item under review. This is usually the author of the specification, but not always, since the specification may have been authored by someone who specializes in a certain type of equipment, such as distillation columns. In some cases the sponsor will be the engineer responsible for the P&ID that shows the particular equipment item.

The sponsor's duty is to walk the approval documents through the review process, having one-on-one conversations with each reviewer as the documents are dropped off and picked up, something that only need take a few minutes with each reviewer. The sponsor must be satisfied that the reviewer has examined the pertinent features. The sponsor must also note a marking or comment that may be of interest to a previous reviewer and cycle the document back for further consideration.

Additional details of responsibility regarding vendor documents are given in App. B. With few exceptions, there are two vendor submittals: approval drawings and certified, final drawings. The approval drawings are all-important at the time of their review—other activities must take second place. The marked version returned to the vendor (with the appropriate instructions from the purchasing department) constitutes an important basis of the purchase contract. The certified, final drawings are mostly important from a procedural† standpoint only.

Up to this point, the discussion has been concerned with approval drawings. The certified final drawings are far easier to handle. For one thing, the certified copies are hardly ever (if ever) on the critical path. For another, the review of the certified copies is just to make sure that they incorporate the markings and comments of the ap-

---

*The set returned to the vendor will be stamped with stamp 21 only. As before, the clerk will fill out the boxes on stamp 21 for each drawing. In the block under *Fabrication Released by*, the clerk will place the initials of the sponsor.

†The certified drawing can become evidence in a court of law. Furthermore, some companies require certified, final drawings for a piece of equipment before an arrangement drawing can be issued for construction.

proval set and that they contain a mark of certification. These tasks can be carried out by a junior member of the design staff—perhaps the document clerk.

The whole of what has been covered in this section is covered extensively in App. B.

LAST COMMENTS

It is worthwhile to reflect one last time on what takes place during the design process. Summing it up concisely, we arrive at this: *Design for process facilities is the plan which enables the economic* construction and operation of a process facility. This plan is developed on paper. It is communicated on paper. It is recorded on paper.*

As a final comment, the following thought is offered as an unproved axiom: No thing can be built, whether it be a living cell or a kazoo, without instructions.

---

*The reader is reminded of the definition of economic activity (see page 76).

References

1. Petr Beckman, *A History of Pi*, The Golem Press, New York, 1971, pp. 62–72.
2. Paul Arthur Schilpp (ed.), *Albert Einstein*, Tudor Publishing Co., New York, 1949, pp. 392, 684.
3. Thomas J. Peters and Robert H. Waterman, Jr., *In Search of Excellence*, Warner Books Inc., New York, 1984.
4. Gene Koretz, "Capital Spending Isn't Growing Where It Counts," *Business Week*, June 26, 1989, p. 23.
5. Thomas M. Nourse, "U.S. Competitive Problems," Nourse Associates, Inc., San Diego, 1990.
6. David S. Jordan, *Investments*, Prentice-Hall, New York, 1929, pp. 6, 9.
7. Max S. Peters and Klaus D. Timmerhaus, *Plant Design and Economics for Chemical Engineers*, McGraw-Hill, New York, 1992.
8. H. F. Rase and M. H. Barrow, *Project Engineering of Process Plants*, John Wiley & Sons, New York, 1957.
9. W. Edwards Deming, *Out of the Crisis*, Massachusetts Institute of Technology, Cambridge, MA, 1986, p. 405.
10. Warren Bennis, *Why Leaders Can't Lead*, Jossey-Bass Publishers, San Francisco, 1989, pp. 23–24.
11. Frank Caropreso (ed.), *Making Total Quality Happen*, The Conference Board, New York, 1990, p. 41.
12. Myron Tribus, "Deming's Way," *Mechanical Engineering*, January 1988, pp. 28–30.
13. Mary Walton, *The Deming Management Method*, Perigree Books, New York, 1986, p. 85.
14. W. Edwards Deming, *Out of the Crisis*, Massachusetts Institute of Technology, Cambridge, MA, 1986, p. 86.
15. Michael Dertouzos, Richard K. Lester, and Robert M. Solow, *Made in America*, Harper Perennial, New York, 1989, pp. 72, 119.
16. Elizabeth Hayward, "Portrait of a Practical Man," *Road and Track*, May 1969, p. 112.
17. *Engineering Times*, May 1991, p. 5.
18. Mary Walton, *The Deming Management Method*, Perigree Books, New York, 1986, p. 124.
19. Warren Bennis and Bert Nanus, *Leaders*, Harper and Row Publishers, New York, 1985, p. 22.
20. Robert Townsend, *Up the Organization*, Alfred A. Knopf, Inc., New York, 1970, p. 114.
21. W. Edwards Deming, *Out of the Crisis*, Massachusetts Institute of Technology, Cambridge, MA, 1986, p. 76.
22. Jerry O. Dalton, "The Rights of Management," *Chemical Engineering*, October 1989, p. 174.
23. Michael Dertouzos, Richard K. Lester, and Robert M. Solow, *Made in America*, Harper Perennial, New York, 1989, pp. 161–162.
24. Richard Foster, *Innovation*, Summit Books, New York, 1986, pp. 242–243.
25. Warren Bennis, *Why Leaders Can't Lead*, Jossey-Bass Publishers, San Francisco, 1989, p. 23.
26. Mary Walton, *The Deming Management Method*, Perigree Books, New York, 1986, p. 32.
27. Thomas J. Peters and Robert H. Waterman, Jr., *In Search of Excellence*, Warner Books Inc., New York, 1984, p. 292.
28. Eli Nesenfeld, "One Overlooked Specification Haunts Control System Design," *Control*, February 1991, pp. 56–61.
29. George S. Birrell, letter to *J. Constr. Engg. & Mgmt.*, 113 (2): 343–345, June 1987.
30. *Engineering News Record*, January 20, 1992, p. 90.
31. *The Richardson Rapid Construction Cost Estimating System*, Richardson Engineering Services, Inc., Mesa, AZ, 1992.
32. William D. Mahoney (ed.), *Building Construction Cost Data*, R. S. Means Co., Inc., Kinston, MA, 1992.
33. W. T. Nichols, "Capital Cost Estimating," *Industrial and Engineering Chemistry*, 43(10):2295–2298, October 1951.
34. Thomas J. Ward, "Estimate Profitability Using Net Return Rate," *Chemical Engineering*, March 1989, pp. 151–155.
35. Benjamin A. Horwitz, "The Mathematics of Discounted Cash Flow Analysis," *Chemical Engineering*, May 19, 1980, pp. 169–174.
36. Kate Ballen, "The New Look of Capital Spending," *Fortune*, March 13, 1989, p. 116.
37. Elizabeth Hayward, "Portrait of a Practical Man," *Road and Track*, May 1969, p. 112.
38. Robert Townsend, *Up the Organization*, Alfred A. Knopf, Inc., New York, 1970, p. 55.

39. J. W. Mellor, *Inorganic and Theoretical Chemistry*, vol. 11, Longmans, Green and Co., London, 1931, reprinted 1966, p. 812.
40. Ju Chin Chu, Shu Lung Wang, Sherman L. Levy, and Rajendra Paul, *Vapor-Liquid Equilibrium Data*, Ann Arbor, MI, J. W. Edwards, Publisher, Inc., Michigan, 1956, p. 55.
41. Theodore C. Fowler, *Value Analysis in Design*, Van Nostrand Reinhold, New York, 1990.
42. Don W. Green, James O. Maloney, and Robert H. Perry (eds.), *Perry's Chemical Engineer's Handbook*, 6th ed., McGraw-Hill, New York, 1984, pp. 6-35 to 6-37, 6-46 to 6-53.
43. R. H. Warring, *Seals and Sealing Handbook*, Gulf Publishing Co., Houston, 1981.
44. Nicholas M. Raskhodoff, *Electronic Drafting and Design*, 5th ed., Prentice-Hall, Inc., Englewood Cliffs, NJ, 1987, pp. 374–376.
45. Don W. Green, James O. Maloney, and Robert H. Perry (eds.), *Perry's Chemical Engineer's Handbook*, 6th ed., McGraw-Hill, New York, 1984, pp. 24-9 to 24-13.
46. Claude Polgar, *Design of Relay Control Systems*, Iliffe, London, 1968.
47. Charles Seymour Siskind, *Electrical Control Systems in Industry*, McGraw-Hill, New York, 1963.
48. George E. Russell, *Hydraulics*, 5th ed., Henry Holt and Company, New York, 1946, p. 74.
49. O. G. Tietjens (ed.), *Fundamentals of Hydro- and Aeromechanics*, based on lectures of L. Prandtl, translated by L. Rosenhead, Dover Publications, Inc., New York, 1957, p. 114.
50. Warren L. McCabe and Julian C. Smith, *Unit Operations of Chemical Engineering*, McGraw-Hill, New York, 1956, pp. 60–61.
51. Ranald V. Giles, *Fluid Mechanics and Hydraulics*, 2d ed., McGraw-Hill, New York, 1962, pp. 249, 250, 257.
52. C. E. Lapple and C. B. Shepherd, "Calculation of Particle Trajectories," *Industrial and Engineering Chemistry*, 32(5):605, May 1940.
53. Warren L. McCabe and Julian C. Smith, *Unit Operations of Chemical Engineering*, McGraw-Hill, New York, 1956, pp. 396–397.
54. Peerless Pump Company, Indianapolis, Brochure B-2340, 1989, pp. 18–19.
55. C. R. Westaway and A. W. Loomis (eds.), *Cameron Hydraulic Data*, 15th ed., Ingersoll Rand Company, Woodcliff Lake, NJ, 1977, pp. 1.29, 1.30.
56. Ibid., p. 1.27.
57. W. Roy Penney, "Inert Gas in Liquid Mars Pump Performance," *Chemical Engineering*, July 3, 1978, pp. 63–68.
58. Mao J. Tsai, "Accounting for Dissolved Gas in Pump Design," *Chemical Engineering*, July 26, 1982, pp. 65–70.
59. C. R. Westaway and A. W. Loomis (eds.), *Cameron Hydraulic Data*, 15th ed., Ingersoll Rand Company, Woodcliff Lake, NJ, 1977, pp. 1.28.
60. Lansing Lamont, *Day of Trinity*, Signet Book, New York, 1965, p. 182.
61. John L. Alden, *Design of Industrial Exhaust Systems*, 5th ed., The Industrial Press, New York, 1982, Fig. 2.2.
62. Jerry R. Johanson, *Chemical Engineering/Deskbook Issue*, McGraw-Hill, New York, 1978, p. 13.
63. Frederick A. Zenz and Frederick E. Zenz, "The Gravity Flow of Gases, Liquids, and Bulk Solids," *Industrial Engineering Chemistry Fundamentals*, 18(4):347, 1979.
64. F. A. Zenz, "Size Cyclone Diplegs Better," *Hydrocarbon Processing*, May 1975, pp. 125–128.
65. Warren L. McCabe, Julian C. Smith, and Peter Harriot, *Unit Operations of Chemical Engineering*, 4th ed., McGraw-Hill, New York, 1985, p. 764.
66. William Strunk, Jr., and E. B. White, *The Elements of Style*, The Macmillan Company, New York, 1959, p. xi.
67. Hubert G. Alexander, *Language and Thinking*, D. Van Nostrand and Co., New York, 1967, p. 52.
68. E. Cassirer, *An Essay on Man*, Yale University Press, New Haven, 1944, p. 24.
69. Hubert G. Alexander, *Language and Thinking*, P. van Nostrand Co., Inc., Princeton, NJ, 1967, pp. 54–55.
70. Jeremy Campbell, *Grammatical Man*, Simon & Schuster (Touchstone), New York, 1982, p. 165.
71. Greg Benz, letter to *Chemical Engineering*, February 1990, p. 7.
72. Daniel W. Mead, *Contracts, Specifications and Engineering Relations*, vol. 2, McGraw-Hill, New York, 1933, p. 179.
73. Joseph Jacobs, "Engineering and Construction: An Industry in Transition," *Chemical Engineering Progress*, June 1988, pp. 26–29.

Appendix A
Sample Proposal Letter, Scope of Work, and Basic Data

This appendix contains a proposal by an engineering company to an owner/operator. Included are a proposal letter, scope of work, and basic data. The scope-of-work and basic data documents are rewritten versions, based on the owner's submittal that accompanied the RFQ (not shown).

PROPOSAL LETTER

AJAX Engineers
323 New Orleans St.
Joplin, MO
November 11, 1994

Ms. Carla Temple
Plant Engineer
Mix Chem Corporation
1133 Andrews Street
Paducah, KY

PROPOSAL: Engineering Services, New Blend Tank

Dear Carla,

Thank you for inviting us to present our proposal for engineering and other services leading to a ±10 percent capital cost estimate for a new blend tank at your Paducah plant.

The attached Exhibit A describes the services we plan to perform. These services include preparation of a P&ID, specifications, sketches, takeoffs, vendor inquiries, environmental support, and cost estimating. Exhibit B lists design parameters that will be used in performing the work described in Exhibit A. Figure A-1 is a flow diagram showing the extent of the proposed project. Figure A-2 gives the approximate location of the mix vessel.

John Hardy, who is well known to you, will supervise the work; however, his involvement will be limited to about 10 hours per week, as this small job will not require his full attention. Under John, working full-time will be Ruben Diaz, also known to you.

We will provide the services to you under the existing national contract between Mix Chem and AJAX (your reference number 79-801).

We estimate our services will come to $62,000. We plan to submit the ±10 percent estimate for your review no later than 12 weeks after your instructions to proceed.

We look forward to being of service to you.

Very truly yours,

William Byrd
Manager, Business Development

cc: John Hardy

EXHIBIT A: SCOPE OF WORK

1.0 General

Engineers will provide services necessary to obtain a ±10 percent capital cost estimate for the installation of a polymer blender/reactor (see Fig. A-1). Site for the installation is the Mix Chem operation at 1133 Andrews St., Paducah, Kentucky. The reactor is to be indoors, adjacent to existing tank T-7 (see Fig. A-2). The reactor is an existing one, originally built in 1957. It has been in mothballs at the Cincinnati plant since 1990.

2.0 Process description

A polyol, received in tank cars, is to be blended thoroughly with a proprietary monomer, designated R33. This will be done in the blender/reactor vessel. A slow-turning anchor mixer plus a high-

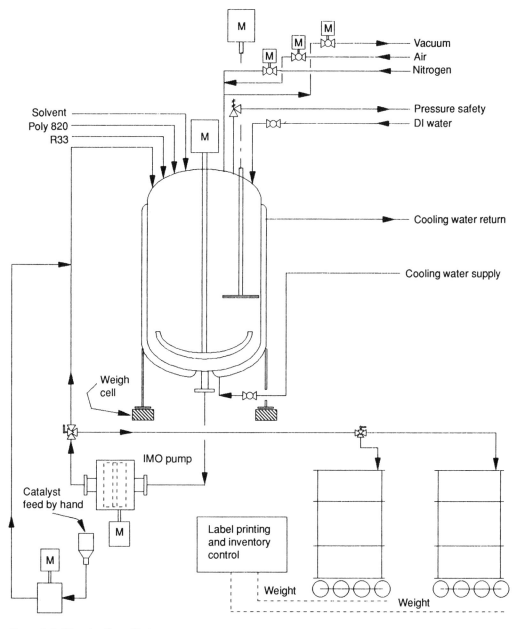

Figure A-1 Blender flow diagram.

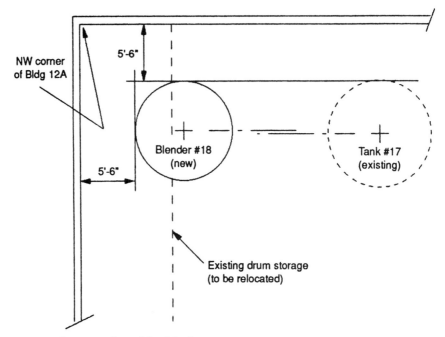

Figure A-2 Location of new blend tank.

speed, high-shear disperser will be used to blend the liquids. A dose of catalyst will be rapidly added via a recirculation line external to the reactor. The catalyst will cause R33 to rapidly combine at certain locations on the polyol chain, making a new product.

The full sequence of operations is shown in the Basic Data, attached.

The reaction is mildly exothermic. The heat is to be removed via cooling water circulating in the reactor jacket.

Product will be weighed into 45-gal drums or 5-gal pails. The weighing device must print a shipping label (with a bar code) and must also transmit production information to the plant mainframe computer.

3.0 Process engineering

The process engineer will prepare a rigorous mass balance based on the approximate data provided by the owner. Said mass balance shall include provisions for reprocessing substandard product. A detailed analysis of reaction by-products and the ultimate destination of these by-products shall accompany the mass balance.

The process engineer will examine the owner heat-of-reaction data and prepare a summary report of provisions needed for cooling the reaction, plus provisions for a safe operation.

The process engineer will prepare a process flow diagram (PFD) with stream information. The stream information shall be on $8\frac{1}{2} \times 11$ sheets, separate from the PFD sheets. The stream information shall consist of (as a minimum)

- Average flows
- Design flows
- Stream compositions
- Design temperatures
- Design pressures

The process engineer will prepare a P&ID showing line sizes, line numbers, piping materials, and fluid commodities. Said engineer will provide the insulation takeoff for equipment and piping. Said engineer will work with engineers and designers of other disciplines in the preparation of their documents and material takeoffs. Said engineer will write specifications for and obtain firm quotes on the following items:

- Three Imo pumps
- Anchor agitator (50 hp)
- Disperser (50 hp)
- Circulation pump
- Tank weighing system (including batch controller)

The process engineer must also work with the instrument engineer to provide a suitable pressure safety device (maybe a rupture disk in front of a self-closing relief valve). Previous safety devices at this site have been based on a shut-in vessel partially filled with solvent—assuming energy input from fire. This vessel must be reviewed independently of past practice.

The process engineer will review (or supervise the review of) the disperser from the standpoint of (1) batch size versus blend time, (2) heat transfer, and (3) whether the old vessel (1957) can take the new agitator.

4.0 Electrical engineering
The electrical engineer will prepare the following:

- A single-line diagram
- A general electrical specification
- An electric motor specification
- A specification for a motor control center
- A formal inquiry for the motor control center
- A material takeoff for the estimate

5.0 Instrument engineering
The instrument engineer will work with the process engineer to establish the required controls and to represent them on the P&ID, using ISA conventions. The instrument engineer will prepare an instrument list, with numbers. The instrument engineer will define the tie-in between weighing, label printing, and inventory tracking.

Formal quotes for panels and the weighing system will be obtained for the estimate. Approximate prices from previous projects will be used to estimate the balance of the instruments.

6.0 Piping design
The piping designer will perform general equipment and layout work. Said designer will provide one study grade plan (D size) at $\frac{1}{4}$ in = 1 ft and a material takeoff. The piping designer will also review Mix Chem piping specifications and issue a revised copy according to the requirements of this job.

7.0 Structural engineering

The structural engineer will provide one $8\frac{1}{2} \times 11$ sketch of the tank foundation. The structural engineer will also provide one $8\frac{1}{2} \times 11$ sketch of a typical pipe support foundation. The structural engineer will provide takeoffs of steel and concrete. A 3×3 ft platform must be included, mounted above the tank, for access to the agitator and the pressure safety device. The platform is to be supported from the tank. Bollards must be provided east of the field panel along the aisleway.

8.0 Mechanical engineering

The mechanical engineer will add a new nozzle on the tank roof to accommodate the new high-speed disperser. Some existing nozzles may require relocation. The mechanical engineer will define necessary steps for obtaining a new ASME section VIII certification. Costs associated with recertification must be included in the estimate.

9.0 CADD group

The following D-sized (6-ft^2) sheets will be done by computer-aided design: a P&ID, a PFD, and an electrical single-line.

10.0 Estimating group

The estimator will take the information provided by the above designers/engineers and, using appropriate unit costs and labor rates, will prepare an estimate.

11.0 Environmental group

The environmental consultant shall review secondary containment, operating permit, and hazardous materials management plan (HMMP). Findings shall be written in a brief memo to the project manager and project engineer.

12.0 Scheduling group

The scheduler will work with the project manager to provide a project schedule for completing the design. A separate schedule for the construction phase will also be required.

13.0 Project management

A full-time project manager will not be required. The project manager will monitor work to make sure it meets Ajax and Mix Chem standards, monitor cost and schedule performance, and issue a monthly letter report to Mix Chem.

14.0 Amenities

Needs for the following amenities have been reviewed with the annotated results:

	Need?
Telephone	Yes
Public address	No
Bathrooms	No
Lunchrooms	No
Parking	No
Laboratory or shop	No
Furniture	Yes*

*Rostrum for logbook and sample sheets.

15.0 Facilities and structures

- Types of buildings: not applicable
- Floor or platform live load: 75 lb/ft^2 for tank platform
- Occupancy: to be determined, per UBC

16.0 Sitework
Needs for the following sitework have been reviewed with the annotated results:

- Survey: not applicable
- Soil report: use existing
- Site preparation and demolition: saw-cut floor, remove portion to make room for new tank foundation
- Roads, railroads: no
- Drainage: no
- Containment: no change from existing

17.0 Other requirements
Needs for the following additional requirements have been reviewed with the annotated results:

- Sprinklers and hydrants: OK as is
- Safety showers and eyewashes: OK as is
- Bathrooms: OK as is
- Drinking fountains: OK as is
- Bollards/guardrails: See "Structural Scope"
- Handicap access: OK as is

EXHIBIT B: BASIC DATA

(This is a checklist format; as such, some spaces are left empty.)

1.0 Materials

1.1 Raw materials

Name	How received	Frequency of receipt	Lot received, gal	Composition
1. Poly 820	RR tanker	2/mo.	30,000	See attachments
2. R33	RR tanker	1/mo.	30,000	
3. Catalyst	5-gal drums	1/mo.	2,000	See attachments
4.				
5.				

1.2 In-process materials

Name
1.
2.
3.

1.3 Products and by-products

Name	How shipped	Frequency shipped	Lot shipped	Composition
1. Star 820	Drum		45 gal	See attachments
2. Star 820	Drum		5 gal	
3.				

NOTE: Weight tolerance = +0.10 percent; –0.07 percent.

1.4 Limits of impurities:

1. Raw materials: See attachments

2. Products: See product specification for Star 820, attached

1.5 Other requirements: TBD*

2.0 Properties

2.1 Common properties

Name	Viscosity	Temperature	Specific gravity	Temperature
1. Poly 820	200	180	1.13	Approx. for all
2. Poly 820	800	100	1.13	temps.
3. R33	150	180	1.29	
4. R33	400	100	1.29	
5. Star 820	880	180	1.31	
6. Star 820	2100	100	1.31	

Units: Poise, °F

2.2 Special properties: TBD

	Temperature	Temperature
1.		
2.		
3.		
4.		
5.		

*TBD means to be determined.

3.0 Capacity

3.1 Operating hours/day: 24

3.2 Operating days/week: 5; therefore, shifts: 3

3.3 Operating days/year: $52.18 \times 5 - 14 = 247$

3.4 Unscheduled maintenance interruptions: 80 h/yr

3.5 Therefore, operating hours per year: $247 \times 24 - 80 = 5848$

3.6 Annual production of in-specification material: 10,000,000 lb

Recycle off-specification material: $\underline{\quad 200,000 \text{ lb}}$

10,200,000

(or about 20,800 of 45-gal drums). Therefore, average
production rate = 10,200,000/247 = 41,300 lb/day
(84 drums/day)

3.7 Design production rate: 47,500 lb/day ($41,300 \times 1.15$)
(97 drums/day)

Note: This is the process design rate. Additional factors must be
added to accommodate process control and particular considerations for each operation in question. Design rates for equipment
will be specified on the process flow diagram.

3.8 Time cycles

Operation	Duration, h
1. Verify order number and batch weights	0.15
2. Fill Poly 820	2.16
3. Fill R33	0.95
4. Pull vacuum	0.48
5. Blend	0.94
6. Purge with N_2	0.48
7. Pull vacuum	0.48
8. Purge with N_2	0.48
9. Add catalyst	0.05
10. Blend	1.24
11. Check/adjust	1.09
12. Package product	12.00
13. Clean out	2.00
14. Slack time	$\underline{1.50}$
	24.00

3.9 Tanks: Calculated requirement + 20 percent*

3.10 Overcapacity for control:*

1. Pumps, piping, valves: Design production rate + 15 percent

2. Heat exchangers: +30 percent

3. Control valves: Pump/system curve mandatory

4. Conveyors: Design production rate + 20 percent

3.11 Overcapacity for future:*

1. Boiler/heater: NA†

2. Air compressor: NA

3. Cooling tower: NA

3.12 Jacket dirt factors:*

Cooling water: 0.006 h · ft^2 · °F/Btu

---

*These are initial guesses to be used if no other information is forthcoming. Use
judgment.

†NA means not applicable.

3.13   Corrosion allowance: $\frac{1}{16}$ to $\frac{1}{8}$ in for aqueous contact*

4.0 Process conditions

4.1   Temperature and pressure

Process area	Design temperature	Design pressure
Blending	300	30 and full vacuum

Units: °F, lb/in^2 gauge.

For further information, see attachments.

4.2   Special materials of construction

1. Tank, 304 SS

2. Piping, per Mix Chem specification P-901-B

3.

4.3   Special safety precautions

1. Solvent is flammable.

2. Polymers are skin irritants.

3.

4.4   Containment

1. General policy: Require secondary containment

2. Sumps: Per secondary containment

3. Chemical sewer: Per secondary containment

4.

5.

4.5   Additional information

All piping for Poly 820 and catalyst must be removable for cleaning.

5.0. Standards

5.1   Piping: Mix Chem specification P-901-B

5.2   Atmospheric tanks: API

5.3   Pressure vessels: ASME

5.4   Pressure safety: API 500

5.5   Pumps: ANSI, ASTM

5.6   Exchangers: TEMA

5.7   Electrical: Mix Chem specifications E-23-H and E-818-D; require UL label

6.0 Conventions

6.1   Dimensions are to be in U.S. units.

6.2   Drawing size is to be the Mix Chem D size: 22 × 34 in

6.3   Scale for arrangement drawings is to be no less than $\frac{3}{8}$ in = 1 ft

7.0 Equipment and materials suppliers

Qualified foreign suppliers accepted: Yes

Exceptions: None

---

*These are initial guesses to be used if no other information is forthcoming. Use judgment.

8.0 Utilities

8.1 Cooling

	Temperature design		Pressure design	
	Max.	Min.	Max.	Min.
1. Dry bulb	105	−8	NA	NA
2. Wet bulb	84	−8	NA	NA
3. Cooling water supply	92	45	90	40
4. Cooling water return	115	NA	30	28
5.				

Units: °F, ft WC.

8.2 Electrical

	Kilowatts	
	Required	Available
1. 480 V		Adequate
2. 120 V		Adequate
3.		
4.		
5.		

Capacity calculations: NA.

Tie-in locations: Motor control center for building 12A.

8.3 Other utilities

	Flow		Pressure	
	Required	Available	Required	Available
1. Instrument air		Adequate		Adequate
2. Plant air		Adequate		Adequate
3. Nitrogen		Adequate		Adequate
4. Plant water		Adequate		Adequate
5. Steam		Adequate		Adequate
6. Condensate		Adequate		Adequate
7.				

	Temperature		Tie-in
	Required	Available	Location and remarks
1. Instrument air		Adequate	TBD
2. Plant air		Adequate	TBD
3. Nitrogen		Adequate	TBD
4. Plant water		Adequate	TBD
5. Steam		Adequate	TBD
6. Condensate		Adequate	TBD
7.			

9.0 Instrumentation

9.1 CRT or graphics panel: CRT

9.2 Programmable controller: Yes

9.3 Stand-alone analog controllers: Yes

9.4 Printer: Use existing

9.5 Uninterruptible power supply (UPS): No

9.6 Start/stop: (Field, ~~Control Room~~)

9.7 Emergency stop: (~~Field~~, Control Room)

9.8 Field panels: Yes

10.0 Installed spares

   10.1 Process: No

   10.2 Electrical: No

   10.3 Instruments: No

11.0 Jurisdiction

   11.1 City: Paducah

   11.2 County: McCracken

   11.3 State: Kentucky

   11.4 Regulatory: TBD

12.0 Economic studies

   12.1 Hurdle ROI: 20 percent (before taxes)

—Appendix B— Procedure for Handling Vendor Documents

This procedure should be in the hands of all key project personnel.

INTRODUCTION

On any project that involves design, one task is always on the critical path: approval of vendor documents. No single event can have a more beneficial effect than the receipt of accurate, clear vendor information at an early date. Such an occurrence enables design to get off to a quick start and minimizes rework.

The quality of our product (and, therefore, our reputation) depends heavily on the quality of our vendor information.

Small errors in vendor documents can eventually lead to large amounts of wasted design. This translates to losses on lump-sum work and the appearance of being slow and "expensive" on cost-plus work.

The purpose of this procedure is to define what we must do so that our vendors will work with us more effectively.

SUMMARY

This procedure relies on three principles:

- Good communications
- Economic incentives
- Assignment of responsibility

During the inquiry phase, vendors will be clearly told what is expected of them. A partial payment will be made once appropriate documents have been approved. Each vendor data package will be assigned to a person whose duty will be to push it through engineering/design groups.

RECEIPT OF VENDOR SUBMITTALS

When approval documents from a vendor arrive, they should consist of three sets of bluelines or bond-paper copies plus other enclosures which may or may not be relevant. The arriving package should have been addressed to the purchasing expediter. After evaluating completeness and taking care of purchasing logs, the expediter should

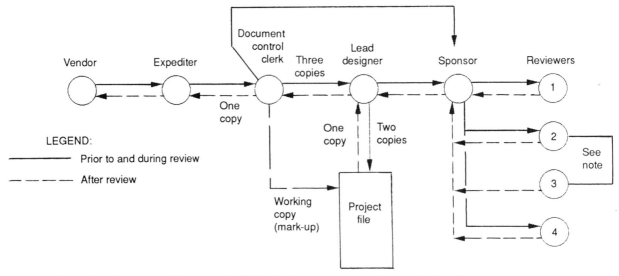

Figure B-1 Flow of vendor approval documents. (*Note:* Reviewers can pass documents directly, but sponsor should be notified.)

hand-carry the submittal to the person designated as the *document control clerk* (sometimes hereinafter called *document control*).

Here the submittal should also be reviewed for completeness and separated into logical "packets" while the superfluous and nonapproval parts are removed (see Fig. B-1). Each sheet for approval will be stamped with the stamps shown in Fig. B-2. The clerk will check with the lead designer to make sure the packets constitute stand-alone information and logical separation. With the concurrence of the lead designer, the clerk will log the submittals in the vendor data log (Form 132), stamp each sheet of one set with stamps 18 and 23, and fill in the blanks of stamp 23 (for each page). This stamped set is for circulation among the reviewers.

The clerk will turn the resulting collated, stamped groups of documents over to the lead designer. The lead designer will file two copies and give the third (stamped) copy to the sponsor. The sponsor's copy is walked through the approval process, and at the end, any markings on the approval copy are duplicated on one of the file copies un-

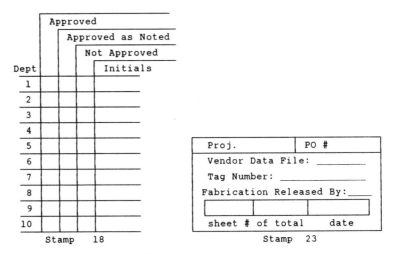

Figure B-2 Stamps for vendor drawing review.

der the direction of the document control clerk (see Fig. B-1). The final disposition of the three copies is as follows: (1) Original markup is placed in project file for use as a working copy,* (2) clean copy of markup is returned to vendor, and (3) unmarked copy of submittal is also in project file (under a separate heading, as backup).

RESPONSIBILITY

At the beginning of the review process, the document control clerk places each group of drawings inside an 11×14 manila envelope and marks the vendor print number prominently on the envelope. A vendor drawing route slip (Form 137) is enclosed or stapled to the outside. The sponsor for that package is designated in the upper left-hand part. The sponsor has four responsibilities:

- To get the package through the design groups in a timely manner
- To make sure the vendor information is correct and meets the specification
- To make sure the unit under review will perform correctly when operated
- To make sure the unit under review will fit in place during construction

Designation of the sponsor is normally the duty of the lead designer. The sponsor will normally be the person most intimately connected with the subject of the vendor data—often the author of the specification. The lead designer will select the reviewers, but the sponsor, who will always be the first reviewer, will determine the review sequence and make sure he or she agrees with the reviewer list.

REVIEW PACKAGES

In general, a vendor data package will be a grouping of drawings and tabular information that stands alone without further supporting information. Each vendor data package will have its own vendor print number and its own manila envelope—even if the "package" consists of a single sheet. Ten tank drawings will go out as ten packages if each tank drawing can stand by itself. Ten drawings of a gas compressor will go out as one package because all ten drawings are dependent on each other.

By breaking down vendor data into the smallest possible packages and assigning logical, undivided responsibility, the job of reviewing vendor information will be easily manageable. The flow of information back to vendors will start earlier, because one item still undergoing review will not hold up the approved items.

COMPLETENESS

A key concept of this procedure is completeness. A condition of completeness exists when a vendor gives us the documents we ask for. Our inquiry letter will ask for a complete set of approval documents. Vendors will be warned at the time of inquiry that partial submittals will not be accepted (see Exhibit C).

---

*In manila envelope; see Chap. 14, *Paper*.

Acceptance of partial submittals cannot be tolerated for several reasons. First, they encourage the vendor to think that the approval requirements are finished. Second, they indicate that the vendor's design is still in a state of flux, so if we use a partial submittal, we run the risk of wasting design man-hours. Third, we lose sight of what is needed: We tend to think that such and such a vendor has given us 90 percent of what we need, whereas the reality is probably closer to 20 percent. We let our guard down. Finally, if we are hard-nosed, our vendors will treat us with respect. Sloppy submittals should be the exception, not the rule.

The concept of completeness applies only to approval of vendor data and not to the purchase order as a whole. For example, the receipt of one tank drawing (on an order of a dozen tanks) may be complete because it is stand-alone and needs no accompanying documents for review. As a matter of fact, vendors should be encouraged to transmit stand-alone information as it develops instead of waiting for the development of other nonrelated data. The question to ask when considering completeness is, Can design groups use this package as it stands, or is more information needed?

Components of packaged equipment should be kept together even though they may seem to be stand-alone. This is to facilitate checking and to help understand overall package drawings. Also what may appear to be a stand-alone item may in reality depend on other items in the package.

ROUTING

The sponsor should examine the package prior to other design groups. The first duty is to check for completeness. The next duty is to determine the review sequence. The sponsor may feel, for example, that instruments should come before electrical and that piping should come first and structural last. A typical vendor package will contain a half dozen sheets, but a package with one sheet is not uncommon, and neither is a package with twenty sheets.

The sponsor should walk the package through the several disciplines. Noteworthy features are identified in person as the package is walked through. Questions are answered on the spot. The sponsor is assured of understanding the markings made by each discipline. Disciplines get to see each other's markings as they logically develop. When the sponsor leaves a package with a design discipline, the sponsor should get a commitment as to when work will be finished on the package.

When a vendor data package has been fully reviewed, the sponsor takes the package to the lead designer. The lead designer examines the markings and assigns a drafter to transfer the markings to a second copy. The lead designer carries the marked copy and the transmittal letter to document control. Here the status of the review is noted in the vendor data log, a requisition is filled out, and the package is hand-carried to the purchasing expediter, who will mail the processed submittal back to the vendor via one-day mail.

PURCHASING

In commercial matters, the purchasing agent is the primary point of contact with the vendor.

The vendor is first advised of his or her responsibility to supply approval documents at the time of inquiry. Purchasing shall include the following statements in the inquiry letter:

> An essential part of the order that may result from this inquiry is approval documents. As a consequence, the terms of payment shall be 10 percent upon approval of a *complete set* of approval documents, plus 5 percent upon receipt of a complete set of certified documents.*
>
> Your proposal shall include two delivery dates: (1) approval drawings and (2) equipment. Lack of performance for drawing delivery will be construed as lack of performance on the order as a whole and can cause us to exercise provisions for recision of contract.

Purchasing will also include general information regarding the approval process (Exhibit C).

At the time an order is placed, the Ajax expediter's name and telephone number will be included in the cover document. One week after issue of the purchase order, the expediter will call the vendor to obtain the name of a contact for monitoring document status. At this time, the expediter will discuss documents required by Ajax and make sure the vendor understands the obligation to provide the documents. The expediter will ask the contact person to stay on top of document preparation.

On crucial pieces of equipment, the sponsor will visit the vendor engineering department for at least 2 or 3 h to answer questions and help expedite preparation of the vendor drawings.

Upon receipt of vendor documents, the expediter will examine a copy of the pertinent specification under the section entitled *Drawings and Documents.* If there is reason to suspect that the submittal will not be satisfactory, the expediter is to confer with the lead designer to determine the likely sponsor. Then the expediter is to confer with the sponsor.

If a submittal is unsatisfactory, the vendor must be contacted immediately by telephone. The vendor will be advised about what to do to achieve an acceptable submittal. A confirmatory telefax or letter will also be sent.

In some cases, one or two sheets of additional data are all that is needed for completeness. This being true, the expediter can sit on the partial submittal until the remaining data arrive. In cases where the vendor's design is obviously incomplete, the submittal should be returned to the vendor in its entirety with a cover letter asking that the design be further developed prior to submittal. Purchasing is responsible for preparing the transmittal letter that accompanies the returned documents.

DOCUMENT CONTROL

Document control takes the vendor information from the expediter, breaks it down into discrete review packages, and affixes review stamps to the sheets. Document control also maintains log sheets naming types of documents, document numbers, sponsors' names, due dates, etc. Document control reviews the log sheets on a daily basis. Two days prior to a due date, document control is to call the sponsor to remind him or her of the due date coming up. When a due date is overdue, document control should check with the sponsor to find out what has caused the overrun. If need be, a new due date

---

*These percentages are negotiable.

should be established; then either the sponsor or document control should advise the project engineer of the new date.

Occasionally, more data will be submitted than are required for design (for example, maintenance instructions). These data should be removed from the approval package and forwarded to the sponsor.

Certified documents may be submitted only *after* approval documents have been approved.

When certified copies are received, they are to be checked by document control. Only with rare exceptions should certified drawings differ from approval drawings. (For example, if drawing DB-0042-A is sent out "approved as noted," it should come back with appropriate changes and with a certification mark. If a different, though similar, drawing is sent back instead, the new drawing must be returned to the vendor with a request for a certified copy of the original drawing. Document control is responsible for establishing the one-to-one identity between approval drawings and certified copies. This is not to say document control should examine the content of the drawings; document control just establishes that what comes back certified is the same document that was sent out approved.

One of the purchasing expediter's duties is to make sure the certified copies are submitted by the vendor in a reasonable time. The expediter will hand-carry these to the lead designer when they are received.

LEAD DESIGNER

The lead designer has sole responsibility for ensuring that the certified copy corresponds to the record markup. Very often the lead designer will have the drafter who made the duplicate markup also check the certified copy. Document control allows 2 days for this check, then notes in the vendor data log that final, certified data have been accepted. The following bears emphasis: *The object of checking certified copies is to make sure our comments and requirements as shown on the record copy are in agreement. Approval is a one-step process.* A full, multidiscipline check is not needed for reviewing certified copies.

Most of the lead designer's duties have already been described above. In summary, he or she

- Chooses the vendor data sponsor
- Selects the reviewers
- Is responsible for transferring markings to the duplicate copy
- Is responsible for keeping the record bluelines
- Is responsible for making sure the certified copies agree with the record copies

SPONSOR

The sponsor is the primary point of contact on technical matters concerning a piece of equipment. The sponsor also has the obligation to move the documents through the system in a timely fashion. Since the sponsor's review is first, he or she can single out items for the attention of different design disciplines. Then they need not waste time uncovering what is pertinent to their review. In passing the approval documents along, the sponsor will be on hand to discuss important features and answer questions.

Since the sponsor is the expert on the item being reviewed and understands how the item fits into a larger whole, the sponsor is in an excellent position to settle conflicts that may arise among design groups. The sponsor also has a personal stake in ensuring that the equipment will perform properly, since it will be part of a plant area under the sponsor's responsibility.

Most of the sponsor's duties are described above under "Responsibility." One additional duty falling specifically on the sponsor is that of answering questions that arise during review. A review document cannot be approved if unanswered questions are among the comments. Approval of a document containing unanswered questions violates rules of logic. Either the document must be returned "not approved," or the vendor must be contacted to resolve the question. Another possible solution is to rephrase questions as statements.

On expensive pieces of equipment with long deliveries or complex "packaged units," the sponsor should visit the vendor when the order is placed to assist the vendor in the initiation of engineering and design (see above).

REQUEST FOR DOCUMENTS

Two types of documents are required: design documents and installation and maintenance documents. For Ajax the most important documents are the design documents. Almost all the discussion up to here applies to design documents.

Both kinds of documents should be referenced in the body of the specification under a section entitled *Drawings and Documents.* Figure B-3 gives an example of a request for documents. Note that non-design information is requested separately. This is to help vendors distinguish between immediate design needs and eventual project needs.

The specific approval requirements are determined by the author of the specification. The author begins with Fig. B-4 as a guide. Then, depending on the nature of the application (flammability, toxicity, corrosivity, etc.), the author determines whether more or less information is required. Consultations with other employees who have dealt with similar equipment are recommended. In no case is a copy of Fig. B-4 to be attached to the specification in the hope that the vendor will read it and determine the appropriate approval data. Approval requirements must be determined prior to inquiry.

DOCUMENT REVIEW

A major objective of document review is to guide the vendor in her or his design efforts. The vendor's initial submittal will be the result of having read our specification. We alter this first submittal to fit our particular needs. Then (after some haggling over price changes) the vendor incorporates our requirements in his or her design and issues certified drawings that are in accordance with our requests. Only in the rarest of circumstances should an equipment item (or package) require more than one approval. If so, it will be because screening for completeness has broken down.

A uniform marking procedure should be used so that each reviewer

SPECIFICATION

Customer: Great Sands Inc.   Proj.: CV - 930
Location: Pomona, CA   Page 19 of 28

Description: Hammer Mill   Tag Nos.:   11900, etc

11.0   Shop Painting

Shop painting and/or surface preparation shall be in accordance with specification S-88.

12.0   Shipping

All openings should be securely closed to prevent entry of moisture and foreign matter in transit.

Unit shall be shipped on its side, assembled to the greatest extent practicable. Unit shall be covered by a tarp.

The gearbox shall be drained of lubricant (from testing) prior to shipment.

13.0   Drawings & Documents

As stated in our inquiry cover letter, we require drawings and documents for approval. Once approved, these same drawings and documents shall be certified and resubmitted. The number of copies for each submittal are:

approval: three bluelines or bond copies
certified: seven bluelines or bond copies

Please note: maintenance manuals and installation instructions are not approval documents. They should not be sent at the time approval documents are sent. They should be included with the certified documents.

For the equipment, subject of this order, we require the following approval drawings:

o   assembly drawings
o   equipment cross-sectional drawings
o   dimensioned outline drawings
o   supports and anchor-bolt arrangement drawings
o   static/dynamic loading diagram
o   views showing maintenance access and clearances
o   electric motor data sheet
o   gearbox drawings

Form   141

Figure B-3 Example of a request for vendor data.

Figure B-4 Examples of documents required from vendors (process and mechanical equipment).

Document	Agitators	Bins, Hoppers, Etc.	Boilers and Water Heaters (1)	Bucket Elevators	Centrifuges	Collectors (particulate, dry)	Columns	Compressors	Conveyors (belt, screw, etc.)	Cooling Towers	Crushers, grinders, etc.	Crystallizers	Cyclone Separators	Dryers	Evaporators	Exchangers, heat	Fans & Blowers	Feeders (for solids)	Filters (with moving parts)	Fixed Equipment (ex. bolters)	Hoists, cranes & elevators	Mobile Equipment	Pneumatic Conveyors	Pumps (liquid)	Pumps (vacuum)	Reactors	Refrigeration Units	Rotary Valves (& such)	Screens & Size Separation	Scrubbers (wet)	Tanks (& atm. vessels)	Vessels (pressure) (1)	Weigh Scales
1. Arrangement drawings, equipment (sections & plans)	X	X	X	X	X	X	X	X	X	X	X	X	X	X	X	X	X	X	X	X	X	X	X	X	X	X	X	X	X	X	X	X	X
2. Arrangement drawings, piping (sections & plans)			X				X			X														X			X				X	X	
3. Assembly drawings	X	X	X	X	X	X	X	X	X	X	X	X	X	X	X	X	X	X	X	X	X	X	X	X	X	X	X	X	X	X			X
4. "Buy-outs" (data and drawings)		X		X	X	X	X	X	X	X	X	X	X	X	X	X	X	X	X	X	X	X	X	X	X	X	X	X	X	X			
5. Center of gravity location drawing	X	X	X	X	X		X	X	X	X	X	X	X	X	X	X	X	X	X	X	X	X				X	X		X	X			
6. Clearances required for maintenance	X	X	X	X	X	X	X	X	X	X	X	X	X	X	X	X	X	X	X	X	X	X	X	X	X	X	X	X	X	X	X	X	
7. Equipment cross-sectional views	X	X	X		X	X	X	X	X		X	X	X	X	X	X	X	X	X	X	X	X	X	X	X	X	X	X	X	X	X	X	
8. Fabrication drawings							X																							X	X	X	
9. Gearbox drawings and data	X	X		X	X		X	X	X		X	X		X	X	X	X	X	X		X	X		X		X	X		X	X			
10. Interior details	X			X	X	X	X	X	X	X	X	X	X	X	X	X	X	X	X	X	X	X	X	X	X	X	X	X	X	X	X	X	
11. Loading diagram (static & dynamic loads)	X	X	X	X	X	X	X	X	X	X	X	X	X	X	X	X	X	X	X	X	X	X	X	X	X	X	X	X	X	X			
12. Nozzle and connection schedules		X	X	X	X		X	X	X	X	X	X	X	X	X	X		X	X	X	X	X		X	X	X	X	X	X	X	X	X	
13. Outline drawings, showing dimensions	X	X	X	X	X	X	X	X	X	X	X	X	X	X	X	X	X	X	X	X	X	X	X	X	X	X	X	X	X	X	X	X	X
14. Parts drawings		X		X	X	X	X	X	X		X	X	X	X	X	X							X	X	X	X	X	X	X	X			
15. Parts list, with material call-outs	X	X	X	X	X	X	X	X	X		X	X	X	X	X	X	X	X	X	X	X	X	X	X	X	X	X	X	X	X	X	X	
16. Performance data	X	X	X	X	X	X	X	X	X	X	X	X	X	X	X	X	X	X	X	X		X	X	X	X	X	X	X	X	X			
17. Piping & Instrumentation Diagrams (P&IDs)	X																							X		X	X			X			
18. Piping specifications		X				X	X	X	X		X	X	X	X	X		X	X	X		X		X	X	X	X	X			X			
19. Seal details (including section views of seals)	X				X	X	X	X	X		X	X	X	X	X	X					X		X	X	X	X	X		X	X			
20. Support & anchor bolt location drawings	**X**	X	X	X	X	X	X	X	X	X	X	X	X	X	X	X	X	X	X	X	X	X	X	X	X	X	X	X	X	X			X
21. Tube sheet details															X	X																	
22.																																	
23.																																	
24. Bill of materials, electrical		X	X	X	X		X	X	X	X	X	X	X	X	X	X		X	X	X			X	X	X	X	X		X	X			X
25. Bill of materials, instruments		X	X	X	X		X	X	X	X	X	X	X	X	X	X		X	X	X		X	X	X	X	X	X		X	X			X
26. Electrical control schematics		X	X	X	X		X	X	X	X	X	X	X	X	X	X		X	X	X			X	X	X	X	X		X	X			X
27. Electrical elementary diagrams		X	X	X	X		X	X	X	X	X	X	X	X	X	X		X	X	X			X	X	X	X	X		X	X			X
28. Electrical tie-in locations		X	X	X	X		X	X	X	X	X	X	X	X	X	X		X	X	X			X	X	X	X	X		X	X			X
29. Hydraulic system drawings	X	X		X			X	X			X	X		X	X								X	X	X			X					
30. Logic diagrams		X		X	X		X	X	X		X			X	X								X	X	X	X	X		X				
31. Motor data	X	X	X	X	X		X	X	X	X	X	X	X	X	X	X	X	X	X	X		X	X	X	X	X	X	X	X	X			X
32. Motor drawings	X	X		X	X		X	X	X	X	X	X	X	X	X	X	X	X	X	X		X	X	X	X	X	X	X	X	X			
33. Physical wiring diagrams		X	X	X	X		X	X	X	X	X	X	X	X	X	X		X	X	X			X	X	X	X	X		X	X			X

Notes: 1. When necessary, ASME code calculations should also be requested.

understands previous markings and so that final transfer of markings to the return copy can be done accurately and efficiently. The color code for marking the blueline is as follows:

- Red: Correction
- Yellow or green: No change; okay
- Blue ⎫
- Silver ⎬ Cover up, simulating erasure
- Paper overlay ⎭

Comments for transmittal to the vendor are to be marked in red; comments for internal use are to be marked in ordinary pencil or blue. When markings are transferred to the return copy, the same color scheme is used. The return copy should also call attention to changes by encircling them with clouds when possible. Purchasing is to attach a copy of our color code to the return copy.

SUMMARY OF DUTIES

The key duties of vendor drawing review are as follows:

- *Sponsor:* Responsible for eventual operation of equipment. Must make sure that disciplines understand equipment and that their reviews are pertinent. Must resolve questions. Will work with purchasing on commercial adjustments.
- *Purchasing:* Expediter will pursue, receive, and transmit drawings. Purchaser will execute commercial adjustments.
- *Document control:* Logs in and numbers documents. Checks on progress.
- *Lead designer:* Assigns sponsor and reviewers. Reviews markings. Makes record copy. Reviews certified copy. Maintains vendor print file.

EXHIBIT C: APPROVAL AND CERTIFICATION INFORMATION FOR VENDORS

(This exhibit should be attached to all inquiries.)

General

Ajax's performance depends very heavily upon the ability of its vendors to supply information in the early stages of a project. Your equipment has a much better chance of being applied properly when complete approval information is made available at an early date.

Definitions

Approval means that you are released to commence fabrication. Prior to approval you may undertake procurement activities, but actual fabrication is not to commence until approval is obtained. A limited approval designated *Approved as Noted* means that fabrication may commence as long as you, the vendor, are in agreement with the modifications noted by Ajax. If you agree with the modifications but think a price change is warranted, please call the Ajax purchasing agent immediately. If several vendor drawings are involved and some are returned approved while others are not approved, the pieces shown on the "approved" drawings may be started through fabrication.

Certification is the step that follows approval. Basically it is an assurance by you, the vendor, that the dimensional information will not change and, in fact, that the dimensions of the delivered equipment will correspond to those shown on the drawings (within a reasonable tolerance). Certification also applies to nondimensional information such as handedness (right or left), number of connections, and the inclusion of appurtenances. Once approvals have been obtained, certification should follow easily and naturally. It is to both Ajax's advantage and your advantage to obtain certification as early as possible.

Procedure

Upon notification of a successful bid, vendors should refer to their own bid documents to remind themselves what they have promised to deliver. They should also refer to the Ajax inquiry documents. If any questions arise, they should contact the author of the specification, whose name will be listed on the specification. Ajax requirements are to be found in this specification under *Drawings and Documents.*

Basically, vendors will note that they are to provide some drawings and data to Ajax by a certain date. Once the drawings and data are ready for a complete submittal, they should be sent by one-day delivery in care of the Ajax drawing expediter. Partial submittals are acceptable only by prearrangement during bid negotiation. Any other partial submittal will be rejected.

Prior to sending out an approval package, vendors should assure themselves that every page is marked as stated in "Document Identification" below. Failure to mark pages properly will also result in rejection. When Ajax has obtained the approval documents, they will be examined for conformance and suitability. It is the Ajax intention to help vendors tie down their designs as early as possible. It is also our intention to make sure vendor-supplied items perform to the best of their ability. For these reasons the Ajax review is mutually beneficial.

For the most part, notations on approval documents will be minor. Each document will be stamped as in Fig. B-5.

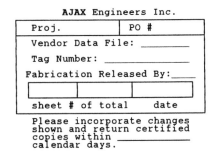

AJAX Engineers Inc.

Proj.	PO #

Vendor Data File: _____

Tag Number: _____

Fabrication Released By:____

sheet # of total		date

Please incorporate changes
shown and return certified
copies within _____
calendar days.

Figure B-5 Stamp 21 (for return copy to vendor).

This will constitute our approval to proceed with fabrication as long as the vendors are in accord with the comments and markings. The following step for vendors is to incorporate whatever comments there may be. If some question arises as to cost or schedule, vendors are to contact the Ajax purchasing agent immediately. Once the vendors are satisfied, they are to submit a certified set of drawings to Ajax. These drawings are to be stamped with a mark of certification, and somewhere near this mark a responsible party places his or her initials and the date. Certified copies are then sent to Ajax via first-class mail. Partial submittals of certified drawings are permitted; however, complete submittals are recommended.

Submittal of a drawing with a certification stamp prior to its approval or the existence of a certification stamp on an approval drawing will result in rejection. If a drawing is incomplete or unreadable or does not meet requirements of the specification, it will be returned "not approved."

If one or two drawings of a submittal are not approved, they will be returned to vendors along with approved drawings. Complete approval will not occur until all drawings and requested documents have been approved.

Once certification has occurred and Ajax has had a reasonable time to examine the certified copy, the vendor's obligation for this part of the work is complete.

Other documentation is required, but it does not need approval and is due at a later date (see "Additional Requirements," page ____ of this specification).

The Ajax review and approval of vendor drawings do not relieve vendors of their responsibility for the accuracy of dimensions and the consequent fit of parts and materials.

Document Identification

Each page submitted for approval or as a certified copy must show Ajax identifying numbers in a convenient location. Vendors' failure to provide these numbers will cause an automatic nonapproval. The numbers required are

- Equipment number
- Ajax project number
- Ajax purchase order number

A good place for this information is above the drawing title block. For convenience we ask that vendors also provide a space measuring about 3 × 5 in above the identity numbers. This space will be used for approval stamps (see Fig. B-6).

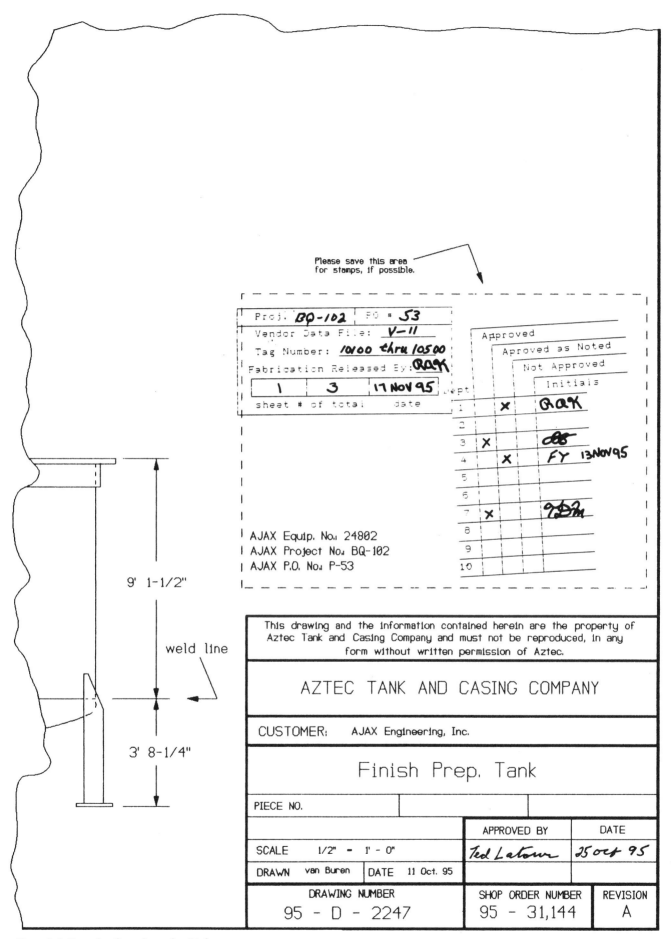

Please save this area
for stamps, if possible.

Proj. *BQ-102*	PO # *53*
Vendor Data File: *V-11*	
Tag Number: *10100 thru 10500*	
Fabrication Released By: *RQK*	

| 1 | 3 | 17 NOV 95 | ...ept |
| sheet # | of total | date | |

Approved
Aproved as Noted
Not Approved
Initials

1	X	*RQK*
2		
3	X	*d85*
4	X	*FY 13NOV95*
5		
6		
7	X	*9D2m*
8		
9		
10		

AJAX Equip. No. 24802
AJAX Project No. BQ-102
AJAX P.O. No. P-53

9' 1-1/2"

weld line

3' 8-1/4"

This drawing and the information contained herein are the property of Aztec Tank and Casing Company and must not be reproduced, in any form without written permission of Aztec.

AZTEC TANK AND CASING COMPANY

CUSTOMER: AJAX Engineering, Inc.

Finish Prep. Tank

PIECE NO.

	APPROVED BY	DATE
SCALE 1/2" - 1' - 0"	*Ted Latour*	*25 Oct 95*
DRAWN van Buren	DATE 11 Oct. 95	

| DRAWING NUMBER | SHOP ORDER NUMBER | REVISION |
| 95 - D - 2247 | 95 - 31,144 | A |

Figure B-6 Sample of vendor submittal.

— Appendix C —
Forms Used during Project Work

This appendix contains samples of forms used to guide the flow of and keep tabs on project documents. As much as anything, this is an appendix of Chap. 14, *Paper.* A list of forms is given in Table C-1.

For the most part, these forms provide a logical method for filing. There is a more subtle point to them, too. This lies in helping to establish procedures. In doing so, they save time and promote teamwork.

These forms are presented with portions done in handwriting. This is to emphasize that the recommended method for tracking documents is a mix of hand and machine. Thus the reader can appreciate from these samples the part to be done by hand and the part to be done by machine. A good example is the project letter log (Form 126). Copies of the blank form are retained on a computer floppy disk. When a project is initiated, the project secretary customizes the blank to include specifics pertinent to project CV-322, including file numbers yet to be assigned. To start, five pages can be prepared, with numbers from 1 through 95. These pages would be placed in a three-ring binder on the secretary's desk (see Chap. 14). The logging in would take place as the project progresses. File numbers are assigned without question, without thought.

The hand entries shown are simple, quick, and permanent when done in ink. Entry of such information into an electronic data base does not make sense. On the other hand, a few forms such as the equipment/commodities list and the vendor data log should be updated regularly and issued regularly. Here electronic data processing can be used advantageously.

Both the copy room and the project task area keep drawing logs. The one in the copy room (drawing log C) is used to archive tracings. The one in the project area (drawing log P) is used to assign revision numbers. This assumes that the tracings (vellums) are archived in the copy room and that CADD is used to make the drawings. When CADD is *not* used, the second log can be eliminated, since the tracing itself contains the log. With CADD, tracings from previous issues can lurk around unless one is careful. Drawing log P is a safeguard against these old tracings.

The major function of a log is to assign document numbers in an orderly fashion. A secondary function, almost as important, is that the log becomes the index of the documents.

The forms presented here are not meant to be used for scheduling or checking progress, and in general, they are not adaptable for that use. A description to help with the use of the form is included in some cases. The reader is encouraged to use these forms.*

---

*Therefore, permission is granted for their use. Furthermore, for use on projects, the usual requirements for acknowledgment are waived. For presentation in a publication, acknowledgment is required, however.

TABLE C-1 List of Forms for Document Handling

Prefix for file number	Form number	Title
Two alpha characters	121	Project Log
S-	122	Specifications Log
	123	Equipment/Commodities List
	124	Requisition
	125	Conversation Confirmer Log
	126	Project Letter Log
	127	Project Memo Log
	128	Requisition Log
Q-	129	Inquiry Log
P-	130	Purchase Order Log
D- and E-*	131	Drawing Log P
V-	132	Vendor Data Log
W-	133	Owner Drawing Log
	134	Client Correspondence Log
	135	Transmittal Letter Log
	136	Copy Room Work Order
	137	Vendor Drawing Route Slip
	138	Vellum Possession Log
D- and E-*	139	Drawing Log C
	140	Specification Cover Sheet
	141	Specification Page (see Fig. B-3)
	142	Bid Analysis Details (see Fig. 12-1)

*These refer to the most common drawing sizes. Prefixes A-, B-, and C- are also possible.

EXPLANATIONS OF SOME FORMS

Form 123

This form is not only an equipment list, but also serves as a file reference list. The abbreviations are as follows:

> spec. # = specification file number
> inqy. # = inquiry file number
> PO # = purchase order number
> VP # = vendor print file number
> diag. # = principal diagram depicting the item
> OD # = owner drawing file number

The example shown is for the process equipment, so it is labeled *Process Group.* If it had been for ventilating equipment, it would have been labeled *HVAC Group*; for electrical equipment, *Electrical Group*; and so on.

The column labeled *pr* gives a priority code: H, M, or L for high, medium, or low. When it is blank, the meaning is either low or undecided. A zero means the item has traversed the procurement process and cannot be further expedited. As the job progresses, the early, high-priority items will decline in priority (from an *engineering* or design standpoint) and other items will move up the scale, until even the lowliest hose (a commodity item) will eventually have its brief period in the sun, when it receives intense but short scrutiny.

The quantity column is not used for equipment, as even identical equipment pieces have different item numbers for reasons of (motor) control identification (see Chap. 11, *P&IDs*). The quantity column is used for commodities.

Form 124

A sure sign of the completion of preliminary *engineering* is when this form attains currency. Informal, noncontractual contacts between engineer and vendor occur continually during the course of any job, and even before most jobs materialize. It is a beneficial fact of commercial necessity for both parties. The requisition ends this, however.

The use of Form 124 signals the beginning of formalities. It must be filled out by the originator and hand-carried through approval and onward the purchasing department. The file number is obtained from the appropriate log. The yes or no concerning revisions can be discerned from the log.

Form 132

The vendor data log should be maintained in an electronic data base. Either the purchasing secretary or the project secretary can be designated as responsible for making entries. Each individual (presumably sponsors) wishing to make changes should do so via markings on a copy of the log sheet. The marked sheets can then be submitted to the secretary. Once vendor drawings start to arrive, the log should be reissued weekly.

The column headed *days* contains two entries for each file number. The first entry is the days from purchase order (PO) issue until an acceptable submittal is received. The second entry is the days required by the review process.

Note that the drawing numbers used by the fabricator or vendor are *not* listed. They are not needed. If a question should arise as to the vendor's identification number, the appropriate manila envelope is opened and the drawings themselves are consulted.

Also note that a satisfactory review ensues regardless of whether the drawings were marked with revisions. Thus the log makes no comment along this line. To discover whether revisions were required, the drawings themselves should be consulted.

Form 133

In the example shown, 40 drawings have been stored quickly and are easy to retrieve. Owner drawings are grouped into logical units and stored in manila envelopes in the same way as vendor drawings (see Chap. 14, *Paper*). Filing the drawings in this way greatly simplifies their storage and retrieval.

When thousands of owner drawings are archived, the same method is recommended, but it may become necessary to set up an electronic data base to identify individual owner drawings. For the typical project of $5 to $20 million, such a measure is not necessary.

Form 136

The copy room work order is designed so that copy room personnel can execute an order with little, if any, outside help. Because the tracings are kept in the copy room, handling is simplified.

Form 136 is used for the following:

- Obtaining a new, numbered blank vellum
- Obtaining a tracing from the file
- Obtaining copies of drawings on bond, blueline, or sepia (reproducible) format (column C of form 136 is used)
- Issuing drawings and specifications (When used this way, the form also serves as a transmittal letter for the issue. The example on page 313 shows the form used in this manner.)

When copies or vellums are obtained, the order can be delivered, or the requestor can pick it up. Formal issues are handled by delivery only.

Other types of copying, such as of magazine articles, calculations, sketches, memos, and the like, is done outside the copy room on local copy machines.

The example on Form 136 is for a formal issue of a specification and a drawing. A vendor (Mesa Fiberglass) is included in the distribution, along with the project team, client, and purchaser. Note 1 instructs the requestor to include a requisition with the work order. This note also instructs the copy room to deliver Mesa Fiberglass's copies to the purchaser.

Form 137

This form accompanies the vendor drawing package as it is hand-carried through the approval route (see Chap. 14, *Paper*). When each reviewer finishes, he or she notes the return date on the form and either hand-carries the drawing package back to the sponsor or calls the sponsor to advise that the package is being sent to the next reviewer. The first course is used when the reviewer feels the sponsor should be notified of some particular point. When the last reviewer has finished, he or she returns the package to the sponsor.

The sponsor reviews the package and initials the fabrication release stamp (stamp 23, Fig. 14-6). The package is then given to the lead designer who also examines the package and decides which draftsman or junior designer will be responsible for transferring the markings on the vendor drawings onto a clean copy for return to the vendor. The vendor copy will carry only one stamp per sheet: stamp 21, Fig. 14-6. A senior designer will check this duplicate against the original. The sponsor's initials will be marked on each sheet in the appropriate space of stamp 21. The new duplicate should be hand-carried to purchasing along with Form 137 for return to the vendor. The marked-up original should be archived with vendor drawings.

Form 138

Whenever tracings are returned to the copy room, the *first* task of the copy clerk is to log them in and note whether the tracing has changed revision status. If so, the drawing file should be checked to make sure the preceding revision has been removed from the file (with non-CADD drawings this should not be a problem). If the previous revision is still in the file, it must be removed, marked as void, and returned to the person who sent in the current revision. This person must nullify the void copy.*

---

*The correct procedure is to request the CADD tracing while readying a revision; then, when the new version is ready, destroy the old one. Furthermore, make only one vellum copy.

When a new (blank) vellum is requested, the word *new* should be written in the revision column.

On large projects, where more than 100 vellums may be checked out at once, preprinted 3 × 5 in cards should be used to note possession. These are kept in numerical order in a card file. Obviously with these chits in numerical order, their retrieval, upon return of a tracing, would be easier. For most projects the simple log is easy enough to use, however.

Form 139

The only function of this log is to assign numbers and to record who requested the action. When a request for a new vellum is received (Form 136), drawing log C (this form) is consulted for the next available number (or block of numbers, if requested).

If CADD is not being used, the numbers assigned in the log are copied neatly onto the vellums, in the appropriate blocks. The vellums are then rolled up and sent to the requestor. If CADD is being used, the numbers assigned in the log are copied neatly onto the request form, or an attached sheet, and the form is returned to the requestor.

The requestor must check the newly assigned numbers against drawing log P (Form 131). Then drawing log P must be updated.

Two "B" numbers are shown in the sample form. These designate sheets 11 × 17 in in size. The smaller sheets cannot be placed in the same physical location as the larger sheets, so they must be filed separately. A copy room clerk must know this when searching for a vellum.

Form 140

As page 1 for all specifications, the two main purposes served by this form are to document the history of the specification and to provide a visible format for approval signatures.

On the example given, the client is shown to have signed only one time, to approve the concept. This is usually the case as the client is included in copies of all revisions, which will mostly be minor. Some clients may demand to sign all revisions.

In the example given, all the revision blocks have been used. A subsequent issue can either add another Form 140 as page 2 or replace page 1 and record this fact under "Remarks."

PROJECT LOG

	Entry Date	Project #	Company	Location	State	Area	Scope	Job Description
1	20 Nov 94	CV – 022	Mix Chem (1)	Paducah	KY	—	E,P	Polymer blend tank T18; installation
2	20 Nov 94	CV – 023	Maxiroyal	Dayton	OH	Compound.	E,P	New compounding line (#11)
3	21 Nov 94	CV – 024	Octane, Inc.	Baytown	NJ	G-22	E	Evaluate heat XG-R5
4	21 Nov 94	CV – 025	Old Soldier	Elko	NV	—	E	60 T/D Barite Mill (+/- 30% Estim.)
5		CV – 026						
6		CV – 027						
7		CV – 028						
8		CV – 029						
9		CV – 030						
10		CV – 031						
11		CV – 032						
12		CV –						
13		CV –						
14		CV –						
15		CV –						
16		CV –						
17		CV –						
18		CV –						
19		CV –						

Notes: 1. This was part of C4 – 885. Now a separate project.
2.
3.

Form 121

SPECIFICATIONS LOG

Customer: Greg's Modern Calendars
Location: Donelson, TN

Proj.: CV 083

	File No.	Description	Date	By	Revision Number					
1	S-1	Site surveying	2 Sept 1995	SM	A 2Sep	B 8Sep	0 16Sep	1 2Fe	2 Apr	
2	S-2	Soil testing	3 Sept 1995	SM	A 3Sep	0 7Sep				
3	S-3	Electric Motors	15 Sept 1995	AL	A 15Sep	B 20Sep	0 2Feb			
4	S-4	Inst. (Included w/ equip)	15 Sept 1995	AL	A 15Sep	0 2Feb½	1 11Mar			
5	S-5	Overhead crane	21 Sept 1995	GAK	A 21Sep	B 29Sep	C 11Oct	0 1Feb		
6	S-6	Tanks (field fabricated)	28 Sept 1995	GAK	A 28Sep	B 15Oct	0 2Feb			
7	S-7	Agitators	28 Sept	RGW	A 28Sep 2Feb½	0				
8	S-8	Pumps (Screw Type)	29 Sept 1995	RGW	A 28Sep 15Feb	0				
9	S-9									
10	S-10									
11	S-11									
12	S-12									
13	S-13									
14	S-14									
15	S-15									
16		(continued from above)								
17										
18										
19										

Notes:
1.
2.
3.

Form 122

Forms Used during Project Work   299

Customer: Old Soldier   Proj: CU - 850
Location: Elko, NV   Date: 16-SEP-94

Process Group

	area	tag number	pr	quan tity	name	spec.# inqy.#	PO # VP #	diag # OD #	motor HP	description
1	18	20105	O		Slurry Tank	S- 31 Q- 27	P- 30 V- 14	K- 24		2000 gal
2	18	20106	M		Slurry Agitator	S- 29 Q- 25	P- 28 V- 13	K- 24	5	
3	18	20107	O		Slurry Pump #1	S- 18 Q- 16	P- 18 V- 6	K- 24	7.5	120 gpm; 85' TDH
4	18	20108	O		Slurry Pump #2 (spare)	" "	" "	K- 24	7.5	idem
5	18	20200	O		Overflow Filter Press (existing)	NA	NA	K- 24 W- 2		Relocate from B'tle Mount. 19 plates & frames; 3x3
6	18	20201	L		Dump Chute	S- 88 Q- 73	P- 52	K- 24		custom-made, see J- 5
7	18	20202	O		Shovel	NA	NA	K- 24		By plant
8										
9										
10										
11										
12										
13										
14										
15										
16										

Notes: 1.   page 4 of 7
         2.
         3.
                                                                              Form 123

Circle One: (I) Inquiry   Revision? Y Yes
           P Purchase   (N) No

```
┌────────────────────────────────────────────────────────────────────────────┐
│                              REQUISITION                                     │
│  Customer: King's Mills, Inc.                    Proj.: CV 322               │
│  Location: Camden, S.C.                          File No.: Q-19             │
├────────────────────────────────────────────────┬───────────────────────────┤
│  Vendor #                                        │ Date Required: 29 oct 94  │
│  V'dr. Tele.# (   ) -                            │ (M) Mail                  │
│                                                  │  S  Ship                  │
│  Vendor:  (bid list attached)                    │                           │
│  Address:                                        │ Attn: G. James            │
│  City:                    State:                 │      (Purchaser)          │
│  Attn:                    Zip:                   │                           │
├───────┬──────┬───────────────────────────┬──────────┬────────────┬──────────┤
│ Item  │ Qty. │       Description          │ Per Item │   Total    │          │
├───────┼──────┼───────────────────────────┼──────────┼────────────┼──────────┤
│  #1   │  12  │ 8' diam. x 5' high, 20ga., │          │            │          │
│       │      │ 304 SS creel tubs per      │          │            │          │
│       │      │ attached specification S-29│          │            │          │
│       │      │ Rev C and dwg. D-73        │          │            │          │
│       │      │                            │          │            │          │
│       │      │ Note: bidding instructions │          │            │          │
│       │      │       attached.            │          │            │          │
│       │      │                            │          │            │          │
├───────┴──────┴───────────────┬────────────┴──────────┴────────────┴──────────┤
│ Copies: Project File          │ Originator: E. a.      Date: 3 oct 94         │
│         Purchasing            │                                               │
│         Field                 │ Authorized by: Franks   Date: 4 oct 94        │
│         Originator            │                                               │
│         Other                 │     Customer: BJ        Date: 7 oct 94        │
│                               │                                               │
└───────────────────────────────┴───────────────────────────────────────────────┘
```

Form   124

CONVERSATION CONFIRMER LOG

Customer:_____   Proj.:_____
Location:_____

	File No.	Subject	By	Date	Between &
1	1					
2	2					
3	3					
4	4					
5	5					
6	6					
7	7					
8	8					
9	9					
10	10					
11	11					
12	12					
13	13					
14	14					
15	15					
16	16					
17	17					
18	18					
19	19					

Notes: 1.
         2.
         3.

Form   125

PROJECT LETTER LOG

Customer: <u>King's Mills Corp.</u>   Proj.: <u>CV 322</u>
Location: <u>Camden, S.C.</u>

	File No.	Subject	Date	From	To
1	20	Monthly report for Sept.	8 oct 94	Arnold	Lu
2	21	Overtime Approval Req'm't.	11 oct 94	Arnold	Lu
3	22	Bid List of Mechanical Contractors	16 oct 94	Arnold	Lu
4	23				
5	24				
6	25				
7	26				
8	27				
9	28				
10	29				
11	30				
12	31				
13	32				
14	33				
15	34				
16	35				
17	36				
18	37				
19	38				

Notes: 1.
           2.
           3.

Form   126

PROJECT MEMO LOG

Customer: <u>King's Mills Corp.</u>   Proj.: <u>CV 322</u>
Location: <u>Camden, S.C.</u>

	File No.	Subject	Date	From	To	
1	39	Tow line guides	11 oct 94	Arnold	Lee	
2	40	Concrete surface hardening requirement	14 oct 94	Arnold	Lee	
3	41	Crimper elevation	15 oct 94	Jones	Lee	
4	42	MCC location	15 oct 94	Pinson	Lee	
5	43	Schedule for HMMP	17 oct 94	Arnold	Thomas	(1)
6	44					
7	45					
8	46					
9	47					
10	48					
11	49					
12	50					
13	51					
14	52					
15	53					
16	54					
17	55					
18	56					
19	57					

Notes: 1. Health department
         2.
         3.

Form   127

REQUISITION LOG

Customer:_____   Proj.:_____
Location:_____

	File No.	Purpose	Date	By	Dept.
1	20				
2	21				
3	22				
4	23				
5	24				
6	25				
7	26				
8	27				
9	28				
10	29				
11	30				
12	31				
13	32				
14	33				
15	34				
16	35				

Notes: 1.
         2.
         3.

Dept. Codes: 1 = process / mechanical   6 = HVAC
               2 = electrical   7 = structural
               3 = instruments   8 = civil
               4 = piping   9 = plumbing
               5 = architectural   10 = other

Form   128

INQUIRY LOG

Customer: Marco Corporation
Location: Lima, Peru

Proj.: AL 652

	File No.	Description	Date	By	Code	Revision Number							
1	Q – 46												
2	Q – 47												
3	Q – 48												
4	Q – 49												
5	Q – 50												
6	Q – 51												
7	Q – 52												
8	Q – 53												
9	Q – 54												
10	Q – 55												
11	Q – 56												
12	Q – 57												
13	Q – 58												
14	Q – 59												
15	Q – 60												
16	(continued from above)												
17													
18													
19													

Notes: 1.
        2.
        3.

Code: E = equipment, S = subcontract, C = commodity

Form 129

PURCHASE LOG

Customer: United Fibers Inc.
Location: Columbia, SC

Proj.: CT - 880

	File No.	Description	Date	By	Code	Vendor	Revisions
1	P - 16						
2	P - 17						
3	P - 18						
4	P - 19						
5	P - 20						
6	P - 21						
7	P - 22						
8	P - 23						
9	P - 24						
10	P - 25						
11	P - 26						
12	P - 27						
13	P - 28						
14	P - 29						
15	P - 30						
16	(continued from above)						
17							
18							
19							

Notes: 1.
        2.
        3.

Code: E = equipment, S = subcontract, C = commodity

Form 130

DRAWING LOG P
D Size

Proj.: **AC 844**

(project file)
Customer: Andrews Hydrocarbons
Location: Altoona, PA

File No.	Title	Date	By	Dept.	Revision Number								
1	D – 79												
2	D – 80												
3	D – 81												
4	D – 82												
5	D – 83												
6	D – 84												
7	D – 85												
8	D – 86												
9	D – 87												
10	D – 88												
11	D – 89												
12	D – 90												
13	D – 91												
14	D – 92												
15	D – 93												
16	(continued from above)												
17													
18													
19													

Notes:
1.
2.
3.

Customer: Wyoming Recyclers Inc.
Location: Green River, WY

Proj.: CV- 447
Today's Date: 24-Apr-93

	file number	description (tag #)	PO #	pp.	spon-sor	submittals rec'd	ret'd	CF	status	days PO revu	remarks
1	V - 25	Kellogg Boiler 15700 etc.	P-381	17	GJF	08-Mar-93	11-Apr-93		Ret(S)	32 34	
2	V - 26	Vacuum Pump 14200	P-371	8 14	CHF	26-Feb-93 08-Mar-93	26-Feb-93 02-Apr-93		Ret(U) Ret(S)	56 25	no tag numbers, incomplete
3	V - 27	Cooling Tower 13600	P-383	11	SM	08-Mar-93 02-Apr-93	23-Mar-93 NA	X	Ret(S) CF	32 15	
4	V - 28	Exchangers 18303 18304 etc.	P-393	9	CHF	12-Mar-93	24-Apr-93		Ret(S)	19 43	
5	V - 29	Dust Collector Platform	P-389	4	RC	12-Mar-93	28-Mar-93		Ret(S)	24 16	
6	V - 30	Condensate Pumps 15701 15702	P-388	4	GJF	23-Mar-93				36	
7	V - 31	Cooling Water Pumps 13601 13602	P-385	3	SM	24-Mar-93				44	
8	V - 32										
9	V - 33										
10	V - 34										
11	V - 35										
12	V - 36										
13		(continued)									
14											

Notes: 1.
2.
3.

Form   132

OWNER DRAWING LOG

Customer: <u>Griffin Petroleum Corp.</u>   Proj.: <u>CV - 88</u>
Location: <u>Wilmington, CA</u>

	File No.	Subject	Plant Area	Pages	Date Rec'd.
1	W - 203	Pipe rack, south of reformer	12 C	8	12Jun92
2	W - 204	Equipment locations and foundation plans	12 C	3	12Jun92
3	W - 205	Piping elevations and sections at reformer	12 C	10	12Jun92
4	W - 206	Piping plans at reformer (part 1: ground to 60 feet)	12 C	7	12Jun92
5	W - 207	Piping plans at reformer (part 2: 60 feet and higher)	12 C	5	12Jun92
6	W - 208	Reformer drawings	12 C	6	12Jun92
7	W - 209	New Site Survey from tank farm to river	36 E 36 H others	1	9Jul93
8					
9					
10					
11					

Notes: 1.
         2.
         3.

Form   133

CLIENT LETTER LOG

Customer: <u>King's Mills, Inc.</u>   Proj.: <u>CV 322</u>
Location: <u>Camden, SC</u>

	File No.	Subject	Date	From	To
1	20	Draw Machine #3 Comments	8 Aug 94	Lee	Arnold
2	21	Raw Well Water Analysis	15 Aug 94	Lee	Arnold
3	22	Safety Procedures for Site Visitors	19 Aug 94	Lee	Arnold
4	23				
5	24				
6	25				
7	26				
8	27				
9	28				
10	29				
11	30				
12	31				
13	32				
14	33				
15	33				
16	33				
17	33				
18	34				
19	35				

Notes: 1.
              2.
              3.

Form   134

TRANSMITTAL LETTER LOG

Customer: <u>King's Mills, Inc.</u>　　　　Proj.: <u>CV 322</u>
Location: <u>Camden, SC</u>

	File No.	Attachments	Date	From	To
1	20	Creel Layout Study	12 Nov 94	Quinn	Barrett (1)
2	21	Creel, Draw, Crimper P&IDs (2)	02 Nov 94	Nyquist	Barrett
3	22	Creel Tub Specification	33 Nov 94	Nyquist	Barrett
4	23				
5	24				
6	25				
7	26				
8	27				
9	28				
10	29				
11	30				
12	31				
13	32				
14	33				
15	33				
16	33				
17	33				
18	34				
19	35				

Notes:　1. For information
　　　　　2. Five sheets
　　　　　3.

Form　135

COPY ROOM WORK ORDER

Received
Date:_____
Time:_____

Needed
Date: _11 May 93_
Time: _11:30 A_

Proj.: _CV- 212_

Circle one:

Requested By: _Jones_ | _1_
Dept.

    V   Vellum Order
or C   Copy Order, circle one: W will call   or (D) deliver
or (I) Formal Issue, circle one: 1 In house
                                   2 1 + Client
                                   3 2 + ___Inquiries (1)
                                (4) 2 + Vendor (1)
    Y   5 2 + ___Contractors (1)
or (N)   Field Copies ?   6 Other_____
                                            Issue Type

SUMMARY

| Specifications (2) | | | Drawings by Type | | | | | | V |
File #	Rev	Co-pies	File #	Rev	New ?	Bond (M)	Blue (N)	Sepia (R)	Vellums
S-18	1	18	K-41	Ø		17		2	

DISTRIBUTION

C	Issue Type						dept	Send To	Instructions (4)	Copies (3)	Type
	1	2	3	4	5	6					
_	X	X	X	X	_	_	1	M. MacKenzie			M
_	X	X	X	X	_	_	2	D. Smith			M
_	X	X	X	X	_	_	3	R. Brown			M
_	X	X	X	X	_	_	4	K. McClain			M
_	X	X	X	X	_	_	5	L. Thomas			M
_	X	X	X	X	_	_	6	A. Woo			M
_	X	X	X	X	_	_	7	J. Unamunzaga			M
_	X	X	X	X	_	_	8	A. Cutworth			M
_	X	X	X	X	_	_	9	B. Clutterbuck			M
_	_	_	_	X	X	_	10	Mesa Fiberglass	Note 1	1 each	M,R
_	_	X	X	X	_	_		Client: L. Marquez		6	M
_	_	_	X	X	_	_		Purchasing: J.Walker			R
_	_	_	_	_	_	_		Field: E.L.Green		3	M

Notes: 1. Copies are required for purchasing. Deliver copies to
          purchasing. Requisition must accompany this order.
      2. Attach originals. Only one copy per person.
      3. One unless otherwise noted.
      4. Folded unless otherwise noted. Sepias are always rolled.

Additional instructions:

Job Finished
Date: Time: By:

Form 136

Start Date: _14 July 94_

```
┌─────────────────────────────────────────────────────────────┐
│                   VENDOR DATA ROUTING                         │
│                   (please hand-carry)                         │
│                                                               │
│   Customer: Martinsville Chemicals        Proj.: BE 89        │
│   Location: Martinsville, VA              File #: V-32        │
├───────────────────────────────────────────────────────────────┤
```

From: ___R. B. Brown___
           (sponsor)

To: See Below

Please note, each reviewer has __2__ days from
receipt to review, mark up, and return to
sponsor. If there is a problem, please notify
sponsor. If you believe a marking might result
in a price change, please contact the purchasing
agent.

Your approval signifies you agree that the item
may be fabricated as described in the vendor data,
inclusive of revisions and comments that result
from this review.

Routing is as follows:

| | | | | dates | |
code	dept.	name	seq.	rec'd.	ret'd.
1	proc.	Latour	1	14 July	14 July
2	elect.	Jones	3	17 July	18 July
3	instr.	Forth	4	20 July	20 July
4	piping	Able	2	14 July	17 July
5	arch.				
6	HVAC				
7	struc.	McGarvey	5	21 July	23 July
8	civil				
9	plumb.				
10	other				
11	purch.		last		

Note to purchasing: Review has been completed.
This has resulted in (pick one): __3__

    1. no price and/or schedule change
    2. a possible price and/or schedule change
    3. a price and/or schedule change

If 2. or 3., please explain: _Price change only._
    Nozzles #12, and #13 have been added.

VELLUM POSSESSION LOG

Customer:_____   Proj.:_____
Location:_____

	File No.	Rev.	Checked Out By	Out	Back
1					
2					
3					
4					
5					
6					
7					
8					
9					
10					
11					
12					
13					
14					
15					
16					
17					
18					
19					
20					
21					
22					

Notes: 1.
          2.
          3.

Form   138

	File No.	Requested By	Dept	File No.	Requested By	Dept
	(copy room)	**DRAWING LOG C**				
	Customer: C&H Sugar				Proj.: CD- 938	
	Location: Hilo, Hawaii					

	File No.	Requested By	Dept	File No.	Requested By	Dept
1	D-39	Erlanger	1	58		
2	D-40	"	1	59		
3	D-41	Scott	1	60		
4	D-42	Edwards	7	61		
5	B-43	Koyama	5	62		
6	B-44	Koyama	5	63		
7	45			64		
8	46			65		
9	47			66		
10	48			67		
11	49			68		
12	50			69		
13	51			70		
14	52			71		
15	53			72		
16	54			73		
17	55			74		
18	56			75		
19	57			76		

Notes: 1.
         2.
         3.

Dept. Codes: 1 = process / mechanical   6 = HVAC
              2 = electrical   7 = structural
              3 = instruments   8 = civil
              4 = piping   9 = plumbing
              5 = architectural   10 = other

Form   139

AJAX Engineering Inc.

File No. S-304, Rev. 0

<table>
<tr><td colspan="3">(cover sheet)</td><td colspan="2">SPECIFICATION</td></tr>
<tr><td colspan="3">Customer: Great Sands Inc.</td><td colspan="2">Proj.: CV - 930</td></tr>
<tr><td colspan="3">Location: Pomona, CA</td><td colspan="2">Page 1 of 28</td></tr>
</table>

Description: Gyratory Crusher	Tag Nos.: 11900, etc

	Pages:	Date of Issue	Issued For: Internal Review
Rev. A	22	16 Oct 95	
	Approv.	Dates	Remarks:
By	DRT	11 oct 95	
Chk.			
Dept.			Page Nos.: NA
Proj.	OB	16 oct 95	
Client			

	Pages:	Date of Issue	Issued For: Approval
Rev. B	25	4 Nov 95	
	Approv.	Dates	Remarks: General Revisions
By	DRT	1 Nov 95	
Chk.	Wm. A.	1 Nov 95	
Dept.			Page Nos.: All
Proj.	OB	3 Nov 95	
Client			

	Pages:	Date of Issue	Issued For: Inquiry
Rev. C	26	29 Nov 95	
	Approv.	Dates	Remarks: Added "Noise Data Sheet". Revised pp. 20, 21 per client comments.
By	DRT	21 Nov 95	
Chk.			
Dept.			Page Nos.: 3, 5, 20, 21, 26
Proj.	OB	27 Nov 95	
Client	JW	25 Nov 95	

	Pages:	Date of Issue	Issued For: Purchase (Engineering only)
Rev. 0	28	15 Jan 96	
	Approv.	Dates	Remarks: Added lube system. Changed page numbers on pp. 13 - 28.
By	DRT	14 Jan 96	
Chk.			
Dept.			Page Nos.: 3, 13 - 28
Proj.	OB	15 Jan 96	
Client			

Form 140

─ Appendix D ─
Instrument
Society of
America Symbols

	FIRST-LETTER (4)		SUCCEEDING-LETTERS (3)		
	MEASURED OR INITIATING VARIABLE	**MODIFIER**	**READOUT OR PASSIVE FUNCTION**	**OUTPUT FUNCTION**	**MODIFIER**
A	Analysis(5,19)		Alarm		
B	Burner, Combustion		User's Choice(1)	User's Choice(1)	User's Choice(1)
C	User's Choice(1)			Control(13)	
D	User's Choice(1)	Differential(4)			
E	Voltage		Sensor (Primary Element)		
F	Flow Rate	Ratio (Fraction)(4)			
G	User's Choice(1)		Glass, Viewing Device(9)		
H	Hand				High(7,15,16)
I	Current (Electrical)		Indicate(10)		
J	Power	Scan(7)			
K	Time, Time Schedule	Time Rate of Change(4,21)		Control Station (22)	
L	Level		Light(11)		Low(7,15,16)
M	User's Choice(1)	Momentary(4)			Middle, Intermediate(7,15)
N	User's Choice(1)		User's Choice(1)	User's Choice(1)	User's Choice(1)
O	User's Choice(1)		Orifice, Restriction		
P	Pressure, Vacuum		Point (Test) Connection		
Q	Quantity	Integrate, Totalize(4)			
R	Radiation		Record(17)		
S	Speed, Frequency	Safety(8)		Switch(13)	
T	Temperature			Transmit(18)	
U	Multivariable(6)		Multifunction(12)	Multifunction(12)	Multifunction(12)
V	Vibration, Mechanical Analysis(19)			Valve, Damper, Louver(13)	
W	Weight, Force		Well		
X	Unclassified(2)	X Axis	Unclassified(2)	Unclassified(2)	Unclassified(2)
Y	Event, State or Presence(20)	Y Axis		Relay, Compute, Convert(13,14,18)	
Z	Position, Dimension	Z Axis		Driver, Actuator, Unclassified Final Control Element	

Figure D-1 Identification letters. (*From S5.1, Instrumentation Symbols and Identification; copyright 1968, Instrument Society of America; reprinted by permission.*)

Notes for Figure D-1:

(1) A "user's choice" letter is intended to cover unlisted meanings that will be used repetitively in a particular project. If used, the letter may have one meaning as a first-letter and another meaning as a succeeding-letter. The meanings need to be defined only once in a legend, or other place, for that project. For example, the letter *N* may be defined as "modulus of elasticity" as a first-letter and "oscilloscope" as a succeeding-letter.

(2) The unclassified letter *X* is intended to cover unlisted meanings that will be used only once or used to a limited extent. If used, the letter may have any number of meanings as a first-letter and any number of meanings as a succeeding-letter. Except for its use with distinctive symbols, it is expected that the meanings will be defined outside a tagging bubble on a flow diagram. For example, *XR-2* may be a stress recorder and *XX-4* may be a stress oscilloscope.

(3) The grammatical form of the succeeding-letter meanings may be modified as required. For example, "indicate" may be applied as "indicator" or "indicating," "transmit" as "transmitter" or "transmitting," etc.

(4) Any first-letter, if used in combination with modifying letters *D* (differential), *F* (ratio), *M* (momentary), *K* (time rate of change), *Q* (integrate or totalize), or any combination of these, is intended to represent a new and separate measured variable, and the combination is treated as a first-letter entity. Thus, instruments *TDI* and *TI* indicate two different variables, namely, differential temperature and temperature. Modifying letters are used when applicable.

(5) First-letter *A* (analysis) covers all analyses not described by a user's choice letter. It is expected that the type of analysis will be defined outside a tagging bubble.

(6) Use of first-letter *U* for "multivariable" in lieu of a combination of first-letters is optional. It is recommended that nonspecific variable designators such as *U* be used sparingly.

(7) The use of modifying terms "high," "low," "middle" or "intermediate," and "scan" is optional.

(8) The term "safety" applies to emergency protective primary elements and emergency protective final control elements only. Thus, a self-actuated valve that prevents operation of a fluid system at a higher-than-desired pressure by bleeding fluid from the system is a back-pressure-type *PCV*, even if the valve is not intended to be used normally. However, this valve is designated as a *PSV* if it is intended to protect against emergency conditions, i.e., conditions that are hazardous to personnel and/or equipment and that are not expected to arise normally.

The designation *PSV* applies to all valves intended to protect against emergency pressure conditions regardless of whether the valve construction and mode of operation place them in the category of the safety valve, relief valve, or safety relief valve. A rupture disc is designated *PSE*.

(9) The passive function *G* applies to instruments or devices that provide an uncalibrated view, such as sight glasses and television monitors.

(10) "Indicate" normally applies to the readout—analog or digital—of an actual measurement. In the case of a manual loader, it may be used for the dial or setting indication, i.e., for the value of the initiating variable.

(11) A pilot light that is part of an instrument loop should be designated by a first-letter followed by the succeeding-letter *L*. For example, a pilot light that indicates an expired time period should be tagged *KQL*. If it is desired to tag a pilot light that is not part of an instrument loop, the light is designated in the same way. For example, a running light for an electric motor may be tagged *EL*, assuming voltage to be the appropriate measured variable, or *YL*, assuming the operating status is being monitored. The unclassified variable *X* should be used only for applications which are limited in extent. The designation *XL* should not be used for motor running lights, as these are commonly numerous. It is permissible to use the user's choice letters *M*, *N* or *O* for a motor running light when the meaning is previously defined. If *M* is used, it must be clear that the letter does not stand for the word "motor," but for a monitored state.

(12) Use of a succeeding-letter *U* for "multifunction" instead of a combination of other functional letters is optional. This nonspecific function designator should be used sparingly.

(13) A device that connects, disconnects, or transfers one or more circuits may be either a switch, a relay, an ON-OFF controller, or a control valve, depending on the application.

If the device manipulates a fluid process stream and is not a hand-actuated ON-OFF block valve, it is designated as a control valve. It is incorrect to use the succeeding-letters *CV* for anything other than a self-actuated control valve. For all applications other than fluid process streams, the device is designated as follows:

A switch, if it is actuated by hand.

A switch or an ON-OFF controller, if it is automatic and is the first such device in a loop. The term "switch" is generally used if the device is used for alarm, pilot light, selection, interlock, or safety. The term "controller" is generally used if the device is used for normal operating control.

A relay, if it is automatic and is not the first such device in a loop, i.e., it is actuated by a switch or an ON-OFF controller.

(14) It is expected that the functions associated with the use of succeeding-letter *Y* will be defined outside a bubble on a diagram when further definition is considered necessary. This definition need not be made when the function is self-evident, as for a solenoid valve in a fluid signal line.

(15) The modifying terms "high" and "low," and "middle" or "intermediate," correspond to values of the measured variable, not to values of the signal, unless otherwise noted. For example, a high-level alarm derived from a reverse-acting level transmitter signal should be an *LAH*, even though the alarm is actuated when the signal falls to a low value. The terms may be used in combinations as appropriate.

(16) The terms "high" and "low," when applied to positions of valves and other open-close devices, are defined as follows: "high" denotes that the valve is in or approaching the fully open position, and "low" denotes that it is in or approaching the fully closed position.

(17) The word "record" applies to any form of permanent storage of information that permits retrieval by any means.

(18) For use of the term "transmitter" versus "converter," see the definitions in Section 3 of the original by ISA.

(19) First-letter *V*, "vibration or mechanical analysis," is intended to perform the duties in machinery monitoring that the letter *A* performs in more general analyses. Except for vibration, it is expected that the variable of interest will be defined outside the tagging bubble.

(20) First-letter *Y* is intended for use when control or monitoring responses are event-drive as opposed to time- or time-schedule-driven. The letter *Y*, in this position, can also signify presence or state.

(21) Modifying-letter *K*, in combination with a first-letter such as *L*, *T*, or *W*, signifies a time rate of change of the measured or initiating variable. The variable *WKIC*, for instance, may represent a rate-of-weight-loss controller.

(22) Succeeding-letter *K* is a user's option for designating a control station, while the succeeding-letter *C* is used for describing automatic or manual controllers.

Figure D-2 Typical letter combinations.

First Letters	Initiating or Measured Variable	Controllers — Recording	Controllers — Indicating	Controllers — Blind	Self-Actuated Control Valves	Readout Devices — Recording	Readout Devices — Indicating	Switches and Alarm Devices* — High**	Switches and Alarm Devices* — Low	Switches and Alarm Devices* — Comb	Transmitters — Recording	Transmitters — Indicating	Transmitters — Blind	Solenoids, Relays, Computing Devices	Primary Element	Test Point	Well or Probe	Viewing Device, Glass	Safety Device	Final Element
A	Analysis	ARC	AIC	AC		AR	AI	ASH	ASL	ASHL	ART	AIT	AT	AY	AE	AP	AW			AV
B	Burner/Combustion	BRC	BIC	BC		BR	BI	BSH	BSL	BSHL	BRT	BIT	BT	BY	BE		BW	BG		BZ
C	User's Choice																			
D	User's Choice																			
E	Voltage	ERC	EIC	EC		ER	EI	ESH	ESL	ESHL	ERT	EIT	ET	EY	EE					EZ
F	Flow Rate	FRC	FIC	FC	FCV, FICV	FR	FI	FSH	FSL	FSHL	FRT	FIT	FT	FY	FE	FP		FG		FV
FQ	Flow Quantity	FQRC	FQIC			FQR	FQI	FQSH	FQSL			FQIT	FQT	FQY	FQE					FQV
FF	Flow Ratio	FFRC	FFIC	FFC		FFR	FFI	FFSH	FFSL						FE					FFV
G	User's Choice																			
H	Hand		HIC	HC						HS										HV
I	Current	IRC	IIC	IC		IR	II	ISH	ISL	ISHL	IRT	IIT	IT	IY	IE					IZ
J	Power	JRC	JIC	JC		JR	JI	JSH	JSL	JSHL	JRT	JIT	JT	JY	JE					JV
K	Time	KRC	KIC	KC	KCV	KR	KI	KSH	KSL	KSHL	KRT	KIT	KT	KY	KE					KV
L	Level	LRC	LIC	LC	LCV	LR	LI	LSH	LSL	LSHL	LRT	LIT	LT	LY	LE		LW	LG		LV
M	User's Choice																			
N	User's Choice																			
O	User's Choice																			
P	Pressure, Vacuum	PRC	PIC	PC	PCV	PR	PI	PSH	PSL	PSHL	PRT	PIT	PT	PY	PE	PP			PSV, PSE	PV
PD	Pressure, Differential	PDRC	PDIC	PDC	PDCV	PDR	PDI	PDSH	PDSL		PDRT	PDIT	PDT	PDY	PE	PP				PDV
Q	Quantity	QRC	QIC	QC		QR	QI	QSH	QSL	QSHL	QRT	QIT	QT	QY	QE					QZ
R	Radiation	RRC	RIC	RC		RR	RI	RSH	RSL	RSHL	RRT	RIT	RT	RY	RE		RW			RZ
S	Speed, Frequency	SRC	SIC	SC	SCV	SR	SI	SSH	SSL	SSHL	SRT	SIT	ST	SY	SE					SV
T	Temperature	TRC	TIC	TC	TCV	TR	TI	TSH	TSL	TSHL	TRT	TIT	TT	TY	TE	TP	TW		TSE	TV
TD	Temperature, Differential	TDRC	TDIC	TDC	TDCV	TDR	TDI	TDSH	TDSL		TDRT	TDIT	TDT	TDY	TE	TP	TW			TDV
U	Multivariable					UR	UI							UY						UV
V	Vibration, Machinery Analysis					VR	VI	VSH	VSL	VSHL	VRT	VIT	VT	VY	VE					VZ
W	Weight, Force	WRC	WIC	WC	WCV	WR	WI	WSH	WSL	WSHL	WRT	WIT	WT	WY	WE					WZ
WD	Weight, Force, Differential	WDRC	WDIC	WDC	WDCV	WDR	WDI	WDSH	WDSL		WDRT	WDIT	WDT	WDY	WE					WDZ
X	Unclassified																			
Y	Event, State, Presence		YIC	YC		YR	YI	YSH	YSL		YRT	YIT	YT	YY	YE					YZ
Z	Position, Dimension	ZRC	ZIC	ZC	ZCV	ZR	ZI	ZSH	ZSL	ZSHL	ZRT	ZIT	ZT	ZY	ZE					ZV
ZD	Gauging, Deviation	ZDRC	ZDIC	ZDC	ZDCV	ZDR	ZDI	ZDSH	ZDSL		ZDRT	ZDIT	ZDT	ZDY	ZDE					ZDV

Note: This table is not all-inclusive.

* A, alarm, the annunciating device, may be used in the same fashion as S, switch, the actuating device.

** The letters H and L may be omitted in the undefined case.

Other Possible Combinations:

FO	(Restriction Orifice)
FRK, HIK	(Control Stations)
FX	(Accessories)
TJR	(Scanning Recorder)
LLH	(Pilot Light)
PFR	(Ratio)
KQI	(Running Time Indicator)
QQI	(Indicating Counter)
WKIC	(Rate-of-Weight-Loss Controller)
HMS	(Hand Momentary Switch)

Figure D-2 Typical letter combinations. (*From S5.1, Instrumentation Symbols and Identification; copyright 1968, Instrument Society of America; reprinted by permission.*)

— Appendix E —
Useful Dimensional Formulas

The Bernoulli Equation

Fluid	Dimensions of p	
Any fluid	Feet of fluid	$p + Z + \dfrac{v^2}{64.34} = \text{constant}$
Water at 70°F	lb/ft²	$p + 62.32Z + \dfrac{v^2}{1.03} = \text{constant}$
Air at 70°F, 1 atm	Inches of water	$p + .0144Z + \dfrac{v^2}{4470} = \text{constant}$
Air at 70°F, 1 atm	lb/ft²	$p + .0748Z + \dfrac{v^2}{860} = \text{constant}$

One velocity head of air (STP) at 30 ft/s = 0.20 inches WC.

Nomenclature: p = pressure (see units above)
Z = vertical distance above a horizontal reference plane (ft)
v = velocity (ft/s)

Tank Volumes

Cylindrical tank where $d = h$ (ft)

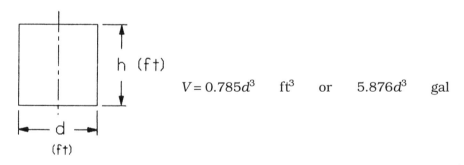

$$V = 0.785d^3 \quad \text{ft}^3 \quad \text{or} \quad 5.876d^3 \quad \text{gal}$$

Cylindrical tank, where $1.5 \times d = h$ (ft)

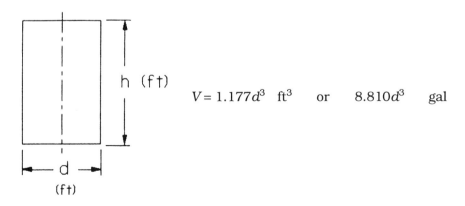

$$V = 1.177d^3 \quad \text{ft}^3 \quad \text{or} \quad 8.810d^3 \quad \text{gal}$$

323

Flow Rates and Velocities

For circular pipes and ducts:

$$v = 0.4082 \frac{f}{d^2}$$

where d = in
     f = gal/min
     v = ft/s

$$v = 3.056 \frac{f}{d^2}$$

where d = in
     f = ft^3/min
     v = ft/s

The 10-4-400 approximation: At a velocity of 10 ft/s, a 4-in line will deliver 400 gpm. Other capacities then follow from linear scaling of velocity and squares of line sizes. For example, a 1-in line at 8 ft/s will flow at

$$0.8 \times \frac{1}{4^2} \times 400 = 20 \text{ gpm} \qquad \text{(approx.)}$$

Reynolds' Number

where d = in
     f = gal/min
     v = ft/s
     μ = cP

For water at 70°F:

$$N_R = 7887 dv$$

$$N_R = 3219 \frac{f}{d}$$

For air at 70°F, and 1 atm:

$$N_R = 500 dv$$

For air at T°F (0–600°F), and 1 atm:

$$N_R = \frac{2.7 \times 10^6 \times d \times v}{1.7t^{1.5} - 10.9t}$$

where $t = \dfrac{T + 460}{1.8}$

For any gas at 70°F, and 1 atm:

$$N_R = 0.321 \times \frac{d \times v \times \text{fw}}{\mu}$$

where fw = formula weight

Easy-to-Remember Conversion Factors

$$\frac{\text{Btu}}{\text{lb °F}} \equiv \frac{\text{cal}}{\text{g °C}}$$

$$\frac{Btu}{lb\ mole\ °F} \equiv \frac{cal}{g\ mole\ °C}$$

which leads to

$$\frac{Btu}{lb} \equiv 1.8\frac{cal}{g} \quad \text{and} \quad \frac{Btu}{lb\ mole} \equiv 1.8\frac{cal}{g\ mole}$$

For flowing fluids the following conversions are easy to remember:

$$500\frac{gal}{min} \cong \frac{lb}{h} \quad \text{for water}$$

$$500 \times \frac{gal}{min} \times sp.gr. \cong \frac{lb}{h} \quad \text{for any fluid}$$

where sp.gr. = specific gravity

── Appendix F ──
Flow Sheet Symbols*

---

*From *Chemical Engineering*, Jan. 1, 1968, with permission.

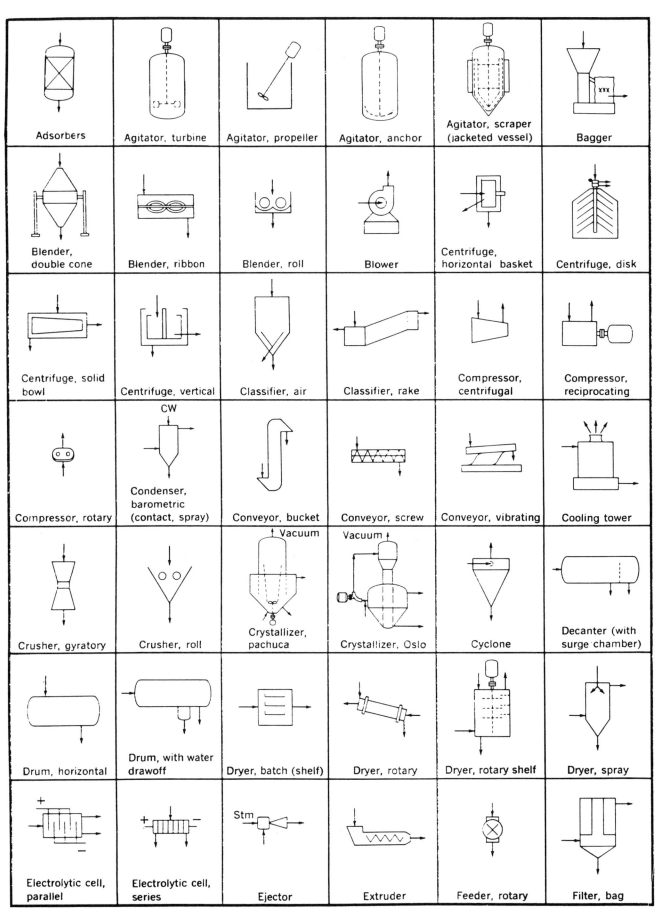

Adsorbers	Agitator, turbine	Agitator, propeller	Agitator, anchor	Agitator, scraper (jacketed vessel)	Bagger
Blender, double cone	Blender, ribbon	Blender, roll	Blower	Centrifuge, horizontal basket	Centrifuge, disk
Centrifuge, solid bowl	Centrifuge, vertical	Classifier, air	Classifier, rake	Compressor, centrifugal	Compressor, reciprocating
Compressor, rotary	Condenser, barometric (contact, spray)	Conveyor, bucket	Conveyor, screw	Conveyor, vibrating	Cooling tower
Crusher, gyratory	Crusher, roll	Crystallizer, pachuca	Crystallizer, Oslo	Cyclone	Decanter (with surge chamber)
Drum, horizontal	Drum, with water drawoff	Dryer, batch (shelf)	Dryer, rotary	Dryer, rotary shelf	Dryer, spray
Electrolytic cell, parallel	Electrolytic cell, series	Ejector	Extruder	Feeder, rotary	Filter, bag

Stm=steam ; CW=cooling water ; Cond=condensate

Filter, leaf	Filter, oil bath	Filter press	Filter, rotary	Furnace, arc	Furnace, fired
Flaker	Gas holder	Grinder, ball mill	Heat exchanger, air cooled	Heat exchanger, bayonet	Heat exchanger, kettle
Heat exchanger, shell and tube	Heat exchanger, spray	Hopper	Kettle	Kiln	Kneader
Mist eliminator, brink	Mist eliminator, mesh	Mixer-settler	Montejus (blowing egg)	Prill tower	Pug mill
Pump, centrifugal	Pump, gear	Pump, in line	Pump, proportioning	Pump, reciprocating	Pump, submerged
Scale and truck	Scale and hopper	Screen	Sphere	Stack	Tank, cone-roof
Tank, floating roof	Thickener	Tower, disk and donut	Tower, packed	Tower, tray	Turbine

Flow Sheet Symbols   329

━ Appendix G ━
Phosphoric Acid Data Sheet (Product Specification)*

---

*Courtesy of Monsanto Company.

Monsanto
Detergents &
Phosphates

PRODUCT: Phosphoric Acid

GRADE: F.C.C.(meets the requirements CODE NO. 7201-765, 768, 855
of the Food Chemicals Codex III)

GENERAL DESCRIPTION: CAS NO. 7664-38-2
Clear colorless liquid with no foreign odor.

FORMULA: H_3PO_4 **MOLECULAR WEIGHT:** 98.0

SPECIFICATIONS:

	75% Code 765	80% Code 768	85% Code 855
Appearance	A clear, colorless liquid		
Odor	No foreign odor		
Specific Gravity @ 25°/15.5°C	1.574 Min.	1.629 Min.	1.686 Min.
% Equivalent H_3PO_4	75.0 Min.	80.0 Min.	85.0 Min.
Arsenic as As, ppm.	3 Max.	3 Max.	3 Max.
Fluoride, ppm.	10 Max.	10 Max.	10 Max.
Heavy Metals as Pb, ppm.	10 Max.	10 Max.	10 Max.

TYPICAL VALUES: (Based on material tested in our laboratories, but variable from sample to sample. Typical values should not be construed as a guaranteed analysis of any specific lot or as specification items.)

	75%	80%	85%
Specific Gravity @ 25°/15.5°C	1.575	1.633	1.692
% Equivalent H_3PO_4	75.1	80.35	85.5
% P_2O_5	54.39	58.20	61.92
Lbs. per gallon	13.17	13.66	14.15
Lbs. P_2O_5 per gallon	7.16	7.95	8.76

NOTE: Both specification and typical values are subject to change from time to time. Please write us for current data sheet.

Handling Precautions: DANGER! CAUSES BURNS. Do not get in eyes, on skin and on clothing. Avoid breathing vapor or mist. Keep container closed. Use with adequate ventilation. Wash thoroughly after handling.*
FIRST AID: If in eyes or on skin, immediately flush with plenty of water for at least 15 minutes while removing contaminated clothing and shoes. Call a physician. Wash clothing before reuse.
IN CASE OF SPILL OR LEAK: Contain spill or leaks to prevent discharge to environment. Emptied container retains vapor and product residue. Observe all labeled safeguards until container is cleaned, reconditioned or destroyed.

*CORROSIVE TO MILD STEEL added here on 75% and 80% acid label.

PHOSPHORIC ACID, F.C.C. GRADE

Production Location: Augusta, GA; Trenton, MI; Carondelet (St.Louis), MO; Long Beach, CA.
Packaging: 3000 gal. tank trucks; 8000 & 12000 gal. tank cars;
   15 gal. and 55 gal. plastic drums (75% & 85% only).
Labeling Requirements: Product Label and DOT CORROSIVE label required by law.
Shipping Classification: 1. In one package of 5000 lbs. or more:
        Phosphoric Acid
        CORROSIVE MATERIAL, UN 1805, RQ; STCC4930248
     2. In one package of less than 5000 lbs.
        Phosphoric Acid
        CORROSIVE MATERIAL, UN 1805; STCC4930248

Key Properties: Monsanto phosphoric acid is made by oxidation and hydration of elemental phosphorus produced by the electric furnace method at our Idaho facility. It contains no more than a few parts per million of the lower oxyacids of phosphorus with only traces of impurities such as iron, arsenic and fluorine. It meets the requirements of the Food Chemicals Codex III.

Current Food Use Applications:

- Generally recognized as safe as a miscellaneous and/or general purpose food additive under 21 CFR 182.1073 (Phosphoric Acid).
- Generally recognized as safe as a miscellaneous and/or general purpose feed additive under 21 CFR 582.1073 (Phosphoric Acid).
- General recognition of safety for flavoring use affirmed by FDA in communication to industry.
- Exempted from tolerance requirements under 21 CFR 182.99 (Adjuvants for pesticide chemicals) when used as a buffer in formulations applied to growing crops or to raw agricultural commodities after harvest (FR June 2, 1970).
- Cleared under 21 CFR 175.300 (Resinous and polymeric coatings), 21 CFR 175.380 (Xylene-formaldehyde resins condensed with 4,4'-isopropylidenediphenol epichlorohydrin epoxy resins), 21 CFR 175.390 (Zinc-silicon dioxide matrix coatings), 21 CFR 176.170 (Components of paper and paperboard in contact with aqueous and fatty foods), 21 CFR 177.1210 (Closures with sealing gaskets for food containers), 21 CFR 177.1350 (Ethylene-vinyl acetate copolymers).
- Cleared as an adjuvant under 21 CFR 177.2260 (Filters, resin-bonded).
- Cleared under 21 CFR 178.3520 (Industrial starch-modified) in starch treated with phosphoric acid not to exceed 6% and urea not to exceed 20% as internal sizing for paper and paperboard (FR April 26, 1968) and as surface sizing and coating of paper and paperboard that contacts water in oil dairy product emulsions, low-moisture fats and oils, moist bakery products, dry solids with the surface containing no free fat or oil, and dry solids with the surface containing free fat or oil (FR Feb. 27, 1971).
- Cleared by Meat Inspection Div. to increase antioxidant effectiveness in lard and shortening at the level of 0.05% 9 CFR 318.7 and 9 CFR 381.147.
- Deemed to be generally recognized as safe by the Flavor and Extract Manufacturers' Association.

FOR MORE COMPLETE INFORMATION ON PROPERTIES AND SAFE HANDLING OF THIS MATERIAL, SEE THE MONSANTO MATERIAL SAFETY DATA SHEET (MSDS).

PERFORMANCE PRODUCTS DIVISION
MONSANTO CHEMICAL COMPANY
a Unit of MONSANTO COMPANY   © Feb. 1992

Sales Offices:

Atlanta, GA	Chicago, IL	Cincinnati, OH	Detroit, MI
404-951-7600	708-250-4400	513-792-2800	313-377-6200
			800 N. Lindbergh Blvd.
Houston, TX	Los Angeles, CA	Westfield, NJ	St.Louis, MO, 63167
713-850-0088	714-855-7760	201-654-9500	314-694-1000

For order assistance, please call our Customer Service Department Toll Free: 800-325-4330

─ Appendix H ─
Sample of
Equipment
Specification

AJAX Engineering Inc.   File No. S-43 , Rev. B

(cover sheet)	SPECIFICATION

Customer: <u>Multi Metallics Corporation</u>   Proj.: <u>BE-423</u>
Location: <u>Reno, NV</u>   Page <u>1</u> of ___

Description: CWS Pumps	Tag Nos.: 11600, 11700

Rev. A

Pages:	Date of Issue	Issued For: Internal Review
12	29 Oct 94	
Approv.	Dates	Remarks:
By NK	4 NOV 94	
Chk. —	—	Page Nos.: NA
Dept.		
Proj. NK	4 NOV 94	
Client JHG	4 NOV 94	

Rev. B

Pages:	Date of Issue	Issued For: Approval
12	8 Nov 94	
Approv.	Dates	Remarks: General Revisions
By		
Chk.		Page Nos.: All
Dept.		
Proj.		
Client		

Rev.

Pages:	Date of Issue	Issued For:
Approv.	Dates	Remarks:
By		
Chk.		Page Nos.:
Dept.		
Proj.		
Client		

Rev.

Pages:	Date of Issue	Issued For:
Approv.	Dates	Remarks:
By		
Chk.		Page Nos.:
Dept.		
Proj.		
Client		

Form   140

SPECIFICATION

Customer: <u>Multi Metallics Corporation</u>   Proj.: <u>BE-423</u>
Location: <u>Reno, NV</u>   Page <u>2</u> of ___

Description: CWS Pumps	Tag Nos.: 11600, 11700

1.0   <u>General Description</u>

   1.1   This specification establishes the requirements for a pair of horizontal centrifugal cooling water pumps.

   1.2   Water is to be pumped from a cooling tower basin to three users (heat exchangers) and back to the cooling tower (see attached sketch).

   1.3   Location will be in a metallurgical plant in the vicinity of Reno, Nevada.

2.0   <u>Codes, Standards, and Additional Specifications</u>

   2.1   The publications listed below form a part of this section to the extent referenced:

AMERICAN SOCIETY OF MECHANICAL ENGINEERS (ASME)

ASME B16.1	(1989) Cast Iron Pipe Flanges and Flanged Fittings

ANTI-FRICTION BEARING MANUFACTURERS ASSOCIATION, INC. (AFBMA)

AFBMA 11	(1990) Load Ratings and Fatigue Life for Roller Bearings
AFBMA 9	(1990) Load Ratings and Fatigue Life for Ball Bearings

HYDRAULIC INSTITUTE (HI)

HI-01	(1983; 14 Ed) Standards for Centrifugal, Rotary and Reciprocating Pumps

Form   141

SPECIFICATION

Customer: Multi Metallics Corporation	Proj.: BE-423
Location: Reno, NV	Page 3 of ___

Description: CWS Pumps	Tag Nos.: 11600, 11700

2.2 In the event of a conflict between referenced codes, standards and specifications, the most stringent shall apply. If Seller cannot readily determine the most stringent, he shall immediately contact Buyer for written resolution.

2.3 In the event of a conflict between this specification and the data sheet, the data sheet shall prevail.

2.4 The following Ajax specification (attached) forms an integral part of this Specification:

S-24   Electrical Motors

3.0 **Operating Conditions**

3.1 Duty

3.1.1 One of the pumps shall operate 24 hours a day, 7 days a week.

3.1.2 Pumps shall be suitable for outdoor installation.

3.2 Rating

3.2.1 Operating conditions are listed on the pump data sheet.

3.2.2 The pump shall be capable of providing discharge capacity and heads when operating at the suction conditions, fluid temperatures, specific gravities and viscosities as listed on the pump data sheet.

3.2.3 The Seller shall advise in the Offering if there are special startup or shutdown operating procedures required due to either power limitations of the driver or other mechanical characteristics of the equipment.

Form   141

SPECIFICATION

Customer: Multi Metallics Corporation   Proj.: BE-423
Location: Reno, NV   Page 4 of ___

Description: CWS Pumps   Tag Nos.:   11600, 11700

3.3 Site Conditions

Elevation: 4500 ft. (approximate)

Temperature:

```
Dry bulb, Summer          120 F
Dry bulb, Winter          -20 F
Wet bulb, Summer (max.)    73 F
Wet bulb, Winter (min.)   -40 F
```

3.4 Utilities

Electrical power is available at 440 volts, three-phase, 60 Hz. and 110 volts, single phase, 60 Hz.

4.0 Equipment

4.1 The Seller shall be responsible for all engineering, design, fabrication, inspection, testing and preparation for shipment.

4.2 The Seller shall provide the following items:

4.2.1 Two pumps (equipment numbers 11600 & 11700)

4.2.2 Electric motors (high efficiency type, see Spec. # S-6)

4.2.3 Couplings

4.2.4 Coupling guards

4.2.5 Pump and motor baseplates

4.2.6 Mounting of motors, pumps, couplings, and coupling guards.

Form   141

SPECIFICATION

Customer: Multi Metallics Corporation	Proj.: BE-423
Location: Reno, NV	Page 5 of ___

Description: CWS Pumps	Tag Nos.: 11600, 11700

4.3 The Buyer will supply the following:

    4.3.1 Foundations

    4.3.2 Anchor bolts

    4.3.3 Motor starters

    4.3.4 Installation

    4.3.5 Instrumentation

5.0 **Design Requirements**

  5.1 It is the intent of this specification that the equipment be the Seller's standard design, modified as required, and suitable for the application and capabilities specified.

  5.2 Pumps shall be designed using hydraulic criteria based upon actual model development test data.

  5.3 Pumps shall not have impeller diameters larger than 90 percent of the maximum diameter of the casing nor less than 15 percent of the diameter of the casing.

  5.4 Available NPSH shall exceed required NPSH by not less than 1-1/2 feet.

  5.5 Pumps of the same duty condition, classification, and accessories, or with specified accessory deviation, shall be identical.

  5.6 The pump and driver shall be mounted on a single, 304 stainless steel baseplate.

  5.7 Rated capacity shall be at least 110 percent of the maximum capacity as specified in the data sheet.

Form   141

SPECIFICATION

Customer: Multi Metallics Corporation   Proj.: BE-423
Location: Reno, NV   Page 6 of ___

Description: CWS Pumps | Tag Nos.:   11600, 11700

5.8   Shaft shall be solid, sleeveless, AISI 400 series
      corrosion-resistant steel, hardened to 425 Brinell in
      stuffing-box area.

5.9   Renewable wear rings shall be provided, both for casings
      and impellers.

5.10 Pump seals shall be mechanical type, using manufacturer's
      standard for this type of service. Casing construction
      shall be such that packing seals may be substituted in the
      field for mechanical seals without machining. Packing-box
      depth shall accomodate six rings of square packing,
      lantern ring, and throttling bushing -- not less
      than five rings of square packing, lantern ring, and
      throttling bushing.

5.11 Impellers shall be fully enclosed cast bronze or
      corrosion-resistant steel, machined and polished.
      Waterways shall be machine- or hand-finished. Impellers
      shall meet maximum and minimum diameter requirements.

5.12 Pump impeller assemblies shall be statically and
      dynamically balanced to within 1/2 percent of W times R
      squared, where W equals weight and R equals impeller
      radius.

5.13 Pump and motor bearings shall be separate and distinct;
      i.e., close-coupled pumps shall not be proposed.

5.14 All systems furnished shall be of standard components in
      general industrial usage for the service intended.

5.15 Seller shall identify all items of equipment (not parts)
      purchased from other manufacturers and furnished as part
      of his supply.

Form   141

SPECIFICATION

Customer: <u>Multi Metallics Corporation</u>   Proj.:<u> BE-423 </u>
Location:<u> Reno, NV </u>   Page <u> 7 </u> of ___

Description: CWS Pumps | Tag Nos.:   11600, 11700

6.0 Degree of Assembly

6.1 Pumps and motors shall be mounted on base plates.

6.2 Pump and motor shafts shall be aligned per manufacturer's standard at manufacturer's shop prior to shipping.

6.3 Units shall be shipped in aligned condition with pumps and motors securely fastened to the base plates.

6.4 Units shall be shipped with the couplings and coupling guards properly installed.

7.0 Drawings and Documents for Approval

Vendor drawings and documents are an important part of the vendor's obligation. They are no less important than the equipment itself. Permission to proceed with the preparation of vendor drawings will occur prior to permission to proceed with fabrication (see Exhibit C, attached).

Drawings and documents shall be provided as follows:

   for approval: three bluelines or bond copies
   as certified: seven bluelines (bond) or one reproducible

Please note: maintenance manuals and installation instructions are <u>not</u> approval documents, yet they are also a necessary part of the vendor's obligation. These are to be sent with the certified documents, <u>not with the approval documents</u>.

For the equipment subject of this specification, we require the following approval drawings:

Form   141

SPECIFICATION

Customer: <u>Multi Metallics Corporation</u>   Proj.: <u>BE-423</u>
Location: <u>Reno, NV</u>   Page <u>8</u> of ___

Description: CWS Pumps   Tag Nos.:   11600, 11700

o dimensioned outline drawings
o support/anchor-bolt arrangement drawings
o views showing maintenance access and clearances
o sectional views of <u>all</u> seal areas showing o-rings, gaskets, packings, lantern-rings, mechanical seals, etc.
o parts lists (showing materials of construction)
o pump curves
o electrical motor manufacturer's data sheet
o seal manufacturer's data sheet
o coupling manufacturer's data sheet

8.0 <u>Testing</u>

8.1 Inspection by Buyer or waiver of inspection, shall not relieve Seller of full compliance with this specification.

8.2 Specific inspection and acceptance requirements as per this specification and the Seller and/or Buyer's inspector are supplements to and do not diminish the requirements of the applicable codes and specifications.

8.3 Buyer reserves the right to inspect and test all material at Seller's plant or any sub supplier's plant during manufacture, upon completion, and at destination before acceptance. Acceptance of goods or failure to ascertain or discover defects shall in no way be a waiver of any warranty or any right buyer may have pursuant to this order.

8.4 Shop measurements of alignment and run-out are to accompany each unit when shipped. These can be placed in an envelope and taped to the motor.

8.5 Rotation shall be tested and proved to occur freely, without binding, without noise.

Form   141

SPECIFICATION

Customer: Multi Metallics Corporation   Proj.: BE-423
Location: Reno, NV   Page _9_ of ___

Description: CWS Pumps   Tag Nos.:   11600, 11700

9.0 Surface Finishes

  9.1 Pump casing, bearing housing and base-plate shall be painted in a light gray or light green color using an epoxy-based paint.

  9.2 Motor finish shall be baked enamel.

10.0 Cleaning

  10.1 Casing and impeller shall be wiped clean of all manufacturing residues prior to assembly.

  10.2 All exterior surfaces must be wiped clean of grease, oil, and dirt prior to shipment.

11.0 Responsibilities and Guarantees

Vendor shall guarantee performance as stated by his pump curves. Vendor shall guarantee that the pumps subject of this order have been factory tested and that the results are shown on the pump curves.

Vendor shall guarantee that all materials employed are new (not reprocessed), free from defects, and made of first-grade raw materials.

Disclaimers avoiding responsibility as to fittness of merchantibility will not be accepted.

It is the understanding on the part of the Buyer that diligence, good manufacturing practice, and good workmanship will have been employed in the manufacture of the subject items.

Form   141

SPECIFICATION

Customer: Multi Metallics Corporation　　　Proj.: BE-423
Location: Reno, NV　　　　　　　　　　　　Page _10_ of ___

Description: CWS Pumps	Tag Nos.:　11600, 11700

12.0 Shipping

    12.1 All exposed machined surfaces and/or other working parts shall be protected with a light grease.

    12.2 All flange faces and other machined surfaces shall be protected with readily removable wood or steel temporary protective cover plates bolted in place with a minimum of four (4) bolts.

    12.3 All threaded connections shall be adequately protected against damage during transit.

    12.4 Unit shall be covered by a tarpaulin while in transit.

13.0 Proposals

    13.1 All bids within 7% (seven percent) of the lowest bid will be treated as equal to the lowest bid.

    13.2 Completeness and clarity of bids will form part of the selection criteria.

    13.3 Drawings showing what is to be provided are considered important.

    13.4 Bidders are encouraged to point out special design features.

    13.5 Bidders shall identify makes and models of seals and bearings being proposed.

    13.6 Bidders shall clearly note any exceptions they might have to approval drawings and documents, listed above under section 7.0.

    13.7 In addition to firm quotes on the equipment, bidder is to quote charges for each of the following: cancellation within 30, 60, and 90 days.

    13.8 Bidders are asked to carefully review Exhibit C, attached.

Form　141

SPECIFICATION

Customer: <u>Multi Metallics Corporation</u> Proj.:<u> BE-423 </u>
Location: <u>Reno, NV   </u>   Page <u>ll</u> of ___

Description: CWS Pumps   Tag Nos.: 11600, 11700

Data Sheet

Number required: Two, identical

Size and model: By vendor

Fluid: Water

Viscosity: Water

Vapor Pressure: Water

NPSH Available: Flooded suction

Temp. (max.): 110 F

Temp. (min.): 40 F

System Curve Points:

   Max. Flow: 140 gpm Head: 30 ft

   Min. Flow: 40 gpm Head: greater than 30 ft

Form 141

SPECIFICATION

Customer: Multi Metallics Corporation   Proj.: BE-423
Location: Reno, NV   Page _12_ of ___

Description: CWS Pumps   Tag Nos.: 11600, 11700

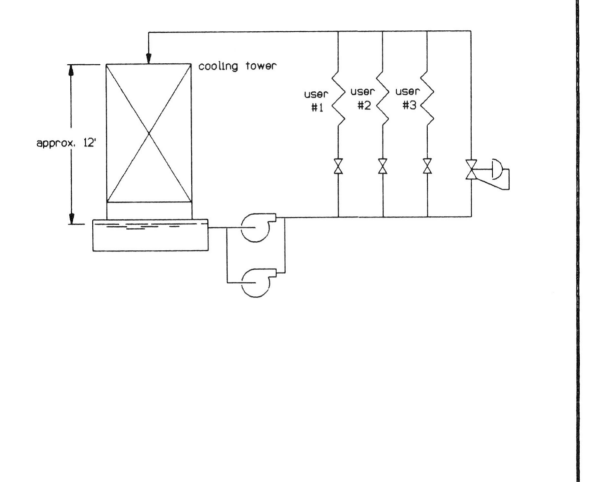

━ Appendix I ━
Text of Article Published in Engineering Times*

Quality Before It's Built

U.S. ENGINEERING DESIGN COMES UP SHORT, SAYS NRC

Engineering design, which accounts for about 70% or more of a product's life cycle cost, is becoming an expensive and losing proposition for most U.S. industries. To change that situation, a new report recommends the creation of a national engineering design consortium and a federally supported engineering design research agenda.

"The decline of U.S. international competitiveness has been ascribed to many factors. A crucial factor that is not often recognized is the quality of engineering design in the U.S.," charges the report, "Improving Engineering Design: Designing for Competitive Advantage," released by the National Research Council (NRC).

The report notes that while effective design and manufacturing are both components of high-quality products, "effective design is a prerequisite for effective manufacturing; quality cannot be manufactured or tested into a product, it must be designed in. The U.S. needs to sharpen its understanding of engineering design theory if it is to realize the competitive advantages of superior engineering design."

Finding Fault

Regarding the current state of engineering design in the U.S., the report concludes:

- The best engineering design practices are not widely used in U.S. industry;
- The key role of designers in the product realization process is often not well understood by management;
- Some U.S. firms use design effectively, but they have had to change their goals and culture to do so;
- Partnerships and interactions among industry, research, and education are so limited that the relevant needs of each are poorly served by others;

---

*May 1991, page 5, with permission.

- Current engineering curricula do not focus on the entire product realization process;

- Industry's internal efforts to teach engineering design—intended to compensate to some degree for these shortcomings—are too fragmented and not institutionalized as natural components of the way business is performed;

- Although universities nominally bear responsibility for producing both practices and practitioners, they do not fulfill this role in engineering design in the U.S.;

- A revitalization of university research in engineering design has begun; and

- The U.S. government has not recognized the development of superior engineering design as a national priority.

A specific example of the U.S. decline in engineering design cited in the report is the speed and cost with which new product concepts and improvements are introduced to the market. A comparison of the lead time required by U.S. and Japanese firms to bring a major body die from concept to delivery shows that Japanese producers take an average of 13.8 months; U.S. firms, on average, take 24.8 months.

Better Every Year

"Manufacturing performance, including adherence to design specifications, flexibility, and efficiency is also involved," the report acknowledges. "But effective design is at the heart of the concept of continuous accumulated improvement—the drive to make the product better and better year after year."

Without a shift to improved engineering design, the report envisions that loss of market share will "likely spread as foreign competition expands into other industries—aerospace, large appliance, and cosmetic industries being likely near-term targets."

Industry, academia, and government each have a role to play in improving engineering design. The report cautions, however, that "half-way measures will not suffice. Simply adopting the design practices of foreign companies will doom U.S. industry to perpetual follower status.

"Companies must reorganize their product realization processes and at least adopt existing best design practices," the report adds. "They must also communicate better with universities in order to secure new design methods and well-prepared graduates. Universities, in turn, must make a high-level commitment to improve engineering design education and research and better relate them to the needs of industry. The government must make engineering design a national priority and encourage research by increasing funding and assisting in the establishment of clearinghouses for design information and teaching materials."

Universities may have the largest role in improving engineering design in the U.S. "Engineering design education is seriously deficient, and strong steps are needed to revitalize it," says the report.

Recommended changes include "assuring that each engineering curriculum fully meets the letter and spirit of the current [Accreditation Board for Engineering and Technology] criteria for undergraduate programs," as well as modernization of ABET's criteria. Regarding the latter, the report states, "Professional societies that are ABET-

participating bodies must take the initiative in revising them."
Similarly directed at professional engineering societies is a recommendation that they "encourage the further education of design teachers and increase the awareness of all faculty members of the importance of engineering design. The guidance of practicing engineers is essential."

To improve engineering design education, the report offers recommendations for undergraduate and graduate curricula. At the bachelor's level, engineering education should "show how the fundamental engineering science background is relevant to effective design; teach students what the design process entails and familiarize them with the basic tools of the process; demonstrate that design involves not just function but also producibility, cost, customer preference, and a variety of life cycle issues; and convey the importance of other subjects such as mathematics, economics, and manufacturing."

Graduate level engineering curricula, according to the report, should develop competence in advanced design theory and methodology; expose students to examples of state-of-the-art design from both industry and academic research; provide hands-on design experience, "preferably during industrial internships"; and require students to perform engineering design research.

Although such research gains made in academia can be assimilated into industrial practice through various routes, the report notes that "even well-developed research results cannot simply be 'given' to industry; new methods must be refined and packaged as products, a task that cannot readily be performed by most universities or by most companies that might take advantage of the results."

To facilitate the transfer of state-of-the-art design technology from university research facilities to industry, the report recommends the creation of a National Consortium for Engineering Design.

The report also promotes the idea of establishing a national engineering design research agenda. Its focus would be 10 research topics deemed by the NRC panel as "crucially important to reforming the practice and teaching of engineering design, and thus worthy of continued expanded effort."

— Appendix J —
Personal Files

In developing one's career, much technical and administrative knowledge must be acquired. To be of any use, it must be filed properly for later use. The information will have many sources: trade magazines, mail, texts, journals, catalogs, notes during seminars, etc.

When an item of interest is identified, it can be copied on a copy machine, or by hand, or if the information personally belongs to the owner of the file, the pages can be placed directly in the file. Catalogs can be dismembered and stored in the file or can be kept whole on a shelf.

Discrimination must be exercised to keep from overloading the file. For vendor brochures and such, a goal of no more than three pages per equipment type is largely obtainable.*

Filing for project documents is covered in Chap. 14, *Paper*. No less important, however, is the professional's file in which equipment information and other information should be kept. This file should also contain information concerning physics, chemistry, secondary containment, etc. As a matter of fact, the file should be subdivided into two major categories:

- Ideas

- Things

The *ideas* portion, of course, should cover topics like heat transfer, fluid flow, properties of substances, and much more—perhaps the root of this file should be one's notes from college. In the *things* category, there should be items such as pumps, valves, membranes, screens, fasteners, O-rings (filed under *seals*), enclosures,† column packings, thermal media,‡ gearboxes, electronic gizmos, temperature switches, ozone generators (filed under *chemical generators*), and so on.

The personal file is a source of knowledge. It is extremely important to the process of brainstorming and invention.

The following Personal File Index has been tested for 25 years or so. It has served the author well. It is probably not a bad starting point for the personal files of many engineers/designers. The user of this index, or any other index, should not hesitate to make changes for personal preference and requirements driven by other needs.

---

*Most items are one page, but some stretch to 20 or more. With some care and attention, but not a great amount, the author's file now is contained in two four-drawer cabinets plus shelves holding about 80 catalogs.

†This is an interesting category in that it includes prefabricated buildings, clean rooms, tents (held by ropes, pressurized, etc.), soundproof booths, glove boxes, fume hoods, and more.

‡Such as Dowtherm, Multitherm, and Therminol.

PERSONAL FILE INDEX

Bases

1.0 Economic Subjects
    1.01   Cost estimates (how to make)
    1.02   Economic data
    1.03   Economic evaluations (ROI, etc.)
    1.04   Engineering/design man-hours
    1.05   Market studies (methods)
    1.06   Prices (ingredients)
    1.07   Quotes (equipment, commodities, subcontracts, etc.)
    1.08   Site selection

2.0 Science, Engineering, Mathematics
    2.01   Biotechnology
    2.02   Chemistry and physics
    2.03   Computer, microprocessor
    2.04   Electrical, electronics (including electrochemistry)
    2.05   Mathematics
    2.06   Mechanical engineering
    2.07   Methods/procedures (engineering and design)
    2.08   Scheduling and network planning
    2.09   Statistics

3.0 Materials
    3.01   Chemicals
    3.02   Coatings
    3.03   Corrosion
    3.04   Heating/cooling media
    3.05   Insulators and refractories
    3.06   Metals
    3.07   Plastics and elastomers
    3.08   Properties
    3.09   Strength of materials

4.0 Engineers/Fabricators
    4.01   Engineers
    4.02   Fabricators and/or subcontractors
    4.03   Laboratories
    4.04   Shop methods

5.0 Processes (flow sheets of diverse kinds)

Operations

10.0 Bulk Transport
    10.01   Flow (liquid, gas, two-phase)
    10.02   Prime movers
    10.03   Solids handling and fluidization

11.0 Separation
    11.01   Absorption
    11.02   Adsorption and ion exchange
    11.03   Cleaning
    11.04   Crystallization
    11.05   Decantation
    11.06   Distillation
    11.07   Drying
    11.08   Evaporation

Materials and Equipment

17.0   Discrete Parts Handling
    17.01   Bagging, palletizing, etc.
    17.02   Conveying
    17.03   Inspection (and label reading)
    17.04   Labeling
    17.05   Miscellaneous
    17.06   Packaging or bottling
    17.07   Transferring

20.0   Bulk Transport
    20.01   Fans, blowers, compressors
    20.02   Pipe, corrosion-resistant
    20.03   Pipe, hose, and duct
    20.04   Pneumatic conveyors
    20.05   Pumps, general
    20.06   Pumps, positive displacement
    20.07   Steam traps
    20.08   Valves, common
    20.09   Valves, control
    20.10   Valves, corrosion-resistant
    20.11   Valves, pressure safety

21.0   Separation
    21.01   Absorbers
    21.02   Adsorbers and ion exchangers
    21.03   Centrifuges
    21.04   Collection equipment
    21.05   Dryers
    21.06   Evaporators and crystallizers
    21.07   Extraction and leaching
    21.08   Filters (gas)
    21.09   Filters (L/S)
    21.10   Flotation
    21.11   Gravity concentrators
    21.12   Liquid cyclones
    21.13   Magnetic and electrostatic
    21.14   Membranes
    21.15   Sieves, screens, trommels
    21.16   Thickeners/clarifiers

22.0   Unclassified Equipment
    22.01   Chemical generators
    22.02   Coating equipment
    22.03   Combustion (boilers and water heaters)
    22.04   Combustion, general
    22.05   Coolers/chillers
    22.06   Dispersion and mixing (see 16.02 for Solids)
    22.07   Equipment installation
    22.08   Extruders
    22.09   Furnaces and high-temperature equipment
    22.10   Heat exchangers
    22.11   Laboratory supplies
    22.12   Plant and office supplies
    22.13   Tanks and vessels
    22.14   Tools
    22.15   Used equipment
    22.16   Water treatment

25.0 Measurement and Control
     25.01   Analytical
     25.02   Controllers, PID
     25.03   Electronic equipment
     25.04   Flow sensors
     25.05   Hydraulic controls
     25.06   I/P converters
     25.07   Laboratory instruments
     25.08   Level sensors
     25.09   Load, strain, weight
     25.10   Meters, recorders
     25.11   Microprocessor-based environments
     25.12   Motor starters
     25.13   Particle detection and measurement
     25.14   Pressure
     25.15   Solenoid valves
     25.16   Switches, relays
     25.17   Temperature
     25.18   Transmitters

── Appendix K── Definition of ±10 Percent Estimate according to One Major Chemical Company

A ±10 percent estimate requires the following inputs:

1. *Major equipment:* Basic specifications and data sheets, firm prices (from several sources when available)

2. *Flow diagrams:* Company-approved, including heat and material balances, and utilities summaries

3. *P&IDs*—including utilities P&IDs

4. *Plot plans and equipment arrangement drawings:* Company-approved

5. *Soil studies*

6. *Instrumentation:*

   6.1 Preliminary instrument list from above P&IDs

   6.2 Computer hardware cost estimate

   6.3 Preliminary control panel definition and sketches

   6.4 Wiring description

   6.5 Hazardous classification drawings (or sketches)

   6.6 General instrument specifications (company-approved)

7. *Electrical:*

   7.1 Preliminary motor list

   7.2 Preliminary lighting specification

   7.3 Preliminary distribution routing

   7.4 Preliminary communications specification

   7.5 Preliminary motor control center definition and sketches

   7.6 Wiring description

   7.7 Preliminary grounding specification

   7.8 Description of tie-ins

8. *Piping:*

   8.1 Material specifications (company-approved)

   8.2 Material takeoff (of piping and valves), based on preliminary layouts

   8.3 Prices based on recent quotes, or representative sampling

9. *Thermal insulation:* Rough material takeoff for equipment and piping; budget prices required

10. *Painting:* For equipment should be included in quoted price. For piping should be based on lineal feet. For buildings should account for type of construction

11. *Site development drawings and specification:* Preliminary grade; estimate based on square footage

12. *Civil and structural:*

    12.1 Preliminary piling, concrete, and steel specifications

    12.2 Preliminary foundation design, based on soil tests

    12.3 Preliminary takeoffs for foundations

    12.4 Preliminary design and material takeoff of structural steel, platforms, stairs, ladders, etc. Pricing based on unit prices

13. *Buildings:* Dimensional sketches based on equipment layouts and allotted square footage; unit prices based on preliminary architectural specifications

14. *Fire protection:* Written description and preliminary layout. Firm prices for major equipment

15. *Schedules:* Detailed design and procurement schedules. Preliminary construction schedule. Schedules to be based on CPM networks

16. *Scope of work:* To include lists of drawings and specifications. To include an estimate of engineering/design man-hours.

17. *Detailed estimate of construction craft labor:* Showing development of projected craft labor rates

18. *Detailed estimate of field supervisory and office staff:* Plus other costs such as construction equipment, tools, expendable materials, etc.

19. *Detailed estimate of insurance and taxes*

Index

ABOUT THE AUTHOR

Scott Mansfield has 30 years of experience in the process industries. Currently, he is a project manager with Jacobs Engineering Group, specializing in engineering design for process facilities. Mr. Mansfield has also worked for DuPont, both in the United States and abroad, and for Foote Mineral Company. He is a member of the American Institute of Chemical Engineers, the National Society of Professional Engineers, and the Instituto Mexicano de Ingenieros Químicos.